The politics of Latin American development

The politics of Latin American development

Third edition

Gary W. Wynia
William Kenan Professor of
Latin American Politics
Carleton College

CAMBRIDGE UNIVERSITY PRESS

Published by the Press Syndicate of the University of Cambridge
The Pitt Building, Trumpington Street, Cambridge CB2 1RP
40 West 20th Street, New York, NY 10011-4211, USA
10 Stamford Road, Oakleigh, Melbourne 3166, Australia

First published 1978
Second edition 1984
Reprinted 1984, 1985 (twice), 1986, 1987, 1988 (twice)
Third edition 1990
Reprinted 1990 (twice), 1992, 1993

Printed in the United States of America

Library of Congress Cataloging-in-Publication Data
Wynia, Gary W., 1942-
The politics of Latin American development /
Gary W. Wynia. - 3rd ed.
p.   cm.
Includes bibliographies and index.
ISBN 0-521-38027-8. - ISBN 0-521-38924-0 (pbk.)
1. Latin America – Politics and government – 1948-
2.. Latin American – Economic policy.   I. Title.
JL960.W6   1989
980.03'3–dc20   89–33232
                                                            CIP

A catalogue record for this book is available from the British Library.

ISBN 0-521-38027-8 hardback
ISBN 0-521-38924-0 paperback

Contents

Maps and tables

Maps

Tables

Preface to the third edition

I have tried to make this edition more instructive than its predecessors. I rewrote the "president's report" in the first chapter so that it better addresses current issues. There is also new material in Part I on the foreign debt issue, the Roman Catholic Church, and the armed forces. But, as might be expected, most of the revising was done in Part II. All of the national cases have been brought up to date, with special attention given to the restoration of constitutional democracies in countries that were previously governed by their armed forces. I have also added more information and analysis on Cuba and Nicaragua.

Anyone familiar with the second edition will notice that I have reorganized Part II. In this edition I begin with Mexico because in my own teaching I have found it to be a provocative starting point for students, all the more so after the 1988 elections and the questions they raised about political change. I have also joined previous chapters on populism with those on military authoritarianism in Brazil and Argentina, to facilitate more systematic comparisons of those nations' movement to authoritarian government and from it, recently, to democracy.

The 1980s have been peculiar and frustrating to Latin Americans. Never have so many countries launched democratic governments in so short a time span, yet never before have so many of them been forced to struggle with enormous foreign debts that they cannot pay. More Latin Americans are voting now, but they are earning less than when the previous editions of this book were published. How much longer they can yield income to their creditors without provoking political rebellion remains uncertain, though no one doubts that discontent will continue to rise.

I am especially grateful to my friends and colleagues in Latin America for the insights they continue to supply. Finally, this edition owes much to my students at Carleton, who enjoy asking questions that I cannot answer, and to my pal Mario, who has dozed through each edition while I wrote it.

G.W.W.

Preface to the second edition

Three things distinguish this edition from the first one. First, each chapter was rewritten and, to varying degrees, reorganized in order to improve the exposition and, in Part II, to make the treatment of each type of politics more complete and the comparisons of countries more meaningful. An entire chapter has been devoted to Mexico, for example, and the discussion of the Allende regime has been moved from the chapter on revolution to the one that deals with democratic reform politics in order to stimulate a discussion of the limits of constitutional government. Second, insights gleaned from recent scholarship are added in several places, including the sections on the Church, the military, authoritarian government, and economic dependency. And third, the analysis has been updated with the addition of new material on the 1982 Brazilian elections, the Argentine military's rise and fall between 1976 and 1983, the Nicaraguan revolution and its aftermath, and the world financial crisis and its impact on the region in the early 1980s.

The book was never intended to serve primarily as a summary of current events, but rather as an introduction to some of the fundamentals of Latin American politics and public policy. That remains its purpose. Nothing has happened to alter these fundamentals. Legitimate governments remain scarce, Latin America is as vulnerable to external forces as ever, the region's militaries – though ruling in fewer countries now than a decade ago – still believe that it is their right and duty to govern whenever they see fit, few of the benefits of economic development have trickled down to those most in need, revolutionaries continue to struggle against heavy odds, and American presidents still believe that they are obligated to block radical change within the hemisphere.

As in the first edition, no effort has been made to present every theory or interpretation of Latin American politics offered by students of the region. No work could do so without sacrificing much of its coherence. The approach taken here is intended to provoke meaningful

xiii

discussion, which I hope will cause those who disagree with it to undertake the kind of study needed to generate conclusions of their own.

Nothing is more pleasing to a teacher than to learn, as I have during the past six years, that many people have gained from one's work. I can only hope that the readers of this edition will discover even more than their predecessors did in the first one.

Preface to the first edition

Latin America is an enduring source of fascination to the student of politics. Within the territory that lies between the Rio Grande and Tierra del Fuego there exist exceptionally diverse forms of political life ranging from the very traditional to the revolutionary. Fundamental issues of politics, economic development, and social justice are still intensely debated throughout the region, and governments continue to experiment with competing forms of political rule and public policy. But Latin America is also a source of frustration to those who try to comprehend its public affairs. Its immense variety and diversity defy simple description, and the behavior of its leaders repeatedly confounds observers. It is no wonder many students of the region prematurely abandon their quest soon after they have begun, convinced that the analysis of Latin America's intrigues should be left to the expert or to those involved in its daily affairs.

Some of this frustration is justified, of course. Latin America is a vast region where 316 million people of European, Indo-American, African, and Asian heritage occupy an area larger than the United States. Its politics are complex, the motives of its leaders often obscure, and its range of experience great. Yet, it is the thesis of this book that Latin American politics, though complex, is comprehensible and that a few basic tools of analysis, consistently applied, can take us a long way toward the development of understanding. To begin with, despite their diversity, the Latin American nations do have many things in common that facilitate systematic analysis. They have, for example, shared a long colonial experience that has had a lasting impact on their social values, economic structures, and political institutions. Most also gained their independence at the same time and spent their formative years struggling with similar nation-building problems. And, most important to the student of the contemporary scene, they now share several conditions, including widespread poverty, uneven and irregular economic growth, and heavy dependence on the more affluent industrialized nations, which provide markets for their exports and financial capital and technology for their development.

There is no better place to begin to develop an understanding of Latin American politics and public policy than with these last three conditions and the ways governments have dealt with them. A rich and diverse array of measures has been tried in recent time. You can still find a few traditional autocrats who endeavor to hold back the forces of change even though self-imposed isolation is no longer possible. There are others who have placed their faith in democratic politics, hoping change will come peacefully through citizen participation in the resolution of development problems. Still others have rejected democracy, claiming that their citizens cannot accept responsibility for self-governance or that a firm authoritarian hand is needed to impose the kinds of growth-stimulating policies that can overcome the region's underdevelopment. And some have decided that only through a revolutionary transformation of their societies under the direction of a mass-based political party can development and social justice be achieved.

The purpose of this book is to introduce you to these governments and to give you some of the intellectual tools needed to analyze their conduct and assess the effects of their decisions on the welfare of Latin Americans. When you complete it, you will not only have become familiar with the different ways governments have dealt with poverty, inadequate economic growth, and dependency, but you will also have acquired some of the skills needed to explore the world of Latin American politics on your own.

A book of this kind cannot be written without drawing on the research of others who have studied Latin American politics and economic life. I am especially indebted to the path-finding work of Charles W. Anderson, William Galde, Celso Furtado, Albert Hirschman, Helio Jaguaribe, Guillermo O'Donnell, and Kalman Silvert. Of course, I alone am responsible for the way their ideas have been interpreted and joined in this book. I have spared the reader footnotes and instead have listed at the end of each chapter the principal English language monographs that were consulted. It is my hope that these brief bibliographies will also serve as points of departure for readers interested in pursuing each topic further. Most of the works cited contain excellent bibliographies of relevant material available in Spanish, Portuguese, and English. In addition, maps of Latin America are provided at the end of this Preface, and data describing each nation's economic and social conditions are included in the Appendix.

This undertaking is the product of several years of teaching Latin American politics to university undergraduates. It represents the culmination of successive attempts to meet the challenge laid down each year by students who insist that they be taught how to understand the political behavior of the Latin Americans who share the hemisphere with them. Had they been less demanding, this project never would have been begun. I have also gained immensely during the past fifteen years from the wisdom of the Latin Americn public officials and private citizens with whom I have discussed the region's affairs during my visits to their countries. I can only hope that this book faithfully communicates their insights.

Several colleagues have read the manuscript and contributed to its improvement. In particular I thank Roger Benjamin, Peter Johnson, and Sue Matarese of the University of Minnesota, along with Sue Brown, who typed the many drafts. I am also grateful to Professors Lawrence Graham of the University of Texas, Richard Clinton of Oregon State University, and William Garner of Southern Illinois University, who gave much needed criticism and advice at each stage of the project's development. Finally, I owe my greatest debt to my teacher, colleague, and friend, Charles W. Anderson, whose intellectual influence on this project is greater than either of us cares to admit.

Map 1. Latin America

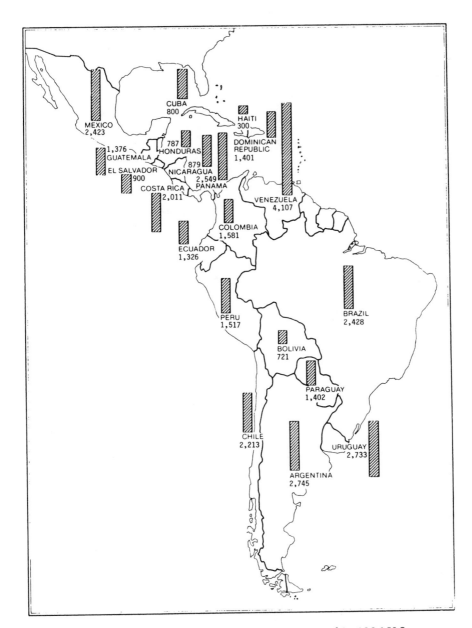

CUBA
800

MEXICO
2,423

HAITI
300

1,376
GUATEMALA

787
HONDURAS

DOMINICAN
REPUBLIC
1,401

EL SALVADOR
900

879
NICARAGUA

2,549
PANAMA

COSTA RICA
2,011

VENEZUELA
4,107

COLOMBIA
1,581

ECUADOR
1,326

PERU
1,517

BRAZIL
2,428

BOLIVIA
721

PARAGUAY
1,402

CHILE
2,213

URUGUAY
2,733

ARGENTINA
2,745

Map 2. Per capita gross domestic products 1987, measured in 1986 U.S. dollars. (*Source:* Inter-American Development Bank, *Economic and Social Progress in Latin America*, 1988, p. 540.)

Part I

Understanding Latin American politics

1. The Latin American predicament

Dissatisfaction runs deep in Latin America. But that is hardly surprising since what Latin Americans desire – be it justice, wealth, security, or liberty – is often denied them. Most North Americans do not share their distress or frustration. Though vulnerable to petroleum shortages, trade deficits, and an occasional stock market "crash," most people in the United States and Canada still feel quite secure. In contrast, many Latin Americans are guaranteed much less in life, and suffer from considerably more discord.

Politically, North Americans confine their feuds primarily to selecting officials and debating public policies, but in Latin America feuds are more fundamental. Unlike their neighbors to the north who read Plato, Machiavelli, Locke, and Marx to understand their intellectual heritage, Latin Americans consult them to find solutions to political problems as yet unsolved. Among them today you will find democrats, authoritarians, and communists who all insist that they know what is best for themselves and their neighbors.

To understand how this all came about and why it persists we need to look into the past as well as the present. In this chapter a fictional president will help us do just that. He does not represent all Latin American presidents; no one could. While these nations share many things, they also differ in important ways, and no single narrative can include everything. Here we will learn how one person understands the Latin American condition and determines what he will do about it. As you read his account, you should judge for yourself his chances for success.

Problems and progress: a presidential assessment

A brief description of my country is presented in Table 1.1. We have approximately 25 million persons, the majority being mestizos (a mixture of Hispanic and Indian); 20 percent of them European, Arab, and Jewish; 10 percent Indian; and 5 percent black or mulatto. If you

3

Table 1.1. *Country profile*

Population: 25 million

Size: 500,000 square miles

Literacy: 70%

Gross domestic product per capita (1988): $2,000 (US)

Ethnic composition:
Mestizo: 65%
European, Asian: 20%
Indian: 10%
Mulatto: 5%

Class structure	*Land tenure*
Upper stratum: 5%	Richest 5% owns 50% of arable land
Upper middle stratum: 15%	Middle 20% owns 30% of arable land
Lower middle stratum: 30%	Poorest 75% owns 20% of arable land
Lowest stratum: 50%	

Distribution of gross national product
Agriculture: 25%
Industry: 30%
Mining: 10%
Services: 35%

Trade

Exports to:		Imports from:	
United States:	40%	United States:	45%
West Germany:	20%	Japan:	20%
Japan:	10%	West Germany:	10%
Great Britain:	10%	Great Britain:	10%
Latin America:	8%	Latin America:	5%
Others:	12%	Others:	10%

---

divide our national product by the number of inhabitants, it is $2,000 per capita, which was just below the Latin American average in 1988.

Agriculture has always been important to us and still generates nearly half of our exports. It would be even more prominent had we not developed a mining industry and substantial manufacturing during the past fifty years. We export coffee, cotton, sugar, iron ore, and textiles, we do our own food processing, and make many consumer goods. Our public utilities and railways are government owned, as are our airline and our petroleum company, having been nationalized some years ago. Foreign investors are prominent in our economy, producing chemicals, pharmaceuticals, appliances, and automobiles in plants

built during the 1960s and 1970s. They also operate our two largest
banks, our iron mines, and an oil company that distributes as much
gasoline as our government corporation does.

We rely heavily on foreigners not only for markets and sophisticated
technology, but also for the capital we need to finance more growth.
Some years ago we benefited from grants and loans from the United
States government, but today its aid goes almost exclusively to countries that are poorer than we are, and to countries like El Salvador
where the United States has strategic interests. We still benefit from
World Bank and Inter-American Development Bank help with financing the construction of hydroelectric dams, highways, and hospitals. In the past fifteen years private foreign banks have also loaned
us substantial capital, eager as they were to invest the "petrodollars"
that were deposited with them by the OPEC nations who had acquired
sudden wealth after raising oil prices in the 1970s. This grand opportunity to borrow and invest in our own development has brought
new problems with it, as I shall explain later in this report.

Social conditions

Our society has changed considerably since 1900, becoming more
urban, literate, and diverse in its composition. Industrialization, new
state enterprises, and more education created a larger middle class and
a dynamic working class. Nevertheless, wealth remains heavily concentrated. In contrast to the more industrialized Western European
and North American nations whose richest 20 percent hold 40 percent
of their national income, our wealthiest 20 percent control nearly 65
percent. At the bottom, widespread poverty persists, the poorest 30
percent earning just enough for minimal subsistence. Moreover, our
population has nearly doubled during the past 30 years, leaving us
with much larger cities and even more poor persons in the countryside.

It is impossible to describe our class structure in any detail since
our census is never very accurate, but its primary features are conspicuous nevertheless. At the top sits a very wealthy 5 percent, the
owners of large rural properties, industries, banks, and investments
all over the world. Just below them is another 15 percent who manage
domestic and foreign firms, operate their own enterprises, own large
coffee or cotton farms, or are successful physicians, lawyers, and en-
gineers. Next comes the 30 percent who compose something that

resembles a middle class, among them military officers, government civil servants, school teachers, office staffs and modest farmers. Just beneath them is everyone else, including an industrial working class, followed by the urban and rural poor, themselves a disparate collection of farm workers, subsistence farmers, menial laborers, street vendors, and domestic servants.

Obviously the lower class has benefited the least from our economic development in recent times. No matter how we promote economic growth in the future, we cannot afford to ignore their plight if we are to develop our entire nation. Currently the lower class neither contributes much to our national economic and political life nor takes much from it. They are preoccupied with local matters, more involved in assuring their own subsistence than in attending party conventions. One marvels at their passivity amidst such deep deprivation, but that does not prevent their mobilization against the system by agitators who wish to destroy it. It is to avert their violent rebellion as well as to improve their conditions that we reformers dedicate ourselves.

But we need first to study our situation and its causes more thoroughly. Looking to the past is always hazardous since it invites blaming our Iberian and pre-Columbian cultures for our predicament even when we know that such conclusions are unwarranted. We are products of our past, but we also have the power to change what we have inherited from it. New ideas, ingenuity, and enterprise can make a difference as we have already seen in countries like Brazil and Venezuela where substantial progress has been made. To assume that we are condemned by history to impotence is to deny our capacity to change.

It all began with the Iberian conquest of the New World five centuries ago. The first conquistadors transmitted social values to the New World that they had acquired when they expelled the Islamic Moors from the Iberian peninsula just before they crossed the Atlantic. By fragmenting the Iberian peninsula into a score of principalities, starting in the tenth century, the Moors had cursed Spanish life with regional economic separatism and local submission. Gradually, over nearly three centuries, however, the Spaniards and the Portuguese pushed the Moors southward, the last battle coming in 1492, the year Columbus reached an island in the Caribbean on his search for a western route to the Orient.

The reconquest of Spain required daring and determination. A premium was placed on military skills, and the heroic military leader established the standard against which all leadership was judged. For their victories the victors were rewarded with land and authority over the peasants who occupied it. For future generations lessons from the reconquest were clear: The quickest route to fame and fortune was through heroic deeds on behalf of the king and queen.

Opportunities to replicate the reconquest were opened by the discovery of the New World at the end of the fifteenth century. Thirty years after Columbus reached the Caribbean islands, ambitious persons like Hernán Cortés and Francisco Pizarro left Cuba for the mainland "to serve God and the king, and to get rich," Cortés by conquering the Aztecs in Mexico in 1519 and Pizarro the Incas far to the south in Peru in 1531. Most of the conquistadors came from Spain's Castilian gentry, themselves modest in wealth, tough and ambitious. Monarchs sent them to find gold for the royal treasury, promising them a place in the New World nobility if they succeeded. They were valiant, cruel, sentimental, aggressive, selfish, and occasionally altruistic, always convinced that they would secure fame and fortune if they succeeded, and salvation from God if they did not.

The conquistadors cleared the way for the Iberian patrimonial monarchy that ruled over its conquests from across the Atlantic. It was unabashedly centralized and authoritarian, reliant on a hierarchy through which the governors dominated the governed. Authority moved in only one direction, from the monarchy in Spain through its viceroys in colonial capitals down to their subjects. Individual citizens were not free agents who could pursue any ends they wished within the new political order; with few exceptions, they had to live within the rank into which they were born and accept the authority of those above them.

According to the Iberian tradition, authority was not granted by citizens to government; it already resided in government and membership within its realm required that citizens relinquish any thought of popular control over authorities. This approach to politics differed fundamentally from the liberal democratic political philosophy that arose in Great Britain and flourished in its North American colonies, where citizens came to believe that political authorities were their creation (i.e., delegates, authorized to make decisions that required periodic public approval). Such ideas were incomprehensible to sixteenth-century Iberians in the New and Old Worlds. The monarch was sovereign, the ultimate earthly authority who defined the rules and enforced them, assisted by a royal bureaucracy; conversely, its subjects were left no choice but to obey their rulers. Only the administration of laws written in Spain and Portugal was subject to appeal, but even that had to be done through courts controlled by the Crown.

The New World was fertile ground for transplanted Iberian values and institutions. Military victories over the Aztecs, Incas, and other indigenous peoples were swift; precious metals were found and shared with the Crown; and thousands were converted to Catholicism. Agriculture became another source of new wealth, nourished by the *encomienda,* a right granted by the Crown to landowners and miners, which allowed them to extract labor from the indigenous people within their domains. Soon a new nobility was built on an economy of mines and large landed estates that generated wealth, social status, and power for their owners.

The landed estates, termed *latifundios,* were unlike the family farms built in North America outside the Deep South. In Latin America land was distributed by the Crown immediately after the conquest. Even though many areas were left unoccupied until this century, the most fertile pieces had been allocated by royal grants by 1600. Labor was even more important than property, for it was by exploiting indigenous labor that the *latifundio* prospered. In North America, in contrast, farmland was distributed gradually, moving from east to west, usually in small parcels to immigrant farmers after indigenous populations had been liquidated or expelled. The notable exception was in the South where plantation agriculture developed using slave labor. But most North Americans earned only a modest income from the land they cultivated; for Latin Americans, in contrast, land was not only a means of production for domestic and foreign markets but also a foundation for social control by a privileged class that believed from the beginning that they deserved a disproportionate share of economic power in colonial society. That is how we Latin Americans inherited a rural society divided between oligarchs and peasants while North Americans escaped both.

Our society was not only more rigidly structured than the North American one, it was also more racially mixed. Throughout colonial times Native American women bore the children of Spaniards, creating the mestizo majority of our population. In addition, slaves were brought from Africa to work in sugar plantations along our coasts, much as they were all over the Caribbean and in northeast Brazil. Some mixed with mestizos, creating our mulatto community. While persons from any race can be in any social class, colonial society left us with racial prejudices at the top that have kept most persons of mixed race outside our upper class which still prides itself on its European ancestry.

The colonial institutions, values, and social structures that were three hundred years old and deeply entrenched by our independence in 1820 have been assailed by new ideas and institutions ever since. Trade in coffee and cotton grew in the late nineteenth century, followed by iron ore a little later, together bringing substantial economic growth to the country. Soon farmers became more productive, cities larger and better equipped, inducing enterprising foreigners to seek their fortunes among us. Simultaneously, a new class of professionals, merchants, bureaucrats, and crafts-workers asserted themselves politically and forced the traditional ruling class to share government with them. The result is a more complex society today, one with remnants from the nineteenth-century economy that coexist with more modern institutions. A few *latifundios* and plantations remain, but they are dwarfed economically by several hundred large- and medium-size coffee and cotton farms and cattle ranches. Most people who live in rural villages or on farms are poor by even the most generous standards, among them tenant farmers, small ranchers, and the landless. Our cities contain substantial variety, including modern, well-educated people living alongside merchants, industrialists, and the descendants of our nineteenth-century oligarchs. At the other extreme are the thousands who occupy our slums and squatter settlements, surviving precariously on their unskilled labor and petty commerce and services. It is a society in which the old tolerates the new and the modern coexists with the traditional. We like to think that we are swiftly moving from our burdensome past to a more productive future, leaving our traditional ways far behind, but that may be wishful thinking. Today we are stuck, unable to achieve elementary social reforms and unsure about how many we really need.

What troubles me is not our inadequate economic growth and modernization, for we have actually grown considerably during the past half century, but the way new wealth is denied nearly half our population. Until greater efforts are made to address this condition, they will stay poor. They are trapped within a vicious cycle of poverty:

Most are unproductive because they have so little capital and so few skills that their low production earns them scanty income, which in turn denies them what they need to become more productive. Until we liberate them from such conditions they will contribute very little to the nation's development or to their own welfare.

Economic underdevelopment and its causes

After colonial times our economy remained agrarian, devoted to producing commodities for both export and domestic consumption. Originally we concentrated on the cultivation of indigo, sugar, cacao, and cattle raising as well as the extraction of gold and silver. When Independence freed us from Spain we merely changed trading partners, looking to England and continental Europe for merchants who were eager to feed their growing populations with our produce. When the nineteenth century ended we had added several new cash crops to our list, starting with coffee in midcentury and cotton a few decades later. As income from our exports increased, we built new ports, modernized our capital city, and, with investments from foreigners, we built railways to transport crops to cities and harbors. Our leaders were proud of their achievements, certain that they had found a lucrative place for us in the world economy. It did not bother them that what we earned from trade reached only a minority of our people, and that most who lived in the countryside remained poor, dependent on cultivating little pieces of land and selling their labor cheaply during coffee, cotton, and sugar harvests. Nor did they feel any guilt for having confiscated native and peasant lands to expand their coffee and cotton farms.

Iron ore was found in 1915, our first mineral discovery since colonial times. Foreign companies developed the mines, sharing 10 percent of their profits with our government and employing several thousand persons. Commerce within the country also increased and some cottage industries emerged, making food products and clothing that were sold in local markets. But it was not until the 1930s that things really began to change.

Until the Great Depression struck in 1929 we had taken it for granted that our export economy would sustain us. Trade had been slowed occasionally by recessions in Europe or droughts at home, but we had always rebounded a few years later. That is why the world depression came as such a shock to us. Suddenly we had lost our markets abroad and had little prospect of getting them back any time soon. Almost overnight doubts about the export economy spread, though initially we did not know what to do about it. It was inevitable, however, that we would turn to industry to save us, if only because we needed goods for local consumption that the depressed European and North American economies could no longer supply.

Industrialization was a difficult and controversial choice since our farmers and exporters feared that supplying our markets with goods produced at home might antagonize the foreigners who had previously supplied then. But we really had little choice because it had become obvious that we could no longer rely on world trade to sustain us in so volatile an international economy. It helped that some of our entrepreneurs were eager to become manufacturers, and that our government was willing to erect tariff barriers to protect them against cheaper foreign imports. After 1935 our industries grew rapidly, supplying more than half of our consumer goods by the end of World War II.

After the war, we were influenced by the United Nations Economic Commission on Latin America which pointed out how we suffered from adverse terms of trade with the industrial nations, a situation that made imports more expensive to us than before (e.g., it took more bags of coffee to purchase an imported item than it had previously). The prices of imported manufactured goods rose, due to higher labor and technology costs abroad, while the prices paid for our commodity exports remained nearly constant or fell when other Third World countries began producing similar commodities. If there had been any doubts about our need to promote more industrialization, they were gone by 1960.

Nevertheless, we lacked the financial capital to build as much industry as we needed because our domestic savings were so low. National savings come primarily from individual savings accounts in banks and other financial institutions and from government taxation. Private accounts are relatively scarce because nearly half of our population is too poor to save. And those who can – property owners, merchants, professionals, and skilled laborers – do so at a lower rate than their counterparts in industrial nations because of well-founded fears that the inflation we occasionally suffer will reduce the value of their savings. Instead, they prefer to consume as fast as possible or buy dollars and deposit them abroad. Capital flight, as the latter is called, accelerates whenever we lose control over domestic prices, and no matter how hard the government tries, it cannot prevent it.

For a time it was left to the government to finance our development. By levying taxes on incomes, business, sales, and imports we tried to raise funds to invest in major infrastructure projects. We also created government banks that loaned money to industries that our authorities wanted built. Unfortunately, this worked better in theory than in practice. Our people have been very adept at avoiding taxes, and our bureaucracy has not improved its ability to collect them. And with our economic performance fluctuating so much, tax revenues from sales, imports, and exports have been very unreliable.

That leaves two obvious sources for financing investment: multinational corporations that are willing to invest in our economy and multinational banks that will loan money to our government and private businesses. Multinational corporations are prominent in several industries, but they have invested little new money in our economy during the past decade. Foreign banks, always modest in our economy previously, rushed in when they needed customers for the funds that the OPEC countries began depositing with them after they raised oil prices in 1973. Since our economy was growing at the time, we welcomed their unusual offer of large loans to government and private enterprises. Though we never borrowed as much as larger nations like Brazil and Mexico did, we did receive enough to finance the construction of a government steel mill, new hydroelectric facilities, and several 747s for our national airline. It was a magnificent windfall for us, but, unfortunately, it was a brief one. We had relied on economic growth and good prices for our exports to repay our loans, but when recessions struck the industrial countries in the early 1980s, we lost crucial markets, and prices for our exports dropped.

The 1980s have been very dark days compared to the 1970s. Instead of borrowing and growing as we did before, we have been forced to slow our growth, drastically cutting our government budget and reducing our imports to save dollars. Stagnation, not growth, has prevailed during the past eight years, causing our per capita income to fall by 10 percent. Thus, at the moment that our economy was beginning to "take off," we suddenly went into a long descent, ending up more dependent on foreign capital than ever before. Our economy is far from collapsing, but to revive it we need foreign credit and investment. Unfortunately, no one is eager to invest in our future at the moment.

Still, we can take pride in some things, most notably our farm production which has doubled during the past thirty years. Had it not done so, we could not repay any of the interest on our foreign loans. But we also know that less than half of our farmers contributed to this change, the rest still farming at the subsistence level. Almost no one starves, but the poorest among them have no clean water, receive little education, and suffer from many health problems that go untreated. Back in the 1960s our government did redistribute some property, dividing pieces of the least productive *latifundios* among sharecroppers, but only 20 percent of those seeking more land received it.

Population growth also constrains our economic development. Between 1900 and 1950 our population doubled; then it doubled again by 1975. Moreover, our capital city (which now has 2 million people) will have more than 5 million by the end of this century, nearly half of them living in improvised, poor housing. No matter how you look at it, we have more persons than our economy can handle. That is one reason why poverty persists among us: We cannot create enough jobs to accommodate those who come into the market each year, especially for people in the lower class where our population is growing the fastest.

Political life: past, present, and future

We gained our Independence from an Iberian monarchy and its colonial bureaucracy nearly 175 years ago but remnants of the colonial experience remain with us. From the beginning we developed a talent for evading the most onerous laws written in Spain for its colonies. Educated in the natural law tradition, we knew that obedience was required, but that never prevented our putting the burden of enforcement on colonial authorities whose power never reached far beyond Mexico City, Lima, and other major government outposts. We were a people who, though raised on an authoritarian diet, developed a talent for abusing or ignoring laws that served the Crown more than they did its subjects.

Colonial rule was ended by rebellions early in the nineteenth century. Those who led our revolt were motivated by a desire to free themselves from the grasp of the colonial trading system, a determination to end political control over us from abroad, and, among a few, a yearning for the kind of liberation that had been championed in the French and North American revolutions. But the task turned out to be more formidable than any of its advocates had realized. No constitutional convention was enough to eradicate the tradition of authoritarian politics and replace it with governments that derived their authority from the people they governed. People just do not change that quickly, especially when they have been educated to resist authorities whose interests were different from their own. Once colonial government was gone, real political power fell to local elites who welcomed the opportunity to control their own regions without deferring to people who issued new rules from the nation's capital. They pretended that they had created replicas of North American constitutional democracy, but in fact it was just a veneer that could not conceal our authoritarian ways of doing politics.

Despite some valiant efforts by new political elites to make democracy work, post-Independence governments were overthrown with regularity by local leaders who commanded private armies. Labeled *caciques* or *caudillos,* they called themselves generals and fought year after year with national authorities and other *caudillos.* Some eventually amassed enough power to rule entire nations by midcentury. Ironically, many who had begun their struggle in order to prevent the centralization of authority in their nations ended up taking over and centralizing it in order to remain in control. Nevertheless, little in our societies changed during those years except the occupants of the presidential palace; our wealthiest landowners retained their wealth and continued to abuse the masses.

Our first political parties arose in the 1860s. Initially, there were only two, one that labeled itself Conservative and the other Liberal. They were not parties in the modern sense, but elites without constituency organizations or mass appeal. More characteristic was their reliance on patron–client relationships in which individuals of low status were made to depend on people of higher status to gain access to resources under the latter's control. Peasants, for example, relied on landowners; the landowners depended on local *caudillos* to maintain order; and they, in turn, depended on national political leaders to keep the nation together. From the landowner the peasant received access to rented land and protection against natural and human enemies in exchange for deference, cheap labor, and support for the landowners' political causes; similarly, landowners were given physical protection by *caudillos* in return for financial tribute and political support. Patron–client politics remain part of our political life. Upward mobility within the political process depends heavily on patronage, and survival in office requires that one serve as a broker between industrialists, farmers, union leaders, peasants, and the government.

The Conservatives, as their name implies, favored the traditional social order, the economic status quo, and a prominent place for the Roman Catholic church in society. The Liberals, though also elitist, were anticlerical, and sought higher profits for themselves by taking lands from the church and from the Native Americans to create larger coffee and cotton farms. It was under the Liberals during the late nineteenth and early twentieth centuries that our economy began to grow at a faster pace, aided by the foreign-financed construction of the railways and ports needed to transport our commodities to foreign markets. The Liberals gave us unprecedented political stability, holding five consecutive elections. Only 10 percent of our adult population participated in those elections, since the franchise was restricted to literate male property owners.

We have already discussed how the 1929 world depression under-mined our export economy and prompted efforts to industrialize. The drive for industrialization was accompanied by new political forces that challenged the traditional elite and its monopoly of economic and political power. In less than two decades our political process was transformed from one in which a few political leaders settled all policy questions among themselves to one in which the representatives of industrial, professional, and labor groups became actively involved in policy making.

The transition had actually begun around 1900. With foreign trade and domestic commerce accelerating we suddenly found ourselves with many more merchants, lawyers, and white-collar employees. Simul-taneously, several hundred thousand immigrants from Europe began new lives in our country, some of them as laborers who brought with them ideas about labor unions and socialist ideologies. Initially, the Liberal Party tried to incorporate its middle-class critics into its ranks, but creating new political parties was far more popular, as were cam-paigns for new electoral laws that gave the opposition a fair chance to win elections. But it was the military, not the new political parties, that finally ended the elite monopoly over public office. Frustrated by the Liberal Party's inability to deal with the economic collapse and social protests that followed the 1929 world depression, the military reluctantly seized the government, ending five decades of civilian rule by the agro-exporter elite. Although they tried to remain neutral, some nationalist officers did much to promote the growth of our industries by nationalizing railroads and several public utilities; creating an industrial development bank; and raising tariffs on imported goods in order to protect those produced here. But, like civilians before them, they ignored the rural economy, leaving its management to the *latifundistas* and commercial farmers who had dominated it for the past fifty years.

After World War II our political life became more complicated. The military had virtually become its own political party, convinced that it had as much right to govern as civilians did. And our Liberal and Conservative Parties were joined by more vigorous, though still small, Socialist and Communist ones, as well as my own left of center Popular Democratic Party, which we created in the late 1930s. The Liberals won the first postwar election but, amid charges of corruption and mismanagement, the military evicted them again in 1950. The Conservatives returned in 1952 and governed until we defeated them in the 1966 presidential contest. We tried to apply ideas that we had taken from progressive economists at the United Nations Economic Commission for Latin America, but implementing them was obstructed from the outset. Opposition in Congress from parties on the left and right delayed passing our agrarian reform and nationalization programs until near the end of our term, and even after they were enacted we were impeded by measures taken in the courts by landowners. Our constituents were disappointed, yet our conservative opponents were fearful, convinced that our reelection would lead us to fight even harder for the reforms they detested.

We were reelected, though just barely, but that was hardly cause for alarm since it was obvious that we would be forced to continue at a slow pace. Then, in the midst of what was quickly becoming another rather undistinguished attempt at reform, violence broke out, only this time it was not the working class or the peasantry that was doing it. One by one, wealthy businessmen were kidnapped and held for ransom, which they reluctantly paid. Banks were robbed and police stations bombed. Clandestine organizations, calling themselves "revolutionaries," were operating in our largest cities. When our police repeatedly failed to capture more than a few culprits we were attacked for being soft on terrorism. No one seemed to appreciate the dilemma we faced. As a democratic government we could not just declare a state of siege and go to war with terrorists. That would give the military too much authority at the expense of what was already a very fragile democracy. Yet, by not dealing firmly with terrorists who refused to negotiate with us, we undermined what little confidence the middle class had in our government. In the end it would not be our choice to make for, with an inevitability that everyone recognized, the armed forces evicted us in 1972 and created a military dictatorship that was unlike any we had known before.

This time they went to war with our own people, determined to eradicate terrorists and revolutionary ideas from our land. A few thousand persons were immediately arrested, some executed without trial, and several thousand more were forced into exile. Convinced that civilians could no longer manage our affairs, the officers in charge announced plans to reorganize our national politics, making law and order their highest priority. We could not help but feel a little responsible for their flight into fascism, yet we knew that it was not entirely our fault. Terrorism was not our creation nor were the military officers who deceived themselves into believing that they could discipline our entire population. But that did not make it any easier for us to spend the next fifteen years living under an authoritarian military regime that outlawed all political parties and denied us our liberties.

Order did prevail after that, bringing with it a new enthusiasm among foreigners for investing in our economy. And for a time the economy grew quite rapidly, this time also with help from banks then overflowing with petrodollars. For a time we were the sensation of the international commercial world, "the country that was finally being run by people who knew how to handle those contentious latinos," is the way a North American business magazine put it. But what goes up usually comes down, as the astonished junta members discovered in 1981 when the international economic boom ended and recessions set in all over the world. New economists were brought in who heeded the advice of the International Monetary Fund which loaned us emergency funds after we agreed to cut back, imposing tight austerity measures on our own economy, cutting the government's budget, and reducing imports.

Seizing the opening that the crisis allowed us, we campaigned with the other parties for a return to democratic government. Initially we made no headway, but peaceful protests against the armed forces grew, and gradually it became obvious that the same middle class that had welcomed military intervention in 1972 was tired of it. It was not long before bickering among the military service chiefs over how to handle our opposition began to tear the ruling junta apart. Even sooner than we had expected, officers offered to negotiate their departure with us secretly, eventually agreeing to hold free elections in exchange for our promise not to take reprisals against any of them. It was not the kind of choice that we wanted to make, but it was too good to refuse. In 1988 elections were held and I was victorious.

Where do we go from here?

Nothing came easily in the past and it is no different now. We must work with what we have without being devoured by the predicament we are in. People to my left already find my proposals too modest and my actions too subservient to powerful forces here and abroad, while those on my right grow anxious about my affection for democracy in all of its uncertainty, and my announced intention to redistribute wealth from the rich to the poor.

My objectives are closely linked to one another, so if we fail with one, the others will be affected adversely. Politically, I want to complete my term and turn my office over to an elected successor, something not easily done in this country. For democracy to endure my administration must survive. It is that simple. Throughout this century we have been trapped within a vicious political cycle: Whenever powerful members of our society decided that democracy was not working to their advantage, they destroyed it; and each time they did, they taught another generation that democracy did not work here. We now have the opportunity to break this cycle and, if I complete my term, I will have taken us another step in that direction.

Democracy has many foes. Our military can end it whenever they wish. They have ideas about how our country should be run and have already demonstrated that they are willing to govern if civilians do not meet their standards. But our military is never as monolithic as it appears, and therein rests our best hope. While some officers are unabashedly authoritarian and detest democracy, there are others who prefer to remain on their bases and give us a chance.

The best way to defend democracy from our armed forces is to make it popular with people of all social classes. While they can shoot their way into the presidential palace at any time of day, they are not eager to do so when they believe a coup will be unpopular with nearly all citizens. They need support from technocrats, industrialists, financiers, and foreign investors, and want the urban middle class to accept them. The latter's opposition to a coup never prevents one, but, when the middle class supports civilian government, it stands a better chance of survival. That is why I am trying so hard to retain middle class support for my government.

The armed forces are not the only threat to democracy. Extremists on the left and right have even less use for it. Leftists come in many different forms, some of them small communist and socialist parties who participate in elections and devote much of their time to disagreeing among themselves over how to represent the proletariat. However, there are others who want to destroy our system in order to create something like Cuba's new society. In the 1960s, young persons who were inspired by Fidel Castro and Ché Guevara tried to imitate them here, but with advisors from the United States our military repelled them. Others attempted insurgency in our cities as I have already stated, provoking the military takeover in 1972.

Today a new effort has sprung up, one that is far less conspicuous than its predecessors. Unlike Castro's little guerrilla army that marched from the mountains to the cities in Cuba, today insurgents occupy no permanent location. Instead they appear from time to time almost anywhere in the country, killing policemen and local officials and planting bombs at public buildings and embassies in our capital city. Then, just as quickly, they disappear, blending back into our community, going undetected. They are swift to take credit for their operations, issuing statements about how they are part of a revolutionary effort to eliminate our corrupt and illegitimate bourgeois government. Clearly, they want to disrupt our fragile democracy by demoralizing our government and injecting fear and violence into our society, but I am determined to resist them. So far there are too few of them to succeed, but the danger remains. Military officers are quick to remind us that more must be done, demanding that we give them greater latitude for hunting suspected insurgents. However, we do not want to fall into the familiar trap created by turning the military loose. We realize that if we do not try harder to police our country, the armed forces and many civilians will turn against us, perhaps even going so far as to evict us as they did in 1972. But if we do turn the military loose, we risk their violating human rights and destroying democracy in the process. Obviously, we must handle this carefully.

Extremists on the right are equally invisible but no less eager to see democracy fail. Dreams of creating a fascist government that keeps the masses under control inspire them. They kill suspected insurgents and radical politicians, using army veterans and criminals to do their dirty work. Because many in our police forces welcome their assistance, they refuse to root them out. We are quickly becoming a nation that trembles by day and fights by night with little hope of ending our barbaric struggle.

Subduing the violent among us is necessary for democracy's preservation, but it is hardly sufficient. At a minimum we also need to provide our poorest citizens with jobs, education, and more medical care. But that costs money, something that is currently in short supply. In the countryside they also need property. That is why I have decided to use the agrarian reform law that we promulgated several years ago to expropriate property that is not currently under cultivation, regardless of who owns it. I will do it carefully, assuring productive farmers that we will not touch their property, but I must do something to make the rural masses believe in democracy. As it stands, most of them think it is a facade that is used to hide middle-class raids on the national treasury. They must be taught that it offers something concrete to them as well.

It is easy to advocate growth and prosperity, but that does not make them any simpler to achieve. We know that we can grow: In 1980 our national product was twice what it was in 1950. But today growth is much harder because of debts whose payment consumes nearly half of the dollars that our exports earn every year. If we have learned anything from our recent experience, it is that economic growth and modernization have not liberated us from our heavy reliance on the supply of capital from abroad. Today we find ourselves not just with a debt to pay, but also with a need for even more capital in order to ignite our growth again, something that forces us to invite foreign industries to invest as much as they can to help advance our industrialization. It seems that we have little choice but to continue to borrow even though we cannot pay everything that we currently owe.

Finally, there is an issue that I am reluctant to discuss for lack of experience with it, namely the appearance of a clandestine narcotics industry. Crime is not new to us, nor is the operation of black markets where people trade secretly in order to avoid government regulation and taxes. Both are commonplace. But we have not known anything that exhibits as much vigor as the narcotics industry. Although drug production is far less intrusive here than it is in countries like Colombia, it involves more persons daily. Poor farmers grow marijuana and coca for traders who pay them ten times what their corn earns them. The traders, in turn, process, pack and export marijuana and cocaine to the United States and Europe where they earn ten or twenty times more than what they paid for it. Allowing this to continue is objectionable on moral grounds, and because it upsets our North American neighbors, but that is not all. Even more threatening is the way it is creating a new force in our society whose leaders can bribe and kill authorities and get away with it. It is as if the *caudillos* of times past have returned to create financial fortresses that no one can penetrate, threatening to establish a semisovereign authority within the nation that operates according to its own rules. Clearly something must be done to stop them, but I am not certain what to do. As long as there is a market for such products abroad, powerful persons in our society will supply it. Do we dare wage a war on our own people if we are not confident of success?

I sometimes wonder why I took this job in the first place. Maybe I am a little too gullible and should know better. Or, perhaps, like most presidents, I am convinced that no one can do the job any better than I can. Only time will tell.

Getting started

What do you think of this president? Does he offer the best solutions to the many problems he describes? How, for example, should the president promote the kind of economic growth that is required to meet the needs of an expanding population that desires an improved standard of living? This mythical nation has tried to free itself from reliance on agriculture and its raw product exports by promoting industrialization, yet its economy continues to rise and fall with the prices of its commodities in world markets. Is it trapped or is there another way out? And what about poverty: How can the condition of the masses be improved? Are radical agrarian reforms the solution? How would they affect the rest of the economy? Should capitalism be abandoned altogether? If so, what should replace it? Then there is the infamous foreign debt. Should a country like this one default on its debt even if that means that no one will loan it the money it needs to import technology that is essential to operate the nation's industry?

And let us not forget politics. Can democracy be preserved? Should it be? Should the government move to the left or to the right to find allies among the other political parties and interest groups? What if the political right urges the armed forces to take over again? What should the government do? How should it respond if insurgents on the left rally people to their cause? And where should authorities draw the line between respecting the liberties of violent persons and silencing them? Obviously, there are no simple solutions to these problems, but decisions are being made daily to deal with them. To understand what is being done we have no choice but to examine carefully everything we can about Latin American politics and economics. By reading the rest of this book you can make a start.

Further reading

Black, Jan Knippers. *Latin America: Its Problems and Its Promise.* Boulder, CO: Westview Press, 1984.

Cardoso, Fernando Henrique, and Enzo Faletto. *Dependency and Development in Latin America.* Berkeley: University of California Press, 1979.

Dominguez, Jorge I. *Insurrection or Loyalty: The Breakdown of the Spanish American Empire.* Cambridge: Harvard University Press, 1980.

Furtado, Celso. *Economic Development of Latin America.* Cambridge: Cambridge University Press, 1977.

Gibson, Charles. *Spain in America.* New York: Harper & Row, 1966.

Glade, William P. *The Latin American Economies.* New York: Van Nostrand Reinhold, 1969.

Harrison, Lawrence E. *Underdevelopment Is a State of Mind: The Latin American Case.* Lanham, MD: University Press of America, 1985.

Lockart, James, and Stuart Schwartz. *Early Latin America.* New York: Cambridge University Press, 1983.

Lombardi, Cathryn L., and John V. Lombardi. *Latin American History: A Teaching Atlas.* Madison: University of Wisconsin Press, 1983.

Morse, Richard M. "The Heritage of Latin America," in Louis Hartz, ed., *The Founding of New Societies.* New York: Harcourt Brace and World, 1964, pp. 123–77.

Sheahan, John. *Patterns of Development in Latin America.* Princeton, NJ: Princeton University Press, 1987.

Stein, Stanley J., and Barbara Stein. *The Colonial Heritage of Latin America: Essays on Economic Dependence in Perspective.* New York: Oxford University Press, 1970.

Veliz, Claudio. *The Centralist Tradition in America.* Princeton, NJ: Princeton University Press, 1980.

2. The rules of the Latin American game

Military dictators, democrats, and communists all governed some-where in Latin America during the past decade. It is hard to find more political diversity in such close proximity anywhere. To make sense of it, we must find ways to generate coherent and convincing expla-nations of the ways Latin Americans behave. In particular, we need to know what government means to them, why some of them disagree so intensely on many fundamental political and economic issues, and how they resolve disputes that are so passionate and profound.

A political game

One way to begin our inquiry is to study politics as if it were analogous to a game. The game idea is helpful not because politics is primarily recreational; obviously it is not. Politics affects the most fundamental aspects of human life, sometimes cruelly. What makes the game met-aphor valuable is the way it helps us see politics as a dynamic process involving contests among people with different ideas about govern-ment and its purpose. It directs us to examine the rules followed, both formal and informal, and to study players and how they collaborate and compete with one another.

Politics is part of social life. It derives in part from a need to resolve conflicts among people who cannot resolve all of their disagreements spontaneously to everyone's satisfaction. Even in what appear to be the most orderly societies disagreements arise over everything from ways to assure personal safety to the amount of taxes that one must pay. So, either by drawing on political traditions that sustain familiar procedures for meeting this basic need, or by organizing new ways of doing so, nations have established ways to deal with their internal conflicts.

However they do it, individual behavior is never entirely predictable. People do not behave like physical particles that function according to natural laws. Though prone to similar behaviors under comparable

24

conditions, people can change their conduct in ways that iron filings cannot. Many things influence the choices they make, and people are not always the same in every instance. That is why we cannot account for their behavior in exactly the same way a physicist does. Nevertheless, we can observe and compare behaviors, using the game idea to discover some of the reasons why people behave as they do.

If relations among persons were always harmonious, the game idea, with its emphasis on conflict resolution, would be of little use. But in nearly all nations today the things that people want are often in short supply, monopolized by a few people, or just never shared in ways that citizens desire, making it impossible for everyone to agree on everything. For many, it is government policy that divides people, each preferring one policy over the others, but many fundamental issues also demand resolution, some of which involve the very nature of government. North Americans sometimes find such profundity a little alien, having grown to maturity in a society that appears to suffer from only minor conflicts. But it was not always that way, as the nation's Civil War reminds us. Nor is it so in Latin America today; instead, vital issues are the subject of intense political and physical combat in some countries and a matter for fervent but peaceful dispute in others. El Salvadorians are deeply divided and at war with one another today; in Peru, authorities cannot deter the aggression of rebels in their midst; in Colombia, cocaine merchants exercise more influence over the nation's judges than does the nation's constitution; and even Mexicans cannot agree on how democratic their politics should be. Our task then is to discover how these and other conflicts arose, how Latin Americans deal with them, and what difference their solutions actually make.

Games come in many different forms. In some players are closely matched and each is given a reasonable chance of winning. Most parlor games are like that. Few political contests are so competitive, however. More common is a type of competition in which the prospects for winning are unevenly distributed, in some cases because the rules discriminate against certain players, and in others because the resources needed to win are distributed unequally. For example, liberal democratic rules favor vote getters and interest groups, whereas communist ones give advantages to Communist Party members. To think of politics as analogous to a game, then, does not mean that we assume that it is always highly competitive or always democratic. On the contrary, games can be rigged by anyone who has the power to write the rules or ignore them.

The game metaphor is not only handy for studying Latin America. Every political process has rules, and comparing them is always enlightening. One can understand politics in Chicago better after examining how its rules contrast with those followed in New York or Miami, for example. Similarly, the way the British play the democratic game, with a prime minister who is selected by a parliament, can be comprehended better by contrasting British rules of conduct with those followed by the president and legislature in the United States. In other words, one can use the game concept to examine all forms of politics, from changes currently under way in the rules followed in the Soviet Union to the detestable way that conflict is regulated in South Africa.

Equally important, we need to be aware that games are not played in a vacuum. Three things will always influence their design and operation: culture, economic structures, and state structures. Each nation has a culture on which citizens rely for many of their beliefs and practices. As we learned in Chapter 1, Latin American society was created when Spaniards and Portuguese forced themselves upon indigenous peoples. Contemporary life is not a replica of colonial life, but it was formed by it and by the many ideas that have intruded upon it during the past two centuries. Today modernity coexists with tradition, each constantly influencing the other. Political and economic ideologies and institutions have been imported repeatedly in a search for better ways of life. The result is a rich and complex mix of beliefs and technologies ranging from the very indigenous to the most contemporary and sophisticated. If we omit tradition and culture from our inquiry, we will miss not only a primary source of political rules and behavior but we will also fail to appreciate what political events mean to players themselves.

The material world in which games are played is also significant. We may not live by bread alone, but we cannot live without it for very long. Economics does not dictate politics, but it always affects it, especially in societies where differences in wealth and power are great. Economic structures give immense political advantages to those who control the means of production, shape what a nation can produce, and affect the way it distributes new wealth. Latin American economies depend heavily on the world economy and on its demand for the region's commodities, as well as on its supply of capital and technology. They simply cannot escape some reliance on others, as even the revolutionary Cubans discovered.

The state's institutional structure is a third feature of the game's environment. Government is seldom a neutral arbiter among players in the political game. Sometimes certain players control it and turn it into an instrument that protects their status and power, as oligarchs did throughout Latin America during the nineteenth and early twentieth centuries. At other times government has been used to redistribute wealth and power in society, as occurred recently in Nicaragua. In every society there exists a "state apparatus" that links public and private institutions in a way that assures public compliance with the dominant social class or way of life. It keeps the society together by enforcing rules as widely as possible. Yet, sooner or later, those who run state institutions develop interests of their own which may or may not coincide with the interests of everyone else. In Brazil, for example, nearly half of the nation's industry is now state owned, making government far more powerful economically than any private institution. With such size comes the kind of power that makes all other players heavily dependent on the state. Who controls whom in this relationship is not easy to measure, since the process is a dynamic one, but it is essential to study how power is wielded by the state as well as by other players. Government is not just a moderator, but a player as well, and its agencies are sometimes among the most powerful players. That is why you cannot assume that winning an election or carrying out a military coup guarantees the victor control over the entire state apparatus.

Identifying political rules in Latin America

When someone speaks of political rules, it conjures up in our minds images of constitutions or laws, but those are only two sources of rules. They may evolve slowly over time, starting as local customs that eventually become codified in law. The ruling monarch of Saudi Arabia, for example, governs under rules that grew from conventions established centuries ago. Others arise from explicit agreements on fundamental principles that are ratified by citizens or their representatives, as happened in the United States with its constitution in 1787, and more recently in the Philippines where a popular uprising led to the creation of a new constitution. On the other hand, rules may be quite arbitrary, constantly amended by autocrats who must coerce compliance with them.

In addition to official, prescribed rules there are many informal ones that discipline political conduct. In some cases, informal rules evolve because constitutions do not cover common practices; few, for example, say anything about political parties and economic interest groups and their exercise of political influence over officials. Informal rules may also develop when citizens choose to ignore the law, as was common in colonial Latin America where local elites disregarded some of the rules issued in Spain or Portugal that did not suit them. Today nearly all of the region's armed forces are disciplined by their own ideas about authority and governance, ideas that are not shared by people from all social classes. Anarchy is the last thing anyone wants, but that has not stopped them from abusing the official rules of the game when they believe it serves their interests to do so.

The weakness of official rules is also evident in the haphazard administration of justice in some Latin American societies. Laws are on the books, most originating in an Iberian society that was built on Roman and Islamic foundations; criminal and civil courts exist, and judges are abundant. But seldom does that guarantee that all laws are enforced. Military governments go through the motions of respecting law but can never resist arresting, and sometimes killing, civilians without recourse to trial, as happened in Argentina and Chile in the 1970s. Even under constitutional governments law enforcement is sometimes indiscriminate thanks to the way powerful civilians intimidate law enforcers and judges. In El Salvador judges have persistently refused to convict mercenaries, who formed "death squads" that were paid by a conservative upper class to liquidate reformers in their midst. In Colombia a private vendetta system has long existed outside of government, operated in the 1980s primarily by powerful drug dealers who murdered the nation's Attorney General and several judges to prevent their incarceration. Many things come to play in this process: bribery, murder, and threats to judges and their families. There are no easy ways to end it, but for authorities to govern they have no choice but to try.

How public office is won and lost

Diversity, not consistency, characterizes the ways nations select their authorities today. Many are liberal democracies where the principle of popular sovereignty prevails and the consent of the governed is expressed through elections and representation. But liberal democracy is only one of several ways to do it. In communist regimes popular consent comes not primarily through elections but via the creation of a collective consciousness and fundamental beliefs about the community and its supervision by a vanguard party.

Latin Americans are familiar with these and many other ways of selecting political authorities. In the 1980s you would have found liberal democracies governed by sophisticated political parties, military regimes intent on eliminating both liberal and revolutionary politics, and even a traditional autocracy. But it was not just the diversity of regimes that was remarkable. Even more striking was the way politics changed within many of the Latin American countries from one year to the next. A nation that lived under constitutional government for a time next found itself under a military one and then returned to democracy. So it was in South America, where all but two of the countries were governed in an authoritarian manner in the 1970s only to try democracy again a decade later. Not every government undergoes frequent change, but the fact that so many do indicates how insecure political rules must be.

This predicament derives in part from the failure of Latin Americans to agree on fundamentals. However people choose to justify their compliance with rules – using philosophical, juridical, religious, cultural, or pragmatic reasons – they must accept the same ones in order for government to operate for very long. But when agreement is absent, the opposite occurs: Nonconformity with rules breeds conflicts, within societies and between citizens and authorities, that defy easy resolution.

Disagreement over political rules was common in Latin America during the nineteenth century. When most of the region's nations achieved their independence around 1820, they adopted a set of constitutional rules, modeled on those written in the newly independent United States, which called for the regular election of public officials who governed according to the principles established in law. But the new post-Independence rules were never universally accepted. In fact, they were followed by only a few members of the urban minority that had originally proposed them. Most citizens were either unaware of the new rules or ignored them because they threatened their more traditional bases of power. What resulted were not stable democracies but political systems in which traditional local power structures that were often personalistic and authoritarian ran roughshod over newly adopted liberal democratic rules, making them entirely ineffective. An impasse was reached that prevented the creation of any form of legitimate government: Neither the antiquated Iberian principles of hierarchy and centralization nor the new democratic one of popular government gained enough support among the most powerful players to prevail. Instead, there developed a strong and enduring habit throughout the region of living by whichever set of rules gave greatest advantage to one's cause; this, in turn, provoked endless debates and fights over how to resolve problems of political legitimacy and authority.

In retrospect, the demise of constitutional democracy after Independence is not surprising. Democratic rules are quite vulnerable to subversion from almost any quarter since they rely primarily on being accepted voluntarily by nearly everyone. North Americans should recall that the initial success of their constitutional government was facilitated by its citizens' familiarity with it, and its acceptance by the most powerful members of the new society. In continental Europe, where tradition was strong and concentrations of wealth greater, democracy did not take hold in most countries until well into the twentieth century. Latin Americans were not alone in their discomfort with the practice of popular sovereignty.

We are left to wonder about the nature of politics in countries where agreement on fundamental rules is lacking. Are they to suffer civil war and anarchy, or is the absence of consensus something that people can actually tolerate? In most Latin American nations, political life has resided somewhere between these two extremes. Disagreement over the rules of politics does not always breed chaos, but neither does it assure much continuity. Rather, people seem to find ways to operate governments even when there is no certainty about how it should be done. Necessity, more than principles, frequently dictates minimal informal accords on the way government functions. Though they appear to be fighting over the highest of political principles, Latin Americans are often quite pragmatic in the ways they keep their countries operating under the worst of political conditions. To comprehend how this occurs we must look beneath rules to the players themselves and how they choose to deal with these problems.

For our purposes a player is any person or group that either wants to occupy public office or seeks to influence the decisions of those who do. Each will employ one or more political resources to accomplish either objective. Physical force is the oldest of them. When we cannot persuade others to comply with our wishes, it is always tempting to force them to do so. That is why physical intimidation and government repression remain the ultimate resource in Latin America, just as they do almost everywhere else. Quite routine under military rule, physical force is exercised by other players as well. Right-wing death squads and revolutionary insurgents rely on violence to force concessions, as do democratic authorities occasionally when "emergencies" dictate their subduing opponents who refuse to play by their rules.

Wealth is another resource. Although it seldom guarantees political influence, it can certainly help procure it, if only because the rich can secure official favors that the poor cannot afford. Economic influence is also exercised more indirectly, as happens when governments make concessions to industrialists, bankers, and farmers in order to promote economic growth in capitalist economic systems. Simply by being essential to the nation's development, producers exercise substantial influence over officials and their policies.

Expertise is a third resource. As governments increase their responsibilities, they must rely more and more on experts in economics, development planning, engineering, and public health. The more dependent authorities are on experts, the more influence the latter will have over them. Economic teams come and go, but presidents rely heavily on each of them when deciding how to invest their resources, promote production, and pay debts. Often local experts are assisted by advisers from international agencies who have their own ideas about how the country should be run. When his economists persuaded Mexican president Miguel de la Madrid to impose harsh austerity measures on the nation to deal with its enormous foreign debt in the mid-1980s, they reduced the incomes of millions of Mexicans, putting more people out of work than anything a Mexican government had done since the 1929 depression. In Nicaragua authorities rely on experts in agriculture when they set prices or expropriate properties. And in Bolivia the government's officials worked closely with an economist from Harvard University when they charted strategies for dealing with their foreign creditors. In other words, crucial decisions affecting national welfare are made all of the time with the assistance of experts whose names many citizens never know. Whether the government is democratic or authoritarian, people who possess the knowledge on which officials must rely will have much to say about what the government does.

Political ideas are also resources. Liberalism, socialism, communism, and fascism appeal to persons who want to base their politics on beliefs about how societies should be run. They accumulate followers who devote their energies to imposing their politics on everyone else. Many domestic and international wars have been fought over such things, and it is no secret that Latin Americans continue to shed blood over their political beliefs. Religious ideas also influence politics, as Iran's Ayatollah Khomeini and his followers have reminded us. In Latin America, Roman Catholicism is the prevailing religion, and today many of its clergy advocate theologies of social justice that have divided church members. The influence of ideas in the game of politics is never easy to measure, yet to ignore it is to deny ourselves access to what often motivates politicians.

Finally, there is the resource of people en masse. When people join together to form movements to protest or vote, they can influence authorities, sometimes toppling governments or electing new ones. Like everyone else, what the masses can do is often constrained by the rules that prevail. If there is a secret ballot, they can create governments; but if elections are prohibited they might have to disrupt society in order to provoke political change. That is why violence is seldom ruled out as a means to achieve one's goals. In Nicaragua, for example, people from all social classes joined together under the leadership of the Sandinista rebels to defeat the dictator Anastasio Somoza and his National Guard in a war that cost 50,000 lives.

Resources like those just described affect the resolution of conflicts in societies, but exactly how much they do is not always clear. Everyone acts and reacts to each other's behavior, calculating, threatening, bluffing, and behaving so as to advance one's own interests. But it is left to us to determine if there are any patterns in their behavior that reveal how the game is really played in their country. Do certain players always prevail over others, or do winners and losers vary from issue to issue? And if there is a pattern, how might we explain it? Is the power structure so entrenched that political variation is impossible, or is conformity determined by other forces, either external or internal? It is to find answers to such questions that we will devote ourselves in Part 2 of this book.

What distinguishes Latin American politics from the North American variety is not the number of resources wielded by players: Force, wealth, expertise, ideology, and mass movements are exhibited in the United States as well. What has characterized Latin America is the way various resources have been employed to abuse and subvert the official rules of the game. In Anglo-America and Western Europe, winning elections determines who governs since the rules require it. Wealth and expertise influence policy, but it is the election, with all its imperfections, that regulates the choice of government officials. But in much of Latin America one cannot rely on elections alone to accomplish that task. Presidents have been elected but many of them have also been removed long before their tenure was completed.

Military coups are accepted by some civilians and many soldiers as necessary to destroy undesirable governments. Even democrats have encouraged military intervention when they could find no other way to eject dictators who denied them free elections. It has become an unfortunate means that is justified by the ends that it achieves. The upper class finds it a convenient way to preserve their property; the middle class, a means to restore political order when they are menaced by protesting masses; and the working class, a way to promote populist politics among nationalist officers. Were it the armed forces alone that wanted coups, it would be a much less prominent means for changing governments.

Insurrections and guerrilla warfare are also employed to depose governments. Peasant uprisings aimed at destroying rural oligarchs have occurred many times in the past. More recently, opponents of incumbents, inspired by the success of national liberation movements elsewhere, have organized small armed units that employ guerrilla tactics to frustrate the nation's armed forces and political authorities. Some operate in the countryside, where they solicit peasant support; others work clandestinely in cities, using kidnapping of the wealthy, assassination, bank robberies, and the destruction of public facilities to undermine governments. Rural guerrilla movements were most active in the 1960s after Fidel Castro's victory in Cuba gave them a model to duplicate. Urban guerrilla warfare followed in countries like Argentina and Uruguay, peaking in the early 1970s before military counterinsurgency efforts forced its leaders into exile or killed them.

More recently rural guerrilla movements have operated in Central America, holding their own in El Salvador throughout the 1980s, and in Peru, where the Maoist *Sendero Luminoso* became a powerful force able to survive the best military efforts to eradicate it. With the exception of the 26th of July Movement in Cuba and the Sandinistas in Nicaragua, no guerrilla movement has managed to carry its insurrection to its conclusion, however.

Governments have also been brought down in less direct ways. Powerful economic interests have devoted themselves to undermining public confidence in authorities. Farmers, industrialists, and bankers, for example, may deliberately derail government economic programs they oppose by not cooperating with them. They may do so even when it is costly to them in the short run, in order to make it impossible for authorities to govern any longer. The routine is well known: The government announces a policy, entrepreneurs protest to no avail, then production falls, public opinion questions the government's competence to run the country, and military officers intervene. None of these phases follows automatically from the other, but everyone knows that together they offer an effective means for weakening, and perhaps destroying, a government.

Domestic interests are not the only ones that weaken a government using economic means. Foreign governments and multinational corporations have assailed the region's presidents and their policies, occasionally working covertly to promote their removal. By cutting off badly needed loans, boycotting a country's exports, withdrawing investments, or covertly supporting opposition groups, they can turn already volatile situations into eruptions that end with a government's demise. What foreign players cannot do by themselves they can do with the assistance of domestic players who share their opposition to incumbents.

Why Latin Americans find it hard to live by a single set of rules is obvious. As we have learned, groups and individuals who discover that existing rules threaten their interests sometimes prefer to ignore or undermine them rather than obey them. There is nothing automatic about this process, however. Players will play by the rules one moment and then abuse them the next. For example, the leaders of large political parties who see free elections as their best route to power may find themselves opposed by players with very small constituencies and no success in elections. The latter may seek to get elections rigged to guarantee victory, or secure their cancellation if they do not win. In turn, the leaders of the larger parties may resign themselves to playing rigged games for a time and then, out of frustration, rise up violently against the minorities who exclude them from government by cheating. The Salvadorians know exactly how it works. In 1972 the armed forces confiscated the ballots after the popular Christian Democrats had won the national election. Furious, the Christian Democrats promoted a countercoup by officers sympathetic to them, only to fail in the effort. Thereafter many in the party resigned themselves to waiting for another opportunity to contest a free election while others gave up on elections and fled to join Marxist guerrillas already at war with the military government. Fifteen years later, long after Christian Democrat José Napoleón Duarte was finally elected president, the war still raged.

Militaries and oligarchs are not the only ones who have excluded their rivals from the game. Revolutionary authorities also do it. Those who built a new government after the Mexican Revolution set out in 1917 to reduce the power of the church, landed elites, the military, and the United States. By denying all of them direct access to authorities and gradually taking away their property, they demoted them. They united organized labor, peasants, and a new middle class within a national party organization that has ruled Mexico ever since. Hardly as exclusive as when it began, the Mexican system has never been as dominated by landed oligarchs and the military as it was before the revolution. The Cuban revolutionaries went even farther after they took over in 1959. They expropriated 70 percent of the nation's farmland, nationalized all private businesses, and built a regime modeled after the Soviet Union that is still supervised by the Cuban Communist Party. And even the Sandinistas in Nicaragua, though unwilling to emulate everything the Cubans have done, were eager to replace the old National Guard with their own army and take control of nearly a third of the economy by expropriating the properties that dictator Anastasio Somoza Debayle abandoned when he fled the country in 1979. In each of these revolutionary experiences the victors took control by eliminating or evicting their most prominent rivals. That, they proudly admit, is what revolution is all about.

How rules affect presidential conduct

Presidents often feel quite insecure in a world in which political rules receive so little respect. How they use their power amidst such uncertainty is a fascinating subject. On the surface Latin American presidents appear quite strong; traditionally they have been freer of legislative and judicial constraints than their North American or European counterparts. Not only do their constitutions give them more discretion in making policy and enforcing laws than do most liberal democratic constitutions, but in actual practice Latin Americans have exercised more authority than their peers in other democratic regimes. Throughout the nineteenth century, when the struggle for national unification was up against a regionalism that resisted central authority, presidents built armies and waged war against those who refused to respect them. Legislatures were always the weaker partner in this process, neither checking nor balancing power with the president.

Nevertheless, presidential power was always circumscribed by the common practice of ignoring presidential authority when one could get away with it. None of the "men on horseback" who united their countries in the nineteenth century enjoyed as much respect as they pretended. Always present was the need to allow local elites to do much as they wished in their domains as long as they did not interfere directly with what the president did in his. It became even more difficult for presidents in this century, as new players joined the game and militaries began to assume more responsibility for the nation's governance. The more that army officers felt that it was their duty to act as guardians of the nation's affairs, evicting presidents who did not live up to their standards, the more insecure presidents became.

Nothing illustrates this better than the ordeals of Argentine presidents during the past thirty years. Even though it is one of the most affluent nations in Latin America, and culturally the most European, the country has endured continuous political instability. Between 1955 and 1982 three presidents were elected, but none was allowed to complete a term by the armed forces. Twelve military presidents gave it a try during the same period, some lasting as long as four years, but most far less. Argentine presidents have suffered not only from military pushing and shoving but also from the stiff opposition of both business and labor, who have openly sought to undermine presidential authority, each for their own partisan reasons. There was no easy way out for civilian presidents who discovered that almost anything they did alienated those who had never wanted them in office in the first place. When they resorted to force to get some control over militant workers, they provoked even more militancy; yet when they yielded to labor's demands, they invited more conservative forces to prod military officers to seize control. Thus, presidents always had to choose between making concessions that risked provoking assaults on their tenure or doing nothing and lending encouragement to those who launched the original confrontations.

Examples of secure, highly institutionalized presidencies are fewer, but they do exist. Take Mexico, for example. A different person is elected president of Mexico every six years. Since the late 1920s Mexican elections have been held on schedule and without interruption. During those years the Mexican presidency has prevailed over all other political institutions, with its occupant serving as both the leader of the nation's dominant party and the head of state. The revolutionary tradition requires that the president give attention to all members of the ruling coalition, among them labor bosses, peasant leaders, and local politicians; and to deal with them he draws upon the resources of the huge bureaucracy that he directs, making his constituents as dependent on his allocation of services to them as he is on their acquiescence with his command of the nation. In other words, both the Mexican rules and power structure have made the nation's president an unusually secure politician. The contrast between the vulnerable Argentine president and the much more sturdy Mexican one is conspicuous. Both ostensibly govern under liberal democratic constitutions yet neither derives authority from those documents. The Mexican president is strong because his party controls the things that nearly every Mexican needs to prosper, while the Argentine president is weak because the nation's power structure is divided into factions who refuse to be governed by one another.

Similarly, Fidel Castro enjoys immense power in Cuba, some of it derived from his popularity as a leader of the 1959 Cuban revolution, but much coming from the way the Communist Party he directs dominates the rest of society. Cubans, whether they support the party or not, know what to expect from it. Serious opposition is not tolerated and all allocations of resources in society are supervised by officials according to national plans. Castro contends that such control is essential to the creation of social cohesion and socialist equality. The true test of the system's durability is yet to come, however, for until Fidel Castro is gone, we will never know for certain how much of his authority is personal and how much of it comes from the rules themselves.

Revolutionary politics is not the only kind that creates secure leaders. Constitutional democracies have generated a few as well. Between

1932 and 1973 the Chilean presidency was among the most stable, and today democratic presidents in Costa Rica and Venezuela waste no time worrying about their removal from office by illegal means. But these cases are the exceptions rather than the rule in modern Latin America, where most presidents still must contend with players who consider it their right to depose governments whose agendas do not conform to their own. In contrast to a president in a consensual system, who knows how and in what form his critics will contest him, the less secure Latin American president does not know when and how his opponents will strike, especially when the military is part of the opposition. He is beset by uncertainty, never sure when laborers will riot or the military will stage a coup. Haunted by a politics of rumored conspiracies, he will devote himself to consorting with allies and developing his own conspiracies to outwit and disarm his antagonists. This is hardly the most productive way to manage the affairs of a nation, least of all one as torn by social conflicts and economic underdevelopment as many Latin American countries are.

The lesson from all of this is that presidential power is a variable rather than a constant in the Latin American political game. Both the amount of presidential power and the manner of its use are heavily influenced by the content and status of the rules operating in each nation. Rules may give the president substantial latitude or they may restrict his authority, but unless all powerful players accept them as their own, authorities will enjoy none of the certitude that rules are supposed to provide.

How rules affect political opposition

One of the most important features of any political process is the relationship between the government and its opponents. The practices that define this relationship are among the principal characteristics of a nation's politics. Liberal democracy, for example, is defined in part by its toleration of political opposition; authoritarian government, in contrast, goes out of its way to exclude opponents and to deny them opportunities to evict incumbents. Both have existed in Latin America, though more often we find games in which some opponents are allowed to participate while others are excluded, by presidents who are intent on preventing anyone who breaks their rules from destroying their governments.

Conflicts over policy may at any time be turned into abuses of authority by presidents, or defiance of it by opponents. For their part, presidents may decide that eliminating those who get in their way is more important than living by democratic rules; meanwhile people who find themselves tormented by authorities may chose to undermine their oppressors. It might seem that such behavior is nothing more than a contemporary replication of what was done throughout the region a century ago. Actually, it is far more intricate, involving a myriad of players who have been added since the turn of the century as well as ideologies that range from the far left to the far right. This only makes the system's regulation all the more difficult and political compromise more elusive.

There are many ways to manage relations between governments and their opponents. The most familiar one is the conventional competitive process practiced in many Western democracies, where political parties compete for public office in elections and private interests are allowed to influence government decisions. Very few Latin American countries have fulfilled the requirements of this purest form of competition, though Uruguay from 1903 until 1973, Chile between 1932 and 1973, Venezuela since 1958, and Costa Rica since 1948 have come close. More common is a less conventional competitive process in which some players are excluded from elections while others are not. For example, communists and socialists have been barred from elections in many countries, as have the Peronists occasionally in Argentina.

Another departure from the pure competitive system is the one in which the government "co-opts" its potential opponents, securing their cooperation by including them in its ruling coalition. Chilean governments during the 1940s and Venezuelan ones in the 1960s strengthened themselves by attracting minority parties to their cabinets. Even more striking was the way Colombians ended a decade of bitter civil strife among members of the nation's two largest political parties by forming a national front government in which the presidency was exchanged between the two parties from term to term for sixteen years after 1958. In essence, the Colombians agreed to suspend competitive rules of the game in order to end a civil war, temporarily transforming national politics into a classroom where combatants could learn to live together amicably again. When violence returned to Colombia recently it was not the work of the Liberal and Conservative Parties, as before, but between guerrillas on the left, drug cartels, and the ruling elite created by the two parties.

Co-optation and coalition building are not confined to political parties. Interest groups of various kinds may also be invited to forgo their opposition in exchange for an opportunity to participate within a government. This practice is quite common in European democracies, where labor leaders, farmers, and business people are often given positions in cabinets or on government committees, where they assist authorities in governing their own constituencies. The same process has taken several different forms in Latin America. In some places informal agreements between interest groups and public officials were made; in others, like contemporary Mexico, the leaders of peasant associations and labor unions belong to the nation's ruling political party, giving them direct access to authorities. In both arrangements co-optation is part of an attempt by authorities to alter the rules of the political process so that they can coordinate and control it. They want well-defined channels of communication and guarantees of co-operation from powerful players so that they can accomplish their political and economic objectives without constantly running up against opposition. It can be an effective device when it makes it hard for co-opted players to pull out and rejoin the opposition. And that is precisely why incumbents do it.

Oppositions have been handled in other ways, too. In one, the government's adversaries are seen but not heard; in another they are eliminated altogether. The first occurs in countries where opposition parties exist and participate in elections, but are never allowed to win even if they have the votes. That is how it was in Mexico, where the Institutional Revolutionary Party (PRI) won nearly all elections for fifty years. Other parties participated and were even guaranteed some seats in the Chamber of Deputies, but when they seriously challenged the PRI, as they finally did in the 1988 presidential election, they were not allowed to win. It operated differently in Brazil when the military governed between 1964 and 1984. Officers created two political parties, one which they controlled and one which all of the opposition joined. By carefully manipulating election laws the military party ruled the country even when it lost elections. Everyone knew that it was a charade, but that did not stop them from participating in it. In both

Mexico and Brazil political opposition was tolerated, but only as long as it did not interfere with the incumbents; criticisms of authorities had to be muted, obedience complete, and hopes of winning future elections abandoned.

One wonders why any opposition is tolerated by governments that have no intention of letting it capture important public offices. Perhaps it is because the ritual of democracy is important to leaders even though the fact of democracy is not, especially when it helps their image abroad. More likely, however, it offers a means, albeit a crude one, for keeping the opposition exposed so that authorities can keep an eye on it. Moreover, it also offers a device for mobilizing the government's supporters against opponents who are allowed to appear threatening to the incumbents.

Oppositions are treated even more harshly in those systems where the government wants unanimity. Cuba is an example. Governed by a Communist party, the country has no place for an opposition. Fidel Castro candidly admits his belief in a communist monopoly, arguing that since there is only one true revolutionary ideology, there is need for only one party to implement it. Dissent over policy, if it occurs at all, should come from within the party and other official organizations. The communists are not unique in this regard, however. Military governments were notorious for their repression of political parties in Argentina, Chile, and Uruguay when they governed in those countries. They liked to declare party politics too divisive, always threatening to destroy the kind of order that antidemocratic officers preferred. None of them succeeded in eliminating parties from their countries, however, something many still regret.

This brief look at political opposition and the way rules affect its behavior in Latin America would not be complete without mention of "antisystem" oppositions. Many opponents of incumbents seek to win public office in elections or to influence the people who do. But Latin American history is also filled with another type that is far more ambitious. Rather than seeking membership in the existing political game they want to demolish it and erect a new one, using violence if necessary. The Mexican, Cuban, and Nicaraguan revolutions have tried to do just that. During the 1960s and 1970s antisystem movements, many of them clandestine, arose all over the region to make war on the political establishments in their respective countries. In South America most of them were crushed in wars with their national

armed forces, though some still operate in Peru, Colombia, El Salvador, and Guatemala.

Choices: pluralism, corporatism, authoritarianism, and communism

Players do not participate randomly, even when they are not disciplined by the same rules. History teaches us that their involvement is
structured either by habit or by design and that the character of the
game is heavily influenced by the form their participation takes. Relations between players and the government that they seek to influence
or control takes at least four different forms, each one with its own
rules about who can play, how they can exert their influence, and
where ultimate authority resides. They are identified by the familiar
labels of pluralism, corporatism, authoritarianism, and communism.

Pluralism involves a process in which many organized private interests compete for influence over public policy. Diversity of interest
and bargaining at all levels of government are its dominant traits. For
pluralism to work political resources must be widely disbursed, and
winners and losers in policy disputes must change from time to time.
Though total equality is not essential, a noncumulative pattern of
"dispersed inequalities" is required; that is, no group can be allowed
to acquire a monopoly of power and influence. Under this arrangement
the state governs not by imposing its control on civil society but by
serving as a mediator or broker among competing private and bureaucratic interests, making policy by bargaining among them. Pluralism is not a neat arrangement, but a mode of policy making whose
openness and competitiveness vary with the distribution of power
among players and the willingness of authorities to leave the initiative
to others. Thus, the politics of some countries, such as the United
States, are more pluralistic than that of others, like Great Britain or
West Germany, though all exhibit many pluralist qualities.

Can pluralism work in Latin America, where resources have been
much more concentrated than in Anglo-America? Doubts exist, as do
suspicions that the state has always been too partisan in Latin America
to serve effectively as a mediator among contesting interests. Yet, in
some societies, organized interests are diverse and competition among
them for political influence is intense. Whether that makes them ex-

amples of pluralism is something we will explore when we examine democratic politics in Chile and Venezuela in Chapters 7 and 8.

Corporatism offers another method of organizing player participation. It rejects the notion of open competition and the principle of government neutrality in favor of a more deliberate effort to organize and regulate public–private sector relations. The government assumes responsibility for directing the society, and private economic and social groups become its instruments for doing so. Instead of competing with each other to influence officials, interest groups deal with them directly and on the latter's terms, gaining what they can by accepting their place in the government's scheme of things. In its loosest form, corporatism may involve a willing collaboration by interest groups with authorities because they believe that it is to their benefit to work together rather than to compete openly for influence. Such is the case in Scandinavia, where a mild form of corporatism has grown from mutual interests in management of economic and social policy. At the other extreme is a corporatism where the state dominates over labor and business, making them little more than deliverers of government orders to their constituents. Italian fascism was an example of such heavy-handed corporatism. But, whatever form it takes, corporatism is attractive to leaders who want to increase their control over public policy and its execution in complex societies where pluralistic competition weakens the state and old-fashioned authoritarianism lacks the means for dealing with dynamic social movements and diverse interests. It seems to offer rulers a way to make labor, business, agriculture, and other groups collaborate with the government as it carries out its plans for the country's development. Nearly all Latin American leaders have been attracted to it at one time or another, and some have actually put corporatist notions to work. The Mexicans adapted corporatist organization to their needs in the 1930s, Argentines and Brazilians to theirs in the 1940s, and military officers to theirs in Peru in the 1970s, as we will learn in Part 2.

There is a simpler way to contain participation: namely, authoritarianism. Autocrats rule over others instead of ruling with them or through them. Organizationally they are more primitive than corporatists, preferring the monopolization of power by a dictator or small ruling elite and the enforcement of rules by repression rather than the use of interest groups to carry out official policy. Whether authoritarian government can accomplish much more than the maintenance of order in increasingly complex Latin American societies is debatable, though that has not stopped autocrats from trying time and again to run some countries. How well they have done will be the subject of Chapters 8 and 9.

Pluralism, corporatism, and authoritarianism are not the only ways that participation and policy making can be organized. Dissatisfaction with all three has led a few Latin Americans to try something very different, namely, communism. Communists do not believe that society has to be divided into separate interests. Instead, they want to create a society in which partisan concerns are eliminated by the socialization of the economy, creating a national community united by a single interest, in which people as equals devote their energies to the pursuit of the common good rather than to their individual aggrandizement. How one goes about doing this and whether it can be accomplished will preoccupy us in Chapter 10, when we look at Cuban communism.

The next step

You are now familiar with the concept of political rules and the role they play in the game of politics. We have discovered that they come in many forms, from constitutional codes to informal norms that shape political expectations and behavior. They influence how political office is won, how presidents behave, and how political opposition is treated. Political rules offer a point of departure in our quest to understand Latin American politics and public policy. It is a tool you can now use to study and compare individual Latin American political systems.

Knowledge about political rules and their abuse cannot furnish all of the answers that we seek, but it does take us a long way toward asking the right questions. For example, when you examine a Latin American political system you can begin by asking about the content of its rules and who respects them. To what extent is a single set followed in practice rather than several competing ones? Are there informal rules that shape behavior? If so, what are they and what is their potency? And what about the consequences of the rules? How do they shape government policy making and to whose advantage do they work? More specifically, who benefits most and who benefits the least from the way the game is played? And last, but certainly not least, what conditions the way various players use rules: self-interest, ideology, social and economic structures, or something else?

Further reading

Ames, Berry. *Political Survival: Politicians and Public Policy in Latin America*. Berkeley: University of California Press, 1987.

Anderson, Charles W. *Politics and Economic Change in Latin America: The Governing of Restless Nations*. New York: Van Nostrand, 1967.

Bailey, F. G. *Stratagems and Spoils: A Social Anthropology of Politics*. New York: Schocken Books, 1969.

Chilcote, Ronald H., and Joel C. Edelstein. *Latin America: The Struggle with Dependency and Beyond*. Cambridge, MA: Schenkman, 1979.

Collier, David, ed. *The New Authoritarianism in Latin America*. Princeton, NJ: Princeton University Press, 1979.

Hirschman, Albert O. *Essays in Trespassing: Economics to Politics and Beyond*. New York: Cambridge University Press, 1981.

Journeys toward Progress: Studies of Economic Policy-Making in Latin America. New York: Norton, 1973 edition.

Klaren, Peter F., and Thomas J. Bossert. *Promise of Development: Theories of Change in Latin America*. Boulder, CO: Westview Press, 1986.

Linz, Juan, and Alfred Stepan, eds. *The Breakdown of Democratic Regimes: Latin America*. Baltimore: The Johns Hopkins University Press, 1978.

Malloy, James M., ed. *Authoritarianism and Corporatism in Latin America*. Pittsburgh: University of Pittsburgh Press, 1977.

Powelson, John. *Institutions of Economic Growth: A Theory of Conflict Management in Developing Countries*. Princeton, NJ: Princeton University Press, 1972.

Roxborough, Ian. *Theories of Underdevelopment*. Atlantic Highlands, NJ: Humanities Press, 1979.

Silvert, Kalman. *The Conflict Society: Reaction and Revolution in Latin America*. New York: American Universities Field Staff, 1966.

3. Players – I

Now we can turn to the players in the Latin American game. In Chapter 2 we defined a player as any individual or group that tries to gain public office or to influence those who do. Political parties, wealthy landowners, and business people come immediately to mind. There are many others: military officers, peasant leaders, labor unions, foreign governments, multinational corporations, priests, and students, just to name a few. But labels tell us little about each of them. They conjure up images, but image and actual power are seldom identical. To know who players are, what they want from politics, and how much clout they wield, we have to examine each of them.

We should also recall that Latin American political systems are not replicas of the North American and Western European ones. Rules are more varied, and less consensus sometimes exists. And interest groups are neither as well financed nor as well organized in Latin America, and they seldom represent as many people as they claim. Some exaggerate the size of their constituencies in order to impress authorities, and many, like peasant leaders, simply cannot communicate with the scattered millions of persons for whom they speak. As a result, our images of them do not always correspond to reality.

As we examine each player, we will ask four questions. First, who are the people involved, and from what social class, regional, or ethnic sector do they come? What do they share in common and how united are they economically, socially, and politically?

Second, what do they want from politics, if anything? We should acknowledge at the outset that most people in Latin America, as elsewhere, do not devote their lives to politics. Many are disinterested; others expect their leaders to make decisions for them. Some players, in fact, want to be left alone, ignored completely by the public authorities who tax and regulate them. Others want favors, though usually on their own terms. So instead of assuming that they will always influence authorities, we must determine just how much they actually do.

Third, what resources do players have at their disposal and how do they use them to influence authorities? The mere possession of resources does not assure that they will be effective; they must be employed with skill and good timing to accomplish anything.

And fourth, which set of rules do players prefer and how successful are they in getting their rivals to live by them? Players are just as likely to do battle over the rules as over public policy, changing the way the game is played to defend or advance their interests.

Since players may be quite diverse, it is imperative that we include large collectivities like social classes as well as more narrow, highly organized ones. In this chapter we will focus on the former in order to learn about the importance of social structure in shaping a nation's politics. Economic elites, the middle class, and the masses will command our attention here. Then, in Chapter 4, we will turn to some of the more organized political and economic interests, focusing on political parties, the military, the church, bureaucrats, and foreigners. What follows are general, introductory surveys of each. Deviations from these descriptions, and there are many, will be left to the discussion of individual countries in Part 2.

Rural elites

For centuries Latin Americans have complained about the dreaded *oligarquía*. It is the *oligarquía,* we are told, that has monopolized wealth, corrupted politicians, manipulated the military, conspired with foreigners, exploited the masses, and obstructed progress. But who in fact are these oligarchs? Are they a small elite of coconspirators or do they form a large social class? Do they operate openly or do they function secretly, perhaps even bribing officials to do as they wish? What resources do they possess and how do they use them? And are they the same today as they were a century ago, or have their power and their tactics changed along with many other features of their societies?

Today few observers agree on who the oligarchs are and how much power they exercise in politics. To be sure, no one denies that a minority possesses a disproportionate share of wealth and power and enjoys immense political and economic advantages. But that is true in all nations of the world. More important is knowing exactly how much more power they have compared to their rivals.

We can begin in the countryside, where wealth traditionally was concentrated and owners of large estates were almost governments unto themselves during the nineteenth century. Today, rural elites are neither as isolated nor as powerful as they once were. They have enormous clout in the largely agrarian nations of Central America and in the Andean region, but in more industrialized ones like Brazil, Argentina, and Mexico they must compete with an array of powerful urban interests. Though quite willing to exercise as much influence as they can on the national scene, landowners have always been strongest at the local level, where people are most dependent on them for employment and access to property. In political matters landowners have relied heavily on their ability to manipulate local judges, the police, and voters in elections. Their fears are many, but two stand out above the rest: losing access to cheap labor and losing land to agrarian reform. The latter is anathema to the largest landowners no matter how modest it might be, and they are quick to wield their influence at the national as well as local level to prevent or obstruct it.

Large landowners share much in common, but they are no longer as homogeneous as they once were. Some are descendants of the nineteenth-century ruling class, whereas others have purchased large estates after becoming wealthy in finance and commerce during this century. Not only do their operations vary in size and quality, but they also employ different amounts of modern technology, causing some to be far more productive than others. Geography, demography, and local traditions also influence their character: A 100,000-acre cattle *estancia* on the rich Argentine pampas has little in common with massive cotton plantations in El Salvador or with old fashioned, labor-intensive, multicrop farms in Colombian river valleys. Because they differ so much in their purpose and productivity, it is helpful to the political analyst to distinguish between at least two different types of operations, one that resembles traditional *latifundios* and another that is similar to the large modern farms found in most capitalist economies.

Among the former are the landowners who prefer traditional ways of life to modern ones, cultivating enough land to live comfortably while renting the rest or leaving it fallow. They rely on abundant and inexpensive labor rather than new technologies, and are determined to preserve the *latifundio* as a social institution, one that gives them control over landless peasants whose dependence on them assures the preservation of their oligarchic lifestyle. Some of them do not live in the countryside for most of the year, and those who do usually send their children to the capital or abroad for their education.

Modern farmers, in contrast, are devoted primarily to production. Their operations tend to be more capital intensive, employing modern technology when it is profitable. Productive commercial farming is not new to Latin America. Since colonial times there have been plantations and haciendas organized efficiently for money making. But not until the twentieth century has intensive commercial farming come to dominate the rural economies of most Latin American countries. Today nearly every country, no matter how industrialized, still relies heavily on the export of commodities to finance its development, and were it not for vast increases in production during the past quarter century they would be in far worse shape than they are.

The *latifundista* operation is more self-contained than the commercial one, a little economic society unto itself. The more modern farmer, in contrast, looks outward to the nation's capital and abroad for markets, often receiving help from government in the form of guaranteed prices and assured sales. Like farmers in the European Common Market and in the United States their importance to their country's economic growth provides them with substantial leverage that often translates into political power in matters involving economic policy.

The *latifundista* has been on the retreat throughout Latin America in recent times. Some *latifundios* have been divided up by inheritance; others have been transformed into productive commercial operations by a new generation of farmers. Some have also been redistributed to the landless by government land reforms aimed at improving peasant welfare and gradually increasing total rural production. In Mexico, Nicaragua, Venezuela, Chile, Peru, and Cuba, extensive holdings were expropriated by the government and redistributed to peasants or were reorganized as cooperative or state farms. Yet, as comprehensive as these efforts have been in some parts of the region, the *latifundista* is not yet extinct. Many tradition-bound landowners still struggle tenaciously to withstand deliberate attacks on their way of life. They are now on the defensive but, as long as they have wealth and social status, and wield substantial influence over local authorities, they are not defenseless.

What, in addition to guarantees of survival on their own terms, do *latifundistas* want from politics? Generally, very little, for they are confident that if they are left to their traditional devices, they can secure all that they require from the society immediately around them, be it labor or physical protection. They require few government services and have little use for most regulations. Since World War II, few *latifundistas* have sought public office, led political parties, or been deeply involved in making national policy in any but the smallest and most traditional countries. They have relinquished the government's operation to urban professionals, party politicians, and military officers.

What about their political resources? Obviously, they have wealth and eminence at the local level, especially where they are descended from the old ruling class. They sometimes buy favors, bribing tax collectors, land surveyors, and judges, among others. But even that may not be necessary where local officials long ago resigned themselves to getting along with the most wealthy and prestigious persons among them. Social status and familial ties gain favors from public officials, many of whom seek admittance to higher social circles. Traditionally, *latifundistas* have made resourceful use of the regional political bosses on whom the government sometimes depends for political control at the provincial level. The exchange of favors between landowners and local politicians builds mutual obligations that are used to halt the enforcement of undesirable laws. Finally, when all else fails, they have been known to hire assassins to kill agitators who ignore their rules, El Salvador and Guatemala being the most recent examples of such atrocities. The armed forces have also stood beside them, though less because of common family ties than because of a mutual interest in maintaining order. In sum, the *latifundistas,* whose political power is concentrated close to their enterprises, are currently only one of several powerful players in all but the smallest and most traditional societies. They are not without influence on the national scene, but it is their desire to hold off enemies who dare to intrude into their domains that absorbs most of their time. It takes a strong, well-organized, and determined bureaucracy to penetrate Latin America's local political systems; that is why insecure governments, even if popular with large numbers of people, are seldom capable of dislodging landed elites, as Brazilian president José Sarney discovered in the mid-1980s when, after his election, he launched an agrarian reform program only to be forced by powerful landed elites to cut it back drastically.

Finally, do *latifundistas* prefer any set of rules over others? Obviously they see little advantage in elections they cannot win. Even though they can sometimes control votes within their regions, the votes are seldom enough to defeat urban political parties. They may join with commercial farmers and urban elites to organize a conservative coalition, but such coalitions receive no more than one-third of the popular vote in most countries. The *latifundistas* want a set of rules that circumscribes reform-oriented, mass-based political parties and, when the latter are elected, limits their power. They need a government that is either uninterested in penetrating and reforming local power structures or too weak to do so. In practice, this means some kind of elitist constitutional government, as was common in the late nineteenth century, or, in the contemporary age of activist masses, an autocratic one devoted to the protection of the propertied classes.

If our analysis of the landed elite was confined only to *latifundistas,* we would be guilty of ignoring a majority of those who wield power in the countryside. Gradually, but steadily, a more intensive type of farming has spread throughout the region. Today, plantations and large family farms outnumber traditional *latifundios* in most countries. They are important not only to the welfare of those who own and manage them, but to national economies as well. Modern agriculture includes units of all sizes, making it impossible to draw a line between the richest and the rest of the modern farmers. But that should not prevent us from studying the behavior of this large and very powerful community.

Some modern farmers are descendants of *latifundistas* who transformed their estates into modern commercial enterprises; others are the heirs of the commercial farmers of the nineteenth century who produced coffee, cattle, and other commodities for export. Some come from immigrant families, primarily from Europe but also from Asia, who arrived around the turn of the century, began as colonists and tenant farmers, and gradually expanded their enterprises. Modern farms come in many forms and operate with varying degrees of efficiency, ranging from well-organized plantations employing several hundred laborers to family farms engaged in mixed cropping. On the whole, their owners are less prominent socially than the traditional ruling elite, though many have achieved social status from their wealth. They are, however, not as isolated from other economic sectors as the *latifundistas;* some, in fact, are also deeply involved in food processing, banking, and commerce. Many of their enterprises are as modern and efficient as those in North America, although the majority operate at a lower level of efficiency, handicapped by the high cost of technology and their reliance on unstable international markets. In sum, Latin America's modern farmers are a diverse and sizable group that includes, among others, the grain farmers of Argentina, Uruguay, and southern Brazil; the coffee producers of Colombia, Brazil, and Central America; the Mexicans who raise fruits and vegetables for export to the United States each winter; the truck gardeners that surround most large cities; the sugar barons of Brazil and the Caribbean; the banana producers of Ecuador and Central America; and the cotton farmers found throughout the region.

Modern farmers want more from government than do the *latifundistas*. First and foremost, they want policies that promote high prices for their produce. In addition, they lobby for cheap transportation and storage facilities, and against land taxes and agrarian reform. Like farmers everywhere, they want to be protected against adversity but allowed to take advantage of opportunity. And like their counterparts in Europe and North America, they have created organizations to represent them before government officials. Some farmers' organizations unite the producers of a single commodity; others follow regional lines. Modern farmers covet membership on the government boards and commissions that make agricultural policy. They may support some political parties, but devote most of their effort to dealing directly with the officials who make policy, avoiding the broader political issues in favor of concentrating their influence on more narrow agrarian matters.

Success in the political arena depends not only on organization and access to public authorities, but also on the resources one can bring to bear on particular issues. The modern farmers' strength derives from the economy's dependence on what they produce. Most Latin American economies still rely heavily on the export of agricultural commodities for desperately needed foreign exchange, now more than ever, with high foreign debts to pay in dollars. Any interruption of the flow of exports can quickly undermine the economy. Moreover, rapidly growing urban populations must be fed by domestic production if the foreign exchange costs of imported food are to be avoided. Thus, no matter how hostile they may be to farmers in principle, most governments are forced to rely heavily on them. Conversely, by using the country's dependence on them to good advantage, the farmers can often persuade officials to meet their demands.

Finally, there is the question of their preferred political rules. Do farmers have a preference for one set of rules over another? Latin American farmers, like farmers elsewhere, prefer stability in all things. There is already enough uncertainty in their world caused by nature without the addition of political instability. It is not so much the form of the government that matters to them as it is the government's stability and receptivity to farmers. Like the *latifundistas,* they tolerate democratic government as long as it is orderly and not hostile to rural interests. On the other hand, they may also welcome autocratic government, especially if it is well managed and able to carry out supportive economic policies. Rules are a means to an end for them, rather than ends in themselves, as they are for many other players.

We now have some idea of what rural elites expect from politics. Still, when we study the behavior of *latifundistas* and modern farmers, we have to look at what they do in specific instances to determine how influential they really are. We cannot assume that they dominate contemporary politics just because they did in the past, nor can we assume that they are powerless in nations where populations and wealth are now heavily concentrated in urban areas.

Business elites

Wealth has never been monopolized by rural elites in Latin America. Since colonial times, merchants, traders, and bankers have prospered alongside them. In the late nineteenth century, native business people were joined by immigrants, many of whom amassed great wealth within one generation. Today the *Who's Who* of business in Brazil, Argentina, and Venezuela reads like a United Nations' roster, listing persons of Italian, English, German, Jewish, Lebanese, and Japanese ancestry. The 1929 depression that shattered the region also opened the door to enterprising investors who seized on the opportunity to manufacture goods that were no longer supplied by a depressed Europe. Long deterred by rural elites who feared that industrialization would offend their European trading partners, native and immigrant entrepreneurs built industries in the larger countries that soon contributed more to the national income than did agriculture. And the more important that industry became, the more governments committed themselves to protecting it from foreign competition, using high tariffs, easy credit, and government purchases.

The study of business elites should be sensitive to three issues. First is the matter of determining who belongs to the "elite." Obviously, the owners of the largest firms do, and those who own the far more numerous tiny ones do not, but that leaves thousands of others who are somewhere in between. There is no neat line to be drawn in most countries, so we have no choice but to treat all but the smallest members of the business community as potentially influential players in the political game. Firms of various sizes often work together in organizations that were created to lobby the government for their members. Industrialist associations as well as individual firms are frequently important participants in any government's policy-making process.

Second is the issue of ownership. Native investors own some of the larger firms, but foreigners and governments own others. We will examine each of the latter two separately in the next chapter. On many things all three collaborate, such as the preservation of capitalist economics, but on other issues native industry may compete with the multinational firms who sometimes take their markets from them. The result is an intense rivalry between them that often causes native capitalists to seek government protection against foreign firms in order to retain large portions of domestic markets for themselves. Obviously, when we examine how industry and commerce play the game we cannot assume that the managers of all firms think alike or want the same things from government. Within any nation there may be a place for each of them, but their working closely together varies from issue to issue.

The third issue involves the relationship between rural and business elites and the perennial question of how much they conspire. It was once taken for granted that they were the same persons, but that is no longer true in the larger countries. People may own enterprises in both sectors but, generally, the more industrialized the economy, the harder it is for rural and urban players to form a ruling class any more. The wealthiest Brazilians, for example, form a large community that is scattered over several regions of the country, some of them rural and traditional, others quite modern, with interests in industry and commerce as well. They are united in their opposition to any tampering with the existing economic structure of the country, but little more. Moreover, they must contend with and work with the more than 600 enterprises that the Brazilian government runs, as well as hundreds of multinational firms. It is different in little El Salvador where a few hundred wealthy families are far more powerful than the rest of the population, but even they are less homogeneous than before. What continues to unite them is their determination to prevent either the government or the rebels currently at war in the countryside from doing anything to reduce the enormous amount of power that they and the armed forces have traditionally wielded.

What do most people in business want from government? Their rhetoric to the contrary notwithstanding, few actually crave free markets. Most industrialists began behind the shield of high tariffs, which protected them against competition from imported goods, and easy credit, and many still rely on government assistance to operate. Academic economists and ideologues, not native business people, are the only proponents of Adam Smith's version of market capitalism these days. When it comes to actual government policy most industrialists still prefer the helping hand of the state.

Equally high on their policy agenda is the subordination of organized labor. Industrialists have fought labor organizations since their inception, always demanding that authorities regulate them tightly to prevent their interfering with management or agitating for more rights and social reforms. They have not always succeeded, at least not as much as they wished, because unions learned how to trade the votes of the rank and file for greater assistance from the government in countries like Argentina, Chile, Mexico, and Venezuela. Fear of radical politicians has also preoccupied the wealthiest members of the business community, and they have not hesitated to summon the military to evict presidents who threatened their interests. The issue for them is less one of democracy versus authoritarianism than maintenance of the status quo versus efforts to redistribute wealth and property.

The political activities of business are like those of modern farmers. They have organizations that represent commercial, financial, and industrial interests before the government. They seldom work directly through political parties, though they do lobby before legislative bodies and participate as much as they are allowed on government boards and commissions. But, more than any of the other players, business people seek out public officials on their own, trying to gain advantages for their individual firms, in many instances resorting to bribes and other favors to secure what they want. Business people, like farmers, take advantage of their role in the developing economy to persuade authorities to meet their policy demands. When threatened by higher taxes or regulations that raise their costs, they warn of the economic calamities such policies would cause. Because industrial and commercial growth is essential to most development programs, a nation's president is especially vulnerable to such threats. He has little choice but to favor business unless he is willing to call its bluff and risk the consequences. How influential business people become in politics will depend on the credibility of their threats and the government's dependence on each industry and enterprise for economic success. Of course, the government is not helpless. Businesses depend on it for purchases of goods, tariff protection, and utility prices, and they are vulnerable to competition from public enterprises, which together give authorities substantial leverage in countries like Mexico and Brazil where the state's involvement in the economy is so great.

Business people seldom agree on which rules of the game serve them best. Native small businesses that are vulnerable to foreign competition welcome nationalistic political parties even if it means risking the election of officials who are more tolerant of organized labor than they would prefer. The managers of larger, more secure firms, in contrast, tend to be less nationalistic and more threatened by social reformers. Democracy is tolerated by them, but only when it generates the kinds of economic policies that allow them to plan ahead and prosper and prevents interference in their enterprises from either the government or their employees.

Middle sectors

The wealthy have never managed Latin American economies all by themselves. Retail stores and banks had to be run, post offices staffed, upper-class children educated, goods transported, and bureaucracies administered. Educated persons with professional skills were needed to make their societies prosper, and their numbers increased as their economies developed and urbanization grew.

Scholars have never known what to call these people. Some use the concept *middle class* while others prefer to label them *middle sectors* in order to distinguish them from the middle classes in Europe and North America with whom they have little in common. The middle sectors are located somewhere between a wealthy and powerful upper class and the poor masses, much like middle classes, but that is where their similarities end. At the beginning of this century they became active politically in Argentina, Chile, Uruguay, Brazil, and Mexico, demanding admittance to government. But they were never as economically powerful as the middle class in Europe that had arisen with the Industrial Revolution. Instead, they were primarily professionals without much economic clout who had to settle for asking the government to improve their well-being by supplying more public education, subsidizing private businesses, and increasing public employment. For them politics was a means to affluence, unlike in Europe where, conversely, the middle class used its economic power to gain control over national politics.

The middle sectors are an elusive subject for political analysis despite their well-known history. There are several reasons for this, all of them related to their origins in elite-run societies and the way they were forced to rely on politics more than economics for their advancement. First of all, they seldom developed as much class consciousness as did the Europeans before them, but instead remained a diverse community whose members were quite independent of one another. Second, they have not changed their societies as much as the middle classes changed the European ones. This is due in part to the determination of so many of them to join the upper class, or at least imitate it, rather than to destroy or replace it. This is less so today than it was a half century ago, but by starting out as individuals who were eager to live like oligarchs rather than to develop their own distinct identity, they have always found it difficult to operate as a social class with shared subjective interests. And third, the middle sectors have taken an unconventional route to industrial development, creating economies that depend far more on government subsidy and protection for their survival than other capitalist ones do. Government became the residence of many in the middle sectors who were more at home exercising their political talents than their entrepreneurial ones. The result has been the heavy involvement of the state in the subsidization of industrial enterprise and a modernizing economy that is very dependent on government support.

If we were to search today for the descendants of the first middle sectors, we would find them everywhere. As society has grown more complex, the middle sectors have grown more diverse and less united by a common cause. Most of the reform-minded political parties of the 1960s were led by individuals who came from middle-sector families. So did most of the military officers who governed in the 1970s. Some have joined the economic elite as commercial farmers, industrialists, merchants, and bankers. And some are now the technocrats who supervise Latin American government agencies. We would be hard pressed to find a Latin American leader today whose parents did not come from the middle sectors.

They are quite fickle in their politics. At times they have championed the cause of the electoral democracy and honored constitutional rules once in office. Few political parties anywhere were more devoted to democratic practices than the middle-sector-led Radical parties of Argentina and Chile and the Colorados in Uruguay. The democratic preference was not present everywhere, however. In Mexico, for example, the middle sectors enthusiastically supported one-party government, and in Brazil they were content to work within the long-established tradition of elite-dominated regional political machines.

Even more striking is the way middle-sector political preferences have varied over time. The same persons who vote for democratic parties have occasionally abandoned them for military rulers who promised to promote prosperity and protect them against revolts from below. When democracy is accompanied by intense political conflict and economic uncertainty, they are quick to insist on stronger government. And even though they may at times support social and economic reforms, they are seldom receptive to much reform when they, more than the powerful upper class, must give some of their wealth to the poor, either through higher taxes, wages, or inflation. In other words, when their economic self-interest conflicts with their political ideals, they are willing to sacrifice the latter. This will become especially evident in Chapters 8 and 9 when we examine military and democratic governments in Brazil and Argentina.

The masses

Before considering workers and peasants, a word of caution is in order. Two problems haunt the analysis of the masses as players in the Latin American game. The first is the temptation to see them as a homogeneous community whose members share economic and political interests. The mere fact that they are laborers in economies run by owners and managers would appear to give them a common identity, as does their poverty, political isolation, and exploitation. But closer examination reveals differences among them that are as great as their similarities, especially when viewed through the experience of the masses themselves. Race, ethnicity, regional identities, and short-term economic self-interest traditionally have separated Latin America's poor from one another. Moreover, their differences have been exploited by local elites who are determined to obstruct concerted resistance to their authority. Even today the masses are not united to do battle with the rest of society. Instead, if they become involved politically at all, it is usually through an organization that competes with other mass organizations for a share of the national pie.

The second problem that accompanies the study of workers and peasants is that few of them actually belong to the organizations that claim to represent them. Less than one-fourth of the region's urban work force is unionized, and very few peasants and small farmers have organizations. Therefore, we must be cautious when attributing the views of union and peasant leaders to all of the people they claim to lead. They are important players in the political game, but that does not justify our assuming that all of those who speak for the masses enjoy their support.

Organized labor

Restraining organized labor preoccupied ruling elites at the turn of the century, and it still does today. Working-class movements began in the 1890s, led by immigrant workers and intellectuals advocating socialist, anarchist, and syndicalist ideologies then popular in Europe. They achieved little at first, divided within by ideological disputes and harassed and repressed from without by conservative business and reactionary government. They were also victims of the region's underdevelopment. Not until industries and the public sector began to grow in the larger countries in the 1930s did the working class achieve the size needed to threaten the existing order through political action seriously. But even then it was thwarted everywhere except in Mexico by stubborn ruling classes who refused to share their power with an unwelcome intruder who demanded admission to the game on its own terms.

Labor leaders learned many things from their political defeats, the most important being their inability to penetrate ruling circles on their own. How to put this lesson to work became the subject of intense debate within labor movements during the 1930s and 1940s. In the end it was resolved not by labor ideologues but by a new generation of politicians from outside the movement who, lacking a large political base of their own, turned to the working class for support, offering them in return protection by a paternalistic state. By exploiting rank-and-file frustrations and a general malaise caused by the Great Depression and its aftermath, politicians like Getulio Vargas in Brazil, Juan Perón in Argentina, and Lazaro Cárdenas in Mexico built populist coalitions that gave labor a new place in national politics.

A labor movement's political prominence depends in part on the terms under which it gains admission to the national political game. Nowhere is this more apparent than when we compare the political fate of Latin American labor with that of labor unions in the United States. The latter retained their institutional and legal autonomy after becoming a player, and they still act as a relatively independent force, negotiating contracts with employers at the industry level and influencing policy by supporting candidates and lobbying legislators on the national scene. Latin American unions, in contrast, gave up much of their autonomy when they accepted the paternalism of populist politicians. Populist law and political practice made organized labor the ward of a powerful, centralized state. To exist legally, unions had to be officially recognized by the government; moreover, the ministries of labor tightly controlled collective bargaining, access to funds raised by special taxes on workers' salaries, and labor courts. Regardless of whether the nation's politics were democratic or authoritarian, the state was responsible for the supervision and protection of organized labor. In contrast to the United States, where the government occasionally acts as a mediator of last resort when all private modes of conflict resolution fail, in Latin America the government supervises from the outset.

Populist paternalism was never as beneficent as it seemed. When the interests of labor and those of populist presidents clashed, the latter usually prevailed by using the power of the state to keep recalcitrant unions in line. The rank and file were often the losers in the populist scheme, for though they gained official attention and legal recognition they usually watched helplessly as their leaders sacrificed their interests in order to retain the vestiges of power for themselves.

Eventually the populists were deposed or replaced, but state control over organized labor survived them, remaining to this day in most places.

We normally think of organized labor as speaking for the masses, but in fact it speaks primarily for itself. It is really an elite within the working class, representing a minority of workers who have to some extent "made it." Most laborers are not among this fortunate few, but are unorganized, protected by no laws, and without much clout when it comes to collective bargaining. Like most elites, organized labor has become more concerned with its own conquests and their protection than with improvement of the welfare of those not within its organizations. Individual unions expend most of their energy on such bread-and-butter issues as wages, working conditions, and retirement benefits, while their national confederations concentrate on securing government policies favorable to them. Confederation leaders not only resort to strikes, demonstrations, and consultations with officials, but also try to put their leaders in government ministries that make labor, economic, and social policies.

Nearly all economic policy decisions affect labor in some way. Take antiinflation policies, for example. Rising prices reduce purchasing power and force unions to demand higher wages to compensate for their losses to inflation. Wage increases, however, may only provoke higher prices, touching off a wage–price spiral. One solution is to freeze wages temporarily, thereby asking labor to bear some of the burden of stopping inflation. But labor leaders seldom stand by idly while they are singled out to pay the price of fighting inflation. Instead, they use all means at their disposal to see that the costs are shifted to others. In so doing they try to protect themselves from harm in the short term even if they cannot secure the long-term benefits they desire.

Organized labor has many resources at its disposal. In a democratic game, for example, it can offer its votes to candidates who will defend labor interests. Despite the fact that organized workers are a minority of the work force, they can deliver large blocs of voters to their chosen candidates. They can also mobilize their supporters for rallies and demonstrations on a candidate's behalf. But votes count only in elections, and since elections are the exception rather than the rule in many places, organized labor is forced to employ other resources to gain favor. One of the most important is its economic influence. More often than not, unionized industries are vital economically. Workers in transportation, mining, petroleum, banking, and manufacturing have been organized for some time and know how to use society's dependence on those industries and services to good advantage. Through strikes they can not only threaten owners and managers, but also undermine government economic programs in order to force the government to settle a strike in labor's favor or to adopt a particular policy demanded by the labor leadership.

Finally, as a source of last resort there is the general strike or violent protest aimed at securing a desirable presidential response. Such extreme tactics are employed to undermine public order and force presidential concessions. They are especially effective in countries where weak presidents fear military intervention if order cannot be maintained. In such cases the president must decide whether to meet labor's demands and risk criticism from antilabor elites or to deny labor's demands and risk continued disorder and possible military intervention. Labor too runs some risks when it chooses such drastic tactics. A strong president may retaliate with force to break union protests, and should the military intervene, it too might exact a high price from the protesters by closing unions and jailing their leaders.

No matter how rich it is in resources, the labor movement cannot succeed without being well organized. It is not enough for a few leaders to claim to represent the rank and file, they must also have their followers' loyal support. Unauthorized wildcat strikes or, conversely, an unwillingness to join in strikes can undermine labor leaders by destroying the unity they need to maximize their influence. Disunity and internal squabbling, in turn, encourage the divide-and-conquer tactics employed by business and antilabor governments that want to break strikes and hold the working class in check. On the other hand, unity creates problems of its own. For example, once the labor movement is joined into a national confederation, it runs the risk of over-centralization and of the kind of bureaucratization that makes labor leaders insensitive to the needs of union members. The latter situation has led in some countries to the creation of rival union organizations that have sought, in most cases unsuccessfully, to break the monopoly of these unresponsive labor bureaucracies.

We might expect laborers to prefer democratic rules, because they give them an obvious advantage over wealthy elites. But it is not that simple. Remember that most unions secured their place under populist leaders or single-party governments that seldom lived by democratic rules. They learned early that what mattered most was not the form of government but the protection it gave to union organizations. Consequently, most labor unions are more concerned with what a government does to fulfill its obligations to them than the methods by which its office holders are selected. Whether it is democratic or authoritarian is not as important, it seems, as whether it will act as their ally and patron.

Campesinos

The rural poor are still not taken very seriously. They have long been neglected, ignored by politicians and bypassed by the forces of economic modernization. Their world is confined to the *latifundio* or commercial farm on which they work, the *minifundio* (small farm) they occupy, or the village in which they reside. For them, effective political authority rests not in some distant capital but with the landlords, village mayors, parish priests, and local military commandants.

Latin American peasants have not always accepted their subjugation by local elites passively. The region's history is filled with peasant revolts, and violence is still common in the countryside. In this century, dispersed protests have been accompanied by organized campaigns to secure government intervention on the peasants' behalf. Throughout the hemisphere governments have responded with diverse reforms aimed at redressing peasant grievances. Agrarian reforms have yielded impressive results in a few countries, most notably Mexico, Cuba, Venezuela, Nicaragua, and Peru. Nevertheless, most of the rural poor survive at or just above the subsistence level, either untouched by agrarian reform or given land but no capital or technology to develop it. For many peasants, agrarian reform has been a disappointment, little more than a means for promoting large-scale modern farming rather than improving the welfare of the rural poor.

To understand why reform has benefited so few, we must look more closely at the Latin American campesinos, their political goals and resources. By campesinos we mean the mestizo, indigenous, and Negro farmers and laborers who populate rural Latin America. Nearly all of them earn barely enough for their physical survival and enjoy few opportunities for improving their condition. At the same time, they differ from each other in important ways. When grouped according to their means of employment, they fall into at least four distinct groups.

The first are the *colonos,* who work as laborers on the *latifundios* or as sharecroppers or tenant farmers. They have probably resided in the same region for generations and are bound to their employers by debts incurred over several years. Some *latifundistas* have taken their responsibilities as *patrones* seriously, protecting the *colonos* and their families from catastrophe and providing them with a subsistence income in order to maintain the *latifundio* as an organic, self-sufficient community. Others have treated them more harshly, ignoring their basic needs and abandoning them during hard times. As one might expect, they are rather isolated from national politics by their physical separation from national capitals. When they vote in national elections, they are sometimes closely supervised by their *patrones.* Moreover, they are hard to organize politically because of their dispersion throughout the countryside and their subordination to the *latifundistas.* The latter can discourage campesino organizers by using the local police, economic control over their workers, and their influence in local courts. It is not difficult to understand why campesino movements have seldom survived without help from outside, for without public officials or party leaders to protect them from the reprisals of local elites, organizers stand little chance of success.

A second type of campesino is the wage laborer. Many of the crops produced on Latin America's commercial farms are harvested by hand. This is especially true of cotton, coffee, sugarcane, fruits, and vegetables grown in areas with an abundance of labor. Many of those who work in the harvest are migrants who leave their villages and return at the end of the season. Some own their own land but must seek employment elsewhere because they cannot produce enough to meet the needs of their families. Others have become landless through population pressures or the loss of their land to creditors. They are the Mexican *braceros* who migrate legally and illegally to California and Texas, the coffee pickers who descend from highland villages in Guatemala and Colombia, and the cane cutters in northeast Brazil. Like migrants everywhere, they exist on the fringes of the political process and are seldom reached by government programs. They can ill afford to become involved in political protests during the harvest for fear of losing an entire year's livelihood. In the off-season they return to their villages and blend back into the local populations, out of reach of labor organizers.

Plantation workers are a third type. Like the *colonos,* they are bound to one place year round, but like the migrant they work on modern establishments rather than traditional farms. Plantation workers have more in common with factory workers than they do with most of their fellow campesinos, for they work in highly organized settings in which modern technology is applied to the production of commodities for export. In some instances, their employers are foreign corporations like the banana companies of Central America and Colombia, though they are just as likely to work for domestic firms or individual families. The relative ease of organizing plantation workers explains in part why the number of plantation worker unions has increased. They work in close proximity, communicate regularly, and develop skills that are needed by their employers. Thus, if the leadership is available, they are organizable, much like factory workers. To succeed, however, they must overcome the resistance of plantation owners, who are often backed by sympathetic government officials.

Not all campesinos work on *latifundios,* plantations, or commercial farms; many own land or occupy small plots to which they have no legal claim. They employ only the most primitive technologies and farm primarily for their own subsistence, selling a small surplus in local markets. They take few risks with new seeds or fertilizers, most of which they cannot secure because of their poverty and lack of access to short-term credit. If they want to ship their small surplus to distant markets, they must rely on private traders, who easily take advantage of their isolation and dependent status. Subsistence farmers confront agrarian reformers with one of their toughest problems, for if they are given land, they may use it inefficiently for lack of technology; yet if agrarian reform is to lead to higher production, something must be done to increase the efficiency of such units. Usually the only alternatives considered are government financing of small-farm modernization, which is quite costly, or farm reorganization into more efficient cooperatives or state-run units that can spread the use of modern technology, a solution often resisted by the very independent campesinos.

What do campesinos want from politics? Unfortunately, they have seldom been asked, and when the question has been raised, others, notably landed elites, reformers, and revolutionaries, have answered it for them. Moreover, as we have seen, they are a very diverse group, separated by economic interest, region, and ethnicity, and they seldom speak with a single voice. Nevertheless, even though they are not united by a single set of policy demands, time and again they have made their basic needs and wants clear to any who would listen.

They want to improve their life chances and the welfare of their families on their own terms. How that is to be done is not always clear. Some of them demand greater protection against exploitation by landlords and employers; some want land of their own, storage facilities, and markets. With only a few exceptions, their concerns are personal, local, and specific, rather than general and self-consciously ideological. They are not as opposed to innovation or the expansion of their production as is often assumed. If they appear to be risk averting, it is because they cannot afford to take chances when their annual crop is all that stands between their families and starvation. New technologies require expenditures they can ill afford, especially if they lack access to credit. Only the government, through its supply of subsidized technology and redistribution of land, can break the vicious circle in which most campesinos find themselves. Thus, even though past experience has taught the rural poor that government is unwilling or ill equipped to meet their needs, it remains the only source of their salvation. Understandably, however, they continue to be suspicious of grand promises, skeptical about the possibility of progress, and alert to the betrayal of their cause. But their apparent passivity should not be mistaken for apathy, for, like other players in the game, campesinos want a larger share of the nation's wealth. If they lack anything, it is confidence in their ability to secure that share.

The political strength of campesinos is yet to be fully tested in most Latin American countries. Their principal resource is their immense size as a social group, a resource they have seldom been permitted to use. Because they are numerous in some countries, they would appear to have much to gain from elections and democratic processes. Yet, although many of them dutifully march to the polls, their votes are usually the exclusive property of their employers or the local elites. Only where modern political parties have recruited the peasantry into constituency organizations, as in Venezuela and Mexico, has their participation affected electoral outcomes. Where electoral influence is denied them, they can resort to violent attacks on their oppressors.

But armed revolts are risky, especially against well-entrenched rural elites and their allies in local law-enforcement agencies. Nevertheless, occasionally rural revolts have been successful, as they were in Mexico in 1910 and Bolivia in 1952.

Given their limited influence in elections and the high risks of violent protests, how can campesinos affect national policy? To have any impact at all, they must overcome several obstacles. One is organization. It is not especially hard to organize wealthy landowners, business people, or labor union members into effective political action groups. They are usually united by physical proximity, an agreement on basic issues, and their ability to finance a permanent staff. The rural poor, in contrast, are separated physically, often do not perceive their common interests, and cannot finance their own organizations. Another is the communications obstacle. They are separated not only by physical distance but also by ethnicity and regionalism, especially in countries with large indigenous populations. As a result, issues and solutions that satisfy one group of them may be inappropriate to the needs of others. Their organizational problems are aggravated by the fact that their enemies exploit their weaknesses in order to limit their success. It has been by taking advantage of their isolation, fear, and inability to communicate over large distances that the landowners and their allies have until recently so successfully prevented the development of viable peasant organizations.

As fears of campesino emancipation have grown among members of the rural elite, so has the brutality of their repression. In some places, most notably Central America in the 1980s, the appearance of guerrilla movements drew the militaries deep into the countryside in an attempt to head off campesino collaboration with insurgents. Even when they chose to be inhospitable to the rebels, they were attacked by authorities, the elite strategy being one of intimidation intended to deprive the guerrillas of potential village sanctuaries. Too often they had little choice but to flee their traditional homes in order to avoid becoming victims of one side or the other. It was not uncommon to find entire villages empty in the Guatemalan highlands, their former residents having been either massacred or forced to flee. Death tolls of several hundred per week were quite common.

Their vulnerability to landowners' divide-and-conquer tactics have made the campesinos more dependent on help from outside, especially from the government, than any of the other players. Ambitious aspirants for public office began reaching out to them during the postwar years, offering agrarian reform and other measures in exchange for political support. Central to their political strategy was their mobilization of campesinos into constituent organizations that could deliver the rural vote. Modeling their tactics after the highly successful organization of the Mexican peasantry by President Lazaro Cárdenas in the 1930s, reform parties throughout Latin America have tried to break the monopoly of local elites over other voters and use the latter to defeat their opponents at the polls. Some campesinos have been organized locally and regionally much like urban labor unions with delegates to national party councils and the legislature. Their goals have been reformist rather than revolutionary, and in countries like Venezuela, Chile, and Mexico they have worked within the system rather than against it. In Venezuela, for example, thousands were organized by the Acción Democrática party in the early 1940s and were rewarded with an agrarian reform program after the party took office in 1947. When the military overthrew the Acción Democrática a year later its rural organizations survived clandestinely to reemerge after the party was restored to power in 1959. The ability of Acción Democrática to win subsequent elections was due in large part to the peasant support it had retained.

Despite its many accomplishments, the kind of reformist agrarianism practiced in Venezuela, Chile, and Mexico is not without serious limitations. Democratic governments which are vulnerable to countervailing pressures have not always fulfilled their promises to their rural supporters. Government fears of retaliation by the rural elite or the military, as well as the desire to increase productivity by encouraging modern rather than peasant farms, have seriously hampered the fulfillment of commitments to the rural poor. In short, even though reformist agrarianism opens the policy-making process to leaders of the rural masses and meets some of their demands for rural reform, it is vulnerable to countervailing pressures that often leave the peasants much as they always were.

Campesinos need not follow the peaceful path of reformist agrarianism. They can choose instead the more direct route of violent revolt, taking matters into their own hands and seizing the land in order to force public authorities to meet their demands. The campaign of Emiliano Zapata during the Mexican Revolution is a classic example of this. Zapata was revolutionary only in the sense that he wanted to change the rural status quo. His was not a utopian vision of a new society, but a simple desire to regain for his village the land that had been taken away by local sugar barons with the government's encouragement. It was a struggle of armed peasants against tyrannical landlords who had destroyed their way of life. But Zapata's is not the only example of revolutionary agrarianism. In Cuba the rural cause was taken up by Fidel Castro's insurrectionists, and in Nicaragua by the Sandinistas. Theirs were not peasant revolts, but the campaigns of urban-bred ideologues who acted in the name of the peasantry as well as other members of the masses. Once their revolts had succeeded, campesinos were among the first beneficiaries of the revolutionary program.

Rural insurrection has been treated harshly by the region's governments and their military guardians in recent years. Nevertheless, revolutionaries continue to struggle. Those who have chosen guerrilla warfare as their mode of attack have been plagued by many problems, not the least of which is the reluctance of suspicious campesinos to support their cause, either directly by joining in the armed struggle or indirectly by not betraying them to authorities. The challenge laid down by guerrillas confronts them with a more difficult choice than might first appear: If they do not support the revolutionaries, their condition is not likely to change, but if they do support the guerrillas, they risk retaliation from landowners and local police; moreover, if revolution does succeed, they have no guarantee that the results will be to their liking. This is why many revolutionaries have discovered to their disappointment that the exploited and potentially explosive campesinos are often reluctant participants in their struggle.

Finally, what about the rules of the game? As the least active and least encouraged participants in the conventional game, they have seldom been given the opportunity to shape the rules by which it is played. Moreover, regardless of the type of political system in which they live, they still find themselves on the receiving end of decisions made by others. In traditional autocracies, for example, they are dominated by local landlords and law-enforcement agents; in reformist democracies, a few peasant leaders and government bureaucrats usually manipulate them. And in revolutionary societies party leaders and government agents reorganize their lives for them. Their choices, it seems, are among being ignored, represented by a few well-intentioned reformers, or transformed by a party elite that claims to act in accord with their objective interests.

The campesinos' weaknesses confront them with a serious problem. Without strong allies among those in political authority, they have little chance of affecting the course of rural policy. Yet, if they do secure an alliance with other players, they risk being absorbed and used by their new allies. The fact that most leaders of peasant movements have been small-town professionals or urban functionaries with very weak loyalties to their rural constituents makes their co-optation even more likely. Moreover, internal conflicts are as common to peasant movements as they are to the interest groups of the rich, perhaps even more so, making them vulnerable to manipulation by competing peasant leaders and politicians. Whichever path they choose, the campesinos will end up with less than optimal results.

The economic development of Latin America depends on the progress made in the rural sector in the years ahead. The region's rural populations are increasing too rapidly and their migration to overcrowded cities is too great to be ignored. Although most governments in Latin America acknowledge this, few have demonstrated that they can do anything about it.

Further reading

Rural elites

Barraclough, Solon Lovett. *Agrarian Structures in Latin America: A Resume of the CIDA Land Tenure Studies of Argentina, Brazil, Chile, Colombia, Ecuador, Guatemala, Peru.* Lexington, MA: Lexington Books, 1972.

de Janury, Alain. *The Agrarian Question and Reformism in Latin America.* Baltimore: The Johns Hopkins University Press, 1981.

Dew, Edward. *Politics of the Altiplano: The Dynamics of Change in Rural Peru.* Austin: University of Texas Press, 1969.

Feder, Ernst. *The Rape of the Peasantry: Latin America's Landholding System.* Garden City, NY: Doubleday (Anchor Books), 1971.

Kaufman, Robert. *The Politics of Land Reform in Chile 1950–1970: Public Policy, Political Institutions, and Social Change.* Cambridge: Harvard University Press, 1972.

Keith, Robert, ed. *Haciendas and Plantations in Latin American History.* New York: Holmes & Meier, 1977.

Smith, Peter. *The Politics of Beef in Argentina.* New York: Columbia University Press, 1969.

Smith, T. Lynn. *The Process of Rural Development in Latin America.* Gainesville: University of Florida Press, 1967.

Business elites

Austin, James E. *Agribusiness in Latin America.* New York: Praeger, 1974.
Cardoso, Fernando Henrique. "The Industrial Elite," in Seymour Martin Lipset and Aldo Solari, eds., *Elites in Latin America.* New York: Oxford University Press, 1968, pp. 94–114.
Davis, Stanley M., and Louis Goodman, eds. *Workers and Managers in Latin America.* Lexington, MA: Heath, 1972.
Evans, Peter. *Dependent Development: The Alliance of Multinational, State, and Local Capital in Brazil.* Princeton, NJ: Princeton University Press, 1979.
McDonough, Peter. *Power and Ideology in Brazil.* Princeton, NJ: Princeton University Press, 1981.

Middle sectors

Gillin, John P. "The Middle Segments and Their Values," in Lyman Bryson, ed. *Social Change in Latin America Today.* New York: Random House (Vintage Books), 1960, pp. 28–46.
Johnson, John. *Political Change in Latin America: The Emergence of the Middle Sectors.* Stanford, CA: Stanford University Press, 1958.
Portes, Alejandro. *Latin American Class Structures: Their Composition and Change during the Last Decades.* Baltimore: The Johns Hopkins University Press, 1984.
Wagley, Charles, "The Dilemma of the Latin American Middle Class," in Charles Wagley, ed., *The Latin American Tradition.* New York: Columbia University Press, 1968, pp. 194–212.

The masses: organized labor

Alba, Victor. *Politics and the Labor Movement in Latin America.* Stanford, CA: Stanford University Press, 1968.
Alexander, Robert. *Organized Labor in Latin America.* New York: Free Press, 1965.
Berquist, Charles. *Labor in Latin America.* Stanford, CA: Stanford University Press, 1986.
Latin America Bureau. *Unity Is Strength: Trade Unions in Latin America.* London: Latin America Bureau, 1980.
Morley, Samuel. *Labor Markets and Inequitable Growth: The Case of Authoritarian Capitalism in Brazil.* New York: Cambridge University Press, 1982.
Spalding, Hobart. *Organized Labor in Latin America: Historical Studies of Workers in Dependent Societies.* New York: New York University Press, 1977.

The masses: campesinos

Alschuler, Lawrence, ed. *Dependent Agricultural Development and Agrarian Reform in Latin America.* Ottawa: Ottawa University Press, 1981.

Grindle, Merilee. *State and Countryside: Development Policy and Agrarian Politics in Latin America.* Baltimore: The Johns Hopkins University Press, 1986.

McClintock, Cynthia. *Peasant Cooperatives and Political Change in Peru.* Princeton, NJ: Princeton University Press, 1981.

Singelmann, Peter. *Structures of Domination and Peasant Movements in Latin America.* Columbia: University of Missouri Press, 1981.

Wolf, Eric. *Sons of the Shaking Earth.* Chicago: University of Chicago Press, 1959.

   Peasant Wars in the Twentieth Century. New York: Harper & Row, 1969.

Womack, John. *Zapata and the Mexican Revolution.* New York: Knopf, 1969.

4. Players – II

Political parties

In Western democracies we take political parties for granted, confident that they will offer candidates, contest elections, and create governments. But it is not so everywhere because party behavior always depends on what other players allow parties to do. For example, we learned that elections are not the only means for creating governments in Latin America and, even where they are used, winning them does not guarantee the victors a full term in office. The military may step in and evict elected officials, foreign governments may subvert them, and opponents within the nation may use violence to bring them down. As a result, party politicians know that winning elections ensures nothing.

Parties play at least three roles in the Latin American game. First, many of them do compete in elections. In some countries, like Costa Rica and Venezuela, their life is fairly simple, requiring little more than intense campaigns aimed at winning free elections. But in others, like Argentina and Brazil, much more is required because, until recently, respect for constitutional rules was lacking. In Argentina, for example, between 1952 and 1982 three presidents were elected but none of them was allowed to complete a single term. Just as important as their vote totals was their failure to prevent their opponents from endorsing their removal by military officers who believed themselves more able than civilians to rule over their nation.

Second, parties also have played the part of conspirators. When other players disregard constitutional rules, party politicians sometimes feel compelled to do likewise. Even the most sincere democrats have found it necessary occasionally to seek the help of military officers or armed civilians to evict authoritarians who could be removed by no other means. Moreover, parties who stand no chance of winning elections but crave power sometimes conspire with undemocratic players to eject the parties that defeated them in fair elections. But conspiracies generate counterconspiracies, adding to the incivility of

73

national politics. One can imagine what France would be like if the parties who stand little chance of winning began provoking violence and encouraging the armed forces to settle civilian conflicts. The Fifth Republic constitutional government would be torn apart if such practices were allowed to become common.

Third, parties sometimes create political monopolies. Rather than live by competition or conspiracy, they may seek permanent tenure. The creation of the one-party government, tempting though it is, is not easily done, as many unsuccessful efforts demonstrate. Critical to its achievement is the ability of the party to secure and retain military approval, and substantial support from the middle sectors and organized labor, as did the Mexicans and Cubans for many years after their revolutions. The product of a rebellion that ended in 1917, Mexico's Institutional Revolutionary Party did not face real competition in any presidential or senate election until just recently in 1988. Using its control over the Mexican state to distribute patronage and wealth to its loyal supporters in all social classes, it denied other parties the constituencies they needed to pose a threat at the ballot box. The Cuban Communist Party, like most communist parties in power, is even more monopolistic, claiming that political truths in its exclusive possession justify its leadership of Cuban society.

Just as the roles played by political parties differ, so do the party systems that they create. The term *party system* refers to the number of parties and the degree of competition among them. We usually speak of one-party systems, two-party systems, and multiparty systems composed of three or more parties. Within the last two catagories different degrees of competition are present; in some countries several parties are close in their popular vote and exchange office frequently; in others, one or two parties dominate. Party systems in Latin America offer examples of nearly every type. For instance, at various times since 1945, you could find two-party systems in Colombia, Uruguay, and Honduras; multiparty ones in Argentina, Chile, Costa Rica, Venezuela, Brazil, Panama, and Ecuador; and governments monopolized by a single party in Mexico and Cuba. In many ways, Latin America provides one of the largest laboratories in the world for the analysis of party systems.

Latin American party systems do suffer from occasional closings by the armed forces, yet despite interruptions of democratic government and substantial political repression, most parties survive and compete with one another time and again. If anything characterizes Latin America's political parties in this century, it is their incredible durability despite the best efforts of their armed forces in recent years to eradicate them. In Argentina, the Radical and the Peronist Parties were closed by the armed forces in 1966, reappeared in 1973, were closed again in 1976, and then ruled the nation once more starting in 1983; and in Chile, the Christian Democrats and Socialists were closed in 1973, then returned and successfully defeated General Augusto Pinochet in his referendum in 1988. Clearly, there is much to learn from the Latin American experience.

There are many ways of classifying and comparing political parties. You can focus on professed ideology, organization, leadership, sources of support, or election strategy, among other things. In studying Latin American parties it is also important to examine them within their historical contexts. Different kinds of parties have arisen in response to different circumstances. Their histories tell much about a country's political evolution since parties often arose at critical points that allowed them to reshape the nation's politics, not just in Mexico or Cuba, but in Argentina and Venezuela as well.

The first organizations to call themselves political parties were little more than cliques drawn from the oligarchy, which ruled during the last half of the nineteenth century. They differed not so much over who should govern – they all believed in elite rule – but over what policies the government should adopt. Those who called themselves Conservatives came primarily from the ranks of landowners and traders, and wanted government to do little more than preserve the prevailing hierarchical social and economic structures. Their opponents, usually termed Liberals, were more ambitious, desiring to use government to promote commercial agriculture and commodity exports through the redistribution of church and indigenous lands to ambitious rural entrepreneurs. Election contests between Conservatives and Liberals were exclusive affairs, seldom involving more than five percent of the adult male population.

In a few countries, such as Colombia and Honduras, Liberal and Conservative Parties forged deep and lasting loyalties that persist today, but in most of the region their monopoly was gradually broken by the rise of new parties at the turn of the century. As long as party politics were dominated by the elite, the new generation of immigrants, urban business people, professionals, and small farmers that emerged in the larger Latin American countries between 1900 and 1920 had little hope of gaining a voice in domestic politics. No matter how hard they might try to affect government decisions, they were usually rebuffed by the leaders of traditional parties, who were unsympathetic to their pleas. Their only recourse was to create political parties of their own and use them to agitate for electoral reforms that would give them an opportunity to compete with the established parties. In several countries middle-sector politicians succeeded not only in securing electoral reforms but also in gaining public office. Calling themselves Radicals in Chile and Argentina and by other names elsewhere, they used urban constituency organizations and the personal popularity of their leaders to defeat traditional elite parties and fill the public payrolls with their supporters while implementing some modest educational and urban reforms, as we learned in Chapter 3.

The 1929 depression was a severe blow to the middle-sector parties, for it revealed their inability to solve the problems raised by world economic crises. They were attacked by Conservatives and, in a few cases, evicted by the military. After World War II they were forced to compete for popular support with new political movements that had been unleashed by the depression and its aftermath. The most important of these were the populists.

The populists were ambitious and skillful political opportunists who took advantage of the rapid industrialization of their countries during the 1930s and 1940s and the rising aspirations of a growing urban proletariat, as well as the latter's neglect and persecution by Radicals, Liberals, and Conservatives. They relied more on the personal magnetism of leaders and the talent of their lieutenants than on sophisticated party organizations to keep their movements together. Once in office, the populists divided the spoils among their supporters and helped native entrepreneurs by promoting industrialization.

The populists were never accepted by most intellectuals and professionals, who resented their demagoguery and strong-arm methods. Consequently, at the same time populism was on the rise, other anti–status quo politicians were busy creating the nucleus of mass-based democratic reform parties. Their goal was to make democracy work by combining the democratic ideals of Radicals with the mass appeal of the populists and the sophisticated party organization developed by socialists and social democrats in Europe. They sought to involve not just the middle sectors, as did the Radicals, but also laborers and campesinos. The two essential ingredients in their campaign were a sophisticated national party that penetrated to the grass roots and the recruitment of rural voters using peasant organizations. They also offered a commitment to reforming traditional economic institutions and to development planning. Democratic reform parties were created in most Latin American countries during the 1940s and 1950s, but they were successful in only a few – those like Chile, Venezuela, and Costa Rica, where populism had never gained a foothold, and where peasants were physically accessible to party organizers.

There are essentially two types of reform parties, one secular and the other religious in origin. The first began with the Alianza Popular Revolucionaria Americana (APRISTA), led by Peruvian Raúl Haya de la Torre and dissident students in the 1920s who were inspired by reformist Peruvian philosophers and modern socialism. The APRISTAs were persecuted throughout most of their history and never allowed to occupy the presidency until the 1980s, when they finally governed Peru. The Acción Democrática (AD) party of Venezuela was more successful, however, governing briefly in the late 1940s and then for all but two presidential terms since 1958. Similarly, the National Liberation Party of Costa Rica has held the presidency on five occasions since its creation in 1948. The success of these parties in the late 1950s convinced some people that Latin Americans had finally found the vehicle needed to build democracy throughout the region. Their hopes proved premature, however, and democratic government did not spread beyond a handful of countries until the 1980s, when various forms of democracy were tried in all but a couple nations.

The second type is labeled religious because of its association with Christian democracy, a movement that was begun by Roman Catholics in Europe and later spread to other Catholic countries. Inspired by the political thought of French philosopher Jacques Maritain, the Christian Democrats aspire to a democratic society that is neither socialist nor capitalist, but one that combines the former's belief in the common good with the latter's respect for the individual. Though not formally tied to the Roman Catholic Church, the party draws heavily on modern Catholic philosophy and the more progressive papal encyclicals for its ideology. Initially quite moderate in their goals and political techniques, the Christian Democrats gradually came to resemble the secular reform parties, expanding their organization to include laborers and peasants and preaching the doctrine of agrarian

reform and national planning. Like the secular reformers, they organized parties throughout Latin America; however, they have been
successful only in Chile, where they governed in the mid-1960s, and
Venezuela, where they held the presidency for two terms in the 1970s.
They too were regarded as a major vehicle of democratic rule and
reform policy, but with the exception of the two countries named,
they have not lived up to their promise.

Last but not least are the revolutionary parties. Revolutionary movements have received much attention of late, but they are certainly not
new to the region. There have been essentially two types of revolutionary parties in Latin America, one inspired by Marxist thought and
example and the other non-Marxist. Among the first are many socialist
and all communist parties. Socialists first organized parties in the late
nineteenth century, primarily under the direction of European immigrants. After the Russian Revolution of 1917, communist parties were
also formed, some of them merging with the socialists, and others
becoming rivals because of the socialists' refusal to accept Soviet leadership of the international revolutionary movement. Thus, at the same
time the Radicals were organizing the emerging middle sectors, small
socialist and communist parties, led by intellectuals and labor leaders,
were trying to build a following among the working class. Proletarian
revolution and social justice were their causes; strikes, demonstrations,
and the education of the masses their weapons. Seldom, however, did
they speak with a single voice, for doctrinal disputes and personal
rivalries bred divisive factionalism within their ranks. Throughout the
1930s and 1940s most were on the fringes of their nations' politics,
often being forced underground or into exile by hostile governments.
Moreover, they had to compete with populists in the 1940s and democratic reformers in the 1950s and 1960s for the support of the proletariat, and they frequently fared poorly against both movements'
more native appeal and ability to deliver on promises of moderate
social legislation. There have been exceptions, most notably Chile,
where Marxist parties that had secured labor support in the 1920s
were admitted to Popular Front governments in the 1930s, and finally
won their first presidential election in 1970.

The Latin American laboratory of political experience offers three
examples of Marxist parties in power. In Communist Cuba we have
witnessed thirty years of social reconstruction, giving us a remarkable
example of how a Marxist society can be built on a Latin American

foundation. Salvador Allende's ill-fated Popular Unity regime in Chile, on the other hand, provides an example of Marxist rule that differed sharply from Cuba's in its intent and achievements, by governing under a democratic constitution until the military evicted it in 1973. And in Nicaragua we find the latest experiment, one led since 1979 by the nationalist Sandinista movement whose leaders espouse their own version of Marxist–Leninist ideology.

The principal non-Marxist revolutionary party is the Institutional Revolutionary Party (PRI) of Mexico. Whether the party is truly revolutionary is much disputed: Critics argue that it has been revolutionary in name only, interested more in maintaining political control over the Mexican electorate and preserving the power of the party elite than in achieving real social and economic equity. On the other hand, the party's defenders claim that during its first sixty years its government went further toward reducing the power of the old upper class, the Church, and foreign investors than has any other non-Marxist government. By comparing the PRI with ruling parties in other countries, in Part 2 of this book, we can assess the performances of Marxist and non-Marxist revolutionary parties.

Revolutionary movements who do not call themselves political parties also appear from time to time, some of them resorting to violent tactics to undermine and evict authorities. They are often clandestine, usually young persons who become skilled at kidnapping wealthy persons and holding them for ransom, or at using explosives to destroy public facilities. In the early 1970s the Tupamaros in Uruguay and the Montoneros and People's Revolutionary Army (ERP) in Argentina fought until they were brutally defeated by the armed forces and forced to flee.

The Sendero Luminoso (Shining Path) operates today in Peru. Organized in the southern Andes by philosophy professor Abimael Guzmán, the very secretive and disciplined organization first struck in 1980. Its pamphlets claim radical revolution akin to the Maoist variety as its objective, declaring the indigenous cultures the only legitimate ones in Peru and promising to destroy everything else. But they are as ruthless with Native Americans and members of the country's Marxist parties as they are with the bourgeois mestizos they abhor. It seems that nothing less than total dedication to their cause is acceptable within the movement. We know little about how its leadership operates and lack information about the size of its membership. What is known is that nearly a decade after its creation it was stronger than ever, the government having failed to prevent its expansion. The fact that it has united Peruvians on the left and right against it reduces the probability of its achieving a military victory any time soon, but the war that it wages in villages and cities, including Lima, leaves Peruvians frightened and with little hope of ending it.

Finally, it is obvious that we have omitted some parties from this brief introduction. Recent Latin American history is littered, for example, with transitory, personalistic parties. Loyalty to a single leader rather than to a platform holds such parties together. Many rise and fall with a single election, beginning as splinter groups in existing parties or starting from scratch and then withering once their candidates are defeated. Personalism is a factor in nearly all parties from the most conservative to the revolutionary, but some parties are organized to survive the loss of a leader, whereas those we have labeled personalist are not. During the nineteenth and early twentieth centuries one could also find regional parties in Latin America. Their purpose was not to capture the presidency, but to represent a regional point of view in legislatures and to force Conservative and Liberal governments to accept their demand for local autonomy. There have also been fascist parties of one kind or another. Modeled after the fascist movements that arose in Italy, Spain, and Germany, they remained on the fringes of national politics in most countries, though they did attain some notoriety in Brazil and Chile and influenced politics and attitudes in wartime Argentina.

The analysis of Latin American party systems would be much simpler if all countries conformed to the history of party development outlined in the foregoing discussion. But they do not. Instead, we find several different patterns throughout the region. Some approximate the course of gradual evolution; in others change has been more abrupt and results dissimilar, such as in the one-party systems of Mexico and Cuba. But regardless of the form each party system takes, parties too are players whose influence on public officials varies with their political resources, skills, and determination. A party supports rules that help its cause and sometimes opposes those that do not. The ones that enjoy widespread support obviously have more to gain from elections than do those without it. Conversely, a party that stands no chance of winning an election might be persuaded that it can gain more from a military coup or insurrection than from an election. But even a party that commands the support of a majority of the electorate may from time to time resort to nonelectoral means to remove a tyrannical government, to block threats from militant opponents, or to create some kind of populist autocracy. Life has not been easy for political parties during the past few decades. They have been attacked by extremists on the Left for being corrupt, self-serving, and intransigent, and by conservatives, especially in the business community, for being demagogic, narrow-minded, and incapable of creating orderly government or achieving steady economic progress. But are political parties really anachronisms, remnants of the liberal democratic state that is in retreat throughout the region? That is how it seemed when the armed forces ruled in most of the South American countries during the 1970s, but ten years later the parties were back, governing once more in nearly every country.

The military

Military involvement in politics is a familiar feature of Latin American life. When not ruling directly, the armed forces often exert their influence on civil authorities, affecting the composition of governments, the treatment of political oppositions, and the content of public policy. We need not dwell on the fact of military political participation, for it is obvious; instead we need to understand why military officers are so deeply involved in politics in the first place. And to do that we must begin with the military itself.

Once poorly educated and unsophisticated, most Latin American militaries have become professional organizations led by highly trained officers who command troops equipped with modern weapons. Nearly every country has an army, air force, and navy, with the army being by far the largest. Its size varies from 297,000 active troops in Brazil to 1,500 in Costa Rica. The Brazilian Army is composed of seven divisions; its Navy has an aircraft carrier, seven submarines, and ten destroyers; and its Air Force has 195 combat aircraft. The Brazilians spent $3 billion (U.S.) on its armed forces in 1987; the Argentines, $2 billion; and the Cubans, $1 billion, and with substantial assistance from the Soviet Union the Cubans kept 40,000 soldiers in Africa, most of them fighting to defend the Angolan government against insurgents. Nearly 3.5 percent of the Cuban population was in uniform, while it was 1.5 percent in Chile, and 1.0 percent in Brazil.

But what does all of this mean for politics? Clearly size, even when measured in relative terms, does not by itself account for the military's involvement in politics. Small as well as large armies have been active politically. Once there is a professional officer corps with a few thousand well-armed troops under its command, the armed forces can evict civilian presidents. To explain its conduct, then, we must turn to other factors.

The military's disciplined, hierarchical organization is one possibility. Without it, coups would be improbable undertakings. To carry out a coup the officers who command major units must support one another or refrain from hindering those among them who decide to take control of their country. Weapons available for the defense of the country can easily be employed to force unarmed civilians from office. But the capacity to carry out a coup is hardly sufficient to explain the decision to intervene. It is a capability but not a motive, making the coup possible but not causing it.

What about the origins of officers and their social class affiliations? Analysts used to argue that officers intervened to protect the *oligarquia* from which they came. This may have been true before 1930, but as an explanation of current military behavior it is quite inadequate. The class background of military officers has changed substantially during the last quarter century. Increasingly, officers are recruited from the middle and lower middle sectors. In place of the offspring of the *latifundistas* one now finds the sons of small-town merchants, skilled laborers, and former military officers, the latter supplying nearly half of the officers in many countries. They seldom represent the urban and rural poor to any large degree, but they are more diverse and less tied by blood to traditional elites than ever before. If they intervene in public affairs to protect the upper class, it is less from a desire to serve them than from a desire to pursue military interests whose achievement often benefits elites who feel threatened by the same political opponents. Radical change is no more welcomed by military officers than it is by big industry or farmers.

Military education helps define officers' political interests and preferences. Officers mature in virtual isolation from everyone else, beginning at secondary military schools at age thirteen or fourteen. After graduation they attend service academies, then take advanced training in specialty schools at home or abroad. There are no ROTC programs at universities or Officer Candidate Schools for university graduates, the armed forces preferring to retain substantial isolation from civilian education. The result is an officer with a strong corporate identity that separates him psychologically, and often socially, from civilian politicians.

Equally important is the content of military education. Most military learning concentrates on traditional concepts of strategy and tactics, organization and administration, and technical training, especially engineering. Beyond rudimentary instruction in foreign languages, history, and economics, little attention is given to the social sciences until the officer enters a war college in midcareer. What results is near total acceptance of a disciplined, tightly organized way of life that is just the opposite of civilian life. If officers learn how to debate and bargain over policy, it is usually within the confines of their own little world, one that breeds little tolerance for the more open and raucous behavior characteristic of civilian politics.

At the same time, officers in the three services are seldom in complete agreement with one another about their nation's politics. Although they will unite to defend the armed forces against their adversaries, they often disagree among themselves over how civilians are to be treated, the economy managed, and foreign affairs conducted. Just as the military as a whole is separated from civilian society, the three services are often separated enough from one another to breed substantial distrust among them. Interservice rivalry plagues the armed forces in other parts of the world as well, but its effects are more consequential when the military attempts to govern the entire nation. The Argentine Army, for example, is notorious for its disputes with the nation's Air Force and Navy, evinced in their shooting at one another in 1962 as well as their implementing contrasting strategies when the country went to war with the British over the Falkland Islands in 1982. The inability of the three services to agree on a new course for their seven-year-old government after the war led to their abdicating to civilians one year later.

Special efforts have been made since World War II to concoct ideologies that give clearer purpose to military politics. War college curricula in countries like Brazil, Argentina, Uruguay, and Peru include courses on national development as well as defense, where officers are taught geopolitics, development economics, and advanced management by civilian as well as military instructors. In some countries, such as Brazil, they are joined in the classroom by civilian students from government bureaucracies and private industry. Together they have defined the military's mission as its defense of the nation, internally as well as externally, along with its preservation of the national way of life, however they choose to define it. Rather than relying on civilians to ask for their intervention, gradually they took it upon themselves to decide what was best for the nation and to act accordingly.

But politics was not their only concern. Increasingly in the postwar years the armed forces in nations like Brazil and Argentina also concerned themselves with their nations' economic development. Frustrated by the repeated failures of civilians to achieve sustained economic growth, they decided to play a more prominent role in the development process, promoting the government's creation of basic industries and assigning responsibility for their management to the military. In the process they vested substantial interest in national production, and in a few countries achieved some sophistication in engineering and management, both of which would make them hard to dislodge from their increasingly prominent position within public enterprises.

Military officers also have considerable institutional self-interests to protect. The Cuban and Nicaraguan revolutions taught them that they would be the first to go in a revolutionary society. In both countries officers were not only defeated by guerrillas, but were either tried and convicted for committing crimes against their nations or were forced into exile. Informed by such events, the military instinct for self-preservation often generates a paranoia about potential threats to their survival that causes them to suspect even moderate reformers of sinister intentions. Of course, they also have privileges to preserve. Without wars to fight or serious threats to national security to deal with, they have been known to vest themselves with sinecures that they refuse to relinquish for even the best economic reasons. The result is an entrenched military bureaucracy that is no more tolerant of reform than are most civilian ones.

Though not a political party or conventional interest group, the armed forces are a major participant in the political process. Constitutions try to subdue them, but only the exercise of real power by other players can ever do it. Defining a more limited role for the military and making them conform to it is one of the most difficult tasks that a civilian government faces after it replaces a military government. In some countries the armed forces are accustomed to running ministries of defense unmolested by civilians and to managing armaments and other industries. They also supervise intelligence operations and believe it is their right to define subversion and deal with it. Laws are never enough to define authority and responsibility under such conditions; working relationships must be established and, no matter how many votes they receive, civilian presidents are seldom powerful enough to define all of them as they wish.

With so much military participation in national politics you might expect to find hundreds of civilians in each country who are experts in military affairs. Yet the opposite is true. Very few civilians are prepared to work in defense ministries and supervise the nation's armed forces for the president. Understandably, it is not a popular profession in countries where the armed forces are often despised by civilians, but that only makes it harder for elected presidents to administer their own defense policies. Without staff members who can read a military budget and assess the claims of officers, presidents must rely on generals and admirals to do it for them, which is exactly how the military wants it. They do not have to threaten a coup to get what they want; they may simply win disputes because there is no one out of uniform able and willing to rebut and rebuke them.

No introduction to military political forces would be complete without mention of foreign militaries and their involvement in Latin America. The region's officers are no less subject to foreign influence than civilians are. Traditionally, they have secured armaments, advanced training, and technical assistance abroad, primarily from the United States after World War II, with the exception of Cuba and Nicaragua, who look to the Soviet Union and Eastern European militaries for assistance. Latin Americans belong to regional defense organizations and purchase weapons wherever they can find them. With such collaboration often comes the reinforcement of shared political ideologies, such as the anticommunist containment strategy launched by President Harry Truman and sustained by all United States presidents after 1947. Most Latin American militaries thrive on defending their countries against "communists" within and without, and they have seldom resisted the temptation to lure foreign assistance from governments who are eager for them to carry out that task.

It would be a mistake to conclude, however, that the region's militaries are nothing more than the passive instruments of foreigners. A close relationship can develop, but its exact character depends on many things, ranging from how dependent the local military is on foreign support to how determined the foreigner is to make the local military a central part of its strategy. Most countries have been trying to reduce their dependence on any single foreign government by diversifying their sources of armaments. Today the Brazilians, Argentines, and Peruvians rely very little on the United States for their supplies; Brazil and Argentina manufacture many of their small arms and all three buy heavily in Europe. In 1970, for example, all but 100 Latin American military aircraft came from the United States; by 1982, 1,500 had been purchased elsewhere.

Tensions between Latin American militaries and the United States arise occasionally, as happened during the war over the Falkland/Malvinas Islands in 1982 when the Reagan administration sided with the British against Argentina, causing sharp criticism of the United States by officers in several countries. But despite the Latin Americans' greater independence, there remains an alliance of sorts between the United States military and the Latin American officers who share its fundamental conservatism on hemispheric political matters. Each has been educated in the school of anticommunism, and they are reluctant to abandon each other completely.

In sum, Latin American armed forces are not monolithic in their goals or behaviors. Nor is their political behavior caused by a single factor. Yet most officers do share an institutional identity that separates them from civilian society and often makes them feel superior to it. Theirs is a bureaucratic culture dependent on hierarchy and command, one that does not cope easily with the uncommon and the unusual, especially when either appears to threaten their prerogatives. They are happiest when they have a clear mission, one that makes them feel important and causes them to be appreciated by their compatriots, something that still eludes them in most places. Long ago they confined themselves to protecting conservative oligarchies, but today life is far more complicated. They want economic development and power for their nations, they fear ideologies and insurgents on the political Left, and they distrust most civilian politicians. How they play politics depends as much on conditions in their societies as on the personal ambitions of service commanders. Their education and military culture filter what they see, causing them to be uncomfortable with the give and take of conflict. This does not mean that they never tolerate constitutional government and party politics; obviously they have done so for many years in some countries. But they do try to have things their way, contending daily with the other players, tolerating some while doing all they can to frustrate others.

Now that we have learned a few of the military's capabilities and motivations, can we predict when and where the next coup will occur? Probably not. An ability to understand military involvement after the fact does not give us the power of prediction. But coups per se are not what should interest us. We can learn little about Latin American politics by viewing the military as an intruder that steps in and out of the game. It is more instructive to see the military as a player much like any other, with its own interests and tactics. Wishing it were not so will not change the fact of military involvement. As every civilian politician knows, the armed forces will continue to play politics whether anyone else likes it or not.

The Roman Catholic Church

One-half of the world's Roman Catholics live in Latin America, and 90 percent of the people in the region claim Catholicism as their religion. For more than four centuries the Roman Catholic Church lent its support to the prevailing political order, praying for the souls of the poor while consorting with the rich. Then in the mid-nineteenth century its role began to change, starting with attacks on the Church by upper-class politicians who were determined to deprive it of its property to expand their plantations. Thereafter, the Church was forced to confine itself primarily to a religious mission, leaving economic matters to entrepreneurs and political ones to civil authorities. Nevertheless, the conduct of the Roman Catholic clergy has been the subject of controversy ever since.

Only a few decades ago the clergy was attacked by political reformers for conspiring with the oligarchs who exploited the masses, especially in the countryside. By preaching salvation in another life they pacified the poor, denying them the incentives needed to improve their condition. In their own defense, church leaders argued that they had no choice since their earthly mission was clearly a spiritual and not a materialistic one. Today, in contrast, the criticism of the clergy comes from the opposite side, with conservatives accusing a reform-minded clergy of forsaking their spiritual mission in favor of a radically different earthly one. Why the sudden change? And why has it occurred within an institution that was thought for so long to have been one of the least interested in improving social and economic conditions?

The Roman Catholic Church is still a hierarchical organization that is supervised from the Vatican by the Pope. But within this structure the beliefs and practices of individual clergy have been changing. Some of the initiative came from the reformulation of church doctrines by authorities in Rome. But most of it originates far from the Vatican, prompted by the frustration of priests, nuns, and laity with the condition of the poor.

The doctrinal sources of revised theology can be traced to two encyclicals, *Mater et Magistra* (1961) and *Pacem in Terris* (1963), which, among other things, stressed the universal rights to education, a decent standard of living, and political participation; and to the Second Vatican Council (1965), which established a certain equality among laity, priests, and bishops. In Latin America the doctrinal reformation was translated to policy by the Latin American Episcopal Conference of Bishops (CELAM) at Medellín, Colombia, in 1968, where Pope Paul VI himself declared that the Church "wished to personify the Christ of a poor and hungry people."

Words are one thing, their translation into action something else, and few ever agree on how to carry out a new mission in the real world around them. Conservative bishops insisted that the clergy confine themselves to the pulpit, whereas the reformers insisted on pastoral involvement in the mobilization of their poorest congregations for social action. An attempt to resolve these differences was made at the CELAM meetings in Puebla, Mexico in 1979, but instead both sides went away claiming victories and their differences remained. Conservatives continued to condemn the theologies of liberation that became prominent in the 1960s, claiming that theologies that relied on Marxist concepts of social class to explain the plight of the masses, interpreted the gospel as advocating communal societies, and promoted revolution were wrong. Reform-minded clergy, in contrast, insisted that revisions in thinking and behavior were essential to serving the poorest among them and bringing justice to entire societies long denied it.

Equally instrumental in promoting innovation within the Church were the thousands of parish organizations known as *comunidades de base* that were formed all over the region during the past three decades. Originally intended to involve parishioners in administering the local church's affairs where clergy were scarce, they often became village or neighborhood organizations that sought to promote greater effort to improve the plight of the poor. Though seldom revolutionary in their politics, they nevertheless posed a threat to local authorities and employers. Local elites feared that efforts to promote self-help projects would increase the economic independence of the rural poor and deprive them of their control over the lower classes. As a result, many of the priests and nuns who promoted *comunidades* became the targets of assassins in Central America and the Andean nations. But the *comunidades* survived nevertheless, though they were often forced to confine themselves to more pedestrian activities.

Many Church officials also stood up against the military authoritarian governments that became prominent in the region during the 1970s. In countries where the military chose to rule harshly, using its weapons against civilians, the Church became one of the few institutions able to oppose it and survive. Political parties can be closed, labor unions repressed, and protest movements defeated militarily, but the armed forces cannot liquidate the entire Church hierarchy. To be sure, priests and nuns have been jailed and killed, but the cardinals and bishops are too visible nationally and internationally to be treated likewise, the notable exception being Salvadorian Archbishop Oscar Romero who was assassinated by right-wing death squads. Consequently, when they chose, they could denounce government violations of human rights, especially in Brazil, Chile, Nicaragua, and El Salvador.

Lest we rush to conclude that the Church has become a new instigator of political revolution, it is important to recognize that revisions in doctrine and grass-roots activism have done more to change the Church than to change the region's politics. The clergy are well located to help the poor do more to defend themselves, but the Church itself is neither organized nor highly motivated to lead political revolutions in Latin America. Moreover, it continues to be divided over what its earthly mission should be. Examples of these political limitations abound.

The Brazilian Catholic Church has more members than does the Church in any other country, an enormity that requires nearly 300 bishops to administer it. It has been for some time the region's most progressive national church, one that devoted itself to defending human rights during the twenty years that the military ruled the country after 1964. But when the military stepped down in 1985 it was not the Church that deposed it. Though many clergy had morally condemned the armed forces for their actions and helped sustain a belief in the illegitimacy of military government, other Catholics defended it, and in the end it was the military itself and civilian politicians and not the Church that caused it to hold elections and step down.

Similarly, the Church is a crucial player in the Nicaraguan game today, but the nation's six bishops are not powerful enough to determine the nation's political fate. Instead, they are entangled in bitter disputes among themselves and with secular authorities. Themselves supporters of the insurrection that deposed dictator Anastasio Somoza in 1979, a few clergy went on to defy papal prohibitions against their holding public office and became ministers in the Sandinista government, some at the cost of expulsion from their clerical order by the Vatican (e.g., dropped by the Jesuits). Moreover, after a couple years of cooperation between the Church and the government, the Pope and most of the Nicaraguan bishops turned against the new authorities, declaring that they had created a Marxist–Leninist government that was manipulating the Church for its own ends, trying to enhance its legitimacy by encouraging the clergy to rally their parishioners behind authorities who professed a dedication to the goals of liberation theology. They feared that secular ideologies would undermine Christian theology by changing it beyond recognition. As a result, many in the Nicaraguan Church leadership lent their support to foreign-financed rebels who sought to depose the Sandinistas. For their part, the Sandinistas felt threatened by the Church's opposition, concerned that it would hinder their completion of the revolution by promoting resistance to them. The result was a divided population with Catholics and clergy on both sides, each seeking respect from the other while fearing its subversion by them.

The lesson from Brazil and Nicaragua is that the Roman Catholic Church, new or old, conservative or reformist, is a powerful player with some special advantages, but not enough to transform a nation's politics on its own. The Church has changed in many regards, especially at the parish level, but it remains too divided and decentralized in actual practice to accomplish what its more revolutionary theologians want and its conservative clergy dread. But to ignore the clergy, the church leadership, or the *comunidades de base* at the grass roots is to miss one of the most prominent forces in Latin American life today.

Government bureaucrats

Why include bureaucrats as players in the game? Do they not serve the interests of the politicians and the military officers who command them? It is tempting to dismiss them as irrelevant to the political contest, but we cannot afford to do so. They do not contest one another in elections but they do influence policy, and therein rests their importance. Moreover, while presidents and generals come and go, sometimes quite frequently, most bureaucrats hang on.

Patronage runs high throughout Latin America, but so does career government service. Many work at routine tasks, but there are always a few who manage government banks, airlines, oil companies, railways, and the like. As government responsibilities have grown, so has the number of technocrats who make policy. They are educated at the London School of Economics, the Sorbonne, Harvard, MIT, and the University of Chicago, as well as universities within the region. Though often short on political skills, they proudly display their technical expertise, convinced that their educations have given them a right to shape their nations' development policies.

The rapid growth of the public sector in Latin America is relatively recent, but it has had an enormous effect on contemporary political life. During the past fifty years, Latin American governments have gone from regulating domestic and foreign trade to promoting industrialization and implementing ambitious development programs. Governments that did little more than build roads and deliver the mail a half century ago now produce a wide range of goods and services, from iron and steel to television programs. This sudden change has not come without some problems, however. Latin American governments, despite their immense formal authority, are still quite weak in many areas, especially when it comes to enforcing regulations, and they are always hampered by insufficient financial resources and managerial talent at the lower levels.

Frustration with unfulfilled development plans and with inefficiently managed state enterprises has become commonplace, prompting a renewed interest in strengthening the state and its bureaucratic capabilities. Military officers and technocrats, who occasionally seize control in many of the region's governments, often claim that they will halt patronage and reduce corruption in order to make government more efficient, though they seldom deliver on their promises.

It should now be clear why we should regard bureaucrats as players who have their own interests and resources. Whatever their historical experiences or policy preferences, the people who manage government institutions share many things in common. First, they desire to preserve and expand their influence over public policy. Second, they seek to administer their programs with as little interference from political authorities as possible. And third, they want to dominate those who depend on their goodwill. What they enjoy most is the power they derive from citizens' needs for the goods and services they provide. To a large degree they are the modern patrons of the industrialists, traders, farmers, laborers, and peasants who work in a private sector that depends heavily on the state for licenses, loans, roads, railways, housing, and innumerable regulations and social services. In return they expect deference, tribute, and compliance with their demands.

The potential power of bureaucrats is evident when we recognize that no matter how noble a government's goals or how sophisticated its development plans, it accomplishes little without the support of administrators. Bureaucrats are supposed to be the servants of the political officials, but political officials often find themselves the captives of their bureaucrats. They rely on them to design policies as well as to implement them. If bureaucrats disagree with official policy or find it threatening to their organizational interest, they have recourse to many weapons, which they can use to sabotage the government's efforts. Political officials cannot afford to sit back and assume that their programs will succeed simply because they are needed. If they do not closely supervise program implementation, making sure that policy goals are met and services delivered, their best efforts will likely come to naught.

In recent years many Latin American presidents have taken it upon themselves to reduce the size of their governments in order to halt rapid increases in their budgets. Various measures were proposed, from selling government corporations to private interests to cutting back on government services. But in few cases have they been successful. In some the same military presidents who proposed such changes were the first to halt efforts to reduce military budgets and those of the public enterprises that they ran. In others it was government-employee unions that fought back. This has not prevented new efforts to reduce public spending during the 1980s when austerity became a way of life for the region's heavily indebted governments, but only the slowest progress has been made.

The weakness of political analyses that focus primarily on "politics" rather than "government" is that they miss the impact of administrators on what governments actually do. If we are to understand why some countries do well when they try to solve fundamental development problems and other do not, we cannot halt our analysis after examining legislatures and presidents and their policy choices. Instead, we must go a step further and ask what the government does with its authority and what consequences, if any, it has on the welfare of its citizens.

Foreign players

Some analysts blame foreigners for the Latin American condition. This is not surprising. For over a century critics of capitalism have argued that it has survived by exploiting Africans, Asians, and Latin Americans, reaping huge profits from the extraction of minerals, the purchase of low-priced agricultural commodities, and the export of expensive manufactured goods. For its part the Third World has gained little but poverty, economic stagnation, and autocratic government, they argued.

Even if one disagrees with this view, the fact of foreign influence throughout the region is indisputable, making it impossible to leave foreigners off our growing list of players. Foreign players are citizens of other countries who influence the politics and economic well-being of Latin Americans through direct involvement in the region. There are principally three types: those who represent other governments, those who work for international agencies, and those employed by private business. Here we will look briefly at a foreign government, the United States, and then at multinational enterprises to illustrate the roles played by foreigners.

The United States government is represented by several persons in each Latin American nation. A U.S. embassy, for example, houses officials who work for the State and Defense Departments, the Treasury, the Departments of Commerce and Agriculture, and the Central Intelligence Agency. They are supposed to work together to achieve a coherent set of objectives set by the president of the United States, but the ambiguity and complexity of U.S. government aims in each country leave much room for each agency to pursue its particular aims.

Since World War II the United States has given highest priority to the exclusion of communists from the region, fearful that communist government would increase Soviet influence and reduce U.S. power in Latin America. The creation of a communist regime in Cuba followed by the Cuban missile crisis in 1962 reinforced a fear that the Soviet Union was gaining strategic advantages over the United States through the creation of anti-American and pro-Soviet regimes like Cuba's. The methods employed to suppress communism have varied, ranging from financing the election campaigns of anticommunist parties to training paramilitary forces to fight guerrillas. Some, like President Jimmy Carter, tried to promote economic reform and respect for human rights in order to undermine the political Left and win friends for the United States. President Ronald Reagan, occasionally with help from the U.S. Congress, financed the Contra insurgents in their attempts to harass the Marxist Sandinista government in Nicaragua throughout the 1980s. But whatever the means employed, the anticommunist objective has stayed essentially the same. A second and complementary goal is U.S. access to Latin America's natural resources and markets. Although most U.S. trade is with Europe and Canada, Latin America is an important supplier of essential minerals and a rapidly growing market for U.S. technology. When we put these two objectives together, it is apparent why the United States prefers the status quo to rapid political change in the region, even when it means tolerating autocratic governments alien to U.S. political values. Creating democracies has never been as important for U.S. presidents as preventing anti-Americanism and communism.

How does the United States government influence Latin American governments, given the objectives just described? At the diplomatic level it tries to convince host officials of the merits of its case, using logical arguments and technical expertise. But logical argument is seldom sufficient to get one's way with officials whose national interest often competes with that of the United States. Therefore, the United States government also relies heavily on the resources that give it advantages over Latin American governments. On the economic front it takes advantage of Latin American reliance on U.S. markets, investments, and foreign assistance, threatening now and then to reduce the flow if its demands are not met. Similarly, it uses its power within international lending agencies to block funding of projects in nations whose governments threaten U.S. interests.

A second resource, and one that has received much attention of late, is direct intervention through covert action. To secure the kind of government or politics they want, agents of the United States government may enter directly into the political game by giving funds to the players they favor, directing hostile propaganda against those they do not, bribing officials and party leaders, fomenting unrest, and encouraging military intervention. As noted, in the early 1980s the Central Intelligence Agency financed an army that sought to overthrow the Sandinista regime in Nicaragua. Even though such techniques frequently fail to achieve their objectives, their availability and the threat of their use may bring a government into line with U.S. wishes.

Finally, there is the threat of direct U.S. military intervention. Popular at the turn of the century during the era of dollar diplomacy, direct U.S. military intervention in Latin American countries seldom occurs today. Nevertheless, the ability to intervene with troops, especially in the Caribbean, as occurred in the Dominican Republic in 1965, and in Grenada in 1984, remains a weapon that can be employed to deter certain undesirable behaviors. More often than not, however, U.S. policy makers are content to use their influence over Latin America's militaries to secure the results they desire.

In sum, what the United States government wants most from Latin America is the region's collaboration with the pursuit of its strategic and economic objectives. A United States president has many assets to command, but success is never automatic. The Latin American game is never simple and its results are influenced by many things, the efforts of foreign governments being only one, though an important one. Moreover, pressure has to be applied skillfully, a requirement not always fulfilled by clumsy foreign governments. Furthermore, as Latin American countries have grown and diversified their markets and sources of capital, they have reduced their vulnerability to any single nation's foreign policy, even one as powerful as the United States. When the United States halted the sale of weapons to Brazil and Argentina in the late 1970s, for example, both countries bought them elsewhere, ignoring U.S. demands, as did General Noriega in Panama when President Reagan tried to force his departure from Panama in 1987 by cutting trade with the country.

Foreign governments may receive the most attention in the press, but more foreigners are sent to the region by private corporations than by governments. As the Latin American economies grew after 1950 so did foreign investment, especially in the larger ones like Mexico, Brazil, Argentina, and Venezuela. Mexico, for example, though noted for its nationalism, still relies heavily on foreign investment. Over one-half of the 500 largest U.S. manufacturing firms have operations in Mexico. Moreover, multinationals accounted for as much as 64 percent of Mexico's production of transportation equipment, 51 percent of its chemicals, and 21 percent of its processed food. These figures are significant, for it is not the size of a firm's share of the entire economy that makes it powerful, but its dominance in industries on which a government heavily relies to meet its citizens' needs. The days when one or two foreign firms ran a nation's economy are long gone, but dependence on a few firms for an essential technology or product is quite common.

Not surprisingly, given their importance and influence, multinational firms are among the most criticized institutions in the region, accused of forcing native entrepreneurs out of business, extracting excessive profits, bribing local officials, and resisting regulation. Criticism has prompted many measures designed to reduce their influence, ranging from restrictions on how many foreigners that firms can employ to sharing a firm's ownership with native investors, as in Mexico where foreign firms in some industries were asked to place 51 percent of their operations under Mexican control. And governments can also nationalize foreign firms, which is quite a risky step but one taken successfully by several Latin American governments.

Foreign firms want a favorable investment climate conducive to a high rate of return for as long as possible. Not surprisingly, investments decline rapidly under the worst of conditions, as occurred during the mid-1980s when bouts of hyperinflation and deep recession struck the larger Latin American economies. Multinational firms want freedom to operate as they wish, an accessible but docile labor force, and the lowest possible cost of operation. And they prefer a government whose actions are predictable, especially in economic affairs. They need to know what the economic rules of the game are and to be assured that they will remain the same in the future. What the multinational firm does not want is a government that is hostile to investors and that continually harasses them with unanticipated measures that limit their operations and reduce their profits. Nor does it welcome the economic uncertainty caused by rising prices and chronic balance-of-payments problems. Nevertheless, they have survived quite well under less than optimal conditions, tolerating what they cannot change while exerting their influence on government policy makers to secure what advantages they can.

The multinational firm's major sources of influence are the resources and products it contributes to the host country. The more the local government wants what the firm offers, whether it be the extraction of minerals, the production of toothpaste, or the provision of jobs for rapidly growing populations, the more vulnerable it is to the firm's demands. It is Latin America's misfortune (and conversely the multinationals' good fortune) that today the region finds itself needing much more technology and capital, both of which are most readily supplied by the multinationals. Officials who are in a hurry to raise the production of goods and services may find the multinationals, with their transferable technologies, capital, and managerial skills, the swiftest means for achieving their growth objectives. On the other hand, they know that there is a price to be paid for foreign investment, most notably the absorption of domestic enterprises by the multinationals and increased foreign economic control.

Not to be overlooked are some of the less advertised ways in which multinational firms try to influence policy. Bribes are occasionally given to secure favorable government decisions. Some even cynically argue that bribes are justified as a kind of informal tax on the rich by the poor. A more indirect form of influence is the ability of multinational firms to block a country's participation in international markets. Boycotts of products, embargoes on exports, and debunking a nation's creditworthiness are all techniques that have been used against Latin American nations in recent times.

It is worth noting that not everyone in Latin America believes that relations with multinationals have to be unhappy ones. Many persons, including some economists, consumers, and industrialists, believe that foreign firms can make important contributions to their economies. For them, it is not a question of nationals versus foreigners, but rather of how the country can efficiently employ its resources. Labeling these persons "lackeys of imperialism" ignores their arguments that foreign investment may be the best available means for financing necessary development projects.

Prominent among multinationals (certainly so in the 1980s) were the foreign banks to whom Latin Americans came to owe billions of dollars. Borrowing money abroad to finance businesses and government programs has always been a common practice in the region, but only in the 1970s did private banks in the industrialized nations begin to make enormous loans to Latin Americans. When the Saudis, Kuwaitis, and other OPEC members made deposits in private European and North American banks after price increases in 1973 had transferred immense wealth to them, the banks rushed to find customers to whom they could lend the money. That they did so with such abandon was caused not only by the enormity of deposits falling into their hands, but also by radical changes made in the international banking system to increase profit.

The invention of the *Eurodollar* created a very different kind of market, one that became far more lucrative than anything before it. Traditionally banks were geographically bound, constrained by the regulations of the country (as well as states, in the United States) where they were registered and by their practice of confining most deposits to that nation's currency (i.e., dollars in the United States, pounds in Great Britain, marks in Germany, etc.). Moreover, in the United States banks are required to hold a certain percentage of their deposits in reserve to make sure that they will have enough cash on hand to meet demands for withdrawals. But they cannot earn any interest on reserves, only on the 80 to 90 percent that is loaned. Generally it has worked well for banks, depositors, and regulators by guaranteeing a secure financial system. But then banks discovered that if they put their dollar deposits outside the United States, they could avoid such regulations. In other words, they could loan and earn interest on every dollar deposited with them if they so wished. With this in mind major U.S. banks set up little offices "offshore" in London, the Bahamas, the Caymans, and other places and went into business. Suddenly billions of dollars were flowing from OPEC countries and other Eurodollar banks to these offices which paid higher interest rates than onshore banks yet still earned more because they had more to lend. Moreover, because loans were often very large, many of them put together by consortia of large and small banks, they earned immense returns (e.g., a $1 billion loan at 10-percent interest could bring in $100 million). Eager to find customers, bankers began rushing all over the Third World after 1973.

Ready and waiting at the other end were Mexico and Venezuela who, though oil exporters, needed additional funds to pay for their ambitious development programs; Brazil, an oil importer, also anxious to finance rapid growth; and Argentina, whose military government was trying to finance its economy's conversion to freer trade. Almost before they knew it, each had borrowed record amounts and accumulated unprecedented debts to the likes of Chase Manhattan, Citibank, the Bank of America, Deutsche Bank, and Barclays. Unfortunately, the entire episode, prompted as it was by avarice and ambition, was built on a tragic illusion: that creditors and debtors alike could accurately predict history. For it to work – for Latin Americans to prosper and repay their debts so that their creditors would flourish – the world economy had to continue to grow at rates achieved in the late 1970s. But it didn't. Instead, government efforts to halt inflation in the industrial nations touched off a world recession in 1981 and 1982, interest rates rose, and Latin American debtors came up short, earning too little income from their exports to pay interest on their record debts. Had there not been so many countries in trouble at the same time, the situation might have been handled easily, but with Mexico and Brazil plagued by debts of over $80 billion, Venezuela and Argentina of over $20 billion, emergency measures became necessary. These and other debtors in the Third World could not be allowed to default, but neither could their creditors let them continue with the same high-powered development strategies. Someone had to pay, and the banks and their governments decided that the debtors would be the first to do so.

Putting their heads together, the Latin Americans, bankers, officials from the International Monetary Fund (IMF), and the U.S. government responded as they had to all of the international financial crises that had arisen since 1945. They lent the debtors more money to tide them over in the hope that eventually they would recover. The International Monetary Fund had been created precisely for that purpose after World War II, and for three decades it had served the industrialized nations as a creditor of last resort responsible for preventing the collapse of the international system. It had done the same for Third World countries unable to pay their accounts abroad. But the IMF's assistance did not come without a very high price tag. In exchange for new loans, each Latin American country had to agree to put its own financial house in order, following strict IMF guidelines that required unpopular cuts in expenditures and reduced subsidies to consumers and local business. The moral of the story was quite clear: In order to continue to operate within the confines of the international trade system, the Latin Americans once again had to accept the terms dictated by their foreign financiers. Moreover, it did not take much insight to see that in becoming more ambitious in their own development plans, some of the Latin American governments had, for the time being, increased their dependence on the foreign powers from whom they were trying to free themselves.

Debts made the 1980s a dismal decade for many Latin American countries. We will examine their effects in specific countries in Part 2. Unprecedented pressures to conform with the demands of multinational enterprises and foreign governments forced the abandonment of expensive development programs. Instead, countries had to pay up to half of their export earnings to their creditors. Moreover, in order to secure more loans to pay the interest on old ones, they were required by their creditors to cut government expenditures and reduce consumption at home, all of which made it harder on the middle and lower classes to survive economically.

Further reading

Political parties

Coniff, Michael C., ed. *Latin American Populism in a Comparative Perspective*. Albuquerque: University of New Mexico Press, 1982.
Maolain, Ciaran O., ed. *Latin American Political Movements*. New York: Facts on File Publications, 1985.
McDonald, Ronald. *Party Systems and Elections in Latin America*. Chicago: Markham, 1971.
McDonald, Ronald, and J. Mark Ruhl. *Political Parties and Elections in Latin America*. Boulder, CO: Westview Press, 1988.
Radu, Michael, and Vladimir Tismaneanu. *Revolutionary Organizations in Latin America: A Handbook*. Boulder, CO: Westview Press, 1988.
Williams, Edward J. *Latin American Christian Democratic Parties*. Knoxville: University of Tennessee Press, 1967.

Military

Bahbah, Bishara. *Israel and Latin America: The Military Connection*. New York: St. Martin's Press, 1986.
Comblin, José. *The Church and the National Security State*. Maryknoll, NY: Orbis Books, 1979.

English, Adrian J. *Armed Forces of Latin America: Their Histories, Development, Present Strength, and Military Potential*. London: James Publishing, 1984.

Johnson, John. *The Military and Society in Latin America*. Stanford, CA: Stanford University Press, 1964.

Lieuwin, Edwin. *Arms and Politics in Latin America*. Praeger, 1961.

Looney, Robert E. *The Political Economy of Latin American Defense Expenditures: Case Studies of Venezuela and Argentina*. Lexington, MA: Lexington Books, 1986.

Lowenthal, Abraham, and J. Samuel Fitch, eds. *Armies and Politics in Latin America*, rev. ed. New York: Holmes & Meier, 1986.

Nun, José, "A Latin American Phenomenon: The Middle Class Military Coup," in James Petras and Maurice Zeitlin, eds., *Latin America: Reform or Revolution?* Greenwich, CN: Fawcett, 1968, pp. 145–185.

O'Donnell, Guillermo. *Modernization and Bureaucratic-Authoritarian Studies in South American Politics*. Institute of International Studies. Berkeley: University of California Press, 1973.

Rouquie, Alain. *The Military and the State in Latin America*. Berkeley: University of California Press, 1988.

Wesson, Robert, ed. *The Latin American Military Institution*. New York: Praeger, 1986.

Church

Berryman, Phillip. *Liberation Theology: The Essential Facts about the Revolutionary Movement in Latin America and Beyond*. New York: Pantheon Books, 1987.

Bruneau, Thomas C. *Religiosity and Politicization in Brazil: The Church in an Authoritarian Regime*. Austin: University of Texas Press, 1981.

Cleary, Edward L. *Crisis and Change: The Church in Latin America Today*. New York: Orbis Books, 1985.

Guitierrez, Gustavo. *A Theology of Liberation: History, Politics, and Salvation*. Maryknoll, NY: Orbis Books, 1973.

Lernoux, Penny. *Cry of the People*. Baltimore: Penguin Books, 1982.

Levine, Daniel, ed. *Churches and Politics in Latin America*. Beverly Hills, CA: Sage Publications, 1980.

Religion and Political Conflict in Latin America. Chapel Hill: University of North Carolina Press, 1986.

MacEoin, Gary, and Nivita Riley. *Puebla: A Church Being Born*. New York: Paulist Press, 1980.

Mainwaring, Scott. *The Catholic Church and Politics in Brazil 1916–1985*. Stanford, CA: Stanford University Press, 1986.

Smith, Brian. *The Church and Politics in Chile: Challenges to Modern Catholicism*. Princeton, NJ: Princeton University Press, 1982.

Government bureaucrats

Anderson, Charles W. *Politics and Economic Change in Latin America: The Governing of Restless Nations*. New York: Van Nostrand, 1967, Ch. 6.

Greenberg, Martin. *Bureaucracy and Development: A Mexican Case Study.* Lexington, MA: Heath, 1970.

Grindle, Merilee S. *Bureaucrats, Politicians, and Peasants in Mexico.* Berkeley: University of California Press, 1977.

Saulniers, Alfred H., ed. *Economic and Political Roles of the State in Latin America.* Austin, TX: Institute of Latin American Studies, 1985.

Wirth, John, ed. *Latin American Oil Companies and the Politics of Energy.* Lincoln: University of Nebraska Press, 1985.

Wynia, Gary W. *Politics and Planners: Economic Development Policy in Central America.* Madison: University of Wisconsin Press, 1972.

United States

Agee, Philip. *Inside the Company: CIA Diary.* New York: Stonehill, 1975.

Black, Jan Knippers. *Sentinels of Empire: The United States and Latin American Militarism.* New York: Greenwood Press, 1986.

Blaiser, Cole. *The Hovering Giant: United States Responses to Revolutionary Change in Latin America.* Pittsburgh: University of Pittsburgh Press, 1985.

Guttman, Roy. *Banana Diplomacy: The Making of American Policy in Nicaragua 1981–1987.* New York: Simon & Schuster, 1988.

Hayes, Margaret Daly. *Latin America and the U.S. National Interest: A Bias for U.S. Foreign Policy.* Boulder, CO: Westview Press, 1985.

Kryzanek, Michael J. *United States–Latin American Relations.* New York: Praeger, 1985.

Lowenthal, Abraham F. *Partners in Conflict: The United States and Latin America.* Baltimore: The Johns Hopkins University Press, 1987.

Middlebrook, Kevin J., and Carlos Rico. *The United States and Latin America in the 1980s.* Pittsburgh: University of Pittsburgh Press, 1986.

Molineu, Harold. *United States Policy toward Latin America: From Regionalism to Globalism.* Boulder, CO: Westview Press, 1986.

Newfarmer, Richard S., ed. *From Gunboats to Diplomacy.* Baltimore: The Johns Hopkins University Press, 1984.

Schoultz, Lars. *Human Rights and U.S. Policy toward Latin America.* Princeton, NJ: Princeton University Press, 1981.
National Security and the United States Policy toward Latin America. Princeton, NJ: Princeton University Press, 1987.

Multinational corporations

Barnet, Richard, and Ronald Muller. *Global Reach: The Power of Multinational Corporations.* New York: Simon & Schuster, 1974.

Evans, Peter. *Dependent Development: The Alliance of Multinational, State, and Local Capital in Brazil.* Princeton, NJ: Princeton University Press, 1979.

Goodman, Louis Wolf. *Small Nations, Giant Firms.* New York: Holmes & Meier, 1987.

Gwynne, S.C. *Selling Money.* New York: Penguin Books, 1987.

Jenkins, Rhys Owen. *Transnational Corporations and the Latin American Auto Industry.* Pittsburgh: University of Pittsburgh Press, 1987.

Newfarmer, Richard S. *Profits, Progress, and Poverty: Case Studies of In-*

ternational Industries in Latin America. South Bend, IN: University of Notre Dame Press, 1985.

Sigmund, Paul. *Multinationals in Latin America.* Madison: University of Wisconsin Press, 1980.

Watkins, Alfred J. *Till Debt Do Us Part: Who Wins, Who Loses, and Who Pays for the International Debt Crisis.* Washington, DC: Roosevelt Center for American Policy Studies, 1986.

5. The stakes in the game

Politics obviously involves much more than winning elections and launching military coups. Players also want to influence people who manage the economy, administer justice, educate citizens, provide social services, and protect the nation against foreign adversaries. Seldom, however, does everyone agree on how all of these tasks should be done. Commonly, entrenched elites contest with the middle and lower classes over how wealth should be distributed and justice delivered, and persons who represent agriculture, industry, commerce, and labor frequently disagree with one another on how to achieve economic development.

There are many kinds of public policy worthy of study, but limited space prohibits our looking at all of them. Consequently, we will confine ourselves primarily to policies designed to affect economic development and social welfare. Few things stir more controversy or are more important to the well-being of citizens than the ways that wealth is created and distributed. This is what much of the political contest in Latin America is about today, so in limiting ourselves to economic and social policy we need not worry about missing the most important political conflicts being fought in the region.

Economic underdevelopment

Latin America's economic and social maladies are no secret. Poverty is immense in most nations despite substantial economic development throughout the region during the past half century. Evidence of modernity is not hard to find anymore, but only a few blocks from the skyscrapers, modern hotels, and enormous factories sits some of the world's worst squalor. Poverty as well as affluence are basic features of Latin American life and will remain so well into the future.

Everyone wants to know what causes such poverty and underdevelopment. Single causes are appealing because they simplify things, so it is not surprising that people desire them, even for so complex a

104

phenomenon as underdevelopment. In Latin America some people blame the region's poverty on its tradition-bound Hispanic culture, claiming that it has hindered the kind of innovation and economic modernization that are believed to be necessary for the region to progress. Others fault unsettled politics, notorious for their desta-bilizing effects on everything from investment decisions to law enforcement.

More recently many Latin Americans have taken a slightly different approach, putting the blame less on culture or politics than on the world economy and the way it has inhibited the region's development. Called *dependency theory,* this approach traces the problem back to colonial times when Iberian monarchs were more consumed with ex-tracting wealth from the Americas than with building economically viable new nations. Primary-product, export economies resulted, econ-omies that changed customers after independence and eventually added new commodities to their exports, like coffee, meat, grain, copper, petroleum, and bauxite, but that always remained bound to selling their commodities in world markets. By relying as much as they did on the export of primary products the Latin American nations were extremely vulnerable to sudden changes in foreign demand for their commodities, their worst predictions coming true in 1929 when a world depression drastically reduced markets abroad and shattered any remaining hopes of relying on primary-product exports to achieve economic development.

To alleviate the problem some nations tried industrialization after 1930, convinced that it would reduce their dependence and vulnera-bility. But their industrial achievements, which were impressive during the next forty years, did not bring the emancipation they sought. Instead, industrialization brought a new kind of dependence with it by requiring that Latin Americans import vast amounts of capital, technology, and raw materials from abroad to construct and operate their industries. Where once they had relied on foreigners to purchase their commodities, they now needed them to supply their new indus-tries. In a curious way, industrialization made them even more de-pendent since it required both the import of capital and technology and the continued sale of primary products to earn the foreign ex-change that was required to make such purchases.

Using this dependency argument, Latin Americans have sought to refute theories of "modernization" once popular among scholars in

Europe and the United States that blamed the region's economic re-
tardation primarily on its people, their culture, and traditions. Modernization theory argued that economic development would occur only
if Latin Americans changed their attitudes and social values, replacing
an ascriptive culture with a more achievement-oriented one. Only by
replacing traditional forms of thought and behavior with the ration-
ality, organization, and acquisitive values of Western industrial society
could Latin Americans invest and produce in the amounts necessary
to become prosperous, it was said.

Dependistas rejected such ideas, claiming that they were contra-
dicted by their own experience. As they saw it, economic structures,
not culture, were responsible for their underdevelopment. Inspired by
the research of Raul Prebisch and his colleagues at the United Nations
Economic Commission for Latin America in the 1950s, they argued
that modernization theory ignored early formations that prevented
Latin America from achieving the kind of economic development attained in Western Europe and North America. Latin Americans were
too dependent economically on the wealthier industrial nations to
replicate their paths to development. Consequently, rather than stress
changes in culture as the means to modernity, one should begin with
the world economy, and with how the structure and performance of
the Latin American economies have been conditioned by their being
forced to reside on its periphery, a reality that drastically reduced the
options available to them.

Dependency also had political consequences. It was apparent long
ago that Latin American presidents would have to cater to foreign
traders and investors far more than they would have preferred. Consequently, when they desired to redistribute wealth from foreigners to
natives, and from the rich to the poor, presidents always hesitated,
always being careful not to impair their relations with their trading
partners. Very often they even colluded with the foreign and national
capitalists who financed the nation's development, using physical
repression against society's more progressive forces whenever they
threatened to interrupt the process.

Brazil is the most frequently cited example of this. Since the 1950s,
Brazilian authorities have promoted the country's economic development by encouraging trade and investment by state, national, and
multinational corporations. When civilian authorities proved themselves incapable of managing the system effectively in 1964, the armed

forces and a legion of technocrats took over to restore international confidence in the country, fostering its most rapid economic growth in this century during the next decade. According to dependency theory, military government in Brazil was not the result of the personal ambitions of military officers or animosities between officers and civilian politicians, but was necessary to preserve the country's very dependent form of development.

The dependency explanation for underdevelopment has its critics, not surprisingly. At one end of the ideological spectrum are those who call it self-serving, a product of frustration written by persons who refuse to face domestic economic realities. Blaming others may give them some consolation, but that does not make it any more accurate or constructive. Self-sufficiency is impossible and trade essential for every modern economy, so instead of worrying about dependence, critics of the dependency explanation insist, Latin Americans have no choice but to play by the existing rules of the international economy, and work even harder to exploit them for their own benefit as several Asian countries have done lately.

At the other extreme are those who contend that the concept of dependence does not go far enough; imperialism, or involuntary economic domination and exploitation of Latin American economies by the more powerful industrial nations, is a more accurate description of the region's plight. They argue that Latin America is the victim of a deliberate effort by capitalist nations and their multinational corporations to enrich themselves by extracting what they need from less developed countries. As a result, foreigners control far more of Latin American life than even the dependistas admit. To end it, very drastic steps must be taken. The nationalization of some industries or the formation of cartels to set prices is not enough. Rather, Latin American nations must sever their ties to the capitalist world economy, "going it alone" if necessary.

The first of these two criticisms of dependency theory is advocated by the proponents of a *conservative modernization* development strategy that we will examine shortly, whereas those who call for more drastic changes propose *socialist revolution* as the solution. Closer to dependency thinking are the proponents of the *progressive modernization* strategy. But before we take a closer look at these, a brief review of economic development and how governments promote it is necessary.

Managing an economy

Managing an economy, be it socialist or capitalist, involves a few fundamental tasks. To design an economic development program you would begin by becoming more familiar with your economy's most basic features. For example, you need to know as much as you can about the country's human capital: the size of its population, its growth rate and age distribution as well as its literacy, skills, and mobility. Physical capital should also be assessed, taking into account energy supplies, existing technology, and the adequacy of transportation and telecommunications. If you governed in a country like the one described in Chapter 1, you would learn that a third of your rapidly growing population was illiterate, that you were still very dependent on the export of a few commodities, that your physical stock was insufficient to service a larger, more industrialized economy, and that you already relied more than you preferred on foreign banks and multinational corporations to finance your development.

Current economic conditions come next. How rapidly is the economy growing, what is the level of employment, what is the rate of inflation, and how is it affecting growth and development? What is the size of your foreign debt and how much of your export earnings go to your creditors to pay the debt? And what about your crops? Is production as great as you hoped, and are prices in world markets what you expected? You cannot predict how each of these conditions will change in the days ahead, but you may try. Of course, no matter how accurate your predictions, you will be forced to adjust to unanticipated events. A doubling of the price of imported petroleum, for example, might require that you spend all of your foreign exchange on energy rather than on projects aimed at promoting economic growth. Or it might force you to borrow much more abroad than you had planned. In other words, no matter how sophisticated and well prepared your plans, you will sooner or later have to adapt them to conditions that you cannot anticipate.

Third, and most important, you must design and execute a set of development policies. This requires identifying specific objectives (such as desirable rates of economic growth, appropriate price levels, and the distribution of income), and choosing the instruments that will achieve them (such as how much to tax and spend, how much currency to allow in circulation, whether to regulate private transactions, and whether to redistribute basic resources, like property, and so on).

In order to match instruments with objectives you also need a model of the economy that tells you how it works. Economic models are abstractions that show how economic activities, in theory at least, are related to each other. Like an engineer who wants to know how much thrust it takes to send a satellite into space, the economist desires knowledge about how much the government should spend to increase the level of growth and employment. There is no single model for all situations, unfortunately. A model is nothing more than a representation of how you think the economy works based on your experience, observation, and logic. If you are convinced that individual conduct in the marketplace sets prices, then you will create a model based on the logic of market behavior. In contrast, if you believe that the government can control the behavior of producers and consumers, you will design a model that facilitates management by central authorities. Whichever you prefer, your model will be your guide when you select instruments to achieve your objectives.

A model never guarantees success. Economic life is far too complex to be captured perfectly by any intellectual construct of reality. Moreover, people do not always behave as one might expect them to, since they can be affected by unanticipated events and unpredictable states of mind, for example, sudden fits of panic. And the data you need to understand prevailing conditions are seldom quickly supplied. Consequently, economic policy is at best a mix of crude theory and guesswork.

The result of all of this effort is an economic strategy that guides specific decisions. One of our goals as analysts of Latin American politics is to identify the strategies chosen by governments, determine their contrasting strengths and weaknesses, and then assess their effects on actual policies. To distinguish among strategies we will focus on four attributes: the theory of development that lies behind the strategy, its specific goals, the policies needed to achieve those goals, and its principal beneficiaries, that is, the players who gain the most from it (see Table 5.1).

Economic strategies are built on assumptions about economic development and its causes. Some of these assumptions are taken from ideologies like capitalism and socialism, and others from observation

Table 5.1. *The dimensions of economic strategy*

Why:	Causes of underdevelopment
What:	Policy objectives
	Production
	Distribution
	Foreign trade
How:	Policy instruments
	Public–private mix
	National–foreign mix
	Coercion–spontaneity mix
For whom:	Beneficiaries
	Immediate
	Long range

and experience. They can steer strategists in many different directions, obviously. For example, one theory might hold that the causes of underdevelopment are found within natural endowments, whereas another might claim that it is due largely to the policies of governments. Obviously, promoting development would be much easier if the second view were more correct than the first. Another crucial distinction is the importance that one's theory places on foreign over domestic forces as determinants of the nation's economic performance. The more important that foreign trade, borrowing, and investment are to the nation's development, the less domestic policies can do to promote it. The crucial issue is whether the strength of external forces can be reduced at all. In sum, development theory and economic strategy go hand in hand, and how well one does in achieving development goals will depend in part on how appropriate one's theory is to the situation at hand.

The second attribute involves the strategy's objectives. Three types of objectives are most prominent. The first involves "production," or the goods and services desired and the rates at which the production of each should be increased. The second objective is "distribution," or how products and wealth are to be divided among citizens, which is obviously a matter of controversy and great political importance. Either by accepting the existing distribution of wealth or by trying to change it, the strategist takes a stand on the distribution issue. It cannot be avoided. The third objective is "trade," including the relationships desired with foreign economies. Foreign trade has been crucial to Latin American development until now; yet many Latin American leaders feel that it has not always worked to their advantage and that somehow old practices should be discarded or revised.

For any of these objectives to be achieved, appropriate instruments must be selected. Governments have at their disposal a wide range of powers that they use to influence economic behavior. They may collect taxes and spend money, regulate the creation and circulation of money, set exchange rates, regulate imports and exports, operate industries, provide services, and control prices, wages, interest rates, and other economic activities. We will focus on three sets of dimensions. First is the mix of public and private economic activities. We want to know how much of the economy is owned and operated by the state and how much is left to the private sector. Second is the mix of foreign and national participation in the economy. Latin Americans continue to disagree about the appropriate role of foreign capital in their development. They have, however, begun experimenting with innovative ways of handling foreign investors, many of which we will discuss in our examination of individual countries in Part 2. The third is the mix of coercion and spontaneity permitted by the government. Essentially we want to know the extent to which the government tries to coerce private conduct in order to achieve its objectives. Once the government decides how much of the economy it will leave to the private sector, it must still determine how free private entrepreneurs should be. Will it, for example, give entrepreneurs free rein within their domains, or will it set the wages they pay, the prices they charge, and the interest rates at which they borrow money? Whether to rely on the market mechanism to promote commerce and investment or to intervene in the marketplace is an unresolved issue that haunts capitalist economics.

Finally, there is the matter of who benefits economically and politically from each strategy. Most development policies greatly favor some players over others. It is important that we determine the effects of development policy not only in terms of its impact on the size of the gross national product or per capita income, but also in terms of its effects on the lives of all people. Players usually try to secure the adoption of policies favorable to them. Conversely, when policies threaten them, they often react, sometimes violently, against the officials responsible. Consequently, when we examine the beneficiaries of development policy we not only want to know what they have gained or lost, but also how they respond to policy politically and how their actions affect the government's ability to achieve its objectives.

Economic development strategies

Latin American leaders did not suddenly discover one day that economic development was desirable. Most of the region's economies have a long history of respectable, if uneven, change and development. What changed after 1930 was not the notion of economic development as a desirable objective, but attitudes about what economic development really meant and the ways to achieve it. Where a single, seldom-questioned strategy had held sway since colonial times, new ideas were introduced after 1930 to challenge the old ways of doing things.

An understanding of how development was managed before 1930 is necessary in order to comprehend why new strategies were needed and why they were so fiercely resisted by vested interests. A brief description of the traditional mode was given in Chapter 1. It was labeled the primary-product export strategy. Based on the belief that it was advantageous for Latin Americans to devote themselves to the production and export of agricultural commodities and minerals, it accepted an international division of labor in which Latin America supplied raw materials to Europe and North America in exchange for manufactured goods, and foreign investors financed the construction of power plants, port facilities, and railroads, and transported goods to and from the region.

The arrangement brought considerable wealth to those at the top, and economic growth accelerated after 1880 in most countries from their export of meat, grain, coffee, sugar, bananas and minerals like nitrates, copper, gold, and silver. Meanwhile, populations grew, local commerce increased, and confidence in the system was fortified, at least among the elites. But it was actually a more vulnerable and insecure system than it seemed at the time. Essentially, too many countries relied on too few commodities for their growth. Prices and demand from abroad rose and fell suddenly, dragging an entire economy up one year and down the next. Moreover, the ability of Latin Americans to meet demand was undercut now and then by droughts, pests, and other natural disasters. It is no wonder that some people questioned the viability of the system early on. And yet, too much was at stake to abandon it hastily. Powerful players within the region and abroad had invested a great deal in it, and they were not about to give up their investments under the pressure of occasional breakdowns in trade.

When a change did come, it came gradually, induced by the shock of the 1929 world depression and the interruption of trade during World War II. New ideas were plentiful, and eventually they gave birth to three new development strategies that would compete intensely for influence over policy during the next half century. Two were capitalist in nature and the third was socialist. Both of the capitalist strategies recognized that the golden years of the primary-product export strategy were over. The first of them, *progressive modernization,* stressed the need to promote industrialization and to redistribute property from landowners to campesinos in order to bring the poor into a productive modern economy. The second capitalist strategy, called *conservative modernization,* was authored by critics of the progressive approach who claimed that the redistribution of wealth and property was incompatible with the stimulation of industrialization in the capitalist economy; instead they advocated programs that favored investors, both national and foreign, intent on raising production. According to this view, wealth would eventually trickle down to the masses as production and employment rose. The third, or *revolutionary,* strategy rejected capitalist economics entirely, convinced that private investors could meet neither the production nor the welfare needs of Latin Americans. Instead of promoting entrepreneurial initiatives, the socialists assigned the state the primary responsibility for allocating the nation's resources and building an egalitarian society (Table 5.2).

Progressive modernization

Progressive modernization began in the 1940s as a critique of the primary-product export economy and the elitist political system associated with it. Its authors were frustrated by dependence on foreigners, widespread poverty, and economic instability. What began as little more than a desire for more security gradually matured into a new and innovative approach to the region's problems. It took its inspiration from many sources, including the Mexican Revolution, the U.S. New Deal, and Roman Catholic social philosophy, but none was

Table 5.2. *Economic strategies compared*

Strategy	Causes of underdevelopment	Objectives	Instruments	Beneficiaries
Progressive modernization	Concentration of rural land Insufficient industrialization Exclusion of masses from modern economy	Increased rural and industrial production Progressive income redistribution Integration of masses into modern economy Greater economic autonomy	Land reform Industrialization Nationalization of critical enterprises Balance between state power and liberty	State bureaucracy Urban middle sectors Industrialists Organized labor Peasants
Conservative modernization	Misguided nationalism Progressive income-redistribution Excessive regulation of private entrepreneurs	Increased rural and industrial production Closer ties to international economy	Assistance for commercial farmers Promotion of large industries Welcome of foreign investors and traders Imposition of firm political order	Foreign investors Industrialists Commercial farmers Exporters Urban middle sectors
Revolution	Capitalism Imperialism	Redistribution of political power Redistribution of property and income Increased production	Nationalization of private property Equalization of income Severance of trade with capitalist nations Mass ideology and organization	Revolutionary elite Urban labor Peasants

more important than the doctrine of *structuralism* popularized by the United Nations Economic Commission for Latin America and the Caribbean (ECLAC), an organization created in 1949 to promote the region's development.

The structuralists, as their name implies, were concerned with the economic and social structures that impeded the region's development. Foremost in their thinking was the obvious vulnerability of Latin American countries to erratic prices for exports and their victimization by the adverse terms of trade between their primary-product exports and the industrial goods they imported from abroad. The structuralists reasoned that Latin America had been unfairly treated in their trade relations with the industrial nations and would continue to suffer until their dependence on foreign trade was reduced. They were also disturbed by the maldistribution of income within Latin American societies and how poverty restricted domestic consumption. Surveying their economies in the 1940s and 1950s, they saw a rural sector polarized between a minority of large holdings and millions of excessively small ones, an emerging but weak industrial sector, and a working class that could not afford to consume the goods produced in national factories. The same economic structures that elites had accepted as natural, the structuralists saw as obstacles to long-range development and social justice. The only way to progress, they concluded, was to replace the old structures with more productive and equitable new ones.

Progressive modernization contains an important political dimension as well. Only the most naive could ignore the fact that any attempt to reform traditional institutions would be intensely resisted by the well-entrenched elite that had lived off them. Despite their technical sophistication, the proponents of progressive modernization were initially no match for the more powerful elite. What they needed, they realized, was a larger following and the toleration of the military if they were to win their struggle against the defenders of the status quo. Eventually they turned for support to the only place they could, namely laborers and campesinos. The cooperation of the former was essential to the expansion of industrial production and consumption, while the campesinos were needed to improve the rural economy. Moreover, both groups offered progressive modernizers a broad political base that might match the power of the ruling elite and its allies in the military.

In contrast to the traditional elite, which favored production over distribution objectives, those inspired by the structuralist critique of the Latin American condition believed that they could achieve both types of objectives simultaneously. Not only were the two thought to be compatible, but they were absolutely essential to each other. The structuralists were convinced that low rates of growth and excessive vulnerability were caused not just by a shortage of capital, but also by the maldistribution of property and income that had led to inefficient enterprises and insufficient consumption. Therefore, to increase production over the long haul, economic resources had to be redistributed to those who would employ them productively, and the size of the national market had to be expanded by making more citizens, both rural and urban, consumers in the modern economy.

At the heart of the progressive modernizers' program is rural reform since it maintains that the traditional system of landownership lies at the root of the region's underdevelopment. In the 1950s there still remained many large landholdings throughout the countryside, as well as millions of small farmers and landless peasants. Not only was production inadequate, but the rural social structure prevented the integration of the masses into the modern economy. It was imperative, therefore, that the government break up large estates, encourage more efficient land utilization, and bring the rural poor into the marketplace as producers and consumers. This could be done, it seemed clear, through a program of land reform that redistributed property from the large *latifundios* to peasant farmers and then transformed the latter into efficient producers through education, technical assistance, and the introduction of modern farm practices. Land redistribution without better production techniques would obviously come to naught, for even though it might satisfy the immediate demands of the land-hungry rural poor, it would neither increase production nor bring peasants into the modern economy. Finally, there was a need to diversify commodity production if the region were to escape its dependence on only a few farm products. As long as its fate was tied to one or two crops, stable economic growth would be unattainable.

Rural reform is necessary to economic development, but it is not by itself sufficient, according to the proponents of progressive modernization. Depression and war had taught a generation of Latin Americans that they could no longer rely primarily on the production of commodity exports for their livelihood. The lesson was clear: Instead of selling commodities in order to purchase consumer goods abroad, Latin Americans should manufacture their own goods. Some industrialization had begun spontaneously after the 1929 depression, but that was not enough, according to the progressive modernizers. Much more had to be done to build a strong, well-integrated industrial economy.

The third objective of progressive modernization was to reduce Latin America's dependence on the industrial nations. The region's disadvantageous relationship with its trading partners had originally provoked the structuralist critique of traditionalism. To overcome their excessive dependence they sought to strengthen their bargaining power and increase their margin of choice by diversifying their economies, using industrial development and agricultural modernization. They did not reject the idea of foreign trade but only sought to free themselves from excessive reliance on it.

It is one thing to identify the causes of underdevelopment and set some reformist policy objectives, but quite another to execute them in the face of well-entrenched traditions and vested interests that staunchly defend the status quo. Exceptional skill, determination, and good timing, along with ample technical expertise, are required to make progressive modernization work. The reorganization of rural life, the modernization of farming, and the introduction of new crops cannot be achieved without abandoning habits that have been nurtured for decades. Nor can heavy industries be built without careful planning, substantial managerial talent, and the expenditure of large sums of money. But despite the enormous task they set for themselves, the proponents of progressive modernization were convinced they could devise the instruments they needed to get the job done by adapting policies that had succeeded in Europe, Mexico, and elsewhere to their local situations.

The government needed substantial power to make progressive modernization work. No longer could public officials leave economic matters to the private sector alone. Structural change and technological innovation require firm leadership, and the state is the only institution powerful enough to assume that role. Government planners must design development programs and coordinate the activities of private industries through the use of incentives and regulations. To assist in the management of economic affairs, the government must also nationalize public utilities and strategic industries, like iron and steel.

And in those sectors where private enterprise is permitted, the state needs to promote investment using low-interest loans and joint public–private ventures.

In the rural sector, land should be purchased with cash payments or government bonds at market prices or declared tax value, depending on what governments can afford to pay. Land reforms must be accompanied by easy credit and substantial technology in order to increase production. Moreover, all government policies should be directed at the ultimate objectives of redistributing income to the rural and urban poor. Agrarian reform and expanded industrial employment will go a long way toward this end, but the government, through its housing, education, and health programs, must also do a great deal. A decent wage should be guaranteed all workers and, if necessary, food prices should be subsidized.

In the field of foreign economic relations two important policy innovations were encouraged. One was regional economic integration. It is obvious that national markets are too small in most countries to generate large-scale industries. Mass production is impossible as long as domestic markets include only 20 to 30 percent of the country's population and increase very gradually even with agrarian reform. Through the missionary efforts of the economists at ECLAC, who had closely studied the European Common Market in the 1950s, a way was found to combine national markets into large regional ones able to support major industries. Called *regional economic integration*, it required eliminating tariffs on goods produced within the region, and the coordination of foreign exchange policies by the members. By agreeing on a division of industries among the countries involved, each nation could take advantage of the markets that integration guaranteed them.

The second innovation was international commodity agreements to regulate the supply and price of raw product exports. The idea of commodity agreements among producer and consumer nations had circulated for a long time, but it was under the leadership of the proponents of progressive modernization that the idea became an integral part of a Latin American development strategy. Today, agreements apply to many commodities, the most successful being the Organization of Petroleum-Exporting Countries (OPEC) agreement on petroleum, which was originally established in the 1960s under the leadership of the Venezuelan minister of petroleum and mines. It set the price of oil charged by all of its members, and when world demand rose in the 1970s, they were able to raise prices substantially.

The most perplexing issue facing the advocates of progressive modernization is how to mix control with spontaneity in the execution of their programs. As proponents of structural change and economic reform, they know that they must assert their authority over those who would obstruct them. On the other hand, their preference for democratic politics and toleration of private enterprise make them reluctant to use heavy-handed tactics against anyone. A good example of their ambivalence is the implementation of agrarian reform. Clearly, in order to succeed land reform must confront and overcome the power exercised by the rural elite. The mere passage of legislation, assuming the government progresses that far, does not guarantee compliance with the new reforms. Landowners are skilled at forestalling government attempts to deprive them of their property. Consequently, agrarian reform can seldom be implemented without the use of some force by the state. And yet, extreme measures aimed at repressing reform's opponents risk undermining constitutional processes and provoking violent reactions leading to disorder. There is no easy escape from the coercion–spontaneity dilemma faced by progressive modernizers, for if they fail to use sufficient force, their programs may wither and die, but if they use too much, they may invite violent resistance. Failure to resolve the dilemma swiftly poses one of the biggest threats to the success of progressive modernization.

Who benefits from progressive modernization? In theory, the marginal rural producers and urban laborers stand to gain the most, for they will be freed from oppressive economic institutions. But in practice their benefits will come slowly; agrarian reform, industrialization, and regional integration cannot be achieved overnight, but require sustained effort for several years to spread their benefits widely. During the strategy's initial phase, the state and its many agencies stand to gain the most. Regulatory agencies will be increased, new state enterprises added, and planning operations expanded. Next in line come the industrialists who benefit from the state's promotion of industrialization. Labor unions, especially when they are supported by the ruling party, will also gain in power and wealth. So will the professionals in the middle sectors, who stand to profit from economic growth and the expansion of the state. Eventually peasants may be incorporated into the mainstream of the nation's economic life, though much more

slowly than any other group. Less noticed among the strategy's beneficiaries are the foreign corporations in Latin America who are tolerated under the progressive rules of the game. Though some will lose
to nationalization, many others, especially in high-technology fields,
stand to gain a great deal as the consumption of their products rises
with economic growth. Technically trained military officers are also
among the less obvious beneficiaries since they will create their own
industries in order to share in the bounties of industrialization or be
assigned managerial positions in government enterprises.

The last and most obvious question is: Why, if progressive modernization spreads its benefits so widely, has it not succeeded in transforming the entire region during the past three decades? We will
explore this question in Chapters 7 and 8 when we assess the strategy's
application in Chile and Venezuela. Yet, even before we look to the
real world for answers, some problems must be mentioned.

First, there is the question of whether the strategy can work in
countries where widespread agreement on the political rules is lacking.
Its proponents argue that the redistributive character of the strategy
makes it a perfect means for building new faith in government and
laying the foundations for authority founded on popular support. But
even if this is true in theory, achieving it in the face of well-entrenched
opposition is seldom as easy as it seems. Second, progressive modernization carries a very high price tag, which Latin American governments may not be able to pay on their own. The wealth confiscated
from the economic elite is seldom sufficient to cover the costs of the
government's development projects. The government must borrow
abroad, but that may only lead to a large foreign debt burden and the
kind of financial dependence the government had hoped to escape.
Last, there is the problem of fulfilling promises to workers and peasants
without threatening the well-being of middle-sector supporters. If the
government cannot satisfy all of them simultaneously, political conflicts may be provoked that will divide its coalition and undermine
its authority. In sum, there is nothing easy about progressive
modernization.

Conservative modernization

Progressive modernization was heavily criticized from its inception.
Naturally, the defenders of the old order denounced it, though seldom

to much effect since spontaneous industrialization had already undermined the old order. Eventually another type of critic emerged, one
who shared the progressives' desire for industrialization and rural
modernization but opposed their reformist methods. Instead of making
capitalism more productive, these critics argued, social and economic
reform had done the opposite by undermining entrepreneurial confidence and misallocating the nation's resources. Moreover, reform had
raised hopes that it could not satisfy, causing many people to lose
faith in it.

Starting from the premise that capitalist institutions offer the surest
route to economic growth (derived as much from faith as from science),
the advocates of conservative modernization believe that first and
foremost government should stimulate investment and economic modernization, favoring entrepreneurs with its policies. Demagogic politics, expensive social programs, and false expectations must give way
to strong and stable political rule dedicated first and foremost to
restoring the confidence of private investors.

The modernity of the strategy lies in its objectives. It has no interest
in retreating to the traditional single-commodity economies of the past,
but wants to pursue rapid industrial growth and to increase agricultural exports through the use of large, modern farms. It denies that
the redistribution of property and wealth from the rich to the poor is
necessary to promote economic development. On the contrary, if economic growth is to be achieved, resources must be concentrated in
the hands of entrepreneurs who will put them to good use in building
a modern economy. If there is to be any redistribution, it should be
done in the marketplace and not by the deliberate efforts of government bureaucrats. For the time being, social reform should be
postponed and income disparities tolerated. Accumulation, not redistribution, is its primary short-term objective because the deliberate
transfer of income to the poorer classes drains the economy of its vital
resources and hinders productive investment. The benefits of growth
will reach the poor, but only gradually, as new workers are absorbed
into the expanding industrial economy.

In its choice of policy instruments conservative modernization favors
a laissez-faire, market-oriented approach except in those sectors where
only the state is capable of promoting development. Where private
investment is inadequate or where government leadership is required,
such as in the development of energy supplies, utilities, and heavy

industry, public enterprises are appropriate. In essence, conservative modernization is a kind of conspiracy between state capitalists and private capitalists, each needing the other in order to achieve their objectives.

Foreign investment is not a pressing issue for conservative modernization. Foreigners are welcome as long as their efforts contribute to growth objectives. Foreign trade must be encouraged and expanded through the diversification of agricultural products and, where possible, the export of manufactured goods. In addition, the government should help finance the investments of modern farmers. Easier credit, guaranteed prices, better storage facilities, and easier marketing arrangements should be used to help farmers who are already prepared to produce on a large scale. From their exports the country will get the foreign exchange that it needs to finance its industrialization program without borrowing heavily abroad.

Conservative modernization strategies took different forms, each a response to the particular situation of the country where it was applied. It was also prone to fads recommended by foreign economists, the most controversial being attempts to open up Latin American economies by cutting tariffs and forcing local industry to compete with imported goods. Protection of industry had allowed production costs to rise, making the region's industrial products uncompetitive in international markets. Convinced that Latin America would have to export such goods in order to prosper, economists wanted to reduce protection and force local industries to compete with cheaper imports in the hope that it would force them to lower their own costs and produce more efficiently. Owners of the larger industries, many of them multinationals, welcomed the opportunity, but the smaller ones that had thrived on protection were seriously threatened by freer markets. They often fought back, creating deep divisions among industrialists who made the strategy's implementation difficult. Too many entrepreneurs had been raised on import substitution to suddenly give it up because some adventuresome economists offered theories that claimed that everyone would benefit in the long run.

Underlying all of conservative modernization's proposals is an important political requirement: To succeed, its unpopular measures need to be enforced by a strong government. Its policies will exact high social costs that may provoke discontent. Labor unions, peasant organizations, and mass-based political parties do not welcome the benefits of economic growth being monopolized by entrepreneurial and bureaucratic elites. The proponents of conservative modernization recognize this and are prepared to take harsh actions to deal with resistance. They see an important relationship between political and economic life but, unlike the progressive modernizers, who perceive politics as the means for reforming the economy, conservative modernizers believe politics, especially the competitive variety, is an obstacle to economic progress. It is the intervention of the state into the marketplace as a means of winning popular support from the disadvantaged that destroys the effectiveness of the market mechanism and undermines entrepreneurial confidence, they argue. Thus, politics, as practiced by many popular Latin American leaders, threatens capitalist economic development. To restore steady growth, competitive politics may have to be suspended, and recalcitrant labor unions and party politicians repressed with force.

The immediate beneficiary of conservative modernization is the investor, both foreign and national, in agriculture, commerce, or industry. Obviously the multinational corporation is the best prepared to take advantage of the strategy, though many national investors will gain as well. Less apparent among those it favors is the new generation of technocrats, and, in some places, the military officers, who design and execute development policy. They will be joined in the winner's circle by the professionals and white-collar workers who staff growing public and private enterprises. Left out in the short run are the campesinos, who will be confined to their small plots or continue to work as rural laborers on commercial farms, and urban laborers, who will be forced to accept low income in order to help finance capital investment.

Like all development strategies, conservative modernization raises many unanswered questions about its ability to achieve its objectives. Few would deny that capital must be accumulated in order to promote economic growth. Nor is there much doubt that a government can stimulate entrepreneurial investment by holding down wages and opening doors to multinational corporations. Less certain is how long it can deny well-organized urban laborers the gains they have come to expect in modernizing societies. Sooner or later the government will have to seek working-class acceptance if it is not to rely on permanent repression. And when it does, it may have to pay a high price for its past neglect of the masses in the form of wage increases and social expenditures that could undermine the confidence of conservative entrepreneurs. Another question is: How long can the government tolerate increased dependence on foreigners? Even though the immediate economic benefits of foreign investment may be great, the loss of national control over critical economic activities may prove costly, especially if it deprives national authorities of freedom to chart their own course. A third problem concerns the "trickle-down" effect. Critics of conservative modernization argue that it leads to enclave capitalism rather than widespread affluence. With profits being repatriated abroad and social programs in suspension, the benefits of economic growth trickle down to the masses at an appallingly slow rate, if at all, thereby doing little to alleviate widespread poverty. Finally, there is the question of legitimizing a government that chooses conservative modernization. Undoubtedly, the strategy will generate strong support from the 10 to 30 percent of the population that profits immediately from it. But what about those who are left out? How long can the government survive in the face of their opposition? Force, intimidation, and public apathy will facilitate the government's task, but they will not eliminate the need to expend much energy and valuable resources on protecting the government from its subjects.

Socialist revolution

What do the two strategies we have just examined have in common? According to their advocates, very little; they are two quite different ways of solving the development problem. There is, however, a third school of thought that says that they are not as far apart as they claim.

Despite their disagreements over objectives and instruments, both progressive and conservative modernization strive to create a society in which public authorities and private entrepreneurs jointly manage the economy. They are in essence merely two ways of organizing the capitalist economic system to meet the needs of Latin Americans. But what Latin Americans need, say the proponents of this third approach, is not capitalism but revolutionary socialism. Latin American underdevelopment, they claim, is not caused by a shortage of resources or by misguided policies, but by capitalism itself and the system of exploitation inherent in it. Neither progressive nor conservative modernization can overcome poverty and underdevelopment because they both try to extend the life of capitalism. Only through a revolutionary effort to seize public authority and reconstruct society can Latin America be saved from the dual evils of imperialism and capitalist exploitation. The revolutionary strategy is dedicated to that end.

What revolutionaries see when they examine their society is not the progress evinced by modern airports, high-rise office buildings, and cities congested with automobiles and buses, but the dehumanization and alienation of the Latin American masses. They are victims not only of traditional institutions like the *latifundio*, but of the modern factory as well. Modernization, if allowed to take the capitalist form, will do little to alleviate this condition. Private property, competition, and the pursuit of narrow self-interests – the motivating forces of capitalism – cannot eliminate poverty and exploitation. Only through the reconstruction of society around the principles of equality and community can underdevelopment and poverty be overcome. Revolutionaries offer their fellow citizens the vision of a world in which the squalid present is replaced by a more just future, one that appeals especially to those who are disillusioned with reform and appalled by the inequities of conservative modernization.

Socialist revolutionaries are more concerned with the distribution of wealth than with its creation. This does not mean that they ignore production, for only the most naive revolutionaries believe that prosperity automatically follows the destruction of capitalism. But, once produced, goods must be used to meet the needs of all citizens rather than only some of them. The entire nation should be fed, clothed, and educated in an egalitarian manner. Accordingly, all property has to be socialized and all wages equalized, ending class distinctions once and for all. Once placed in a state of equality, citizens will labor for the good of all rather than for personal gain, according to the revolutionary strategy.

The country's external economic relations also have to be changed drastically. Revolutionaries believe that, under capitalism, resources are siphoned from Latin America by the industrialized nations. The only way to change that is to break the ties that bind the developed and underdeveloped economies together. One should begin with the eviction of foreign corporations from the country and the severing of trade relations with those who have exploited the nation in the past. Only after this objective has been achieved can the socialist economy be launched. Naturally there are costs to be paid for the sudden loss of one's trading partners, and the costs are especially high if in the past the country relied heavily on foreign trade and the importation of capital from abroad. But revolutionaries have little choice but to pay them if they are to gain the power of self-determination that they so desperately want.

To create the socialist society, radical instruments are needed. The first is the transformation of the state from the regulator of private economic affairs to the owner of the means of production. Nearly all private property must be expropriated by the state and reallocated to cooperative or state-run production units. The rate of transfer will depend on how fast the state can assume its new responsibilities and overcome counterrevolutionary forces. Second, central planning must be instituted to manage the newly nationalized economy. The implementation of development plans is still a matter of dispute among revolutionaries. Some, especially those who emphasize distribution, favor decentralization and virtual autonomy for local production units; others, most often bureaucrats who place highest priority on the expansion of production, prefer firm central control over all economic processes. And third, during the initial phase of the revolution, a revolutionary elite must assume full control over the nation's economic and political reconstruction. Loyal to the masses they represent, they must make and enforce policies aimed at the fulfillment of revolutionary objectives. They should be guided by revolutionary ideology and their understanding of the needs of the masses rather than by their individual interests or the demands of separate players.

There is no mystery about the means socialist revolution uses to free the nation from imperialism. Foreign properties are expropriated and all trade relations reorganized according to principles set down by the new authorities. But to desire economic autonomy is one thing; to achieve it is something else. Few nations possess all the raw materials or produce all the consumer goods they require. Sooner or later they will either trade with other nations in order to meet their needs or do without some basic materials. If revolutionaries choose complete autonomy, they initially must accept a lower standard of living and severe constraints on national development; if they choose to retain ties with some other nations, they must either select trading partners who share their ideology or turn once again to the capitalist nations, though hopefully on more favorable terms than before. The same is true when it comes to financial assistance and foreign technology. As much as possible they will seek out nations that support their revolution, reasoning that if they must be dependent on anyone, it should at least be an ally in the revolutionary cause rather than someone who desires the restoration of capitalism.

It might at first appear that revolutionaries handle the question of mixing control and spontaneity with ease. Their goal is social reconstruction and they can leave nothing to chance, so whenever necessary they resort to controls without hesitation. Attitudes, institutions, and work habits must be changed, political loyalties transformed, and a new order quickly established. And counterrevolutionaries have to be deterred and made to respect the strength of the new regime. None of these objectives can be accomplished without the use of force. But what happens after the transition to socialism is achieved? Will real power be turned over to the people as promised? There is no simple formula. Revolutionaries live with a dilemma created by their need to use force to create a new society. Their solution often is not to choose between control and spontaneity, but to try to combine them in a special way. The key is the ideological reeducation of the masses. If they can be taught to follow the community ethic of socialism, control will eventually become unnecessary. Individuals will be motivated not by fear of the government but by their belief in a shared ideology. Spontaneity will be redefined to include all behavior consistent with the ideology. But reeducating the population, so compelling in theory, is not easily achieved in practice. Values and habits built up and reinforced during centuries of Iberian rule and decades under capitalism do not yield quickly to a new ethic that is centrally imposed. Resistance and counterrevolutionary acts may persist for some time, requiring the constant use of force by central authorities. The greatest danger is that in their determination to transform society, revolutionaries will lose sight of their ultimate objectives and never relinquish control for fear of losing power altogether.

Who benefits from socialist revolution? Ideally, the peasants and laborers who were exploited under capitalism have the most to gain. The elimination of the *latifundista,* commercial farmer, and factory owner should benefit the masses. So, too, should their admission to schools and hospitals that previously excluded them. But how rapidly will the condition of the poor be improved under socialism? The rate of redistribution depends primarily on how much of its resources the government allocates to capital accumulation and how much it reserves for social welfare. If it chooses to emphasize capital accumulation, as it did in some socialist nations such as the Soviet Union, the masses will have to wait until substantial economic development has been achieved before their condition can be improved significantly. On the other hand, an emphasis on social services may immediately advance their welfare, but at the expense of rapid economic growth. In either case, however, it is the new revolutionary elite that profits the most at the outset of the socialist revolution. Its members gain status, power, and personal comfort from their positions of leadership. Only gradually, as the economy develops and the supply of goods increases, will the masses gain access to important though very basic services.

The losers under socialist revolution are obvious. Landowners, industrialists, merchants, bankers, foreign investors – all members of the capitalist elite – are deprived of their property and power. Some will survive longer than others depending on how much the revolution temporarily requires their services, but eventually nearly all will go. There is no way their continued existence can be tolerated in a society dedicated to egalitarianism and central direction. Survival of a large private sector means the revolution has failed, so only by eliminating it can revolutionaries demonstrate that they have achieved their objectives. Among the other losers are many in the middle sector who refuse to live by the socialist ethic, the prerevolutionary military, and labor leaders who are replaced by others more loyal to the revolutionary elite.

Despite its obvious appeal to anyone frustrated by the failures of other strategies to cure Latin America's ills, revolutionary socialism is no easier to implement than other strategies. In fact, because it is more ambitious it faces enormous obstacles. First, the eviction of foreign and domestic investors exacts a high price in the loss of liquid capital and managerial talent. When the revolutionary regime deprives entrepreneurs of their property, it alienates many of the professionals and technicians who depend on entrepreneurs for their livelihood; although some join the new regime, many flee in search of better opportunities elsewhere, denying the new government their talents. Second, in executing radical social change, revolutionaries risk making very large mistakes. The sudden transformation of the rural sector, for example, may lead to a breakdown in agricultural production, and new industrial organizations may prove inefficient on a large scale. Revolutionaries must take chances if they are to achieve their objectives, but when they err they often do so on a grand scale and entire programs have to be abandoned, setting back the revolution by months or years.

It is also apparent that the creation of a revolutionary regime does not by itself guarantee that the new programs will be implemented. To succeed, the revolution must penetrate deeply into society and transform the attitudes and values of citizens. An elaborate and well-organized bureaucracy must impose its will on areas of life that were previously ignored by public authorities. In the larger Latin American states an immense effort would be needed to reach remote areas and bring their isolated populations under the central government's control. And finally, revolutionaries must continually grapple with the growth–equity dilemma. On the one hand, they wish to spread wealth throughout the society in order to achieve equality. On the other, they recognize that they have to concentrate their resources in order to build solid foundations for sustainable economic growth. The problem is especially troublesome for revolutionaries because, unlike conservative modernizers, they are committed, in theory at least, to equality. Seldom, however, can they afford to sacrifice their economic growth objectives to achieve it. To discover how they cope with all of these problems, we will examine Cuba and Nicaragua in Chapters 10 and 11.

Large populations and enormous debts

The economic strategies that we have examined are not new to the region. The revolutionary one has been around for over a half century and the modernization strategies for almost as long. They were designed to deal with problems that have long plagued Latin America: underdevelopment, poverty, and dependence. But they must also deal with current problems, two of which have plagued Latin Americans greatly in the 1980s and will no doubt continue to do so for some time.

Population growth rates accelerated after 1940, reaching a peak in the 1960s. Between 1960 and 1970 the annual average growth rate for the region was 2.8 percent, with highs of 3.8 percent in Mexico and 3.5 percent in El Salvador. During the following decade the rate fell to 2.6 percent, and it appears that it will continue to decline slowly in the future. Yet, because of the relatively large size of the younger populations, the effect of the decline in growth rates will not be felt until well into the next century. A population growing at a rate of 3.5 percent doubles in twenty years; one increasing by 2.5 percent annually will double in twenty-eight years. Assuming that the birthrate continues to decline slowly, it is estimated that the Latin American population (now at 370 million) will reach 600 million soon after the year 2000. Urban populations are growing even faster as people continue to migrate from the countryside and small towns to larger cities in search of work. Whereas 50 percent of the region's people lived in the urban areas in 1960, 66 percent do today. Mexico City alone, one of the fastest-growing cities in the world, will be inhabited by 30 million people by the end of this century.

Long ignored, population growth became a major public policy issue throughout the region during the 1970s. All governments began to address it in some fashion, though their dedication to its reduction varies a great deal. In some countries, like Mexico, clinics were opened and an estimated 40 percent of Mexican women under the age of 44 were taught to practice some sort of family planning. But resistance to population policy, or at least some of its methods, remains strong. One of the most entrenched sources of opposition is the leadership of the Roman Catholic Church. Their influence is much greater among the poor than among the more affluent, where education and economic self-interest, not the teachings of the Church, seem to guide behavior; as a result, birth rates are lower in middle- and upper-class families.

Another source of opposition comes from politicians who, though not necessarily against family planning per se, distrust the population planners sent to their countries by international and foreign agencies. Foreign advisers come, they insist, because of fear that a larger Third World population will consume the resources the industrial nations want for themselves. The redistribution of wealth and resources from the rich countries to the poorer ones, and not population control, is the answer, they claim. However, as it becomes more and more evident that no one gains from rapid growth, the nationalist argument has fewer takers than it did a decade ago.

But even if religious and political opposition to birth control were overcome, other obstacles would persist. The greatest impediment of all is poverty. In contrast to middle-sector couples, who can gain economically by limiting the size of their families, many of the poor believe they benefit from large families. Working children bring in desperately needed income and, once they are adults, they can care for their parents when the latters' working years have ended. Clearly, if family-planning programs are to have any effect in the less affluent Latin American countries, they must begin by changing the attitudes and institutions that have perpetuated poverty and the survival-through-numbers ethic.

In sum, though they would prefer to ignore it, economic strategists are being forced to face the frustrating population-growth problem. The achievement of their development objectives depends not only on their expertise and political skill, but also on whether they allow their achievements to be undermined by a failure to keep up with the demands placed on their economies by ever larger numbers of constituents.

Another problem stems from the huge foreign debts that Latin Americans are expected to pay. In the last chapter we learned of the region's unprecedented indebtedness to foreign banks. Before concluding this chapter we need to put it within the larger context of the region's development strategies.

In the 1970s many Latin American officials had hoped that a new era of rapid growth was under way, enough growth at least to permit them to borrow and repay the new loans being offered them by private foreign banks. But their hopes were misplaced, as they discovered when recession struck the world economy in 1981. By August 1982, when the Mexicans went to the International Monetary Fund meetings in Toronto to report that they could no longer pay their debt, the borrowing binge was over and a new era of debt crises began all over Latin America.

Existing economic strategies suddenly seemed irrelevant to the resolution of an unanticipated crisis. Moreover, disagreements over how to overcome it plagued relations among debtors and creditors from the start. It had to be handled jointly, but how to do so to everyone's satisfaction was never obvious. Old rules did not hold much appeal to debtors, who insisted that creditors acknowledge their unusual plight and reduce their debts in order for them to recover economically. But bankers and their home governments resisted, preferring conventional methods which relied on their dealing with each country on an incremental, case-by-case basis in an effort to secure as much debt repayment as possible.

They disagreed from the outset over whether the crisis was one of *illiquidity* (a temporary shortage of dollars) or *insolvency* (an inability to ever pay). If the former, then additional loans by creditors and some austerity in the debtor nation could get it through its crisis. According to this view, the debt crisis was temporary and could be handled through immediate policy changes within the debtor nations. In contrast, if insolvency were the problem, much of the debt would never be paid, and the sooner everyone recognized this, the more effective they could be in getting on with the region's development. Naturally, debtors pleaded that they were suffering from insolvency while creditors and most economists in the industrial nations preferred the illiquidity explanation.

It was left to Latin Americans to worry about the social and political consequences of necessary austerity policies that lowered public consumption and reduced government paternalism. The Mexicans had not experienced such economic distress as a nation since the 1930s, and though their political system is an unusually sturdy one, there was reason to wonder just how tolerant an urban population accustomed to three decades of economic growth would be. Argentina and Brazil were especially shaken by events that forced newly created democratic authorities to postpone the rewards they had promised their constituents in order to pay their debts. Previously, both had relied on authoritarian governments run by the military to execute such regressive measures, but now it was up to democrats to demand unprecedented sacrifices by their populations. That they were willing to do so was due in part to the belief, fostered by creditors, that economic recovery in the industrial nations was imminent, and that by 1985 or 1986 economic growth would be restored to Latin America. More trade and better prices would follow, generating higher national incomes and a larger surplus to invest.

It was not the first time that indebted nations, creditors, and international agencies like the International Monetary Fund had dealt with debt problems, but the enormity of the task they faced after 1982 was unprecedented. Textbooks offered little advice on how huge debts and economic recovery could be managed simultaneously in several countries. Initially Latin Americans had little choice but to renegotiate individually, accepting terms granted them by creditor cartels and the IMF, which put most of the packages together. Default was not a real option at the time since it carried very high costs, among them the denial of short-term credits necessary for foreign trade. Most imports are paid for immediately, so the loss of short-term credit could prove

Table 5.3. *Decline in per capita GDP, 1981–6*

	Percentage change in per capita GDP (1981–6)	Growth in export volume since 1980	Growth in export revenue since 1980
Argentina	−15.5	30%	−13%
Brazil	4.0	50%	22%
Chile	−6.2	38%	−12%
Ecuador	−3.3	49%	−19%
Mexico	−10.4	57%	−12%
Peru	−10.1	95%	−36%
Venezuela	−21.9	93%	−53%

Source: Data provided by Alfred Watkins, Democratic Staff Member of the Joint Economic Committee, Congress of the United States.

disastrous. Talk about "going it alone" was cheap, but unless export receipts were generating a positive balance, defaulting would deprive factories of the materials they imported and their employees of jobs. That is why formal defaults by the larger nations seemed out of the question, regardless of how nationalistic they were.

By 1986, presidents who had asked their people to trust them as they engineered painful recoveries suddenly found themselves with almost nothing to show for their efforts. They had cut imports and public spending and raised exports, but more exports did not assure more income. Between 1980 and 1986 Argentina increased its export volume by 30 percent, Mexico by 57 percent, and Venezuela by 93 percent, but their export revenues fell by 13, 12, and 53 percent, respectively (see Tables 5.3 and 5.4); the major exception was Brazil, whose export volume grew by 50 percent and revenues by 22 percent. Their terms of trade had worked against them, the prices of their exports having fallen and their imports risen, and there was no indication that they would improve any time soon.

They could not help but conclude that the deck was stacked against them. Whether it actually was or not mattered less than the perception of victimization. They had watched as commodity prices fell to their lowest level in decades in 1986. Reducing their imports had always improved trade balances previously, but the results were far less this time. They simply could not earn enough from trade both to pay their debts and finance their own development. Moreover, they continued

Table 5.4. *Debts and export incomes, 1981–6*

	Cumulative growth of external debt (1981–6)	Cumulative growth of export revenues (1982–6)	Ratio of interest payments to exports (1986)
Argentina	41.3%	−7.9%	51.8
Brazil	27.3%	21.9%	37.7
Chile	32.9%	10.8%	39.2
Ecuador	29.3%	−13.0%	32.2
Mexico	33.5%	−35.9%	40.0
Peru	49.0%	−27.3%	27.3
Venezuela	7.2%	−46.0%	

Source: Data provided by Alfred Watkins, Democratic Staff Member of the Joint Economic Committee, Congress of the United States.

to face barriers to trade with Europe and North America at a time when creditors on both continents were insisting that they export far more in order to pay a reasonable interest on their debts. Add to this the fact that real interest rates, though somewhat lower than previously, remained high for the debtor.

Capital flight added to their woes. Difficult to measure, it is obvious that substantial amounts of dollars fled indebted economies at a time when capital was desperately needed. According to one estimate, between 1983 and 1985 $6.6 billion left Brazil (33 percent of what it borrowed during that period), $16.2 billion left Mexico (180 percent), and $5.5 billion Venezuela (100 percent). A great deal of this represents money invested abroad by people who have little or no faith in the management of their own economies, but much of it consists of billions of dollars rushed away by corrupt officials and wealthy individuals who want to guarantee their economic futures.

Latin Americans felt trapped. Indebtedness required austerity measures intended to improve their capacity for long-term growth. But austerity, accompanied by very slow recovery in the world economy, prevented growth. In other words, cutting inflation, increasing exports, and reducing imports were supposed to restore price stability and renew investor confidence, but instead they perpetuated recession and dampened the enthusiasm of investors. After making debt payments, little remained to pay for the imports needed to achieve recovery. In short, they could not pay debts and grow simultaneously.

The debt burdens accumulated by Latin American countries made progressive economic strategies inoperative in the 1980s, because no government could afford them anymore. Even revolutionary Cuba, after borrowing from European private banks and finding itself unable to pay, chose to impose austerity at home in order to get through the crisis. Latin Americans, who did not need reminding, learned once more how vulnerable their economies were to forces beyond their boundaries; even more troubling, they also discovered that regardless of their economic ideology, there was no easy way out.

However one looks at it, the 1980s were a dismal decade economically. The region's real gross domestic product (GDP) grew by an average of 1.5 percent a year between 1980 and 1987, but the population grew faster, leaving the real GDP per head in 1987 nearly 5.5 percent below what it was seven years before. The sharpest declines in per capita GDP came in the poorest countries (e.g., Bolivia where it fell by an average of 4.5 percent annually; Guatemala and Venezuela, by 3.0 percent; and Nicaragua, by 2.8 percent annually). But even more-affluent Argentina saw its fall by an annual average of 2.3 percent, while Mexico's dropped by 1.5 percent annually. Even if trade incomes improve in the 1990s, and some of their debts are repaid or canceled, it will be some time before the region's per capita product will accumulate enough to make up for a decade of losses.

But more on this later. Now we are ready to return to the political games currently played in Latin America. In Part 2 we will start with Mexico, a nation which, though familiar to North Americans, is actually one of the least well understood. Perhaps that is how Mexicans prefer it, but with the nation's politics becoming unusually competitive and raucous in the past few years, and its economy more troubled, it is imperative that we make a greater effort to comprehend it.

Further reading

Anderson, Charles W. *Politics and Economic Change in Latin America: The Governing of Restless Nations.* New York: Van Nostrand, 1967.
Anglade, Christian, and Carlos Fortin, eds. *The State and Capital Accumulation in Latin America.* Pittsburgh: University of Pittsburgh Press, 1985.
Chilcote, Ronald H., and Joel C. Edelstein. *Latin America: Capitalist and Socialist Perspectives.* Boulder, CO: Westview Press, 1985.
Chilcote, Ronald H. *Theories of Development and Underdevelopment.* Boulder, CO: Westview Press, 1985.
Dietz, James L., and James H. Street. *Latin America's Economic Develop-

ment: Institutionalist and Structuralist Perspectives. Boulder, CO: Lynne Rienner Publishers, 1987.

Economic Commission for Latin America and the Caribbean (ECLAC). *External Debt in Latin America: Adjustment Policies and Renegotiation.* Boulder, CO: Lynne Reinner Publishers, 1985.

Frank, Andre Gunder. *Latin America: Underdevelopment or Revolution.* New York: Monthly Review Press, 1969.

Glade, William P. *The Latin American Economies.* New York: Van Nostrand Reinhold, 1969.

Hartlyn, Jonathan, and Samuel A. Morley, eds. *Latin American Political Economy: Financial Crisis and Political Change.* Boulder, CO: Westview Press, 1985.

Hirschman, Albert O. *Essays in Trespassing: Economics to Politics and Beyond.* New York: Cambridge University Press, 1981.

Kim, Kuan S., and David F. Ruccio, eds. *Debt and Development in Latin America.* South Bend, IN: Notre Dame University Press, 1985.

Loup, Jaques. *Can the Third World Survive?* Baltimore: The Johns Hopkins University Press, 1983.

Murdoch, William. *The Poverty of Nations: The Political Economy of Hunger and Population.* Baltimore: The Johns Hopkins University Press, 1980.

Muñoz, Heraldo. *From Dependency to Development: Financial Crisis and Political Change.* Boulder, CO: Westview Press, 1983.

Roxborough, Ian. *Theories of Underdevelopment.* Atlantic Highlands, NJ: Humanities Press, 1979.

Sheahan, John. *Patterns of Development in Latin America: Poverty, Repression, and Economic Strategy.* Princeton, NJ: Princeton University Press, 1987.

Stallings, Barbara, and Robert Kaufman, eds. *Debt and Democracy in Latin America.* Boulder, CO: Westview Press, 1988.

Watkins, Alfred J. *Till Debt Do Us Part: Who Wins, Who Loses, and Who Pays for the International Debt Crisis.* Washington, DC: Roosevelt Center for American Policy Studies, 1986.

Wesson, Robert. *Coping with the Latin American Debt.* New York: Praeger, 1988.

Part II

The political games played in Latin America

6. Mexico: Whose game is it?

The Mexicans rebelled eighty years ago, bringing down a dictatorship that had lasted for more than a quarter century. But what resulted from their rebellion remains in dispute to this day. Boasting of their dedication to social justice and strident nationalism, the victors revised Mexican politics in fundamental ways, yet Mexicans disagree about how much they really accomplished.

Differences of opinion about what Mexicans have achieved are not surprising. Debate and disappointment always follow promises of radical reform. But in assessing contrasting interpretations of the Mexican experience we need to keep the standards we are using in mind. Comparisons of contemporary Mexico with the nation run by a wealthy oligarchy before 1917 yield one kind of conclusion, whereas contrasting it with a socialist revolution like Cuba's will spawn dissimilar ones. Mexico has come a long way from the darkest days of its subjugation a century ago, but it has not progressed as far as was promised. Never socialist in its objectives nor Leninist in its methods, the Mexican revolution adapted the country's deeply entrenched traditions to twentieth-century needs without changing some attitudes and ways of doing politics. Only by carefully reviewing this debate and the political practices that it describes can we begin to discover the rules of Mexican politics and their beneficiaries. And to do that we must begin with what the Mexicans call *La Revolución*.

The revolt: 1910–17

The revolt began in 1910 as a campaign to block the "reelection" of Porfirio Díaz, the dictator who had ruled the nation since 1877, and it ended seven years later with the drafting of a new constitution by the victors who had deposed him. It was a chaotic time, in which makeshift armies were led by men as dissimilar as Emiliano Zapata, a peasant leader; Francisco "Pancho" Villa, an enterprising outlaw; Venustiano Carranza, a landowner politician; Alvaro Obregón, a small

139

farmer; and Francisco Madero, a cultured gentleman from an upper-class family in the far north. It was incredibly costly in lives, not just among the masses who fought it but even among its leaders after the fighting ended: by 1928, Madero, Zapata, Villa, Carranza, and Obregón had all met violent deaths.

Prominent among the underlying causes of the revolt was the accumulation of opposition to the Porfiriato, as the regime of Porfirio Díaz was known, from the middle sectors, especially in the north, as well as from labor leaders and many long-repressed campesinos. Díaz, who inherited the liberal regime founded by reformer Benito Juárez in 1857, dedicated himself to the economic development of Mexico by opening the nation's resources for exploitation by foreign and domestic capitalists. He wielded a heavy hand against anyone who resisted his reign, especially the campesinos who opposed the confiscation of their village lands by ambitious plantation owners and commercial farmers and the laborers who protested harsh conditions and depressed wages in mines and factories. An informal hierarchy with Díaz at the top, the system relied heavily for enforcement on local political elites and a police force, known as the *rurales*, that defended them. The Mexican economy prospered as never before after 1880, but its product was monopolized by a small minority of wealthy Mexicans and foreign corporations. This could not help but frustrate those in the middle sectors, peasantry, and working class who were denied larger shares of the expanding economic pie.

When Díaz announced in 1908 that he would not seek reelection and then backed away from his pledge, he provoked a violent reaction from his frustrated opponents. Inspired by the radical writings and agitation of intellectuals like Ricardo Flores Magón, many of them turned to the more moderate Francisco Madero for leadership. Madero, the son of a wealthy northern Mexican family, was dedicated to the restoration of constitutional government rather than to radical economic or social change. As the candidate of the Anti-Reelectionist party, he campaigned vigorously against Díaz before the 1910 election, only to be arrested and jailed for his efforts. After his release Madero reluctantly took to arms, joining an uprising already in progress in several parts of the country. One year and several minor battles later, Madero's forces captured the border city of Juarez, embarrassed Díaz's army, and forced the seventy-eight-year-old patriarch to abandon the presidency and flee into exile in Europe, where he spent the last four

Table 6.1. *Mexico: historical background*

1821	Independence from Spain
1848	Texas ceded to United States in Treaty of Guadalupe Hidalgo
1857	La Reforma revolt led by Benito Juárez creates new constitution
1872	President Benito Juárez dies in office
1877	General Porfirio Díaz becomes president and creates a dictatorship that lasts for thirty-four years
1911	Porfirio Díaz forced to resign by revolt led by northern democrat Francisco Madero, who becomes president
1913	President Madero overthrown and killed by troops of General Victoriano Huerta; civil war follows
1914	General Huerta resigns and flees
1916	Truce declared and constitutional convention called
1917	New constitution; Venustiano Carranza becomes president
1920	Carranza forced to flee and killed by rival revolutionary generals; General Alvaro Obregón, ex-ally of Carranza, made president
1924	Plutarco Elias Calles elected president
1928	General Alvaro Obregón assassinated while campaigning for election to presidency; Revolutionary Party (PNR) created by Calles
1934	Lazaro Cárdenas elected president; agrarian reform accelerated and foreign petroleum companies nationalized; Revolutionary Party reorganized along corporatist lines with peasant, labor, and popular sectors; renamed the Party of the Mexican Revolution
1940	Manuel Avila Camacho elected president
1946	Miguel Alemán Valdés elected president
1952	Adolfo Ruiz Cortines elected president
1958	Adolfo Lopez Mateos elected president
1964	Gustavo Díaz Ordaz elected president
1970	Luis Echeverria elected president
1976	José López Portillo elected president
1982	Miguel de la Madrid elected president Economy hit by debt crisis; austerity imposed
1988	Carlos Salinas elected president with a bare majority; first time a PRI candidate was threatened by the opposition

years of his life. What followed, however, was not the kind of simple transition that added a few new players to the game, but a decade of turmoil and civil war that changed many aspects of Mexican life.

The first phase (1911–1913; see Table 6.1) was dominated by the figure of Francisco Madero, elected president after Díaz's departure. Madero's goal was not the economic transformation of Mexico, but the creation of political democracy whose procedures individual Mexicans could use to improve their condition. He was a constitutional democrat concerned more with political means than socioeconomic ends. Instead of eliminating the traditional elite and Díaz's army and bureaucracy, he invited them to accept a place in the new constitutional order. And rather than responding immediately to the demands of Emiliano Zapata and other peasant leaders for the return of the village land sugar planters had taken from them, he asked them to wait until their claims were duly processed and evaluated by the new authorities. Nevertheless, it was not Zapata or Madero's other disappointed supporters who did him in: Instead, it was Victoriano Huerta, an army general backed by antidemocrats in the elite and by archconservative American ambassador Henry Lane Wilson (who sought the restoration of a government more sympathetic to foreign investors), who deposed and killed Madero on February 22, 1913.

Huerta's coup, which represented a last-ditch attempt by the followers of Porfirio Díaz to regain political control, touched off the second and most violent phase of the Mexican Revolution (1913–1916). Those who had seen their reformist aspirations frustrated by the proceduralism of Madero and ignored altogether by Huerta's vengeful autocracy turned to the battlefield to accomplish what they could not secure through the political process. Northerners Carranza and Obregón wanted to create a constitutuional democracy and promote Mexican nationalism; peasant leaders like Zapata wanted their land returned; labor leaders wanted their rights protected by the state; and an assortment of urban intellecturals aspired to lead Mexico down a path of liberty and social reform. Between 1913 and 1916 they waged war, first against Huerta, who was forced to resign in 1914, and then against one another. In late 1914 Villa and Zapata took control of Mexico City; in 1915 both were evicted by Obregón and Carranza. For nearly three years Mexico was engulfed by one of the most violent struggles in Latin American history. It was, in the words of revolutionary novelist Mariano Azuela, "like a hurricane, and the man who enters it is no longer a man, but merely a miserable dry leaf beaten by the wind."

Exhaustion and the military superiority of the forces led by Carranza and Obregón finally brought peace in 1916. Soon thereafter the generals met in Queretaro to settle their differences and write a new constitution. Conspicuously missing were the *latifundistas,* clergy, bureaucrats, and army officers who had been the mainstay of the old Díaz regime; it was the opposition middle sectors from northern Mexico, intellectuals, and labor and peasant leaders who convened. Though most of the document was inspired by the same kind of liberalism that had influenced the 1857 constitution written under the leadership of Benito Juárez, the proponents of reform did secure the inclusion of significant new powers that would later enable the implementation of social and economic reforms. Article 3 limited the power of the Church by prohibiting religious instruction in Mexican schools. In Article 27, the traditional right of the Spanish Crown to all land and water within its domain was given to the Mexican state, as was the right to expropriate land and pay for it at declared tax value using twenty-year bonds with a 5-percent rate of interest. And laborers were guaranteed an eight-hour day and given the right to strike in Article 123.

These statutes finally opened the door to social and economic reform in Mexico. Or so many hoped in 1917. Still to be settled were equally important issues of how the new Mexican political game would be organized, who would dominate it, and how dedicated revolutionary leaders would be to fulfilling the promises contained in the 1917 constitution.

On paper the masses had won the revolution, but in actual fact they had become the subjects and not the owners of the new government. Provincial elites from the northwest and petit bourgeois warriors from the various states who had sided with Carranza and Obregón in their wars against the oligarchs and in their elimination of Villa and Zapata were the persons in charge. Campesinos and laborers were not neglected, but they were forced to negotiate their new status on terms set by the victorious generals who promised to look out for them as long as they played by the rules that the generals wrote for their new revolutionary regime. Mexicans had liberated themselves from the few thousand oligarchs and the U.S. investors who had ruled over them for a half century, and their society would never again be as closed as it was before 1910; that alone was revolutionary. But by itself it never guaranteed that everyone would achieve the things that prompted them to make war in the first place.

The consolidation of power

Popular insurrections produce political vacuums that must be filled quickly. But the creation of new institutions is often hindered by disagreements among rebels about the exact form the new regime should take. In Mexico conflicts among members of the insurrectionary coalition developed immediately after the fighting stopped and lasted for over a decade. What later came to appear as one of the most cohesive, well-organized regimes in the region started slowly and suffered many strains before achieving the qualities for which it is known today.

The generals who emerged victorious in 1916 were handicapped by two weaknesses when they began. First, they had no coherent plan or ideology to direct their reconstruction of the Mexican state. Second, they were a disparate group with diverse interests, who had fought almost as much with one another as they had with the Díaz regime. In 1916 Mexico was emerging from the chaos of a long and destructive war. New aspirations had been codified in the 1917 Constitution, but the truce was an uneasy one. The constitution allocated formal authority to the president and the legislature, but political power remained in the hands of the many armed leaders whose forces had shared in the victory. Only by establishing some control over such groups could anyone hope to govern the war-ravaged country.

It is helpful to view the consolidation of power in postrevolutionary Mexico as involving a series of choices among only a few real options. First came the matter of whom to include in the new game. Clearly the old order would never be the same again. The revolution had destroyed the army, broken the grip of the regional bosses who had enforced the will of the Díaz regime, drastically reduced what was left of the power of the Church, and weakened the strength of the landed elite. There was no question of restoring any of them to power. Rather, it was a matter of deciding which of the victors would rule. The most obvious choice was the revolutionary generals, men like Carranza and Obregón, each the leader of an army that had fought in the revolt. All of them expected rewards, either in the form of sinecures in the new government or some of the property and other spoils of war. But they were not alone. Also demanding entry into the new regime were the campesino leaders who, like Zapata, demanded some assurance that their village lands would be returned to them by the new government. Some had seized hacienda lands during the war but needed legal recognition of their titles, and state protection against their recovery by the rural elite. Labor leaders also wanted a place at the top, fearing that without their participation the rights given them by the new constitution would go unenforced. Last but certainly not least were the middle-sector professionals and intellectuals who saw the new government as their means to rapid advancement.

The challenge was to create a government strong enough to rebuild a nation torn apart by a decade of internal war, one that could rise above the narrow interests of any single group or sector yet retain the support of each for its reconstruction program. A handful of revolutionary generals understood this when they seized the initiative after the constitutional convention and gradually built a regime that looked revolutionary only to those in the Porfiriato who were excluded from it. Though they adopted the trappings of liberal democracy, with a president, bicameral legislature, and independent judiciary, what they actually created was a highly centralized and hierarchical political machine whose leaders exercised immense control over the nation.

The study of postinsurrection politics lays to rest the fiction that the revolutionary regime emerged quickly and painlessly. Consolidation came only after intense and often bloody struggles led by Alvaro Obregón, president from 1920 to 1924, and Plutarco Calles, president from 1924 to 1928. They jailed, bought off, or shot their rivals. Zapata was ambushed in 1919, President Carranza was shot while fleeing in 1920, and Villa was assassinated in 1923. Obregón and Carranza had never shared the objectives of their poorer, rural collaborators. While they expressed sympathy for the yearnings of campesinos and urban workers, were nationalistic and anticlerical, and knew that mass participation was essential to the construction of a secure political regime, they were committed to capitalist economics and private property. They had no intention of turning over the rural economy entirely to the Zapatistas and the Villistas, or the nation's businesses to the laborers who worked them. Instead, they wanted to build a country run by a new elite recruited from among their colleagues in the middle and lower middle classes that would supervise the solution of campesino grievances without sacrificing real political power to them.

Piece by piece, Obregón and Calles assembled a coalition composed of the regional revolutionary generals, obliging peasant leaders and labor bosses, and a new class of bureaucrats by offering privileges to each without allowing any one of them to reign. Radical peasant leaders were replaced by moderate ones willing to play by the government's rules, and the labor movement was reorganized to make it more dependent on the state for its entitlements. Mexican nationalism was spread throughout the nation with propaganda, rudimentary education, and art and music, and the Roman Catholic Church was stripped of its remaining property, and its defenders were crushed violently when they resisted the authority of the new state. Thus, after a decade of intense infighting Mexico's new leaders had laid the foundation of the regime that has governed the country ever since.

The Mexican state

Mexican ideology, though nebulous and contradictory to the casual observer, was important because of what it did to legitimize the new regime for the masses. According to the official rhetoric – which has changed little since 1917 – the Mexican government is the servant of a nation that liberated itself from its foreign and domestic oppressors by means of a heroic struggle, and it is dedicated to securing social justice, economic development, and national independence for all Mexicans. The ideology is taught in schools, expressed in popular art, repeated in political campaigns, and recalled in nearly every presidential speech. Many Mexicans consider it a sham, little more than words cynically manipulated by rather conservative authorities to retain their power over the masses, but that has not ended the government's ritualistic reliance on it.

For a long time presidents adroitly exploited popular affection for the nation and its new beginning in 1917, making them the envy of politicians throughout the hemisphere who never had such a powerful resource for securing public acceptance of their politics. Mexican presidents claim inheritance of the right to lead the nation not just because they win elections but also because they are links in a chain that ties them to Carranza, Obregón, Zapata, and Villa. It is as if Democrats in the United States could deny Republicans the presidency by making themselves the only legitimate heirs of Thomas Jefferson, John Adams, and the other founders. Though the duplicity of such tactics may seem obvious, the Mexicans have capitalized on it to great advantage for many years.

Ideas, though important, do not run governments; people and organizations do. When they began, the Mexican rebels needed a means for enforcing the new rules in every region of their rebellious country. Rejecting old fashioned dictatorship, they chose the more modern device of the political party to control national, state, and local governments. The party's creation was made possible by the triumph of Plutarco Calles over his rivals soon after Alvaro Obregón's death in 1928. One year later he launched the National Revolutionary Party, an organization built from a coalition of regional revolutionary generals and their local constituencies. Thereafter, the party adapted to the needs of governing Mexico, the most important reorganization coming a decade later under the direction of president Lazaro Cárdenas. Rather than working primarily through local party officials as Calles had done, Cárdenas wanted direct contact between the president and the leaders of mass organizations. Accordingly, in 1938 he created a corporatist-like party organization composed of three sections: the Mexican Confederation of Labor; the National Peasant Association; and a third, called the "popular" sector, which included teachers, public employees, small farmers, and the military. Now labeled the Institutional Revolutionary Party (PRI), its organization is much the same as it was under Cárdenas, though the military was later removed.

Cárdenas was more than just another tactician. What made his reorganization so effective was his accompanying it with economic and social reforms that sought to renew public trust in the system. He expropriated and redistributed more land than all of his predecessors combined, nationalized U.S.-owned oil companies, and supported the efforts of organized labor to increase its power. Cárdenas realized that some renewal was essential to the survival of the new regime and that only bold populist measures could achieve it. He never trusted the party to accomplish what the government had promised its people, without substantial new effort by the president. By creating a more popular political regime he also facilitated stable economic development in the years that followed. No other Latin American country would achieve industrialization with less rancor and class conflict than did Mexico, governed as it was by an enormous political party that kept organized labor and the rural poor under its close supervision, all the time insisting that it was in their best interests to comply with its dictates.

Equally important was the way Cárdenas handled the armed forces. When he brought the remnants of the revolutionary armed forces into the party, he confirmed their subordination to the political authorities who had created them. It was not a semisovereign military at the time, and Cárdenas made sure that they would not become one afterwards. The Mexicans' subordination of their armed forces is the envy of civilian leaders throughout the region. Emulating Mexico is no easy task, however, since it required the destruction and reconstruction of the armed forces before its subordination to political authority. In other words, control over it came only after he did something that most civilian politicians in other nations are unable to do, either because they have come to rely on the military for their own protection or have too little power to challenge and subdue it successfully.

By World War II the Mexicans had overcome the perpetual conflicts over political rules that still plagued many Latin American nations. A nation that, in the nineteenth century, had experimented with liberal democracy only to see it descend into the dictatorship of Porfirio Díaz, now did it differently, this time using a political party that reached deeply enough into society to bring the masses under its supervision by rewarding some among them with property and greater personal income for joining in the effort. Mexicans paid a price for the new regime, however. A process of political centralization that had begun under the Porfiriato was completed by the PRI, giving the president and his bureaucrats in Mexico City immense control over the nation, making a mockery of constitutional claims of having created a federal republic. Little was done by officials anywhere in Mexico without prior sanction from Mexico City. Elections also took on a special meaning under this system. Winning and losing was not the issue since the same party nearly always won. Instead, they served as a necessary ritual in which the public declared its loyalty to the government and to candidates whom they had not selected while, in return, the president pledged his fidelity to the nation and the values espoused by his predecessors. High prices to pay, perhaps, but a people long plagued by civil strife and by presidents who made pledges to no one understood why they were paying them.

The rules of the Mexican game

The Mexican political game defies simple description. Constitutionally, it retains the trappings of liberal democracy, with a president, legislature, judiciary, and regular elections held every six years. It even guarantees opposition parties seats in Congress. In practice, however, the system is run by PRI leaders and the president, who together control the masses much more than they are controlled by them.

The dependence of the rank and file on the party elite for so long derived largely from the government's immense patronage powers. Rule by the PRI is somewhat analogous to that of the political machines that once governed some of the larger North American cities. It controls access to thousands of public jobs, which it distributes annually to grateful supporters. And, regardless of profession or business, every person is affected by decisions of the economically powerful Mexican government. Favorable treatment is not claimed by right but is secured in exchange for political support, personal favors, and bribes. Moreover, all villages and towns are dependent on central authorities for their public works; should they not support the PRI in elections, they deny themselves access to the resources on which they must rely to meet their minimal needs.

Equally important to the PRI's power is its ability to co-opt opponents before they are strong enough to do the party any harm. Instead of insulating themselves from opponents, pretending that they do not exist, as is the practice among less-secure ruling elites, PRI leaders have until recently absorbed them into the party, offering them government posts and policies aimed at satisfying the people they claim to represent. In this way they persuaded many critics to abandon their cause for an opportunity to pursue their interests from within the government. The critic's choice was seldom easy: To stay outside a government as seemingly invulnerable as the Mexican one usually meant a futile struggle; but joining it allowed one to get some if not all of what was desired.

If the PRI is one key to political control in Mexico, the presidency is the other. Disputes are common at every level of government in Mexico, as elsewhere, and an effective mechanism is required for their ultimate resolution. Few Latin American nations have managed to establish a reliable means for conflict resolution. The Mexicans, in contrast, did so long ago. Ultimate authority resides in the Mexican presidency. For six years one person uses it to supervise the nation, but once his term is completed, he relinquishes all authority to his successor. Thus, by holding to a fixed term the Mexicans have prevented control by any person for more than a single term. And the longer the rotation of the office worked, the more people accepted it as a part of the natural order of things.

The Mexican president is given substantial formal authority by the constitution, but he gets his real power from the PRI's control over society and the nation's tradition of relying heavily on presidential tutelage. He is not an autocrat with unlimited power to do as he pleases. Although it is important that he appear omnipotent, everyone knows that he is their leader, not their oppressor. The informal rules of the Mexican game require that he use his authority constantly, initiating most domestic and foreign policies and arbitrating disputes among governors, cabinet members, labor and management, peasants and commercial farmers, and the like. He is also the supervisor of a very complex economy and the person ultimately responsible for the nation's development. It is this blend of an old and deeply entrenched tradition of imperial authority with a very sophisticated mechanism for supervising the affairs of state by consulting constantly with leaders from all social and economic sectors that has caused Mexicans to accept their presidency as essential to their maintenance.

To sustain his authority, the president must successfully do three things: secure the cooperation of the PRI's labor, peasant, and popular constituencies with official policy; work closely with powerful business interests that are not included in the party; and assure a smooth presidential succession. The first task was managed for a long time using patronage, co-optation, and the adoption of policies aimed at satisfying minimal constituency demands.

The second task is more challenging. The party, though broadly based, is not all-inclusive. Two of the country's most powerful forces – the domestic and foreign business communities – are deliberately excluded in order to maintain the popular character of the party. Private entrepreneurs resent the president's ability to use his immense power against them, yet they are never hesitant to exploit his reliance on them to finance and manage much of the nation's mixed, capitalist economy. Until economic crisis and recession struck the country in 1982 the arrangement had worked rather well for both sides; but now Mexico is in a quandary, its president being told by some economists to give greater freedom to the private sector while being warned by PRI politicians that such a redistribution of economic power will weaken the government permanently.

Finally, Mexican presidents must handle the succession problem smoothly in order to sustain public faith in the presidential institution. Nothing has done more to preserve the system than its prevention of a single person's governing for more than one six-year presidential term. As soon as he is replaced, he is little more than a wealthy citizen removed to the fringes of national politics. But before he is, he must conduct the selection of his successor. Even when they did not like his choice, party members seldom challenged the decision for fear that it would undermine the party unity that was so essential for its remaining in power. Impressively, with the exception of a brief interlude after President-elect Obregón's assassination in 1928, each Mexican president has managed the task successfully, something unimaginable in almost any other Latin American country.

Party primaries and convention battles were unknown to Mexicans until 1988. Usually a member of the cabinet was selected by the retiring president and informed of his appointment twelve to eighteen months before the end of the incumbent's term. Soon thereafter his candidacy was ratified by the national PRI convention, launching a campaign that took him to towns and cities throughout the country to reaffirm the symbolic link between the president and his people. Once this ritual was concluded, the election was held.

The presidency is the last stop for only a few of the thousands of Mexicans who begin their careers aspiring to high office. PRI politicians do not compete for it publicly with one another, but work within the party organization or the cabinet to gain favor with the incumbent. Traditionally, rising even that far has required a person to devote his life to moving up the hierarchy, taking what advantage he can from the personal relationships that abound within party and government. Each office holder relies on networks of colleagues and subordinates devoted to his advancement and their advancement with him. A political career within the PRI usually begins with the aspirant attaching himself to an office holder, serving him as a political operator or technical aide. If his mentor rises higher in the official hierarchy, he may be rewarded with a post in the government or the party. Once established, he then builds his own network of followers whom he uses the same way his mentors used him. If one's leader does not rise, however, the aspirant for higher office will leave him for someone whose mobility is more probable. In short, the successful Mexican politician operates like an investor who hedges his bets by investing in several firms simultaneously, only to transfer his money from the least to the most profitable enterprise as often as necessary. On the surface Mexican politicians appear to be quite cordial, giving the impression of membership in a large, fraternal association. But they are neither as secure nor as collegial as they pretend, for to survive in this very competitive system duplicity and betrayal often become necessary. Ultimately only a few reach the cabinet; nevertheless, thousands of them eventually acquire sinecures for themselves that guarantee comfortable retirement when their climb up the political ladder concludes.

What has changed in presidential politics in recent years is not the process for presidential selection but the type of person being selected. Starting with President López Portillo in 1976, presidents have come from a new class of technocrats rather than from among the politicians who have worked their way up through the PRI apparatus. They are well educated, many of them with advanced degrees from foreign universities, and went to work in the executive branch as experts in banking, budgeting, or other economic matters. In recent years their numbers have increased substantially, as has their control over the Mexican state. They are members of the PRI, but until election time they have largely ignored its organizations. If they are selected to run for president, they expect the party to adopt them just as it has their predecessors, aware that once installed it will be the new president who will distribute the rewards to which their member organizations are accustomed. Such technocratic leadership is the result of an inevitable need for expertise in a government as huge as Mexico's, and for those who are especially adept at using their aptitude in dealings with foreign governments, international organizations, and multinational banks in times of economic crisis. But that does not make them more popular. On the contrary, even though the PRI candidate is assured victory in presidential elections, popular support for them has been declining steadily over the past thirty years.

No introduction to Mexican politics is complete without mention of the "corruption" for which the nation has become notorious. Millions of dollars change hands every day between government officials and citizens. Payments induce police to drop charges, tax collectors to ignore certain taxpayers, and government corporations to sign contracts with suppliers. Is it an abuse of authority? Not according to the Mexican code of political ethics. Persons are neither proud of it nor embarrassed by it; it is too much a part of normal life to excite much consternation. Some people enter politics in order to use authority to extract payment from clients, and clients rely on purchased help to secure assistance in getting through burdensome rules and regulations. It was that way centuries ago and it will not likely change any time soon. Yet there are limits, it seems, as recent "excesses" indicated. The head of PEMEX is not supposed to pocket millions of dollars, nor the police chief of Mexico City to build castles to live in, something each did recently. What was once a normal means of enrichment for those in power suddenly seemed like outright confiscation. Bribery and theft are not the same thing as the Mexicans see it, and demands that the latter be halted are now heard. Drawing the line is not easy, however, since everyone wants the president to start in someone else's domain. As a result, a few arrests were made until recently but even then only for the most outrageous abuses. For everyone else the need to pay for services will continue to be part of the Mexican way of life, enticing new generations of politicians and civil servants to earn as much as their predecessors.

Unrevolutionary economics

Nowhere are the mixed motives behind the Mexican Revolution more obvious than in the nation's economics since 1917. Between 1920 and 1940 substantial land was taken from the *hacendados* and returned to the campesinos, and some foreign enterprises were nationalized. But after 1940 attention turned to the nation's industrialization, and through the combined efforts of the rapidly growing Mexican state and native entrepreneurs, Mexico sustained one of the fastest and steadiest rates of economic growth in the hemisphere during the next forty years. In the 1960s they were joined by multinational firms, who came to see Mexico as the land of opportunity. But the more officials placed their faith in industrialization, the more the gap between the rich and poor grew, for little of the nation's new wealth trickled down to campesinos and unorganized laborers. What the descendants of Obregón and Cárdenas had created, it turned out, was not socialism but a very Mexican version of capitalism.

A closer look at how this occurred needs to begin in the Mexican countryside. In 1910, 97 percent of Mexico's land was owned by just 830 people or corporations, an incredible degree of concentration, even for Latin America at the turn of the century. Ending this condition became the objective of the agrarian activists who fought in the 1910 insurrection. Some seized haciendas in the midst of battle: Campesinos recovered village lands taken from them during the Porfiriato, and revolutionary generals secured their own haciendas. Yet most of the rural elite survived the war, and it was up to the new government to strip them of property and power.

The cause of agrarian reform was embraced by Obregón and subsequent Mexican presidents primarily because it was necessary for the maintenance of order in the countryside. By redistributing land they hoped to deprive the oligarchy of its primary means of control over the masses while at the same time securing the political support of campesinos by making them indebted to their new benefactors in Mexico City. Land expropriation by the government, which began slowly in the 1920s, was accelerated by President Cárdenas during the 1930s; in only six years he expropriated twice as much land as had been taken during the preceding seventeen years. Most of the land was redistributed in units known as *ejidos*, an indigenous mode of organization in which property is owned by the entire village and farmed either communally or in family units. Today 43 percent of Mexican farmland is held by 18,000 ejidos, and 4,000 of them are communally farmed. The other 57 percent is privately owned, nearly half of it held by families or corporations in farms of over 250 acres. In the northwest they often take the form of irrigated farms that supply the United States with fruits and vegetables during the winter months.

Agrarian reform, while necessary for social justice in the countryside, is certainly not sufficient. Most campesinos stay poor and a majority of them are still landless. Debates have raged between the left and right wings of the PRI over what more to do for the rural poor. The left, which praises the *ejido* system, also protests the government's repeated failure to deliver on promises of easy finance and accessible technology, accusing it of deferring to larger farmers who can produce far more than the *ejidos* for consumers in Mexican cities and markets abroad. Conservatives, in contrast, think it time to replace *ejidos* with family-owned plots that can be sowed or sold by their owners. Doubtless more productive, this division of land would also encourage its concentration through purchase by larger farmers, causing even more persons to abandon the countryside for cities, a change the PRI is still reluctant to promote. Consequently very little is changing.

Mexicans today face a supply problem: Once self-sufficient in grains and beans, they are no longer. Starting in 1980 they had to import $2 billion worth of grain from the United States. Farm production, which stagnated in the 1970s, no longer keeps up with population growth. Obstacles to increasing production abound. Only 17 percent of Mexico is arable, and the land that is cultivated is plagued by soil erosion and erratic rainfall. And only 25 percent of the nation's farmers have access to credit, fertilizer, and other things essential for rural modernization. This is no accident, however, for a few decades ago government officials chose to devote their limited resources to assisting the development of large agribusiness operations in northwestern Mexico. Theirs was a choice between spreading resources widely but thinly among the needy *ejiditarios* and concentrating them among a few hundred very productive farms able to earn dollars needed to finance the nation's industrialization. They chose the latter, convinced that economic objectives should prevail over social ones. In doing so they took the revolution another step away from one of its original purposes. Nevertheless, Mexican presidents still claim dedication to elevating the poor farmer, and they have allocated some resources to selected *ejidos*, but it is always far too little to make much difference.

Mexican leaders discovered long ago that the nation could not rely on agriculture and mining to promote rapid economic development. Instead, they chose import-substitution industrialization after 1940, using public enterprise and investment to do the job in areas where private investment was slow in developing. The Mexican government has supplied an average of 30 percent of annual national investment, and by 1970 it had accumulated 600 of its own businesses. What distinguishes the Mexican public sector from that of other Latin American countries is the greater variety of activities in which it has become engaged. Only in Cuba and Nicaragua has the state become so influential in so many markets. This is due, it seems, to the government's need to assure that certain goods and services reach their principal constituents and to supply jobs to thousands, as well as the practice of taking over industries near collapse in order to preserve jobs, especially after economic growth slowed in the 1970s. The result is a powerful and paternalistic government on which most Mexicans depend directly or indirectly for their welfare.

Mexican nationalism, which led to the eviction of many foreign firms in the early days of the revolution, did not prevent their return in large numbers after 1960. Eager for modern technology and for help with financing industrialization, the Mexican government has unofficially encouraged foreign investment. And despite restrictions on foreign ownership of enterprises in some sectors and requirements of Mexican-investor participation in most, foreign investment increased eleven-fold between 1950 and 1979 when it reached $6.9 billion (70 percent of which came from the United States). By 1972 it was estimated that foreign firms were responsible for 35 percent of Mexico's industrial production and owned 45 percent of the share of capital in the nation's 290 largest firms. Here too the Mexican economy has come to resemble those of unrevolutionary Brazil and Argentina more than that of revolutionary Cuba.

Mexico's industrialization was a remarkable achievement. By combining national, foreign, and government investment in new industries after World War II the Mexicans achieved rates of growth that were unprecedented in Latin America. Industry, which grew at an annual rate of about 7 percent for twenty years after the war, accelerated in the 1960s, when it averaged 9 percent annually. It did not matter to those who directed the effort that most Mexicans saw none of its benefits; they had achieved something that made them the envy of their Latin American neighbors who could not keep pace. Though revolutionary in name, they had behaved more like conservative bankers eager to bolster investor confidence in the nation's future than adventuresome rulers of a reformist society. Having begun in 1920 with something resembling the progressive modernization development strategy, they gradually incorporated many of the elements of conservative modernization, emphasizing monetary and foreign exchange consistency and capitalization over distribution.

Private business enjoys a very special relationship with the Mexican government. Officially, it is excluded from the PRI and is often criticized by presidents for its selfish behavior and abuse of its enormous economic power. But this is largely a facade, and everyone knows it. Despite inevitable disagreements over policy, the managers of private and public enterprises rely heavily on one another to make the Mexican economy operate. The nation's pragmatic policy makers want business to succeed because it supplies most of the jobs that are desperately needed to employ a rapidly growing population, produces the goods that are consumed by the middle and working classes, and will, it is

Table 6.2. *Distribution of income: Mexico, Brazil, Venezuela, Argentina, U.S.*

	Poorest 40%	Next 20%	Next 20%	Highest 20%	Top 10%
Mexico	9.9	12.0	20.4	57.7	40.6
Brazil	7.0	9.4	17.0	66.6	50.6
Venezuela	10.3	12.9	22.8	54.0	35.7
Argentina	14.1	14.1	21.5	50.3	35.2
U.S.	17.2	17.9	25.0	39.9	23.3

Source: World Bank, *World Development Report – 1987* (New York: Oxford University Press, 1987), p. 253. Data on Mexico is taken from 1977; Brazil, 1972; Venezuela, 1970; Argentina, 1970; and U.S., 1980.

hoped, manufacture the goods that Mexico must export in the 1990s in order to recover from the disastrous 1980s. It is a marriage of convenience rather than affection, a partnership that is outside party politics; it has its own political system, just out of public view, where private entrepreneurs and government bureaucrats bargain and negotiate over regulations, subsidies, contracts, and favors. Presidents have occasionally gone on the attack, as when President López Portillo nationalized the nation's banks in 1982 to halt the flight of capital, but then they pull back, always searching for ways to promote private investment without succumbing to the private sector's control over policy.

No one in Mexico boasts of creating an egalitarian society. Instead, now they debate how far from it they have fallen. One measure is income distribution, something that reformers try to improve in a progressive manner (i.e., taking from the rich and giving income and property to the poor). Under the Porfiriato income was concentrated in the extreme, a very small number of families owning most property and receiving most income. That has been changed by postrevolution governments, especially during the Cárdenas presidency, but never as much as the term revolutionary might imply. As you can see in Table 6.2, the richest 20 percent of the Mexican population receives almost 60 percent of the national income. The only worse case among the larger Latin American nations is Brazil, which approaches 67 percent. In contrast, in unrevolutionary Venezuela they hold 54 percent, and in the highly industrialized and far more affluent United States it is

40 percent. Such data is never exact, but it does indicate that through its postwar development Mexico has achieved a distribution of wealth not unlike other Latin American nations, its claims of massive redistribution notwithstanding. It has followed a capitalist path, with the state serving as the largest of all capitalists, rewarding investors with enough profit to keep them investing. As in other capitalist systems, those who invest the most may also earn the most. In the process some people do rise from the lower class and join others in the middle, but very little of what is held by the richest 20 percent ever is transferred to the masses.

Mexico's economic boom was losing momentum when a world recession brought it to a halt in 1973. Demand for Mexican exports fell, economic growth slowed, and business confidence faltered for the first time since World War II. The descent was brief, however, for just as authorities were beginning to reconcile themselves to slower growth, new petroleum discoveries were made along the country's eastern seaboard. The timing could not have been better, since the OPEC nations had raised international prices in 1973 and again in 1979, making Mexico's newly acquired oil surplus a source of immense new wealth. The Mexican government, which owns all of the nation's petroleum, quickly recast its plans in anticipation of an unprecedented capacity to finance new development projects. But after soaring to new heights in just a couple years, Mexico's boom came to a crashing halt in 1982. Suddenly a government that had struggled for decades to reduce the nation's dependence on its northern neighbor was forced to go, hat in hand, to its creditors in the United States and Europe to plead for emergency financial assistance to cover the debts that it could no longer pay. Something had gone very wrong in just a few years and everyone knew it.

In retrospect, the reasons for the Mexicans' miscalculations are quite conspicuous. In the early 1970s authorities knew that the economy would have to expand at a very fast rate in order to create the 800,000 new jobs needed annually by its growing population. But doing that was unlikely until new oil discoveries in the Gulf of Mexico suddenly gave them the means to finance it. Officials proceeded cautiously at first, aware that if national income rose too swiftly, high inflation would follow. Accordingly, President López Portillo announced a limitation on oil production, holding output to 2.5 million barrels a day, keeping 1 million for national use and exporting the rest to the United States and Latin America.

Still, it was hard to resist the temptation to launch new development programs aimed at bringing prosperity back to the country. Public expenditures soared and the economy's growth accelerated to 8 percent annually between 1978 and 1981, creating over a million jobs a year, most of them in construction. But government spending rose so fast that oil revenues could not come close to covering it. To finance the deficit the government borrowed heavily abroad, taking advantage of low interest rates and the eagerness of foreign banks to loan the money that other oil producers had deposited with them. As a result, Mexico's foreign debt, which was already a record $33.9 billion in 1978, soared to $87.6 billion by the end of 1982. Then the world recession struck, cutting Mexico's income from trade in half and making it impossible to meet its interest payments. To make matters worse, Mexicans had borrowed at floating interest rates, meaning that what they paid in interest went up or down as rates changed in the marketplace. Real interest rates had been low in the 1970s but they suddenly soared in 1981, the U.S. prime rate reaching 21 percent. At first they just borrowed more money, but soon it was obvious that they could not pay what they owed. Adding to the country's woes, wealthy Mexicans realized what was coming and began buying dollars to protect themselves and rushing them from the country, sending $9 billion abroad in August 1982 alone.

In theory, the government had two options: They could default on their debts, or they could seek help abroad. But as gratifying as it might have seemed at the time, defaulting was out of the question for a trade-dependent and financially conservative Mexican leadership that refused to abandon the international financial system on which they had become so reliant. So they went north and relief came quickly, first with loans from a United States government that wanted to protect its nation's vulnerable banks by making sure that Mexico kept paying its debt, and from the International Monetary Fund, which secured additional private bank loans for Mexico by promising to supply IMF loans and enough supervision to make sure the Mexicans slowed their spending and reduced imports in order to increase their net dollar income. It was a high price to pay, especially for Mexican consumers, for it meant increases in the prices they paid for public services and basic foods and limits on wage increases at a time of record inflation. Yet pay it they did as the Mexican authorities accommodated themselves to the demands of their creditors.

As expected, Mexico's gross domestic product (GDP) fell by 5.3 percent in 1983, then recovered some in 1984 and in 1985. But then the international price of oil fell from $26.70 a barrel in February 1985 to only $8.60 in July 1986, as increased production of non-OPEC nations like Canada, Norway, and Great Britain put oil supplies far ahead of world demand. Mexico's recovery came to a crashing halt, unemployment nearly doubled and inflation soared: In just two years tortilla prices rose 416 percent, bread 1,800 percent, beans 776 percent, and eggs 582 percent while the minimum salary was only 363 percent higher. Mexicans had seen nothing quite like it since 1930.

Tragically, Mexico found itself caught in a kind of catch-22 of indebtedness. To pay their debts they had to recover economically, but recovery, they were told, first required austerity measures intended to improve their capacity for long-term development. Economic growth also depended on the recovery of a world economy that continued to grow too slowly. Mexico, like other nations in the region, increased its exports in order to earn more, but with demand low, prices also stayed low, so earnings were actually 12 percent less.

In 1988 President Miguel de la Madrid ended his six-year term as he began it, asking Mexicans to sacrifice current gains for future benefits. In 1987 prices had risen 160 percent, an unprecedented inflation rate for Mexico, forcing him to call on business, labor, farmers, and government to sign a "Solidarity Pact" that included agreements on wage, price, and foreign-exchange controls aimed at ending the panic that was growing among the middle and upper classes who once more were buying dollars and sending them abroad. Initially it worked – the rate of annual inflation fell to less than 30 percent – renewing some confidence in the economy, as did the return of international oil prices to around $20 a barrel. Nevertheless, the nation's gross domestic product fell by 2 percent in 1987, and real wages, which remained frozen most of the year, continued to fall after having already dropped by nearly 50 percent between 1980 and 1987. It was the price laborers had to pay for playing by the rules of the game.

No matter what happens next, most Mexicans will suffer. Some day they may look back and say, "Thanks, we needed that," but for the time being they see only an unceasing need to pay 32.7 percent of the nation's export earnings to the creditors who own their debt. Debt rescheduling and refinancing, as well as a variety of piecemeal schemes aimed at easing the debt burden, have prevented even greater disaster, but as long as the banks demand payment, Mexicans will be exporting vast amounts of what they earn from exports rather than investing it at home.

A new era?

Where Mexico goes from here economically is uncertain. It still enjoys an abundance of oil and gas and will profit from the sale of both in the years ahead. Yet, as everyone now realizes, petroleum alone cannot solve the more fundamental problems facing the nation. Raising farm productivity is neither easy nor cheap, and even if substantial progress is made, most campesinos will remain landless and without easy access to employment in industry. Moreover, the nation's economic dependence on the United States will continue, even if some progress is made in diversifying Mexico's trade and reducing its borrowing abroad. And a rapidly growing population is making unprecedented demands on its nation's resources. It went from 20 million in 1945 to 83 million today and will reach 100 million by the end of this century. The annual population growth rate, which was 3.5 percent in the 1960s, is estimated to have fallen to between 2.0 and 2.5 percent today as a result of government-sponsored family planning, middle-sector affluence, and several hundred thousand illegal abortions every year, but because 40 percent of the Mexican population is now under 15 years of age, the population will double again in only 35 years.

But however Mexicans deal with their economic problems, their politics will certainly be different. In 1988 the opposition rose up and challenged the PRI in a manner inconceivable just a few years before. According to official figures, the PRI won the 1988 presidential election with just over 50 percent of the vote, though doubts will always remain about whether last-minute tinkering with the tallies was necessary to give them a victory. Whatever the truth, the message was clear: PRI control over the government, though not yet ended, would be threatened for some time to come.

When Mexicans went to the polls the PRI held 95 percent of all municipal governments, all 31 governorships, all 64 Senate seats, and 289 of the 400 seats in the Chamber of Deputies. Together the country's opposition parties had never received more than 35 percent in presidential elections. But opposition to the government rapidly rose in the 1980s as economic conditions deteriorated and consumption declined. It was so manifest in gubernatorial and municipal elections in the northern states in 1986 that the PRI had to rig them in order to win. All of this left party leaders with a real dilemma: whether to run roughshod over increasing opposition or to allow freer elections in an attempt to absorb protests within the existing political process without sacrificing the PRI's domination. In this instance they tried a little of both, though without convincing anyone that they intended to do anything but retain their monopoly over everything that really mattered.

It began with President Miguel de la Madrid selecting his budget minister, Carlos Salinas de Gortari, to succeed him. A thirty-nine-year-old economist who, like de la Madrid, earned a graduate degree from Harvard University, Salinas was another in a line of highly technocratic presidents who had never run for office before. Once again the management of the Mexican economy, more than the pursuit of personal popularity, governed the selection process. Dissidents within the PRI protested Salinas's selection. Calling themselves the Democratic Current, and led by Porfirio Muñoz Ledo, once a prominent PRI boss, and Cuauhtémoc Cárdenas, son of President Lazaro Cárdenas, they were swiftly expelled from the party for their dissidence. It was a costly decision for the PRI for, once outside the party, Cárdenas turned to parties on the Left for support of his own candidacy. His timing could not have been better since it came just after the Mexican Socialist Party (PSM) was created from a merger of five small parties, among them the Unified Socialist Party (PSUM) and the Mexican Workers' Party (PMT). Calling this movement the National Democratic Front, Cárdenas appealed to the urban middle and lower classes to rebuke the "undemocratic and corrupt" PRI by electing him president.

It took the Election Commission seven days to tally the votes, leaving the opposition to suspect tampering to save the PRI from defeat. On July 13 Salinas was pronounced the victor with 50 percent of the 19 million votes cast; Cárdenas, second with 31 percent; and Manuel Clouthier of the conservative National Action Party (PAN), 17 percent, though Cárdenas would claim to no effect that he had actually received 38 percent and Salinas just 36 percent. The impact was felt in Congress as well. The number of seats that the opposition won by direct vote in the Chamber of Deputies increased from 1 to 51, which, when added to the 189 seats that they won through the system of proportional representation, reduced the PRI's majority to 260 in the 500-member Chamber.

Most shocking to the PRI was how its constituency organizations failed to rally their members behind the party. In 1988 the three "core sectors" claimed a membership of 30 million – the National Confederation of Popular Organizations with 6 million members, the National Farmers' Confederation from 10 to 12 million, and the Mexican Labor Confederation 14 million – but Salinas received only 9.6 million votes. Half of the electorate stayed home and did not even bother to vote. Equally stunning was the opposition's winning nearly every major city except Monterrey, and taking the states of Morelos, Michoacán, Mexico, and Baja California, something unimaginable before the campaign began. It was only with votes from the most traditional rural areas that the PRI pulled out a victory. The political *caciques* in the countryside delivered, but their colleagues in unions and popular organizations did not. As a result, most of labor's candidates for the Chamber of Deputies were defeated.

Ironically, Salinas, a president who in his campaign had promised to "modernize" Mexican politics by making it more competitive, was elected by voters in the countryside, themselves the least modern members of Mexican society. The incongruity is obvious and will likely remain troublesome: Salinas says that he is making Mexico more satisfactory to the urban middle class but they refuse to believe him. In the past, social class divisions and political frustrations had little effect on politics in a Mexico that was run by a corporatist political party, but that is no longer so. Salinas knew that many of those persons who had supported his party were now rejecting it. Clearly, the PRI could not continue to govern effectively by rigging elections in a society that was more able than ever before to express itself in public protest. He had no choice but to become more responsive to the demands of his opponents, but there was no guarantee that his doing so would strengthen the PRI.

Mexicans do know, however, that their neighbors to the north will be watching them closely. The United States government has seldom complained about the PRI's autocratic practices as long as it achieved political stability and a prospering Mexican economy eager to make purchases north of the border. It was the first and the fastest to respond to Mexico's financial crisis in August 1982, and quickly sent a couple billion dollars more in loans in 1988 to help Salinas get off to a good start. The United States purchases about 66 percent of Mexico's exports and supplies 65 percent of its imports. Moreover, U.S. capital holds 67 percent of all the direct foreign investment in Mexico. Though Mexicans would prefer to deny the reality of their heavy dependence on the United States, it remains a fact of life with which they must live.

Is Mexico unique?

Until recently Mexicans prided themselves on having avoided the conflicts over fundamental rules that are so common in the rest of the hemisphere. For over sixty years their government was strong, their presidential transitions orderly, and their military subservient to civil authority. No other nation in Latin America could make that claim. But how different is Mexico from the rest? Is it really as unique as it appears?

Actually, Mexico does share a few traits with its neighbors, as comparisons reveal. For example, the PRI, though more successful than most parties, is not the only party to gain its strength from building a coalition of middle-sector politicians, labor unions, and peasant organizations. Venezuela's Democratic Action (AD) Party, we will discover, did much the same thing with substantial success electorally. Where the two parties differ is in the AD's inability to achieve a political monopoly such as the PRI secured in Mexico with a powerful revolutionary mythology that helped raise it above its competitors and legitimize its rule.

Mexicans boast of excluding their armed forces from national politics, yet they sometimes operate in ways familiar to the generals and admirals who recently ran military authoritarian governments in Brazil. Its democratic pretensions notwithstanding, Mexico is governed by a strong central government that uses the power of the state to regulate the conduct of sectoral interests not unlike what the Brazilian military tried to do for over two decades. Where they differ is in the manner in which they have legitimized this kind of heavy-handed, corporatist government: The Mexicans claim that their people want it that way, whereas the Brazilians could do little more than argue that it was the most practical way of governing their rapidly industrializing nation.

Mexico's unusual blend of democratic rules with corporatist and authoritarian practices makes it similar to and yet distinct from the politics found elsewhere in the region. That is what makes it so hard to label accurately. But that is exactly the way Mexican authorities want it. Ambiguity about their principles and practices makes it difficult for their critics to pin them down. The same government that allows an opposition press to function and opposition parties to speak out against them cheats its way to victory in elections, as it did in Chihuahua in 1986 and, many believe, also did in the 1988 presidential election. Yet, time after time, the PRI has demonstrated that it is not without considerable support within the population. Does that make it democratic? Not really.

Mexican presidents mediate and arbitrate among the most important forces in society, from business and industry to farmers and campesinos, and even dictate to them when it becomes absolutely necessary. Everyone recognizes the president as a kind of supreme *patron* who supervises a large and complex political system that has always relied on a powerful leader. But the president's job is far more difficult today in an age when austerity has replaced development, and doubts about the ability of anyone to reverse its current decline are common. Few Mexicans believe that the old system works any more. Their alienation and cynicism, which is currently rampant, may not lead to revolt, but the postponement of rebellion is not much to celebrate.

Mexico's increasing resemblance to its neighbors to the south derives even more from the economic travails that it now suffers. Despite its revolutionary pretensions, Mexico, like Brazil and Argentina, followed the path of import-substitution industrialization, combining a very large public sector with an aggressive though sheltered private one. Later both were joined by hundreds of multinational corporations. It was quite productive in aggregate terms, but industrialization did not increase Mexico's economic autonomy significantly, and today economic independence is as great a myth as ever. Indebted as much as it is, Mexico can only hope for some relief through an increase in oil prices one day, but even that will not allow it to replicate the steady growth it enjoyed before 1970. Nor will it assure employment for a population that will double in size in the next thirty years. If Mexicans once believed that they had escaped the frustrating regressions that have long plagued the region, they do so no longer.

Further reading

Bailey, Norman A., and Richard Cohen. *The Mexican Time Bomb*. New York: The Twentieth Century Fund, 1987.

Brandenburg, Frank. *The Making of Modern Mexico*. Englewood Cliffs, NJ: Prentice Hall, 1963.

Camp, Roderic A., ed. *Mexico's Political Stability: The Next Five Years*. Boulder, CO: Westview Press, 1987.

    Who's Who in Mexico Today. Boulder, CO: Westview Press, 1988.

Gettleman, Judith. *Mexican Politics in Transition*. Boulder, CO: Westview Press, 1987.

Hamilton, Nora. *The Limits of State Autonomy: Post-Revolutionary Mexico*. Princeton, NJ: Princeton University Press, 1982.

Hamilton, Nora, and Timothy F. Harding, eds. *Modern Mexico: State, Economy, and Society in Conflict*. Beverly Hills, CA: Sage, 1985.

Hansen, Roger. *The Politics of Mexican Development*. Baltimore: The Johns Hopkins University Press, 1971.

Hellman, Judith Adler. *Mexico in Crisis*, 2nd ed. New York: Holmes and Meier, 1984.

Hart, John Mason. *Revolutionary Mexico: The Coming and Process of the Mexican Revolution*. Berkeley: University of California Press, 1987.

Johnson, Kenneth F. *Mexican Democracy: A Critical View*. 3rd ed. New York: Praeger, 1984.

Levy, Daniel, and Gabriel Szekely. *Mexico: Paradoxes of Stability*. 2nd ed. Boulder, CO: Westview Press, 1987.

Newell G., Roberto. *Mexico's Dilemma: The Political Origins of Economic Crisis*. Boulder, CO: Westview Press, 1984.

Padgett, Vincent. *The Mexican Political System*, 2nd ed. Boston: Houghton Mifflin, 1976.

Reynolds, Clark W. *The Mexican Economy: Twentieth Century Structure and Growth*. New Haven, CN: Yale University Press, 1970.

Riding, Alan. *Distant Neighbors: A Portrait of the Mexicans*. New York: Knopf, 1985.

Roxborough, Ian. *Unions and Politics in Mexico: The Case of the Automobile Industry*. New York: Cambridge University Press, 1984.

Smith, Peter H. *Labyrinths of Power: Political Recruitment in Twentieth Century Mexico*. Princeton, NJ: Princeton University Press, 1979.

Story, Dale. *The Mexican Ruling Party: Stability and Authority*. New York: Praeger, 1986.

Tannenbaum, Frank. *Mexico: The Struggle for Peace and Bread*. New York: Knopf, 1956.

Ward, Peter. *Welfare Politics in Mexico: Papering over the Cracks*. Boston: Allen & Unwin, 1986.

    ed. *Politics in Mexico*. London: Croom Helm, 1985.

Womack, John. *Zapata and the Mexican Revolution*. New York: Knopf, 1969.

7. Chile: democracy destroyed

Chileans once thrived on democratic government. Their political parties were numerous, ranging from Communists and Socialists on the Left to Conservatives on the Right, and every six years between 1932 and 1970 they elected a new president who peacefully replaced an incumbent whose party he had defeated. But this was ended abruptly in September 1973 by the nation's armed forces. It would be fifteen years before the Chilean people were given an opportunity to try democracy again. In a 1988 plebiscite in which General Augusto Pinochet sought confirmation of his authoritarian government, 54 percent of the Chilean electorate rejected it, forcing him to deliver on his promise to restore democratic government by 1990 if he were defeated. Thus, the nation that had once been one of Latin America's most admired democracies, before it was closed by the armed forces in 1973, chose to dismiss its military dictator and start over. Why this became necessary deserves some explanation.

Democratic rules

Latin Americans have experimented with various forms of liberal democracy ever since they gained their independence over 170 years ago, but from the beginning it was frequently undermined by the most powerful members of their societies. Constitutions modeled on the United States document have been written and rewritten, stressing popular sovereignty, majority rule, minority rights, and free elections, but until the middle of this century most of them only served as pretenses to legitimize the political monopolies of entrenched elites.

It pays to recall that liberal democratic rules are not arbitrary, but are derived from fundamental beliefs about the nature of society and its governance. They start with the notion that separate, diverse, and sometimes conflicting interests among individuals and groups are a normal and permanent feature of social and political life. In other words, people by nature and position differ on many things, and,

167

therefore, cannot be expected to achieve uniformity of interest within society. All that one can do is establish procedures for dealing with the conflicts caused by inevitable differences. Second, these procedures or rules must be agreed upon if they are to be effective. They cannot change with each dispute; if they did, no one would have confidence in them or feel compelled to obey them. And third, conditions must be established that guarantee that the winners and losers of political disputes are not known before the contest is held, be it an election or a dispute over policy. Competition is crucial to motivate everyone to submit disputes for resolution under the agreed-upon rules. The less competitive the game is, the less democratic it becomes, and the less acceptable its results will be for everyone involved. Though no democratic game ever achieves perfect competition, its rules lose meaning without substantial amounts of it.

Democracy has not always failed in Latin America. Political aspirants who wanted freer politics in their nations (many of them young, urban, and reform minded) organized democratic parties in their countries during the first half of this century, and they succeeded in a few countries, briefly in some and for long periods in others. Unwilling to make war on the incumbents, they mobilized members of the middle sectors, urban laborers, and even campesinos to demand political reform, promising their followers greater freedom and economic and social rewards in exchange for their votes. If they needed models to draw upon, they found them primarily in Europe where Social Democrats and Christian Democrats had built powerful mass-based political parties. From them and from the example set by Lazaro Cárdenas and the PRI in Mexico, these reform-minded democrats took ideas about recruitment and constituency organization which they adapted to their own situations, often quite creatively.

Politicians in Chile and Venezuela were among them. Some of them were ideologically sophisticated, often well organized, and seldom reliant on any single individual to lead them. It was never an easy task, for, unlike reform politicians in the United States, Great Britain, and Scandinavia who could take public respect for constitutional rules for granted, most Latin American reformers could take nothing for granted; instead they had to create constitutional regimes in hostile environments at the same time that they were trying to elevate the members of the lower classes who had supported them. As a result, they could not assume that democratic rules would be obeyed by any but their most ardent supporters.

Pluralists in spirit, they believed in the inherent diversity of interests in their societies and were certain that constitutional democracy was the most flexible means for mediating among competitors. But that was not all; they also preferred democratic rules because they considered them advantageous to their own pursuit of power. Not having the economic resources needed to compete with the rich or the weapons required to defeat the military, these predominantly middle-sector politicians concluded that the selection of authorities in free elections gave them the best opportunity to use their organizational skills to secure public office.

Of course, elections alone do not guarantee political triumph. Gaining the elite's respect for rules that permitted their eviction from office was always problematic. Nor could democrats assume that the masses would trust their leadership. In fact, the lower class is often quick to judge democracy a failure when it does not meet their material needs. Democrats are aware of these hazards, but that has not deterred them. If anything characterized their past efforts, it was not naïveté, but their determination to work tenaciously against very heavy odds. Nowhere is this more apparent than in the achievements and failures of democrats in Chile and Venezuela.

The two nations have much in common. Both have relatively small populations (12 and 18 million, respectively, in 1986), most of their people live in close proximity to each other, both have relied on mineral exports for their welfare (copper in Chile and petroleum in Venezuela), and both were governed by sophisticated, well-organized democratic reform parties during the 1960s – Christian Democrats (PDC) in Chile, and the Acción Democrática (AD) party in Venezuela. But there the similarities end. To begin with, they started out quite differently. Constitutional democracy began anew in Chile in 1931, while in Venezuela it did not really get under way until 1958. And second, currently constitutional government continues uninterrupted in Venezuela while it came to an abrupt halt in Chile in 1973, and is only now trying to start over.

These contrasting histories invite many questions. Why, for example, was the democratic game brought to a halt in one country but not in the other? Are the answers found in the strategies of the players, their relative strengths, or the conditions under which the game was played? And what about reform: Did either achieve very much by attempting agrarian and other reforms using democratic means? Finally, what can we conclude about how the distribution of political and economic power in society affected democracy's chances? Did it really make any difference? It is to the search for answers to these and other questions that we shall now turn, first with Chile, in this chapter, and then to Venezuela, in the next one.

Christian democracy in Chile

Chile escaped the *caudillo* wars that plagued most Latin American countries after independence because of the unusual unity of its small political elite and the loyalty of the military to it. The strong, executive-dominated governments that ruled Chile throughout most of the nineteenth century were replaced in 1891 after a brief civil war by a "parliamentary" regime dominated by an elite-controlled national congress (see Table 7.1). The latter, torn from the outset by interparty conflict that manifested itself in continual cabinet instability, collapsed in 1924, and after a succession of brief military governments was replaced in 1932 by a constitutional regime that governed Chile without interruption until 1973. Not only did the Chileans enjoy greater political stability than most Latin American countries after 1932, but they did so using an unusually sophisticated multiparty system and a stubborn commitment to competitive electoral politics. It was a system, however, that was controlled effectively by upper-class and middle-sector parties that tolerated working-class opposition only as long as their interests were not threatened. When working-class parties occasionally did get out of line, they were outlawed, as was the Communist Party between 1947 and 1958.

The Christian Democratic Party did not have to fight for admission against ruling autocrats as in Venezuela. What they needed at the outset was not a plan of political reconstruction but an election strategy that could generate a large enough following to defeat its conservative, moderate, and radical rivals. Two decades after they commenced their uphill struggle, they succeeded. Under the leadership of Eduardo Frei, they won the presidency in 1964 and spent the next six years implementing their program of economic and social reform.

The ascent of Chile's Christian Democrats (PDC) from their origins

Table 7.1. *Chile: historical background*

1818	Independence from Spain
1830	Autocratic republic created under President Diego Portales
1871	Liberal republic created by Liberal, Radical, and National Parties
1891	Parliamentary republic organized to reduce power of strong executive and give supremacy to Congress
1921	Liberal reformer, Arturo Alessandri, elected president
1924	Military closes Congress and installs Alessandri as president, who implements constitutional reforms
1927	Colonel Carlos Ibanez seizes power and creates personal dictatorship
1931	Colonel Marmaduke Grove creates "socialist republic," which lasts six months
1932	Republican government restored and Arturo Alessandri elected president
1938	Popular Front government of Radicals, Democrats, Socialists, and Communists elected
1952	Carlos Ibanez elected president on populist platform
1957	Christian Democratic Party created from Falange Nacional and Social Christian wing of Conservative Party
	Communist and Socialist parties form coalition called Frente de Acción Popular (FRAP)
1958	Conservative–Liberal candidate Jorge Alessandri elected president
1964	Eduardo Frei of Christian Democratic Party is elected president
1965	Christian Democrats win majority in Chamber of Deputies
1970	Salvador Allende, Socialist leader of Unidad Popular coalition, is elected president, with one-third of the vote
1973	Military coup ends Unidad Popular government; Allende killed in his office; General Augusto Pinochet becomes supreme ruler
1980	New constitution adopted in plebiscite; General Pinochet continues as president
1988	Pinochet loses plebiscite held to confirm him for eight more years; election called for December 1989

as an obscure faction of the Conservative Party with a minuscule constituency in the 1930s to winning the presidency in 1964 is an impressive, though unspectacular, story. It was begun by a group of law students at the Catholic University of Chile in the late 1920s. Sons of conservative families, Eduardo Frei, Radomiro Tomic, Bernardo Leighton, and Rafael Agustín Gumucio took their inspiration from philosophers who had sought to revitalize Roman Catholicism as an agent of social change. They had become disillusioned with conservatism, but they wanted no part of the Marxist or anticlerical Liberal parties then active in Chile. For them social Catholicism offered an alternative to the excessive individualism and economic exploitation fostered by nineteenth-century liberalism and the atheism and collectivism of communism. There was, however, no Chilean party ready to embrace their new ideology during the 1930s. The Conservative and Liberal Parties sought only to preserve the power and privileges of urban and rural elites and foreign investors, the middle-sector Radicals were anticlerical and little concerned with social justice in the countryside, and the Socialists and Communists rejected Christian theology. The only option, it became clear in 1937, was to organize a party of their own able to challenge the others.

The young Falangists, as the Christian Democrats were first known, played the game according to the conventional rules of Chilean politics, winning an occasional seat in the legislature and from time to time accepting cabinet posts in coalition governments. Their breakthrough came in 1957 when Eduardo Frei, the party's leader, was elected senator from Santiago, the nation's capital, and a year later polled 21 percent of the popular vote in the national presidential elections. From that election it became clear that by doubling their popular support they could win the presidency in a three-way contest with the Socialist–Communist coalition on the Left and the Conservatives on the Right. It was to that objective that they devoted their energies over the next six years.

They had relied on candidate-based, local constituency organizations during their formative years, but after 1958 the PDC accelerated its efforts to build mass organizations by recruiting the so-called marginal urban slum dwellers, campesinos, and the unemployed who had been effectively excluded from the political process in the past. In doing so they hoped to weaken parties on the Left by denying them their natural constituencies. Chile's Socialist and Communist parties, whose coalition received 30 percent of the vote in 1958, had strong organizations that drew their support primarily from organized labor and intellectuals. In the mid-1950s they became as interested as the Christian Democrats in expanding their ranks by recruiting the rural poor. To neutralize their efforts as well as recruit thousands to its ranks the PDC organized neighborhood associations with the help of

Table 7.2. *Chilean presidential elections, 1958 and 1964 (%)*

Party	1958	Party	1964
Conservative–Liberal Parties		Democratic Front	5
Jorge Alessandri	31.6		
Christian Democratic Party		Christian Democratic Party	
(PDC)		(PDC)	
Eduardo Frei	20.7	Eduardo Frei	55.7
Popular Action Front (FRAP)		Popular Action Front (FRAP)	
Salvador Allende	28.9	Salvador Allende	38.6
Others	18.9		

the clergy and university students and it created campesino organizations and farm worker unions.

Especially helpful to the PDC (as well as to the Communists and Socialists) were electoral reforms adopted in 1962. In 1932 Chilean Conservatives had designed a constitution that restricted participation in elections to middle- and upper-class males. In 1949 they were forced to extend the franchise to women, and finally, in 1962 their congressional opponents secured passage of legislation that extended the vote to nearly all Chileans. Attracting these new voters to their party became the primary objective of the PDC during the next two years.

The support of new voters was, by itself, not enough to catapult the Christian Democrats to victory. They also needed the votes of thousands of citizens who had opposed them in 1958. As we can see from Table 7.2, only 21 percent of the electorate had voted for the Christian Democrats in 1958, whereas almost 30 percent had supported the Socialist–Communist coalition, FRAP, led by Socialist Senator Salvador Allende. The likelihood of the Christian Democrats' taking votes from the Left was remote, for the Marxist parties had, since the 1920s, developed a hard core of supporters, especially in the labor movement. This dictated that the PDC seek some support among those who had supported the Conservatives or Liberals in 1958.

But how does a political party that campaigns on a platform of social and economic reform attract conservative and middle-sector voters? It does it, Frei and his colleagues decided, by convincing Conservatives that the Christian Democrats offered them their only hope of preventing a dreaded Marxist victory in the 1964 elections. The logic of their argument was simple. In 1964 Chileans were locked in a three-way electoral battle involving parties on the Right, Center, and Left, with each standing a chance of victory. Thus, if the Conservatives, Liberals, and Christian Democrats competed with each other, dividing slightly less than two-thirds of the electorate equally among them, they would make possible the election of Marxist Salvador Allende. To avert such a fate, the Conservatives should throw their support to the Christian Democrats, according to this logic. If the Christian Democrats needed some assistance in persuading Conservatives to support their candidates, they received it in March 1964, six months before the presidential election, when a Conservative was upset by the FRAP candidate in a special congressional election for a minor rural seat. They also received it from the United States government, which helped finance the PDC campaign and worked hard to persuade Conservatives to join in the PDC's anti-Marxist coalition, arguing that without it a FRAP victory was certain. Consequently, the threat of a Marxist president suddenly seemed likely, and, exploiting it to the fullest, Christian Democratic candidate Eduardo Frei secured enough Conservative and Liberal Party support at the last minute to block Salvador Allende's path to the presidency. With the assistance of his allies on the Right, Frei, who had received only 21 percent in 1958, polled an amazing 56 percent of the popular vote in the September 1964 election. Thus, playing by the Chilean rules and turning them to his personal advantage, Eduardo Frei concluded a thirty-five-year uphill struggle with one of Chile's most impressive presidential victories.

Reform politics and policy

Election victories open the door to public office, but they do not guarantee success in governing the nation, as reform-minded presidents everywhere will testify. Exceptional skill and substantial good fortune are required to prevail in democratic societies. Unlike the authoritarian who can command obedience, securing compliance using force, the democratic leader must always deal with competitors to whom the rules allow substantial latitude for obstruction.

Chile's Christian Democrats tried hard to deliver on their promises despite strong opposition from the Left and the Right, concentrating their efforts on agrarian reform, increased national control over natural resources, improved social welfare, and accelerated industrial development. Unfortunately for Frei, Chile's was not a parliamentary system in which party victory meant control over the government but a presidential one in which Frei faced a legislature controlled by the opposition. Consequently, his success depended, at a minimum, on his ability to do three things: create and maintain effective legislative coalitions, keep his own party united, and help his party win subsequent congressional and presidential elections.

First came the need for a coalition supportive of reform legislation. Frei had won the 1964 election by attracting Conservative voters to his party. But once the Conservatives had accomplished their objective of denying Salvador Allende the presidency, the coalition dissolved. Consequently, until congressional elections were held in March 1965, Frei could only count on the support of his own party, which held 23 of 147 House and 4 of 45 Senate seats, hardly enough to secure the passage of his program against the combined opposition of Communist, Socialist, Radical, Conservative, and Liberal Party legislators. So instead of seeking a coalition with one of these parties, the Christian Democrats put all their effort into the 1965 elections, asking Chileans to sustain the mandate they had given the PDC in September 1964. The strategy was in large part successful, for the PDC increased its hold on the House by taking 81 seats; however, it gained only 13 seats in the Senate. Consequently, throughout the remainder of his term, Frei had to work with a divided Congress in which the parties of the Left and the Right could unite to block PDC measures in the Senate.

Frei also faced serious divisions within his own party. Throughout his presidency the PDC was divided into three factions: one that supported Frei's moderate course, a second that demanded a more socialistic program, and a third that sought a compromise between the other two. Disputes over the government's program were common, but serious conflicts were initially avoided through the distribution of cabinet posts among members of all three factions. Gradually, however, frustration with the slow rate of reform increased, and disputes among the three wings of the party became more intense, especially during the 1967 party conference. Just as Frei was preparing to introduce austerity measures to deal with rising inflation, he was met with demands for the acceleration of reform through the adoption of the Plan Chonchol, a proposal prepared by agrarian reform minister Jacques Chonchol, advocating greater state control over the economy and more rapid land expropriation. The battle was eventually won by Frei and his supporters in the moderate faction, but their victory came at the expense of the loss of Chonchol and his followers, who left the PDC in 1969 to form their own party, the United Popular Action Movement (MAPU), which allied itself with the Marxist coalition that supported the candidacy of Salvador Allende in the 1970 election.

Frei intended to use popular reform policies to attract the masses to the PDC, making it strong enough electorally to withstand future competition with Conservative and Marxist parties. But the party's constituency changed little under Frei, and in 1970 no more than one-third of the Chilean electorate preferred it to its rivals. What Frei did achieve with his reform politics, however, was the alienation of the Conservatives who had supported him over Allende in 1964. Thus, like so many who start from a position between the two extremes, Frei succeeded in hardening the opposition without drawing many constituents from either one.

The government's development program combined tax and regulatory measures aimed at increasing mass consumption and national production while implementing agrarian reform. Frei's progressive tax reforms and liberal wage policies raised consumption as intended, but rising demand for goods provoked new inflation. When revenues from the new tax and foreign credits leveled off in 1967 and unions became more militant in their wage demands, Frei was forced to cut back on his popular expansionary measures. The decision was an especially bitter pill for his party to swallow, for not only did it threaten its chances in the forthcoming national elections, but it also raised concern within the party about the ability of its leaders to overcome the nation's production and inflation problems. In their own defense, party leaders claimed that the fault was not theirs but belonged to their opponents who delayed their programs in Congress and obstructed their implementation, using their influence within an unresponsive bureaucracy and the labor movement. But whatever the cause, the result was the same: Few Chileans were convinced that the Christian Democrats had solutions to the nation's fundamental problems.

Reform involves much more than new solutions to inflation and production problems. At the heart of the progressive modernization strategy is agrarian reform. Even though it was blessed with fertile lands, Chile had to import substantial amounts of food. In the 1950s, moreover, it suffered from a constant exodus of the rural poor to already overcrowded cities because of the impossibility of economic survival on the land. The causes of low production and rural-to-urban migration were the same: the maldistribution of property and its inefficient use by landowners. By the time Frei had come to power, Chile's rural economics had been extensively analyzed and their deficiencies were well known. The only question that remained was whether the government could do anything about them.

Frei was not the first Chilean president to sign an agrarian reform bill, but he was the first to implement one. In 1962, under the pressure of his coalition partners in the Radical Party, Conservative President Jorge Alessandri had secured the passage of a weak agrarian reform law. But like so many other agrarian measures adopted throughout the hemisphere at the time, it had very limited application, having defined eligible property as that which had been abandoned or was used inefficiently. It is no wonder, then, that Frei made agrarian reform a campaign issue in 1964 and a central part of his legislative program in 1965. Nevertheless, despite its compelling nature, Frei's bill did not become law until 1968 because of the opposition of Conservative and Marxist legislators, the former because they stood to lose property and power under the law and the latter because they did not want the Christian Democrats to be credited with alleviating the land tenure problem with their modest reforms.

The new law contained several innovative measures. First, size rather than use would determine expropriation. Large estates, regardless of how they were farmed, would be broken up. Second, the land would be purchased by the government at its declared tax value rather than its current market value. Because Chilean landowners habitually underdeclared their land value at tax time, this approach would penalize them for such practices as well as save government money by lowering the cost of expropriation. Third, the landowner would be paid only 10 percent of the price in cash with the other 90 percent in twenty-five-year bonds. Finally, the expropriated estate would be turned over to the peasants who had worked it or lived in the immediate area and then organized into an *asentamiento* under the direction of an elected peasant committee and experts from CORA, the government agrarian reform agency. The actual administration varied from one *asentamiento* to another, with some dividing property into private plots, others forming cooperatives, and a few farming collectively. Frei's rural reforms were not, however, limited to the reallocation of property. He also encouraged the organization of farm workers' unions and their efforts to raise rural wages. At the same time, new incentives were given to farmers to increase production, and self-help projects were encouraged in rural villages to build schools, roads, and health care facilities.

Throughout his campaign and during his first year as president Frei had promised to transfer land to 100,000 of the country's approximately 200,000 landless peasant families. But it was a promise that he could not keep. In fact, only 21,000 peasant families had received land by the time Frei left office in 1970. Legislative opposition, bureaucratic delays, technical problems, and obstruction by landowners turned a noble promise into a bitter disappointment and gave Marxist opponents a campaign issue that they could use to attract peasant support in 1970. The Frei government did raise the income of rural workers by an estimated 70 percent, and it increased rural production by an average of 3.8 percent a year, but it became clear in 1970 that despite their bold initiatives the Christian Democrats had not solved their country's rural problems. They had made a beginning, but in the process they had raised hopes that they could not fulfill and had alienated a conservative upper class.

The Chileanization of the foreign-owned copper industry was more easily achieved. Like most Latin American countries, Chile was heavily dependent on the export of a single commodity to finance its development. When copper prices dropped, so did the performance of the nation's economy. Naturally Chileans resented their vulnerability; what made it worse was that foreigners, not Chileans, owned and operated most of the mines. The Christian Democrats and the Marxists had responded to popular sentiments in their presidential campaigns, promising to put the mines under national control. But whereas Allende called for their complete nationalization, Frei proposed a less drastic solution, one he labeled *Chileanization*. Rather than evict the Braden, Anaconda, and Kennicott corporations, the Chileanization law, which gained legislative approval with Conservative Party support, only authorized the Chilean government's purchase of 51 percent of the shares in the largest mine (owned by the Braden Company). The deal, which was supported by moderates within the PDC and tolerated by foreign investors, was severely criticized by Socialists and Communists as a

Table 7.3. *Chilean presidential election, 1970*

Party	Male voters	Female voters	Total	Percentage
National Party (PN)				
Jorge Alessandri	479,104	557,174	1,036,278	35.3
Christian Democratic Party (PDC)				
Radomiro Tomic	392,736	432,113	824,849	28.1
Popular Unity Party (UP)				
Salvador Allende	631,863	443,753	1,075,616	36.6

sellout to foreign interests. Frei nevertheless held firm to his moderate course, arguing that anything more radical would drive foreign investors from the country and severely damage the economy. The issue became one of the most controversial the Christian Democrats faced during Frei's tenure because it forced them to confront directly the costs of compromising with the foreigners whose control over the Chilean economy they were trying to reduce. It divided the party during the 1970 presidential campaign and gave the Marxists another popular issue to use against the PDC.

The limits of Chilean democracy: the Allende years

Under what condition does the democratic game work in Latin America? And under what conditions does it fail? Clearly we are better able to answer the second question than the first, since experience with failures is much greater than with successes. In most instances the democratic game is insecure from the outset because some players simply refuse to live by its rules. But there have been some outstanding exceptions, and none greater than Chile, where for forty years all players tolerated one another and abided by constitutional rules. But even the Chilean democracy did not endure, as the world discovered one September day in 1973 when the Chilean military seized control.

Democracy's destruction began with the 1970 presidential election (Table 7.3). Like the previous one, it started as a three-way contest among the National Party (formed by the merger of the Conservative and Liberal parties in 1966), which nominated ex-president Jorge Alessandri; the Christian Democrats, who chose Radomiro Tomic, leader of the PDC left wing, since Frei could not succeed himself; and Popular Unity (successor to FRAP), which went again with socialist Salvador Allende. Alessandri promised to halt the reformism begun by the PDC, Tomic offered a more radical reformist program than Frei's, and Allende proposed a peaceful socialist revolution. The conservatives once again held the trump card, for if they supported the PDC, it would undoubtedly win, but if they supported Alessandri, the election would be close, with any one of the three the possible winner.

This time the conservatives decided to gamble, now convinced they would gain nothing from another reformist Christian Democratic president. Bolstered by preelection polls that predicted Alessandri's victory, they fully expected to win a three-way race. Tomic believed that another alliance with the conservatives would retard reform and make a mockery of his promise of radical change. Yet, because the leadership of the PDC refused to allow him to pursue a coalition with the Marxist parties, as he desired, he was forced to adopt an electoral strategy that sought to undercut Allende's support by appealing again to the urban and rural poor as well as to the middle sectors.

But when the ballots were counted, Salvador Allende the socialist, not Tomic or Alessandri, was the victor. In the weeks that followed, the National and Christian Democratic Parties had to make some of the hardest strategic decisions ever to face Chilean party leaders. Because Salvador Allende had received less than a majority of the popular vote (36.6 percent), he could not be inaugurated without confirmation by a majority in Congress. And for that he needed the support of the parties outside his coalition since they still controlled two-thirds of the seats.

The Christian Democrats had to decide for themselves if Allende and his socialism were tolerable and, if not, what their refusal to confirm him would do to the democratic system they claimed to respect. The United States government and Chilean Conservatives did what they could to provoke military intervention and PDC opposition to confirmation, including a scheme to vote no and then hold new elections in which Eduardo Frei could legally become the PDC candidate. But their efforts came to naught, and Allende was confirmed with PDC support.

Chile's experiment in socialist government lasted only three years, however, leaving it to us to determine why the nation's constitutional rules were so cruelly broken after being respected for over forty years without interruption. Was it because constitutional government and socialist politics were incompatible, as some contend? Why should they be? After all, socialists have governed recently in Greece, Spain, and France without meeting the Chilean fate. And what about foreign involvement? Was the United States government responsible for Allende's downfall, adding him to its list of deposed leftists it found intolerable? Clearly, the abrupt termination of constitutional democracy in Chile raised a host of challenging questions about the nature of class conflict, foreign intervention, and the strength of democratic institutions. It also offers insights into political tolerance and how it is shaped by economic and political self-interest.

Our search for answers to these questions must begin with Salvador Allende and the challenge that he faced when it all began. Even before his campaign for president was launched his prospects actually looked quite bleak. In fact, his Marxist coalition barely made it to the polls. Many Socialists wanted to boycott the elections to protest Chile's bourgeois democracy, which they claimed had always been rigged against them. Only when half of the members of the Socialist Party's central committee agreed to abstain from its endorsement vote did Allende secure the party's nomination. But even then the Popular Unity (UP) coalition of Socialists, Communists, and three minor parties had no chance of victory if the Conservatives agreed to support the Christian Democratic candidate, as they had done in 1964. But they ran their own candidate and in doing so gave the UP the opportunity it needed.

Once in office Allende still faced divisions within his own ranks. The collaboration of the Socialists and the Communists had been motivated more by political necessity than mutual affection. The Socialists were the more doctrinaire of the two, eager to achieve the immediate creation of a socialist economy, whereas the Communists were pragmatic, more willing to compromise with opponents in order to avoid provoking military intervention. Although the two parties agreed on most of their ultimate goals, their debates over strategy, economic policy, and the mobilization of the masses placed constraints on Allende that would never have been tolerated by Marxists like Fidel Castro in Cuba.

Instead of viewing Salvador Allende as the leader of a typical Marxist party-state, we should see him for what he was: an elected president who was plagued by problems common to the leaders of minority coalitions who still face legislative opposition. The radical character of his program merely made his job harder by threatening Chilean entrepreneurs and causing the United States government to do what it could to prevent Chile from becoming a Marxist success.

As a political strategist, Allende was actually quite cautious. He knew that his electoral victory had been slim and that he lacked majority support in Congress. Although he was eager to achieve his economic revolution, he did not want to antagonize his Christian Democratic opponents. Consequently, he sought to deprive the economic elite of its wealth and power without harming the middle sectors. In practice, this meant a gradual nationalization of large enterprises accompanied by a prohibition on measures that might deprive the middle sectors of their wealth and property. Separating the two sets of interests proved quite difficult in practice, however, since most professionals, technicians, and white-collar workers depended on private enterprise for their livelihood. As Allende's critics within his own coalition warned him, nationalization, even if carried out in a gradual manner, would sooner or later threaten all members of the Chilean bourgeoisie, making the cultivation of their support a hopeless and self-defeating endeavor. Nevertheless, Allende held firm to his original strategy, guided by the belief that his revolution would be achieved only if he avoided a direct confrontation with potential middle-sector opponents.

Allende's development program had two primary goals: the gradual socialization of the means of production and an immediate increase in mass consumption to build a working-class–middle-sector alliance. The first was essential if the state was to reallocate society's resources in a more equitable manner; the second was prompted by Allende's determination to secure a majority of the popular vote in future elections as well as protect his government from its upper-class and foreign enemies.

During 1971 and 1972, the government moved swiftly toward the socialization of Chile's capitalist economy. Its immediate objective was the creation of a mixed economy that included three sectors: one controlled entirely by the state, another composed of public–private enterprises where the state was dependent on the private sector's supply of technology, and a third consisting of small private firms involved in retail sales. The government requisitioned some enterprises without compensation, using an old law that permitted the seizure of firms that refused to produce to capacity. The local plants of multinational firms like Ford, General Motors, and Dow Chemical were among those taken in this manner. Others – for example, all banks, Coca-Cola, Du Pont, and Bethlehem Steel – were purchased at book value. And a few, most notably the Kennicott, Braden, and Anaconda copper mines, were nationalized with congressional approval but denied compensation because, according to Popular Unity officials, they were guilty of extracting excess profits and therefore had already received their compensation. Many foreign firms, however, were left untouched in the initial round because they provided essential goods and services; among these were IBM, Xerox, Mobil, Texaco, Exxon, and RCA. In fact, Allende never went as far with nationalization as his more militant supporters would have preferred or his enemies had feared. Nevertheless, the nationalizations eventually alienated many Christian Democrats who were initially disposed to cooperate with the government; equally important, they also imposed an immense fiscal burden on the Chilean state that heavily taxed its limited resources.

As a Marxist, Allende believed that the proletariat would continue to be exploited as long as it was denied control over the means of production. And as an experienced campaigner and party leader, who had received less than 40 percent of the popular vote in 1970, he knew that his hope of electoral victory in the March 1973 congressional elections rested with the mobilization of the urban and rural poor and many in the middle sectors. Accordingly, he decreed across-the-board wage increases during 1971, expanded public works programs giving jobs to the unemployed, and limited the distribution of scarce foodstuffs primarily to retail outlets that served the urban poor. As a consequence, 1971 was a boom for Chilean workers, whose real income rose by an average of 40 percent during that year alone.

Popular Unity also had a plan for rural development. The Marxists had blamed Chile's failure to feed itself on the inefficient use of farmland. Moreover, the plight of the Chilean poor could be traced, they argued, to the antiquated class structure that prevailed in the countryside. Accordingly, Allende pledged himself to the speedy completion of Frei's agrarian reform program to improve the campesinos' existence and foster a higher level of production. Prompted by a wave of land seizures by impatient campesinos, Allende moved fast, expropriating and redistributing twice as much land in his first two years as Frei had done in his last three. In 1965, 55 percent of Chile's farmland was held by owners of farms that exceeded 200 acres in size, but by the end of 1972 only 2.9 percent was still left in such large, privately owned units. Expropriated lands were reorganized in several different ways, with some turned into agrarian reform centers or large production units controlled by those who worked them, and others, especially those of a more agroindustrial type such as cattle breeding, run as state farms by government administrators.

Four conditions had to be met for Allende's economic program to succeed. First, economic expansion had to be sustained in order to satisfy the demands of working-class and middle-sector consumers simultaneously. If it was not, shortages would develop, inflation increase, social tensions rise, and support for the government, especially among the middle sectors, decline. Second, the government had to gain enough control over the economy through its nationalizations to capture industrial and financial profits for the treasury and pay for its expansion of public works and other job-creating programs. Without substantial increased revenues, it would be forced to borrow heavily abroad or resort to inflationary Central Bank financing of the deficit. Third, exports, especially high foreign-exchange producers like copper, had to be increased to pay for capital and consumer-goods imports. This was crucial since Chile could expect little financial assistance from capitalist nations and international agencies who opposed its economic revolution. Finally, a rapid decline in agricultural production due to land expropriation had to be avoided. A drop in food production at a time of rising consumption would lead either to food shortages or increased imports to cover the deficit, neither of which Allende could afford. Obviously, the Allende program was plagued by high risks. If any one of these conditions were not met, serious problems would arise that might undermine the entire effort. Moreover, any failure could be easily exploited by enemies in the elite or from abroad who were determined to stop Allende's socialist revolution.

At first the program did quite well. In 1971 unemployment was reduced to nearly zero, the gross national product grew by nearly 9 percent, and prices rose by only 20 percent, slightly below the annual average of the Frei years. Despite expropriation and the controversy it caused, copper production also rose slightly. By taking a pragmatic approach to the Chilean economy rather than the more doctrinaire one recommended by members of his coalition, Allende had, it seemed, achieved the kind of economic growth and reallocation of income that would boost his political fortunes without inducing a violent reaction from his opponents.

But Allende's policies, it soon became apparent, were neither as bountiful nor as moderate as they first seemed. Cracks in his economic edifice, which began to appear in 1972, widened rapidly during the first half of 1973. Some were of his own making; others were promoted by his foreign and domestic opponents. Hidden from view in 1971 were several disturbing facts. Although consumption rose, gross domestic investment declined by 5 percent as private firms responded negatively to the threat of expropriation, and the state, already heavily involved in spending to increase consumption, did little investing. Moreover, the fiscal and monetary policies followed at the end of 1971 differed substantially from those proposed by Allende after his inauguration. First, public revenues were much less than intended (owing in part to the refusal of opponents in Congress to authorize tax increases), and expenditures were much greater. This forced Allende to increase the money supply by 100 percent to cover a fiscal deficit that was 71 percent larger than planned. Second, the balance of payments took a turn for the worse, accumulating a $315 million deficit in 1971 after a $91 million surplus in 1970. An overvalued exchange rate, increased imports to meet consumer demand, the accelerated flight of financial capital, and a 30-percent drop in copper prices all contributed to the deficit. To make matters worse on the supply side, agricultural production began to fall during the 1972–1973 harvest as the effects of low prices, a lack of seed and fertilizer, and administrative bottlenecks began to be felt. Finally, although the government managed to contain the inflationary effects of its program in 1971 with price controls, prices began to rise rapidly in late 1972 and continued into 1973, increasing 190 percent during the first nine months of the year alone (Table 7.4).

Inflation and shortages were not new to Chile, and governments had survived such conditions in the past. What made Allende's situation different was both the severity of the economic problems he faced in 1973 and the determination of his enemies to exploit them. Prominent among the latter were the United States government and the multinational firms with investments in Chile.

The administration of Richard Nixon was opposed to Chile's Marxist government and was determined to secure its demise through any means short of direct military intervention. One tactic was to limit

Table 7.4. *Chilean economic performance, 1971–3 (annual growth rates)*

	1971	1972	1973	1960–73
Gross national product at constant prices	8.9	1.0	−5.0	3.5
Gross domestic investment at constant prices	−5.0	1.6	−5.5	3.6
Retail price index	20.0	77.5	353.5	43.5

Source: World Bank, *World Tables 1976.* Washington, D.C., 1976, pp. 74–5.

the flow of financial assistance to Chile. Allende had been careful to make payments on Chile's foreign debt in order to keep his country's good credit rating. The United States government was, however, determined to undermine that rating by cutting off new credit to Chile and forcing Allende to request moratoriums on the payment of Chile's debt, something he reluctantly did in late 1971. As part of its campaign to isolate Chile financially, the United States disbursed only $15.5 million in previously authorized loans in 1971, while Chile was repaying $51.3 million in old debts. At the same time, the United States maintained a generous program of aid to the Chilean military as well as an estimated $8 million in covert assistance to several opposition groups. Pressure was also exerted by the American-owned copper companies, which, displeased with Allende's refusal to compensate them for their expropriated enterprises, tried to block the delivery of Chilean copper to the United States and European ports. The Chileans succeeded in bypassing some of the foreign embargoes and locating other sources of credit; nevertheless, the American blockade reduced Allende's policy options considerably.

The Popular Unity government might have survived the impediments placed in its path by President Nixon, but it could not overcome those imposed by an increasingly intractable and effective opposition within Chile that went to the streets to stop Allende. In September 1973, almost three years to the day after his election, they succeeded, but only after sacrificing Chile's democratic government to military wolves.

Allende had hoped to fortify his government by winning congressional elections in March 1973. As we can see from Table 7.5 the UP

Table 7.5. *Distribution of seats in Chilean Chamber of Deputies and Senate before and after 1973 elections*

Party	Chamber	Senate
Before 1973 elections		
CODE (PDC–PN alliance)	93	32
UP (Socialists, Communists, Radicals, et al.)	57	18
After 1973 elections		
CODE	87	30
UP	63	20

needed to gain nineteen seats in the Chamber of Deputies and eight in the Senate to gain majority control. Socialist and Communist Party organizers had worked hard after Allende's inauguration to enlist new voters, hoping that his initial populist wage and price policies would attract many to their ranks. Recognizing this, the Conservatives and the Christian Democrats joined ranks once again, merging their congressional campaigns to maximize their gains and prevent a UP victory in 1973. When the votes were counted it was apparent that Allende had been blocked once again, for the UP had secured only 44 percent of the popular vote and was still short of a majority in either house.

Elections were not the only way the opposition attacked. Even more effective in the long run was their mobilization of protests that virtually shut down the Chilean economy in mid-1973. After searching for vulnerable points in Allende's armor, the PDC and Conservatives, with financial help from the United States and Christian Democrats in Europe, decided to concentrate on the copper and trucking industries.

In April 1973, miners and technicians at the El Teniente copper mine went on strike. Despite their ideological sympathy for the Popular Unity government, they initially refused to accept its decision to reduce the amount of a promised wage increase in order to fight inflation. A month later a settlement was reached and most of the miners returned to work. However, a hard core of white-collar workers and technicians, encouraged by the PDC, remained on strike until July and did substantial damage to the production of copper. But the critical blow was struck by the trucking industry from June through August. Chile's truckers, most of whom are small, independent operators, had gone

on strike once before, in October 1972, to protest a government proposal to absorb them into a state trucking company. Backed by a
sympathy strike of retailers, they had forced Allende to declare a state
of siege, admit military officers to his cabinet, and eventually withdraw
the proposal. When they went on strike again in June 1973, they were
acting as part of a well-conceived opposition campaign to force the
government to halt its program of nationalization and chart a more
moderate course. There is general agreement that the truckers' strike,
which lasted until the coup of September 11, was the single most
important factor in paralyzing the Chilean economy and fomenting
political chaos during July and August 1973.

In the end, it was the military, emboldened by Conservative and
Christian Democratic protests and provoked by rising civil strife and
economic chaos, that abruptly brought Chile's brief socialist experiment to a close. The Chilean military, known since the 1930s for its
restraint in political matters, had been divided in its assessment of the
Popular Unity government and its program since Allende's inauguration. Some officers were willing to give the government their support
as long as it carried out its revolution in a constitutional manner;
members of this group, whose support Allende deliberately cultivated
and whom he trusted until the day of the coup, went so far as to join
Allende's cabinet in order to help him deal with violent opposition
protests. Others in the military opposed Allende and his attack on
Chilean capitalism from the outset, but did not undertake to overthrow
him until 1973, when increasing civil unrest and the encouragement
of the Christian Democrats gave them the political excuse they wanted.
By then, Allende's frantic last-minute efforts to deal with his collapsing
economy and work out a compromise with his opponents were not
enough to stop officers who were determined not only to evict Marxists
from the government but also to replace constitutional democracy
with authoritarianism.

What can we learn from the Chilean tragedy? First, it reminds us
how tentative and precarious democracy can be. As we learned at the
beginning of this chapter, there is no way of guaranteeing that democracy will work, for its survival hinges on the willingness of society's
most powerful citizens to live by its rules. Although minor lawbreakers
can be punished by the democratic state, the defiance of the mighty
will always undermine it. Liberal democratic politics is, to be sure,
sustained by something more than the narrow self-interests of players.

Constitutional rules are also derived from beliefs in values like liberty and legality. But there is always tension between the maintenance of these values for society as a whole and individual self-interest, and Chile serves to remind us how vulnerable the former is when the vital interests of powerful players are seriously threatened.

Democracy works best when the stakes in the game are not great. The less one stands to lose, the less threatened one is by possible defeat. Conversely, the greater the stakes, the greater the threat and the harder it becomes to achieve peaceful conflict resolution. Political conflicts had always been intense in Chile's democracy but their resolution had exacted few sacrifices by the upper class until the 1960s. The middle sectors and the elite of organized labor gradually gained admission to the game after 1930 and, in exchange for their moderation, were given some of the spoils. The Christian Democrats raised the stakes some-what in 1964 when they tried to reduce foreign control over the Chilean economy, increase workers' rights, and redistribute some rural property. That is why the Conservatives decided to fight back in the 1970 elections. Then Allende and the UP raised the stakes even more, when they attacked the resources on which the Chilean bourgeoisie and its foreign allies had relied for their power and its maintenance.

Rather than ask why Chilean democracy failed to withstand this kind of test, a more appropriate question is why anyone should have expected it to survive. Should not Allende have understood the im-possibility of his task at the outset, given the apparent incompatibility between liberal democracy and radical socialism? Perhaps, but it was not hard for Allende to convince himself that Chile would be different. He was, after all, an experienced politician who knew his country and its politics intimately. And by living by its rules all of his life he was rewarded with an opportunity to govern the nation. Allende had re-jected armed insurrection as a political strategy long before, eschewing violence in favor of living by democratic rules. Consequently, when blocked by the opposition, he relied on what he knew best: political dexterity and the authority of his office, neither of which was enough.

Today Allende's former colleagues, most of whom spent fifteen years in exile, continue to debate the wisdom of his strategy. Some insist that arming the masses was the only way to preserve the regime. The fact that Allende did not do so and was overthrown convinces them of the merit of their position. Others argue that such second-guessing ignores realities of power and political practice within Chile at the time: Arming the masses would have only provoked a coup sooner. The only real option he had, they argue, was moderation. Where he went wrong was not in his failure to engage the military in conflict, but in his excessive populism, which damaged the economy by raising consumption too rapidly, causing rampant inflation and shortages, both of which gave the opposition the issues it needed to mobilize the middle sectors, truckers, copper workers, and other consumers against the regime.

Disputes will persist, but if the Allende experience teaches us anything, it is the vulnerability of the democratic game to the intensification of conflict, especially over fundamental issues of economic development and the distribution of wealth. Tolerance is a fragile thing, and seldom does it survive anywhere when elites find themselves under assault by the masses.

Another chance

General Augusto Pinochet did not restore democratic government to Chile quickly as the Christian Democrats had hoped he would. Actually, he had no intention of doing so when he took over in 1973. Quite the opposite. Placing political order above everything else, and defining it in very conservative terms, he ruled the country tightly, using the armed forces and a sophisticated security organization to strip Chilean citizens of every political right that they had previously enjoyed. Guided by the belief that he was purging the entire society of the individuals and the ideas that were alien to his kind of nation, he became the proficient autocrat who adroitly established personal control over his armed forces by elevating a new generation of officers who pledged total loyalty to him. Hundreds of party leaders, especially from within the UP, labor leaders, student activists, journalists, and scholars were either killed, jailed for an extended time, or exiled. Many other Chileans left of their own free will. Amazingly, a nation that had thrived on competitive politics was suddenly transformed into a very secure police state, a sad reminder of how vulnerable democracy really is.

To his cabinet Pinochet brought civilian conservatives and technocrats whom he asked to replace the welfare state with a free economy that would rely on private capital for its future development. Gradually the effort brought wealth to big investors, and new growth to the economy, though only temporarily, as Chileans discovered when the world recession struck in 1981 and wiped out much of the growth that they had achieved during the previous four years. Chile did recover some a few years later and was singled out by free market economists for continued praise. Unfortunately, not everyone benefited from the gains made. While investors and professionals prospered, the working class suffered low wages and a denial of either economic or political power. Very little "trickled down" in Chile below the urban middle class.

In 1980 Pinochet asked his people to confirm a new constitution, calling it the first stage in a very gradual transition to a more orderly democracy of his own design. The document promised the public a plebiscite eight years later, and the election of a new congress not long after that. With no real choice to make, a majority voted in favor of his proposal.

When another plebiscite was held as promised in October 1988, the choice was different: Confirm Pinochet for eight more years in the presidency and he would allow the election of a new congress the following year; reject him and new presidential and congressional elections would be held within fifteen months. Despite the obvious appeal of the second option to democrats, Pinochet was convinced that he would triumph because he believed that Chileans had become as frightened as he was of real democracy. Having spent fifteen years reminding his people of the "chaos" that had accompanied the Allende government, and warning them that communists would seize their every possession if they were allowed to come above ground once again, he was certain of victory. But he was wrong this time: 54 percent voted against eight more years of Pinochet. Obviously most citizens were ready to restore something that they had once called Chilean democracy. Pinochet was surprised by the results, but he declared that he would keep his promise to hold a free presidential election at the end of 1989.

Further reading

Democracy: general

Hirschman, Albert O. *Journeys toward Progress*. New York: Norton, 1964.
Needler, Martin. *The Problem of Democracy in Latin America*. Lexington, MA: Lexington Books, 1987.

Wiarda, Howard, ed. *The Continuing Struggle for Democracy in Latin America.* Boulder, CO: Westview Press, 1980.

Chile

Allende Gossens, Salvador. *Chile's Road to Socialism,* ed. Joan Garces. Baltimore: Penguin Books, 1973.
Davis, Nathaniel. *The Last Two Years of Salvador Allende.* Ithaca, NY: Cornell University Press, 1985.
Debray, Regis. *The Chilean Revolution: Conversations with Allende.* New York: Pantheon Books, 1971.
De Vylder, Stefan. *Allende's Chile: The Political Economy of the Rise and Fall of Unidad Popular.* New York: Cambridge University Press, 1976.
Feinberg, Richard E. *The Triumph of Allende: Chile's Legal Revolution.* New York: New American Library (Mentor Books), 1972.
Fleet, Michael. *The Rise and Fall of Chilean Christian Democracy.* Princeton, NJ: Princeton University Press, 1985.
Francis, Michael. *The Allende Victory: An Analysis of the 1970 Chilean Presidential Election.* Tucson: University of Arizona Press, 1973.
Gil, Federico. *The Political System of Chile.* Boston: Houghton Mifflin, 1966.
Kaufman, Robert. *The Politics of Land Reform in Chile 1950–1970: Public Policy, Political Institutions, and Social Change.* Cambridge, MA: Harvard University Press, 1972.
Loveman, Brian. *Chile: The Legacy of Hispanic Capitalism.* 2nd edition. New York: Oxford University Press, 1986.
Petras, James. *Politics and Social Forces in Chilean Development.* Berkeley, CA: University of California Press, 1969.
Pollack, Benny, and Herman Rosenkranz. *Revolutionary Social Democracy: The Chilean Socialist Party.* New York: St. Martins Press, 1986.
Roxborough, Ian, Phil O'Brien, and Jackie Roddick. *Chile: The State and Revolution.* London: Macmillan Press, 1977.
Sigmund, Paul. *The Overthrow of Allende and the Politics of Chile 1964–1974.* Pittsburgh: University of Pittsburgh Press, 1978.
Smith, Brian. *The Church and Politics in Chile: Challenges to Modern Capitalism.* Princeton, NJ: Princeton University Press, 1982.
Stallings, Barbara. *Class Conflict and Economic Development in Chile, 1958–1973.* Stanford, CA: Stanford University Press, 1978.
United States Congress, House Committee on Foreign Affairs, Subcommittee on Inter-American Affairs. *United States and Chile during the Allende Years, 1970–1973.* 94th Congress, 1st Session, 1975.
United States Senate, Select Committee to Study Governmental Operations with Respect to Intelligence Activities. *Covert Action in Chile, 1963–1973.* 94th Congress, 1st Session, 1975.
Valenzuela, Arturo. *The Breakdown of Democratic Regimes: Chile.* Baltimore: The Johns Hopkins University Press, 1978.
Valenzuela, J. Samuel, and Arturo Valenzuela, eds. *Chile: Politics and Society.* New Brunswick, NJ: Transaction Books, 1976.
Military Rule in Chile: Dictatorship and Oppositions. Baltimore: The Johns Hopkins University Press, 1986.

8. Venezuela: democracy preserved

There is nothing in Venezuela's history that would have caused one to predict its governance by a democratic regime during the last half of the twentieth century. On the contrary, torn by regionalism and civil war during the nineteenth century and ruled by an old-fashioned dictator until 1935, Venezuela seemed doomed to autocratic politics. Escaping such a fate was a major achievement, one that was made possible by the Venezuelans' having a valuable resource – petroleum – which, for a time, supplied the income needed to finance the nation's development without threatening the wealthy; and by a generation of politicians who proved exceptionally skilled at creating mass organizations, placating the armed forces, and securing agreements among contending players that laid a foundation for constitutional rule.

Acción Democrática

Until 1935 the Venezuelan game was a traditional, dictatorial one. Between 1908 and 1935 the country was governed by Juan Vincente Gomez, a heavy-handed *caudillo* who modeled his rule after that of his nineteenth-century predecessors (Table 8.1). Among the few who protested his brutality was a group of university students who came to be known as the Generation of 1928, for the year in which they started their campaign for democratic government. It was from their nucleus that the Acción Democrática (AD) party was formed a decade later.

Gomez died in 1935, and the Venezuelan oligarchy was quick to replace him with officials who were no more eager to democratize the nation's politics than they were. They ran the nation with little serious opposition, and those who did protest were jailed, exiled, or forced underground. Nevertheless, quietly but diligently, the future leaders of the AD spent a decade roaming the country, clandestinely recruiting campesino leaders and organized laborers into their party, laying the foundation for a broadly based, national political organization. They

193

reasoned that, if they were to rule the nation one day, their chance would come only after they had secured enough popular support to force the ruling conservatives to compete with them in open elections.

The AD eventually succeeded but, when it did, the door was opened by the military and not through negotiated concessions from the ruling elite. To this day Acción Democrática leaders deny that they conspired with the young officers who were responsible for the 1945 coup, arguing that to have done so would have made a mockery of their claims of being different from those who had ruled the nation using military might. Whether or not they actually did conspire, it is clear that with the exception of guerrilla warfare, which the democratically inclined AD leaders had rejected from the start, the coup was the only means available for dislodging the oligarchs at the time.

True to their word, Acción Democrática leaders persuaded the military to hold free elections of delegates to a constituent assembly, which wrote a new constitution in 1947. To no one's surprise, AD polled 79 percent of the assembly vote, and a few months later won the presidency with 74 percent and captured two-thirds of the seats in the new Congress. The magnitude of its victory bore witness to the success of the mass organization strategy, which by 1948 had brought 300,000 urban workers into the AD-controlled Venezuelan Workers' Confederation (CTV), and 43,000 peasants into its Venezuelan Campesino Federation (FCV).

Venezuela's new democracy was short-lived, however (see Table 8.1). In 1948 the conservative opposition struck back with its own military coup, sending the AD leaders back into exile, and disbanding all labor and peasant organizations. Massive electoral victories and a new constitution had not been enough to ensure that all players would conform to the new rules of the Venezuelan game. Acción Democrática's success had been too swift and its break with the past too sharp for the Venezuelan elite. When the government tried to use its mandate to execute a sweeping agrarian reform and revise the petroleum law, conservatives responded with a coup.

AD leaders spent the next ten years in exile reassessing their past campaigns and planning future ones. They came away from their deliberations chastened and less radical, convinced that more caution was required in their relations with Venezuela's agricultural and commercial elite and that more attention had to be given to creating a new role for the military in the democratic game. Despite the immense

Table 8.1. *Venezuela: historical background*

1821	Independence from Spain
1859	Federal (civil) War lasting four years, killing 40,000 and leaving country in economic ruin
1870	Eighteen-year dictatorship of Liberal Antonio Guzmán Blanco begins
1908	Dictatorship of Juan Vicente Gómez begins
1921	Export of petroleum commences
1935	Juan Vicente Gómez dies
	Generation of 1928 student activists, led by Rómulo Betancourt, create Movimiento de Organización Venezolana (ORVE, later the Partido Demócrata Nacional), the predecessor of the Acción Democrática Party
1945	Unión Patriótica Militar, organized by young officers and supported by the Unión Democrática, overthrows conservative government of Isaias Medina Angarita
1947	Under new constitution Acción Democrática wins presidential election and congressional majority
1948	Acción Democrática government is overthrown by military; dictatorship of General Marcos Pérez Jiménez is created
1958	Military overthrows Pérez Jiménez government
1959	Rómulo Betancourt of Acción Democrática elected president
1963	Raúl Leoni, of Acción Democrática, elected president
1968	Rafael Caldera, of Christian Democratic Party (COPEI) elected president
1973	Carlos Andrés Peréz of Acción Democrática elected president
1976	All foreign petroleum and iron-mining firms nationalized
1978	Luis Herrera Campins of Christian Democratic Party elected president
1983	Jaime Lusinchi, of Acción Democrática, elected president
1988	Carlos Andrés Peréz elected president; riots to protest government austerity policies leave 300 persons dead

popularity of democratic government, it was still vulnerable to the economic power and military strength of its opponents. If reform measures were to succeed, it was concluded, they would have to be implemented slowly and carefully, avoiding direct attacks on those who were capable of striking back.

After a decade of exile AD leaders returned to try once again when officers, annoyed by the abuses of dictator Marcos Pérez Jimenez, removed him in 1958 and called for elections. This time Rómulo Betancourt, Raúl Leoni, and their AD colleagues rejected their original vote-maximizing strategy in favor of alliances and preelection agreements with opposition parties and economic interest groups. Confident that they would capture the presidency, they concentrated on sharing power in order to secure the acceptance of the constitutional rules by their competitors. They promised to consult with the other parties when formulating reform policy and to share government patronage with them. They insisted that agrarian reform, government promotion of industrialization, and greater national control over petroleum resources remain their objectives, but promised moderation in the pursuit of each. And, equally important, they gained the support of the Venezuelan armed forces by offering them money to improve facilities and buy new weapons.

The AD strategy reduced fears by reassuring the opponents of reform that moderation would prevail this time; it carried a high price however, for, to meet his obligations, Betancourt had to modify the party's original platform substantially. Instead of redistributing wealth and property, he was forced to draw heavily on government revenues from petroleum sales to finance increased social services and to use public lands to satisfy the demands of the landless.

AD's primary concern when Venezuelans went to the polls in 1959 was not its defeat – for it was confident of victory – but how much larger its opponents had become, among them the Christian Democratic Party (COPEI), formed a decade before by conservatives and Catholic reformers; and the Republican Democratic Union (URD), a party dedicated primarily to the candidacy of Jovito Villalba, a member of the Generation of 1928 who had abandoned his colleagues several years before. Both did cut into Acción Democrática's base of support, leaving Betancourt with only 49.2 percent of the popular vote, compared with the URD's Jovito Villalba's 34.6 percent, and COPEI's Rafael Caldera's 16.2 percent. AD's strength, as before, was in the countryside, where it received 66 percent of the rural vote. Of greater concern for future elections was its failure to gain the votes of more than 13 percent in the cities.

Party government and reform policy

Once elected, Betancourt invited the Christian Democrat and URD Parties to form a coalition government, and together they secured swift legislative passage of the programs they had agreed upon before the election. Subsequently the coalition crumbled, with the departure of the URD in 1960 and the COPEI in 1963, but by then it had served its purpose by reinforcing an ethic of peaceful competition and legislative cooperation among the country's principal parties. Clearly the Venezuelan experience indicates the utility of collusion among the competing parties during the formative stage of constitutional government in countries where a tradition of intense conflict and distrust prevails. Though hardly sufficient by itself, it may be a necessary condition for launching a competitive political process. Competition is quite risky for most participants, especially those who do not enjoy an immediate electoral advantage; only by assuring them that they can trust the victors to involve them in governing the nation can you expect them to play by the rules.

It was not just the other parties that weakened Acción Democrática after 1959. They also had to deal with divisions within their own ranks. From the outset the left wing of the party opposed its conciliatory strategy and policy moderation, and in April 1960 a pro-Castro faction gave up and left the party. A second split occurred in early 1962 when a group of middle-level party leaders broke with Betancourt and the old guard, forming a small party of their own. In 1967 the AD split once again over the selection of the party's presidential candidate. Although the first two splits did little damage, the third one cost it a presidential election. Led by the party president, Luis Beltrán Prieto Figueroa, whom a large minority of the party members supported for president in 1968, the rebels formed their own party when the dominant faction, guided by Betancourt, insisted on the nomination of Interior Minister Gonzalo Barrios. The result was the unexpected victory of Christian Democrat Rafael Caldera in 1968.

This brings us to the third condition that affects the survival of democratic reform parties: their ability to win elections. As we can see from Table 8.2, despite its failure to secure a majority of the vote, Acción Democrática won reelection in 1963, but went down in defeat in 1968. The COPEI victory in 1968 was not, however, as great a threat to AD and its reform program as first appeared. By the time of its election, COPEI had already adopted much of AD's platform and during its campaign had promised to retain most of the reforms already implemented. Consequently, AD's leaders were called upon to do little more than tolerate a familiar and trusted rival whose legislative program was virtually a carbon copy of their own. The primary threat posed by COPEI was not its possible maltreatment of the AD but its exploitation of its newly acquired power to increase its popular sup-

Table 8.2. *Venezuelan presidential elections, 1958–88 (percentage of total vote)*

	AD	COPEI	Others
1958	49.2	15.2	35.6
1963	32.8	20.2	47.0
1968	28.2	29.0	42.8
1973	48.6	36.8	14.6
1978	43.3	46.6	10.1
1983	56.8	34.4	8.6
1988	54.9	39.9	5.2

Source: Venezuelan Embassy.

port, thereby keeping the AD from recapturing the nation's highest office in 1973. But that seemed unlikely given AD's strong, if somewhat diminished, appeal to the Venezuelan masses. Consequently AD leaders stepped aside, proudly boasting that their electoral defeat marked a major triumph for democracy, giving the nation its first peaceful transfer of power from the leader of one party to the democratically elected leader of another.

AD self-confidence proved justified, for after the reunification of the party AD candidate Carlos Andrés Pérez gained 44.3 percent of the popular vote, and the presidency, in 1973. But the AD comeback proved to be only temporary; in 1978 the electorate turned again to COPEI, electing Luis Herrera Campins president in a very close contest. Then in 1983 they brought Acción Democrática back, electing Jaime Lusinchi president in a landslide. Clearly something remarkable was happening: Not only had Venezuelan democracy survived for two decades, but for the fourth time in a row the party of the incumbent president was defeated at the polls. Equally significant, the country's multiparty system had become essentially a two-party one in which the electorate seemed as comfortable with COPEI as it was with the AD.

How do we account for this unusual development? Part of the explanation lies in public acceptance of both parties as the principal founders of the country's constitutional order, which gives them a legitimacy and respect not available to parties created after 1959. It was also caused by their ideological convergence. Previously more conservative than the AD, the COPEI was forced by electoral realities to accept AD's agrarian, social, and petroleum policies. Moreover, after the initial reforms had been put into effect in the 1960s, both parties came to share in the defense of the new order, each relying on the other to protect the privileges of the country's new ruling elite.

Equally important is the riches each party has at its disposal for campaigning. Wealthy Venezuelans, labor unions, and government bureaucrats want to be on the winning side and are eager to help probable winners by donating to their campaign chests. In 1978, for example, AD and COPEI candidates spent an estimated $125 million (or $8 per capita) to discredit their opponents. Moreover, each presidential candidate was advised by a noted North American consultant; the victor, COPEI's Luis Herrera, a rather aloof politician, was converted by media expert David Garth into a folksy, tireless friend of the common people who claimed to stand with them against a new upper class created by AD policies. For two months prior to the election radio and television stations broadcast hundreds of party ads. The more AD spends on its campaign the more COPEI spends to keep up with it, making Venezuela's democracy one of the most expensive in the world.

Few Latin Americans embraced the progressive modernization development strategy more enthusiastically than Romulo Betancourt and Acción Democrática. No wonder, since they were among its original authors. Exiled by the military coup that installed autocrat Marcos Pérez Jiménez in 1948, they took their notions of agrarian reform, industrialization, and social policy with them to the United Nations Economic Commission for Latin America in Santiago, Chile, and to Mexico City where they refined them in dialogues with foreign colleagues who shared their reformist objectives. These collective efforts, along with the lessons that were learned from the policy experiments of the Mexicans in the 1930s and 1940s, gave birth to the progressive modernization approach to development.

The Venezuelans have one advantage over other reformers in the hemisphere, namely, the income needed to finance reform in its earliest stages. The sale of petroleum has paid most of the government's bills since the 1920s. Its actual value to Venezuela has varied, depending on the price it brought on the world market and how much of the companies' profits the Venezuelan government took from the multinational firms that extracted, transported, refined, and marketed it.

As long as there was a large surplus of petroleum on the world market, prices were low and revenues inadequate to finance the AD's ambitious development programs. Moreover, the smaller Venezuela's share of the profits, the less Venezuelans had when prices rose. Therefore, action was necessary on both fronts.

This is why Betancourt placed so much stress on the development of a coherent, nationalistic petroleum policy from the earliest days of the AD party. His proposals consisted of two parts: One was to gradually increase the country's share of the revenues from sales abroad, and the other was to work in collaboration with other petroleum-producing nations to gain more control over the world supply and, therefore, over the world price, with the aim of raising the price as high as possible.

Nationalization of the foreign holdings would obviously have accomplished the first objective but the Venezuelan government was unprepared to manage the industry on its own when the AD first came to power in 1946. What they wanted was a strategy for increasing their income without alienating the firms whose technology and marketing networks were needed to extract and sell petroleum. Their solution was to gradually increase the nation's share, always leaving enough to keep the firms producing. In 1946 they increased Venezuela's portion from 30 to 50 percent; and then, when they returned in 1959, they raised it to 70 percent, where it remained until 1976 when the industry was finally nationalized.

Nationalization had been contemplated for some time but not until the AD lost the presidency to the COPEI and needed a popular campaign issue did AD candidate Carlos Andrés Pérez promise nationalization if elected in 1973. Equally important was that it was finally feasible, for by then several thousand Venezuelans had learned how to manage the facilities. Moreover, the Venezuelan government had accumulated the financing necessary to purchase the installations, thereby avoiding the more risky alternative of confiscating them without compensation to the powerful multinationals. With near unanimous congressional support for the nationalization bill, it was passed in 1975 and implemented in 1976. To assure the stability of the industry, many foreign technicians were hired by PETROVEN, the newly created government corporation, and the original foreign firms were granted the right to market the product as they had done before.

The AD's second objective – securing a high price on the world market – was harder to achieve since most of the forces that determined the price were out of its control. But here too the Venezuelans were patient, persistent, clever, and successful. Under the leadership of Betancourt's Minister of Petroleum and Mines, Juan Pablo Pérez Alonso, the Organization of Petroleum-Exporting Countries (OPEC) was formed by Third World petroleum producers in 1960. Not until the early 1970s, however, when world demand for petroleum had risen to record levels, were the OPEC nations able to take advantage of their cartel. Exploiting the industrial nations' need for abundant supplies of imported fuel, they raised the price from $4.60 a barrel in 1973 to more than $12.00 two years later. The economic impact was immense: The Venezuelan balance-of-payments surplus, which was at a respectable $372 million in 1972, rose to $4.3 billion (American billions) in 1974.

Venezuela's petroleum policies, with their gradual but deliberate assertion of national control, are regarded by many as one of the highest achievements of reformism in contemporary Latin America. It was an impressive feat. Yet before one holds it up as a model for others, it should be noted that Venezuela enjoyed several advantages over its neighbors. Petroleum was a unique commodity during the 1970s, when none other, except perhaps gold, enjoyed such inelastic demand. Moreover, because of petroleum's international visibility and because Venezuela's democratic regime was held in such high esteem in Europe and the United States, political retaliation against Venezuela was out of the question. To their credit the Venezuelans exploited these advantages adroitly, but they were fortunate to have them to exploit.

Agrarian reform was equally vital to the AD program. Not only were reforms needed to bolster the nation's agriculture and improve the condition of the rural poor, but the AD was also compelled to deliver on its promises to the many campesinos who joined the party years before through the Venezuelan Campesino Confederation and supplied most of its votes in 1959. The agrarian reform law was the product of interparty bargaining prior to Betancourt's election. Moderate in design, it required the government to purchase land at market prices, rather than at declared tax value as in Chile, a concession aimed at placating landowners that few countries other than oil-rich Venezuela could have afforded. It authorized the expropriation of private property not in production, grazing lands, and properties occupied but not owned by tenant farmers and sharecroppers, but most of the land distributed was taken from government reserves rather than private holdings, lowering the program's cost and reducing opposition to it. Of the estimated 300,000 families who needed land, approximately 100,000 received it between 1960 and 1970, a major accomplishment in comparison with the performance of most agrarian reform programs in Latin America, though nevertheless one that fell short of government objectives.

The law was intended not only to improve the condition of campesinos but also to promote the more productive use of privately owned land. And here it was even more successful. Under threat of expropriation, farm production increased dramatically after 1960, rising in value by 58 percent in ten years and making Venezuela self-sufficient in most commodities. Nevertheless, in the 1970s the agrarian reform program was still a matter of controversy in Venezuela, though in contrast to the early years the criticism came increasingly from the Left rather than the Right, with the former claiming that agrarian reform had done more for the large commercial farmer than for the rural poor, leaving the country with a rural proletariat that was migrating to the cities in greater numbers than ever before.

The nationalization of oil and agrarian reform laid the foundation needed to accomplish a third objective: the industrialization of the Venezuelan economy. Without industry, AD leaders argued, economic growth would collapse once the nation's mineral resources were exhausted. The Betancourt administration dedicated itself to a program of centrally planned development that included the creation of a large and diverse universal sector to reduce the country's dependence on petroleum exports. Industrial development objectives were set in successive five-year plans drawn up by CORDIPLAN, the nation's planning agency, and supervised by the Ministry of Development and the autonomous Venezuelan Development Corporation. The private sector was to assume the largest burden for plan implementation, but the most spectacular achievements were those of public enterprises like the Venezuelan Guayana Corporation, an organization created to supervise one of the most ambitious regional development projects in Latin America. Located in the basin of the Orinoco River, the project included hydroelectric facilities, iron-ore mines, steel and aluminum industries, and several petrochemical enterprises. The Venezuelan Development Corporation has financed many other public and private ventures; after specializing in import-substitution industries for six years, it switched to intermediate and capital goods enterprises in 1966. Largely because of these efforts, the value of manufacturing in constant dollars was 240 percent greater in 1980 than it was in 1960. Though still heavily dependent on its petroleum industry, Venezuela finally began to construct an industrial base intended to sustain the economy once petroleum resources were exhausted.

The price of petroleum

Prosperity is not assured by the discovery of petroleum, even in the age of OPEC, as the Iranians, Nigerians, and Mexicans will testify. So will the Venezuelans. Twenty years ago they appeared to be more fortunate than the others, for not only were their mineral resources abundant, but their population was also quite small (only 7.4 million in 1960). Moreover, they were governed by a constitutional regime whose leaders shared a commitment to economic development and social reform. Nevertheless it did not turn out the way it had been planned.

The Venezuelans had become accustomed to steady economic growth, only to be shocked when it stopped in 1979. After averaging 5.7 percent annually between 1960 and 1975, the GDP was increased by only 0.9 percent in 1979 and then declined by 1.6 percent in 1980. Simultaneously, the nation's debts to foreign banks suddenly rose, reaching a record $32 million in 1982, one of the highest on a per capita basis for any nation in the world. Why the swift change? The answer lies in the very nature of petroleum-induced development.

In the 1970s petroleum gave some Third World nations unprecedented development opportunities, but like all opportunities it carried some risks. The possession and export of a valuable commodity encouraged officials to hope that its sale would finance an economic development that would lead to reductions in the nation's dependence on foreign finance and trade over the long haul. The vision is compelling, but on the way to making it reality the nation must become heavily dependent on the sale of a single, if lucrative, mineral. Thus, ironically, an increase in short-term dependence is necessary to achieve what one hopes will be greater economic independence. So it was in Venezuela. If one measures a nation's dependence on trade by the ratio of total imports and exports of goods and services to the gross domestic product, it increased from 45 percent in 1970, when oil prices and imports by Venezuela were modest, to 108 percent in 1980 during the oil boom, making it the most trade-dependent nation in South America. (In contrast, the ratio was 80 percent in Chile, 51 in Argentina, and 23 in Brazil.) Venezuela was richer than before, but it also became much more vulnerable.

AD leaders rapidly accelerated economic modernization after 1973, basing their investment decisions on estimates of future income from petroleum exports, convinced that it would rise through the efforts of OPEC to control its supply internationally. If their revenue estimates proved correct, as they hoped, all would go well; but if they were incorrect, they would face a new problem, namely, insufficient income to pay for the expensive investments they had made, just as Mexico had. If that happened, they would have little choice but to borrow heavily abroad to pay their bills, thereby increasing their dependence on foreign banks; or they could close down their projects, which would undoubtedly provoke hostile reactions from the contractors, national business, and consumers who were counting on them. Unfortunately for the Venezuelans their optimism did prove unfounded and, consequently, they faced an unprecedented crisis in 1979.

President Carlos Andrés Pérez had borrowed heavily abroad to pay for the AD projects, anticipating that oil revenues would rise fast enough to handle the nation's debts as payments came due. But he guessed wrong. Energy conservation in the industrial nations, a world recession, and rising interest rates in 1980 cut world consumption of petroleum and with it Venezuelan income. Pérez's successor, Christian Democrat Luis Herrera, a candidate who had exploited the "mismanagement" issue during the 1978 campaign, had no choice but to impose an austerity program, causing a generation of Venezuelans to discover for the first time that their nation's economic growth could not be taken for granted.

The world economy was not the only culprit, however; the ambitions of democratic politicians also bear some of the blame. One of the virtues of democratic government is said to be its responsiveness to the wants and needs of the electorate. Yet wants are unlimited, whereas government resources are quite finite. This may be obvious, but it does not prevent politicians from making promises to constituents that far exceed their capacity to finance them. Moreover, democratic politics encourages short-term thinking by presidents who know they will depart after only five years in office, so it is not unusual for them to try to deliver as much as their constituents demand. What matters, as even the United States government discovered in the 1980s, is how easily they can live beyond the limitations imposed by domestic resources. The United States government borrowed money; and so did the Venezuelans after the new wealth they had acquired by raising oil prices in 1973 bolstered creditor confidence in their ability to repay. For ambitious politicians like President Pérez who wanted to build a stronger and less vulnerable AD and become the Betancourt of his generation, it seemed the perfect opportunity.

Pérez went on a spending binge using oil revenues and borrowed funds to subsidize private business, expand government enterprises, and nearly double the number of public employees in just five years. By the time he stepped down in 1978, an estimated 25 percent of the country's work force was employed by the Venezuelan government and its many enterprises. To make matters worse, most of his projects proved to be much more expensive than originally planned, forcing him to increase the nation's debt rapidly to finance them.

The Christian Democrats campaigned against what they claimed were the excesses and corruption of the Pérez government, promising to end the binge in order to get some control over expenditures without halting the nation's economic prosperity. Their candidate, Luis Herrera, won in 1978, but once in office conditions forced him to slow the economy even more than he expected. For the first time in almost three decades the Venezuelans, who had enjoyed constant economic growth and rising consumption, suddenly began to wonder if they really were as blessed as they believed. No one feared that these new difficulties would undermine their democracy, yet they were no longer certain about where they were headed. Nevertheless, most Venezuelans simply refused to let their doubts take control of them.

After five difficult years under Herrera, the Venezuelans returned Acción Democrática in December 1983, giving Jaime Lusinchi a massive victory with 56.8 percent of the popular vote. But with his triumph came responsibility for a once booming economy that had not grown at all during the previous four years, and one in which confidence had sunk so low that the wealthy were protecting themselves by sending $23 billion of their capital out of the country in 1982 alone. To make matters worse, oil prices, which had reached new peaks a few years before, fell rapidly in 1986. If any doubts about the seriousness of

Venezuela's economic plight remained, they were dashed by these new events. After negative economic growth in 1984 and 1985, Lusinchi tried to raise production by increasing public spending in 1986, and he achieved some success, though at the cost of doubling the rate of inflation. For a time the Venezuelan people were incredibly calm. Yet much of what passed for contentment was due less to public satisfaction with the system than to recognition that there was no obvious alternative to it. Venezuelans complained a great deal about the nation's leadership, the self-serving games that politicians played, and their inability to restore anything resembling the economic prosperity that had been achieved a decade before. However, no one expected their discontent to provoke any serious revolt against the nation's two ruling parties by the masses or to cause the nation's richest members to ask the armed forces to take over.

The nation's leaders had not only created a two-party democracy, but they had also secured substantial collusion between all of the nation's most powerful forces. Business often complained about government intrusions into its terrain, yet it relied on the government for much of its business. And organized labor, which the AD had incorporated into its party long ago, also came to rely on the government for jobs and privileges. Though not exactly corporatist in any formal sense, it was a game that was built on the government's ability to supervise business and labor by making them dependent on the state. Consequently, instead of becoming more radical when economic conditions deteriorated, labor leaders feared turning away from the party and the state enterprises on which they relied for their own power. In short, for the time being there was no one among the masses who could provoke the armed forces to become more politically active, nor were there any among the wealthy or even the middle class who wanted to persuade the military to intervene on their behalf. This contrasted sharply with the conditions that provoked military coups in other South American countries in the 1970s and 1980s as we will discover in the next two chapters.

In many ways the Venezuelan game resembled Mexico's, where a large and powerful government was also devoted to dividing new wealth among its citizens rather than redistributing old wealth after its initial reforms were completed. Both had substantial leverage over business and labor, yet they were heavily dependent on domestic and foreign business to keep their economies growing. As a result, collusion among political and economic elites to maintain peace became common in both systems. Where they differed was in the manner in which they allowed political parties to share in the nation's governance. Until 1988 the Mexican PRI was monopolistic, while in Venezuela, where no revolution had occurred, the nation's major parties were forced to share power in order to secure everyone's acceptance of democratic rules. Monopolization had been tried by the AD in 1945, but the armed forces struck back, so when they were given another opportunity in 1959 they knew that they could govern only if they allowed their competitors to do likewise. So Venezuela remains more competitive than Mexico, though more and more its competitors have come to resemble one another.

Venezuelans received good news and bad news in 1988. Both involved petroleum. The good news was their discovery of new oil fields, raising the nation's proven reserves from 26 billion to 55 billion barrels, and elevating it from the tenth-largest producer to the fourth-largest, worldwide (the United States has 35 billion). Having feared that they would exhaust their reserves by the end of this century, they now knew that they could export far into the next one. The bad news was that the average price of a barrel, which had dropped from $26.00 in 1985 to $14.00 in 1986, was still around $14.00 in 1988. And with the nation's debt reaching more than $32 billion – large for a nation of 18 million people – they had to send $15 billion to their creditors between 1986 and 1988 to service it, years in which oil exports were earning them only $10 billion a year. In short, they were left with far less income to deal with their domestic economic needs than they had enjoyed during the 1970s.

What to do politically when President Lusinchi's term expired in 1988 was solved for the Venezuelans by none other than Carlos Andrés Pérez. After staying on the sidelines through two presidencies, as required by the constitution, he returned to win the AD's presidential nomination in bitter contest with a younger candidate. Then, in December 1988, he won the national election with 54.9 percent of the vote, marking the first time since the 1960s that one AD president succeeded another. Exploiting memories of prosperity during his first presidency, he promised good times again to the rich and poor alike. It was a welcome message even though no one expected him to succeed at it immediately. But few were prepared for how quickly after his inauguration Pérez did just the opposite.

To deal with the nation's continuing indebtedness he asked the International Monetary Fund and the nation's many creditors for more loans, and in return swiftly imposed new austerity measures on the economy, among them much higher prices for public services. An increase in gasoline prices and with it the price of bus tickets provoked protests that turned into riots for several days that ended only after the armed forces killed an estimated 300 looters to restore order. Venezuelans had seen nothing like it before, and hoped never to see it again. But it was clear that economic austerity itself had become a threat to public order if not democracy itself.

Critics of the nation's politics had warned long before that public affection for it was bound to decline, gradually at first and then rapidly. Politicians on the Left claimed that a decade of economic woes had exposed the system for what it really was: an experiment in capitalist development that was doomed to fail by the contradictions inherent in its heavy dependence on the export of petroleum. The Venezuelan masses had been asked to pay a high price for economic failures, they claimed, because two political parties that were essentially elitist in character had refused to make the wealthy pay their share for recovery. If it was a democratic game, it was rigged in order to assure that those with the most wealth and those with new wealth could retain control over everyone else.

In rebuttal, AD and COPEI politicians insisted that they had accomplished much more than had other governments in the region. Of the Andean nations theirs was the most prosperous and their middle and working classes were still the most affluent. Drug cartels had not penetrated the nation's politics as much as they had Colombia's, and there was no successful guerrilla war under way like the one waged by the Sendero Luminoso in Peru. It was a strong defense, but it referred largely to the past. The future of Venezuelan democracy depends on how the system handles a rise in protests, even from organized labor, and how soon it reaps benefits from its debt-management strategies. No one expects revolts or revolutions, but neither does anyone anticipate a swift restoration of complete public confidence in the people who govern them.

Democracy and reform: lessons learned

Chile's Eduardo Frei and Venezuela's Rómulo Betancourt were practical politicians who stubbornly refused to give up their quests for political power until they had taken office. They came from the middle sectors but knew that they needed the support of those outside their social class as if they were to triumph. So they organized campesinos and laborers where they could, giving them the hope of long-sought access to authority in exchange for their votes and other public demonstrations of support. That they succeeded in their political quests within systems ruled by elites determined to block their path is testimony to their skill and persistence. It also lays to rest erroneous notions about the incapacity of Latin Americans to conduct their politics democratically. Clearly, frequent interruptions of democratic government in Latin America are not caused by an inability to understand what democracy requires; on the contrary, it is because some persons comprehend its effects that they choose to undermine it.

Democratic reformism teaches us much about coalition politics. It was as coalition builders that the democratic reformers' skills were most notable. Even though no coalition, no matter how well conceived, could guarantee security from sabotage and military intervention, without one they knew that they stood little chance of securing office and passing reform legislation. But coalition maintenance was no simple task; not only did it require the constant attention of politicians who would have preferred fewer political obligations, but it also demanded programs that were able to accomplish the nearly impossible task of satisfying partners whose demands were incompatible with one another and usually very expensive.

Democracy offers no simple solution for preventing military intervention. Unless the military is neutralized or won over to democratic government and civilian command, it poses a serious threat to the government's survival, as the Venezuelan military demonstrated when it overthrew the AD government in 1948 and as the Chileans did in 1973. When the constitutional regime was restored to Venezuela in 1958 AD leaders were careful to cultivate military support by lavishly financing military budgets, turning soldiers loose against occasional insurgents, and refraining from direct confrontations with the economic elite. In return, the Venezuelan military respected the norms of democratic politics. Chilean democratic reformers were more fortunate initially. After a coup in the late 1920s, the Chilean armed forces left politics to civilians. As long as the Christian Democrats maintained public order, respected the military's institutional integrity, and did not permit the radicalization of Chilean politics, they too were not challenged by military leaders.

Also important was the United States government, which became an important ally of democratic reform governments throughout the hemisphere during the 1960s, thanks in part to the revolution in Cuba and fears of additional ones. In addition to substantial economic assistance, the U.S. government gave nearly $3 million to the Christian Democrats to finance their campaign in 1964 in Chile. And Rómulo Betancourt delighted in posing as the democratic answer to Fidel Castro, whom he personally despised and blamed for an assassination attempt on his life in 1962. He and Frei were held up as models for the kind of reformism that the Kennedy and Johnson administrations believed to be the most tolerable alternative to communism within the hemisphere. They were democratic in spirit, stridently anticommunist, and, though nationalistic, quite tolerant of foreign investment, which they believed to be essential to the achievement of their development objectives. They probably would have succeeded without U.S. assistance, but they welcomed it nevertheless.

The democratic reform coalition, though adroitly conceived, was never as secure as its creators intended. Disputes over the substance and pace of reform haunted it and led to frequent defections, especially by labor and party factions who thought presidents were too willing to compromise with their conservative opponents. Reformers were also plagued by the problem of holding together a coalition that sought to unite peasants with urban workers and both of them with the middle sectors. As long as resources were plentiful it could be held together, but when the competition for scarce resources intensified, as it did frequently in Latin America, each coalition member tended to go its own way in the struggle for survival.

Reform policy was always easy game for critics. Much of the criticism was deserved. To be sure, the reformers did achieve a great deal: the redistribution of rural property, industrialization, and the nationalization of some enterprises. And they increased government responsibilities for the social welfare of their people and improved the condition of many. But they never achieved as much reform as they had promised. Import-substitution industrialization did not secure the kind of national independence and self-sustaining development that was desired. Nor did agrarian reform eliminate rural poverty or substantially improve the welfare of those who were given property, though it did reduce their discontent somewhat. And a larger public sector turned out to be more expensive and less productive than expected. They also had to cope with a very practical problem. They knew what to do, but they were not experienced with agrarian reforms, national development plans, and regional economic integration. Consequently, they were often forced to become incrementalists, slowing down their efforts and abandoning some of their more ambitious schemes when they encountered unexpected technical problems.

Incrementalism was also forced on reformers by the political obstacles they faced. As we learned repeatedly, democratic rules afford one's opponents abundant opportunities for halting reform. In Chile, it will be recalled, agrarian reform legislation was delayed for two years by a coalition of Conservatives and Marxists. But political obstacles are not confined to legislatures. As elsewhere, bureaucrats were amenable to bribes and other means of opposition influence, and judges often intervened to protect the rights of defenders of the status quo, slowing government programs and disappointing their intended beneficiaries.

Much of the democratic reformers' political frustration stems from the trap they fall into when they advocate programs that threaten vested interests on both the Left and the Right. If they concede to their opponents, they must sacrifice much of what they hope to achieve. But if, on the other hand, they go after them, deliberately intending to strip them of their power, they risk eviction from office, as Salvador Allende discovered. Is there no escape from this trap? Maybe not, but that never deters democratic reformers. For them politics does not involve choosing between imposing one's will on society in an authoritarian manner and resigning oneself to political immobility; rather it requires living with hosts of dilemmas and accepting imperfect solutions. To demand that it be otherwise is to ignore the nature of the democratic game. This is why they are so much less disturbed by the paucity of their economic achievements than are their opponents on the Left, who are less dedicated to liberal notions of civil liberty and political competition.

Lest we blame all of the democratic reformers' shortcomings on their domestic politics, we should recall that they operate in the same economic world as all other Latin American leaders, one that treats the highly dependent Latin American economies quite harshly. Import-substitution industrialization and agrarian reform did not free Chile and Venezuela from their need to import a great deal. As their production of consumer goods rose, so did their demand for imported capital goods and financial capital, forcing them to rely as before on the export of primary products to secure the foreign exchange needed to finance their imports. How well they did economically depended as much on economic growth and inflation in the industrial nations as it did on their own policies. Ambitious development programs, like those undertaken in Chile and Venezuela, make a nation even more vulnerable to external forces by increasing the costs of incorrect calculations about the future price of its exports and the cost of its imports. Reformers are optimists who accept short-term risks in order to achieve long-term objectives but, because they take such risks, they are easily undermined when things do not go according to plan. Such was the case in Venezuela in the 1980s. No nation seemed better prepared for rapid development, yet seldom have a government's ambitious programs been reversed so quickly in order to avert financial disaster. But the Venezuelans were not alone in their plight, for it was the same throughout the region. The cause of their problem was not the government's reform politics but the simple fact of the region's economic dependence on nations richer than themselves.

A new democratic era?

Constitutional government has not disappeared in Latin America. On the contrary, there were more governments operating by liberal democratic rules in the 1980s than at any time in Latin American history. Within a few years of one another, Peru, Ecuador, Bolivia, Brazil, Argentina, Uruguay, Guatemala, El Salvador, and Honduras replaced military governments with elected civilian ones. How "democratic" each of them actually became differed substantially. The armed forces and their allies have broken the rules frequently in Guatemala, Honduras, and El Salvador, and they remain important political forces within the other nations. But the mere fact that so many nations tried democracy once again after being told by authoritarians that it was no longer feasible or desirable is significant. Still to be determined by Latin Americans themselves is whether we are witnessing a familiar political cycle whose phases rotate from authoritarian government to the democratic and back again, or the beginning of far more durable political changes.

A closer look at this process is called for, so in the next two chapters we will examine two nations that are known for the way authoritarians and democrats have taken turns at trying to govern them. Brazil gave constitutional government a try starting in 1945, but twenty years later the military took over, only to allow the restoration of civilian government twenty years after that. In Argentina the changes have come more frequently. The officers who took over in 1966 governed for seven years, let civilians back for three, and then returned to govern for seven more. In 1983 they retreated again, allowing a civilian president to govern for six years and another to replace him in 1989. But let's begin with Brazil.

Further reading

Black, David Eugene. *Venezuela: Politics in a Petroleum Republic.* New York: Praeger, 1984.

Ewell, Judith. *Venezuela: A Century of Change.* Stanford, CA: Stanford University Press, 1984.

Herman, Donald. *Christian Democracy in Venezuela.* Chapel Hill: University of North Carolina Press, 1980.

Levine, Daniel H. *Religion and Politics in Latin America: The Catholic Church in Venezuela and Colombia.* Princeton, NJ: Princeton University Press, 1981.

Martz, John. *Acción Democrática: Evolution of a Modern Political Party in Venezuela.* Princeton, NJ: Princeton University Press, 1965.

Martz, John, and David Myers, eds. *Venezuela: The Democratic Experience.* Revised edition. New York: Praeger, 1986.

Powell, John Duncan. *Political Mobilization of the Venezuelan Peasant.* Cambridge, MA: Harvard University Press, 1977.

Petras, James, Morris Morley, and Steven Smith. *The Nationalization of Venezuelan Oil.* New York: Praeger, 1977.

Tugwell, Franklin. *The Politics of Oil in Venezuela.* Stanford, CA: Stanford University Press, 1973.

Yepes, José Antonio Gil. *The Challenge of Venezuelan Democracy.* New Brunswick, NJ: Transaction Books, 1981.

9. Brazil: populists, authoritarians, and democrats

It was once believed that underdevelopment was the cause of military dictatorship. Plagued by widespread poverty, illiteracy, and large rural populations, Latin American nations were thought to be natural breeding grounds for violence and military repression. But with their "modernization" this was supposed to end, since modern countries do not have military governments. Well, they did modernize, some countries industrializing and urbanizing even faster than anticipated, but military governments did not disappear. Instead, starting in 1964 they became more common than ever. Worse still, this time the armed forces took it upon themselves to govern as long as necessary to make fundamental changes in their nations' politics. Latin Americans had seen nothing like it before.

Why military authoritarianism?

Chronic disagreements over political rules are characteristic of the region's politics, as we have learned, as is military involvement in these disputes. But that fact alone cannot explain the new wave of military governments that swept the region in the 1960s and 1970s. Nor does it explain why officers believed that they could actually reconstruct their nations' political systems the way the Brazilians tried to do starting in 1964, the Argentines in 1966, the Peruvians in 1968, the Chileans and Uruguayans in 1973, and the Argentines for a second time in 1976.

No single condition or event accounts for the creation of these military authoritarian regimes, but two circumstances contributed a great deal to their invention, one of them economic and the other ideological. Economically, import-substitution industrialization had never delivered on its promise of greater national independence and steady economic development. Instead, by the 1960s the region's most industrialized economies still found themselves heavily dependent on exporting raw products and acquiring capital supplied from abroad.

214

Moreover, internally they faced demands for higher consumption from an organized urban working class that could not be easily satisfied without some redistribution of wealth downward in the social structure. It did not help that working-class expectations were elevated by political parties that had won the support of the urban lowerclass on promises to give them a bigger piece of a national economic pie that did not always expand fast enough to satisfy everyone. The more assertive and demanding that the working classes became, the more difficult it was for the upper and middle classes to tolerate them. Add to that recognition by elites that these interclass conflicts and the economic instability that they touched off discouraged the investments of multinational corporations they believed to be essential to further industrial development, and you have an economic motive for putting a halt to elected government. Advised by prominent civilian economists that something resembling what we labeled conservative modernization was far more appropriate for their nations' economic progress, and aware how unpopular such a regressive strategy would be with the working class, the armed forces took it upon themselves to assure its implementation over all objections.

In short, the propertied classes, both domestic and foreign, became convinced that their world could no longer be preserved without help from the armed forces. The demands and expectations of the popular classes had become too great and civilian governments too incapable of containing them to be tolerated any longer. As they saw it, the termination of open politics and the implementation of unpopular economic reforms was the only way to preserve their way of life. Military officers who had seen legislators and presidents feud, workers protest, and economies deteriorate were ready to listen to their pleas. Business complained about "irresponsible politicians" and multinational corporation executives warned of "irreparable economic damages" that civilians were doing to their nations' development. One by one the militaries of South America responded.

Yet, as plausible as these economic causes of military authoritarianism may be, they are insufficient without the addition of some powerful ideological motives as well. Intense political conflict and economic crises do not always produce military government. Military officers must have convictions of their own to motivate so drastic a solution as they tried this time, and they found them in the ideology they had acquired after World War II in their war colleges and in regional security organizations located in the United States and Panama. Labeled the National Security Doctrine, it was refined by Brazilian officers in the Cold War atmosphere of the 1950s who spread it swiftly among their peers in neighboring countries.

The doctrine, which draws heavily on old notions of "geopolitics" once advocated by European nationalists, places the nation above the individual. For its own survival in a hostile world the nation must accumulate and exercise as much power as it can, obligating its citizens to do whatever it requires of them. In contrast to liberal democratic thinking, which defends individualism, diversity, and competition, the National Security Doctrine stresses conformity to a single set of values. Its view of human nature is decidedly Hobbesian, stressing the passionate character of human beings, power-seeking creatures whose aggressiveness cannot be restrained by reason alone. Consequently a few persons must exercise control over the rest, preventing them from destroying one another and the nation. Placed in the Latin American context, it was decidedly conservative, relying on an old-fashioned Roman Catholicism to bind its pieces together morally by stressing hierarchical authority, spiritualism, self-discipline, and strong, male domination, starting in the family.

The doctrine resembles the fascist ideology that was once popular in Italy and Spain. Like Italian fascism it seeks to mold national character and unite a people behind powerful leaders. Citizens are expected to dedicate themselves to advancing the interests of the nation, making whatever sacrifices that authorities wiser than themselves ask of them. Like fascism it detests liberalism, multiparty democracy, and the free press, and has little use for reasoned argument. Yet, despite these similarities in substance, the doctrine differs from fascism in one important regard. Mussolini turned fascism into a popular doctrine that was embraced by millions of Italians as a source of emotional security and national salvation. Most civilian Latin Americans, in contrast, never took the National Security Doctrine all that seriously. Conditioned by a history of partisan military rule, they reacted to the military's patriotic proclamations quite skeptically, accepting them as little more than necessary rationalizations for its attempt to preserve the existing socioeconomic order.

Nevertheless, it was easy for military officers to regard themselves as saviors of their nations in the wake of successful revolution in Cuba in 1959 and the threat they perceived of additional insurrections elsewhere in the hemisphere. Inspired by Cuba and their own aspirations, some persons, most of them young, had launched little wars, first from the countryside and later within their nations' largest cities, all of them aimed at undermining incumbent governments and their military guardians. Eradicating such insurgents became an obsession of the armed forces, and preventing any future revolutionary insurrections their long-range goal. With their National Security Doctrine in hand, they believed that they had found the way to create societies in which rebellion would neither be desired nor considered remotely achievable by anyone desiring change.

In retrospect, the doctrine and its implementation may appear naïve and exceptionally foolhardy, but two decades would pass before military officers realized it. And even then some never did, but instead continued to believe that they were right.

Starting with an emperor

Brazilians have always thought big. Over one-third of all Latin Americans live there, and one of its states, São Paulo, is larger, with 42 million people, than every Latin American country but Mexico. Brazil alone accounts for 39 percent of what is produced in this region of over twenty countries (second place goes to Mexico with 18 percent, followed by Argentina with 11 percent). Two-thirds of the region's largest public and private corporations reside in Brazil, and nearly half of the foreign investments made in Latin America go to this country whose gross domestic product is larger than those of countries like Spain and Australia.

But size alone tells us little about the country since there are really two Brazils. Several million business people, professionals, commercial farmers, public servants, and skilled laborers live in relative comfort in one of them, most of them residing in the rapidly developing southern third of the country. They have always shown great confidence in the nation's future and have been quick to advance themselves by modernizing the nation's economy. The other two-thirds of the population live in another Brazil, one plagued by substantial illiteracy, subsistence farming, urban unemployment, and petty crime, all conditions that the more affluent Brazilians, like their peers in other countries, prefer to ignore. Per capita income in São Paulo is $4,000, while in the northeast it is only $600. Once upon a time the poor were largely rural but today 78 percent of the population lives in cities and towns. Some of them will escape poverty just like others before them, but most will not.

For twenty years, beginning in 1964, both Brazils were governed by a military regime, one whose politics was quite different from anything they had known before. It tolerated no real opposition and promised to rule as long as it needed to rescue its economy and reorganize its politics. It became an example that would be imitated in various forms by colleagues in Argentina, Uruguay, and Chile before a decade had passed.

Authoritarians were not a new species in Brazil. When independence from Portugal came in 1822, Dom Pedro, then ruling Brazil as a regent for his father, Portuguese King João IV, lined up on the side of independence and was rewarded with appointment as the new nation's first monarch (see Table 9.1). It was not long, however, before the Brazilian elite, resentful of their new emperor's concentration of power, revolted, forcing Dom Pedro to abdicate in favor of his five-year-old son in 1831. A decade passed before the nation's parliament officially declared fifteen-year-old Dom Pedro II the new emperor, but once on the throne he ruled for forty-eight years over a centralized, pseudoparliamentary regime, bringing order to his very diverse society of white elites, black slaves, and mixed races.

When the emperor was finally deposed in 1889, young military officers led the way, backed by many in the upper and middle classes. Disgruntled with the emperor's neglect of the armed forces and inspired by a positivist philosophy that advocated the promotion of economic modernization under the leadership of private business, the armed forces assumed responsibility for making sure that more progressive civilians ran the country and promoted its development. Thereafter they never again abdicated their role as supervisor of the nation's progress, staying on the sidelines when civilians managed the country well and stepping in when they did not. That is why no one was shocked when they took over in 1964. It was only their announced intention to rule by themselves indefinitely that departed from past practice.

In 1889 they created a constitutional regime that allowed some decentralization of political authority, using federalism to distribute power among regional political machines that ran the nation's states according to local traditions, the poorest of them in a tyrannical man-

Table 9.1. *Brazil: historical background*

1822	Independence declared by Portuguese Prince Dom Pedro, who is crowned Emperor Pedro I of Brazil
1840	Dom Pedro II, aged fourteen, is declared second emperor of Brazil
1889	Army overthrows emperor and two years later creates first constitution of the Republic of the United States of Brazil
1917	Brazil enters World War I on the side of the Allies
1929	World economic depression strikes Brazilian economy
1930	Military–civilian insurrection led by defeated presidential candidate Getulio Vargas ends the Republic
1932	Provisional government of Getulio Vargas puts down constitutionalist revolt in São Paulo
1934	Second republican constitution is adopted, and Congress elects Getulio Vargas president
1937	Just before election of his successor, Vargas leads coup and creates Estado Novo, appointing himself as president with indefinite tenure
1942	Brazil enters World War II on the side of the Allies
1945	Vargas is forced to resign by military after creating Populist movement drawing heavily on support of organized labor
1950	Vargas wins legitimate presidential election with support of Social Democratic Party and Brazilian Labor Party, receiving 49 percent of popular vote
1954	President Vargas commits suicide at age seventy-two
1955	Juscelino Kubitschek, with support of Vargas coalition, elected president, with 36 percent of popular vote
1960	Janio Quadros, nominated by opposition, elected president, with 48 percent of popular vote
1961	President Quadros resigns and is succeeded by Vice-president João Goulart
1964	Military overthrows Goulart on March 31, has Marshal Humberto Castello Branco elected president by purged Congress
1967	Marshal Artur Costa e Silva selected president by military
1969	President Costa e Silva forced to resign by illness; replaced by General Emilio Garrastazu Medici
1974	General Ernesto Geisel selected president
1979	General João Baptista Figueiredo selected president
1982	Elections held for local, state, and national legislatures, and state governors
1985	Opposition candidate Tancredo Neves elected president by electoral college, defeating military party candidate, civilian Paulo Maluf. Neves died before inauguration and Vice-president José Sarney became the first civilian president since 1964
1986	MDB party wins huge victory in congressional elections and national congress writes new constitution in 1988
1988	New constitution written

ner. Thereafter, by agreement among machine leaders, the presidency was exchanged between the two most powerful states, São Paulo and Minas Gerais. But it all came apart in 1930 during a dispute between candidates. Retiring president Washington Luis of São Paulo broke with tradition by selecting another Paulista to replace him instead of accepting Getulio Vargas, the nominee of the Minas Gerais political machine. Soon thereafter Vargas led the military-backed rebellion that brought the forty-year-old republic to an end.

Washington Luis's violation of the electoral agreement was the principal cause of the 1930 insurrection, but not the only one. The 1929 depression and the failure of the Luis government to act decisively to relieve the crisis undermined the confidence of coffee growers, bankers, and traders in his administration. Moreover, the military had grown weary of the old regime and was disturbed by its failure to accelerate the country's economic development. Increasing professionalization, foreign travel, and greater awareness of Brazil's untouched economic potential heightened young officers' distress over the country's insufficient progress. Once firm supporters of the regime, they gradually became its strongest critics, convinced that only a new generation of bold leaders could impose on Brazil the kind of moral order needed to achieve the country's full potential.

What the opposition needed was someone able to unite all of the politicians, the armed forces, business people, and professionals who had grown tired of the corrupt old order. Getulio Vargas was that person. An experienced and well-known politician aggrieved because he had been denied the presidency after winning it under the old rules, he quickly became the obvious choice. From the outset he assured each of the players within the coalition that he would serve their particular interests. Some saw him as the long-awaited founding father of a more democratic constitutional regime. For others he was the promoter of rapid national development, dedicated to uniting government and business to achieve industrialization in the wake of the world depression. For still others, he became the only one who seemed capable of taming the warring political machines through his ingenious wielding of national authority.

Getulio Vargas: populist politician

Populism preceded military authoritarianism in both Brazil and Argentina, Getulio Vargas its proponent in the former and General Juan

Perón in Argentina. The populists' achievements were actually quite modest, but politics was never quite the same again in countries where they plied their trade. Not only did they change a few rules in Brazil and Argentina, but they also invented a new kind of leadership, manipulative in style, nationalist in sentiment, and massive in appeal.

Had the populists launched well-organized, ideologically coherent movements, comprehending them would be easy. Unfortunately, coherence and clarity were not among their virtues. Like other rebels who rose from within a tenacious old order, they were absorbed by the immediate struggle for political advantage rather than by a grander crusade to reconstruct the nation in accord with an elaborate ideology. Though radical in their rhetoric, they were moderate in their behavior. Theirs was not the cause of revolution but the acquisition of political power in order to get a larger piece of the nation's economic pie for themselves and for the urban entrepreneurs and workers who believed in them. They feared the radicalization of the working class as much as did the conservatives they displaced; what made them different was their conviction that the labor movement could be handled more effectively by the government's absorbing it rather than repressing it. Though it seemed a cavalier and risky venture at the time, it turned out to be a simple task for modern Machiavellians like Getulio Vargas and Juan Perón.

The term *populist* may be confusing to anyone familiar with North American politics who envisions agrarian movements protesting against railway monopolies. Latin American populism was quite different, for it drew its support from an urban constituency in the midst of early industrialization during the 1930s and 1940s in the larger Latin American nations. To complicate matters, no populist was an exact replica of another. Vargas and Perón responded to different national circumstances and adjusted populist tactics to take advantage of them. Populism was very much an exercise in personal leadership, always leader-centered and heavily dependent on a single person for cohesion. As a result, its strengths and weaknesses were often those of the person in charge.

Vargas ruled Brazil for thirteen years – from 1930 to 1943 – before he actually launched his populist movement. A lawyer from the southern Brazilian state of Rio Grande do Sul and a member of an upper-class ranching family, he began his political career as a federal deputy in 1924, served as finance minister in 1926, and returned to his home state as governor in 1928. After losing the 1930 presidential election

– an election rigged by his opponent – Vargas led a heterogeneous coalition of disgruntled civilian politicians and young military officers in an insurrection that deposed the incumbent president. For fifteen years thereafter he personally dominated Brazilian politics as the country's president, employing his exceptional mastery of the rules and norms of Brazilian life and his ability to guide the country through the uncertain times of the postdepression era.

Brazilians quickly discovered that Vargas was happier governing as an authoritarian than as a liberal democrat. The turning point came in 1932, when he invited and defeated a revolt by constitutionalists in the state of São Paulo. The revolt's leaders had accused him of postponing the return to constitutional government so that he could increase his power at the expense of the large state machines. They were correct, but by launching and losing their confrontation with him, they only enhanced his image as a patriot defending the government against unruly, self-interested rebels.

Once comfortably in control, Vargas authorized the election of a constituent assembly in 1933. Less than a year later the assembly drafted a new constitution, converted itself into the Chamber of Deputies, and elected him to a four-year term as president. But instead of strengthening the constitutional process, he again dedicated himself to undermining it. And, as before, he provoked opponents and then used the threats they posed to justify his authoritarian methods. This time he encouraged initiatives by small communist and fascist movements, playing each off against the other to make the threat of both to the nation appear much greater than it actually was. The strategy worked and, in 1937, just before an election to replace him, he persuaded the military to overthrow the constitutional regime and appoint him president with indefinite tenure.

An admirer of fascist regimes in Spain, Portugal, and Italy, Vargas desired to emulate them, but never followed through on most of his initiatives. The Estado Novo, as the new order was called, was little more than window dressing to clothe his expansion of state control over Brazilian life. What Vargas really did was join two nineteenth-century Brazilian traditions together and adapt them to the needs of the postdepression era. One was the tradition of paternalistic central authority, which was developed during the imperial rule of Emperor Dom Pedro II between 1841 and 1889; the other was the dependence of private economic groups on the Brazilian government. The regional political machines that had governed Brazil between 1889 and 1930 had weakened central authority but had not destroyed popular longing for it. Vargas drew on the need and desire for firm national leadership and transformed the presidency and the national bureaucracy into powerful promoters of the nation's economic development. He encouraged private investors to take an active role in the nation's development, something they were already doing, and he protected them from organized labor, which was initially restrained by authorities, promising all of them rewards if they played by his rules. A new era was under way, or so it seemed in 1938.

In the early 1940s demands for restoring constitutional democracy rose again, coming primarily from democratically inclined politicians, along with military officers who were returning from Europe where they helped liberate nations like Italy from fascists, and thought that it was time to do the same in Brazil. Always ready to adapt himself to new political realities, Vargas, aware that he needed mass support to defeat opponents when free elections were finally held, chose to become more populist, mobilizing organized labor by using a new Brazilian Labor Party. His scheme came to naught, however, when the armed forces staged a coup to make sure that Vargas would not again subvert the constitutional order as he had done so adroitly in 1937. They forced him to return to his ranch in southern Brazil and watch the 1945 elections from the sidelines. His retirement was premature, as it turned out, for once constitutional rules had been put into practice Vargas worked his way back into the contest. Mobilizing the Labor Party that he had created in 1943 and drawing support from the regional political bosses previously loyal to him, he secured 49 percent of the popular vote and became president once again in 1950.

Vargas tried to play the role of moderator and unifier, rewarding laborers for their support with patronage and social security while simultaneously promoting industry and going easy on rural elites. But Brazil had changed a great deal since his first presidency; the urban middle sectors were more numerous, foreign investors more involved in the country, industrialists more demanding, and economic policy issues more complex and less resolvable to everyone's satisfaction. The techniques that had worked a decade earlier were no longer adequate for keeping opponents at bay. The National Democratic Union, the principal opposition party, repeatedly refused Vargas's invitations to join his government, preferring a major effort to undermine him. His foes encouraged junior military officers, who charged him with excessive patronage and corruption, and foreign investors who denounced his strident nationalism. As the attacks of the opposition gained momentum in 1954, it became increasingly difficult for Vargas to deter them. The end finally came when the mysterious assassination of an anti-Vargas military officer stirred demands for his resignation. The frustrated seventy-two-year-old president refused, then walked alone into his office and shot himself, leaving the country to successors.

Military authoritarianism, 1964–85

Industrialists, urban professionals, bureaucrats, foreign investors, and organized labor had become part of the national political process under Vargas, as had new political parties, when a constitutional regime was launched in 1945. But the latter took on uniquely Brazilian characteristics, eschewing ideology and mass mobilization in favor of regional electoral organizations dedicated primarily to capturing the presidency and seats in the legislature.

Essential to governing Brazil between 1945 and 1964 was the maintenance of a balance among its dominant players by promoting a rapidly growing industrial economy. This required policies that satisfied some of the demands of each player without seriously offending the wealthiest and most traditional of them. Few Brazilian presidents directed this system more adroitly than did President Juscelino Kubitschek between 1955 and 1960. A promoter of national development who built the nation's new capital, Brasília, in the interior, he helped foster expectations that Brazil was finally on its way toward lasting economic prosperity. His successors, however, did not live up to such high expectations and, four years after Kubitschek had departed, the military took over.

The descent began in 1960 with the election of Janio Quadros, a rare kind of politician who campaigned on promises to purge Brazilian government of patronage, corruption, and political balancing acts, all legacies of the Vargas years that had been perpetuated by Kubitschek. What made Quadros unusual was his determination to operate independently of the ruling coalition that had been held together and expanded by presidents since 1930. Instead of acquiring power by becoming an indispensable mediator among coalition members, he sought "man-in-the-street" support for his political purification campaign. It was a bold initiative, but one doomed to fail. In less than a year Quadros had alienated party politicians who had thrived on patronage and bureaucrats who had lived on corruption. He also antagonized industrialists with an antiinflationary, tight credit policy, increased labor opposition with wage controls, and upset the military with a neutralist foreign policy. When a disheartened Quadros suddenly resigned in August, 1961, in an attempt to generate an outpouring of popular support that would overwhelm his opponents, nearly everyone stayed home and watched it on television, turning his leave of absence into permanent retirement.

Vice-president João Goulart, who succeeded Quadros, also upset the traditional equilibrium. Goulart, a former protégé of Vargas, and labor minister in his last administration, initially tried to replicate the development program employed by Kubitschek. He was haunted, however, by his reputation as an opportunistic and unreliable labor operative deeply distrusted by the military. To make matters worse, the Brazilian economy deteriorated rapidly in 1962 and 1963. Kubitschek's acceleration of growth in the late 1950s had left Quadros and Goulart with rising inflation and a slowdown in production followed by a decline in investor confidence. Goulart tried several conventional solutions to the inflation problem, but when none worked and opposition to him grew he looked for another way out.

Under Goulart, educated Brazilians had become divided into two contrasting schools of thought about development. On one side were *reformers,* who complained that Brazil was still a very traditional society in which privilege prevailed over hard labor, making real economic and social progress impossible for the middle and lower classes. Radical by Brazilian standards, they argued that change had to begin with the dismantling of old legal and economic institutions run by the semifeudal and capitalist elites who behaved as if they were an aristocracy in a colonial society. Without doing that, they insisted, government efforts to help the poor would be transitory and fruitless. On the other side were *conservatives,* who denied any need for such reforms. They too criticized the most reactionary members of Brazilian society for their lethargy, but saw nothing to be gained from the persecution of capitalists. Instead, they advocated strong leadership by individuals who would use the enormous power of the state to promote the nation's development, giving entrepreneurs the opportunities they needed to finance growth and build productive enterprises in return for such backing.

In early 1964 Goulart, desperate to shore up his troubled administration, sided with the reformers. He announced a modest land reform, nationalized some private oil refineries, gave illiterates the right to vote, and, most disturbing to the armed forces, took the side of enlisted men when they protested their treatment by commanding officers. It was an enormous gamble that broke two basic rules of the traditional Brazilian game: one that forbade the redistribution of property from one player to another, and the other that prohibited the mobilization of the masses against their masters.

Conservatives were quickly alarmed, and warned the country that communists were taking over. And the louder they shouted, the more recalcitrant Goulart became, polarizing national politics as never before. Gradually it became obvious that the armed forces were the only ones who could settle the dispute swiftly. If they needed any more encouragement, it came from the United States government, which had always feared Goulart's nationalism at a time when American firms were heavily involved in Brazil. When the coup finally did come in April few were surprised. Even Goulart knew enough to flee south to Uruguay.

Military officers are not trained to design political systems, but that is precisely what they hoped to do in Brazil in 1964. Understandably, they began with a clearer idea about the rules and political practices they wanted to eliminate than about what they would create to replace them. Moderate officers wanted to restore economic growth and purge the system of politicians who championed popular causes, leaving conservative civilians to run the country under temporary military supervision. Hardliners, in contrast, sought democracy's termination and replacement by a permanent authoritarian state. Moderates would prevail most of the time, though not without making major concessions to colleagues who were dedicated to running a police state.

To assist them, officers hired some of the nation's most talented civilian technocrats, many of them with extensive international experience in management and economic policy making. Simultaneously they closed all existing political parties and denied labor unions the right to protest or strike. The rural aristocracy and most industrialists were also excluded at first. In a very unique way it was a government directed by self-selected members of the middle class: professionals, bureaucrats, and military officers who were convinced that the nation's upper and working classes were incapable of making a great nation of Brazil. Military president Castello Branco and his cohorts believed that decades of import-substitution industrialization had produced a complacent elite that lived off protection and speculation, making quick profits for themselves without advancing the nation very far. Like juvenile delinquents, speculators had to be put in their place and closely supervised by much wiser persons. Attitudes had to be changed and Castello Branco and his technocrats believed that they were the only ones who could manage the task.

To describe the new government as middle class might seem improper, given how much richer the wealthy became during the next twenty years. But their opulence does not change the fact that the armed forces began convinced that they were placing the interests of the nation above those of any one sector. It was at substantial cost to both the agricultural and industrial sectors that they made war on inflation with unprecedented austerity measures in 1964. Four years later, after they had succeeded, new opportunities for investment arose and, not surprisingly, local entrepreneurs joined state and multinational enterprises in making big profits from rapid economic growth. Yet, throughout it all, it was government and not private business that was in charge of Brazilian development, both because of its size and the technocrats' desire to keep it that way.

Moderate officers wanted new laws and a civilian legislature to sanction them in order to make their enterprise appear more legitimate to the most prominent members of society, reminiscent of what Emperor Dom Pedro II had done when he governed with the assent of an aristocratic congress a century ago. To assure that the legislature complied with presidential wishes while giving the appearance of representing diverse middle and upper class interests, the government created two new political parties, one composed of politicians loyal to the military, called the National Renovating Alliance (ARENA), and the other of opposition politicians, known as the Brazilian Democratic Movement (MDB). In a country where ideology had always played a small part in politics and sophisticated political parties had never existed, it was not surprising that civilians from the middle and upper classes quickly volunteered for membership in parties, some hoping that greater access to government and its wealth would eventually come their way.

The new rules of the game were announced in a series of Institutional Acts decreed between 1964 and 1969. They created a hierarchical government in which the president had as much formal power to exercise as he wanted. If he wished, he could jail anyone, close any newspaper, and dismiss any public official. Brazilian generals and admirals were determined to create a regime in which they, as leaders of the armed forces, would govern the nation rather than turn it over to a single officer who would become a one-man dictator with indefinite tenure. So they selected from the army at regular intervals an officer whom they delegated to supervise the implementation of their plans. Civilians were given no say whatsoever. Disputes within the military over the selection of presidents were common, but officers proved skillful at keeping their internal debates from the public.

At his disposal the president had a repressive apparatus that grew rapidly during the regime's first years. Working closely together with police the armed forces rounded up students, labor leaders, and politicians, sending some into exile and jailing others for a time. Then, when members of the opposition tried to wage a guerrilla war against the government in 1969, kidnapping foreign diplomats whom they tried to exchange for political prisoners, the president turned loose organizations like the National Intelligence Service that arrested hundreds of persons, tortured them, and eventually found and killed those who led them. Official terror was also used in the countryside to destroy peasant organizations and groups demanding agrarian reform. Until 1974 security forces went about their business energetically, totally destroying the guerrilla movement and terrorizing anyone sympathetic with it.

Still, the president's power was not unlimited. To begin with, when making decisions he had to take the opinions of other officers into account. He represented the high commanders as much as he commanded them, and often they did not agree on how far to go in policing and changing society. Second, in matters of economic policy, he was heavily dependent on the bureaucrats who ran state corporations. The president could not just order them to change their operations; most were too large and complex for sudden transformation. They had loans to pay, services to deliver, and income to collect, all of which they did in their own, well-established ways. Huge government steel corporations, mines, airlines, chemical plants were never entirely at his disposal. When his and their interests coincided, as they often did, cooperation was easy, but it was never guaranteed because few economic policies could satisfy all state corporations simultaneously.

It was a bizarre scene in those years. On the one hand, regular elections were held, a legislature and civilian courts operated, and the economy boomed. Yet the election results were not allowed to affect national policy, and judicial decisions were ignored or suspended when they interfered with presidential ventures. Nevertheless, the opposition was never completely silent. When students were jailed, civil rights lawyers ignored, and guerrillas battered, the clergy took it upon themselves to denounce human rights violations. And the same authorities who had repressed nearly everyone, whenever they wished, let up from time to time. It was as if the armed forces knew that they could not control everyone in so complex a society, so they periodically concentrated on those who were most forthright, punishing just enough people to prevent their forcing the government into retreat.

The national security state went through three phases before the military finally withdrew in the mid-1980s. The first, which ended in 1969, laid the foundations, with laws and reorganizations within the executive branch. Then, between 1969 and 1973, the repressive apparatus went to work while civilian technocrats directed an impressive economic recovery. In 1974, when the economy ran into trouble, authorities began a third phase, which involved a process of "decompression," in which the armed forces searched for more legitimacy. They decided to strengthen the state by creating a more pliant system of political representation that could incorporate and manage dissent without yielding any power to dissenters. Moderates in the armed forces had long warned that national security would be undermined by unrestricted efforts to control the entire society by repressing everyone in it. The military was not equipped to govern that tightly nor could they expect a huge capitalist society to function unless its most active members were given some freedom to operate. Somehow the state had to be "legitimized" or accepted as proper by the most powerful civilian players in society, and it was to winning and retaining elite and middle-class support that President Geisel devoted his decompression plan in 1974.

Ironically, it was to elections that he turned, convinced that it was the most obvious way to legitimize the security state's political authority. Having beaten the MDB party in the 1970 congressional elections, he believed that his government could repeat the feat in the

1974 congressional and 1976 municipal elections. What he did not count on, however, was the MDB's use of the media to attack repression, authoritarianism, and the deprivations suffered by most Brazilians during the first six years under the new economic recovery program, tactics that brought them a resounding victory in 1974. Frustrated by his mistake, Geisel immediately restricted opposition access to the media, as if that would somehow diminish its support in the 1976 municipal elections. But it did not work as well as planned: The government's ARENA picked up only enough to barely defeat the MDB.

The MDB made their exclusion from the media the issue in the 1978 congressional elections, mobilizing thousands of grass-roots organizations that won them 57 percent of the Senate vote, and 49.5 percent in the House. ARENA retained a majority of seats in both houses thanks to last-minute changes in electoral laws that increased representation of the conservative northeast, but it was clear that the legitimacy they desired had eluded them. In retrospect, they seem naïve for having tried, but in a country so accustomed to elite rule such tactics are not really surprising.

Economic miracles: real and imagined

After they took control in 1964 the armed forces administered some bitter medicine to the nation's economy. To understand why this became necessary, we must look back a few decades to discover how its predicament began.

The government's reliance on market forces gave way to more direct state intervention after the creation of the Estado Novo in 1937. At the urging of his nationalist military advisers, Vargas accelerated the process of industrialization begun spontaneously after the depression using investment-promoting taxes, exchange and credit controls, import quotas, and the development of state-owned petroleum and steel enterprises. Then came World War II and the interruption of Brazilian trade with Europe once again. True to form, Vargas increased state control in order to protect the Brazilian economy from the war's disruptive effects, making his government the patron and regulator of the country's private entrepreneurs. It was this recourse to state paternalism that made Brazil's economic development so different from that of early industrializers like Great Britain and the United States.

Whereas industrial growth was promoted and managed largely by entrepreneurs in the latter, much greater state intervention and direction were necessary to accelerate it in a late-industrializing nation like Brazil. In addition to protecting coffee producers and promoting industrial growth, Vargas sought to make the state the patron of organized labor and labor the loyal servant of the state, as we have seen. But in doing so he confined his effort to the organized labor elite, leaving most of the working class unorganized and poor, especially in the countryside.

When Vargas returned to the presidency in 1950, the process of import-substitution industrialization prompted two decades earlier by the depression had gathered momentum, but was still far from complete. His initial goal was the acceleration of industrial growth and the diversification of Brazilian production. His economic advisers recognized that Brazil still suffered from structural bottlenecks and a low capacity to import because of insufficient returns on its primary-product exports. What was needed, they concluded, was more domestic production of consumer goods for local markets. Vargas cloaked his program in strong nationalist rhetoric, promising to liberate the country from the tyranny of world markets and economic control by foreigners. But his words could not hide the fact that what he prescribed was actually a modest effort to stimulate economic growth by combining rather orthodox international trade policies with state promotion of industrialization using heavy investments in economic infrastructure, the liberal financing of private entrepreneurs, and the expansion of state enterprises involved in the production of iron, steel, petroleum, and other basic materials.

The skills Vargas had used to dominate the Brazilian polity and stimulate its economic growth after the depression were no match for the task of managing a more complex economy and satisfying the more diverse economic interests that had arisen by the 1950s. For example, when the rate of inflation accelerated and the balance-of-payments deficit reached record levels in 1953, Vargas could devise no solution that pleased all the dominant economic forces. Instead, he chose to bow to economic realities and adopt a conventional economic stabilization program that cut public spending, limited imports, and tightened credit – to the displeasure of industrialists, merchants, and union leaders. To make matters worse, stabilization did not immediately rescue the economy or save Vargas from his critics.

His elected successor, Juscelino Kubitschek, proved more adept at using economic policy to placate the members of the populist coalition while at the same time promoting rapid economic growth. A student in the Vargas school of politics, he recognized that without the deliberate acceleration of economic growth there was little chance of satisfying industrialists, organized labor, and other economic groups simultaneously. So instead of stressing redistribution, he encouraged investment and industrial expansion by promoting the efforts of domestic and foreign entrepreneurs and supporting them with increased public investments in infrastructure and government enterprises. Bolstered by improving external conditions, he achieved impressive results with his program: Industrial production rose 80 percent and the gross national product increased at an annual average rate of 6.1 percent between 1955 and 1961, one of the highest rates in the hemisphere. Equally impressive was Kubitscheck's ability to use his policies to satisfy the demands of competing economic groups. He supplied easy credit and tariff protection to industrialists, price supports to farmers, favorable terms to foreign investors, new jobs and rising wages to labor, and pay raises to the military. Only the peasantry and the urban poor − albeit 50 percent of the population − were excluded from the new bounty, but as nonparticipants in the Brazilian game, they could be ignored without serious political repercussions.

There were other costs as well, namely record budget deficits that boosted inflation and contributed to balance-of-payments difficulties. But unlike Vargas, who had earlier responded to similar conditions by imposing unpopular stabilization measures, Kubitschek ignored the pleas of foreign creditors and International Monetary Fund advisers, who insisted on cooling off the overheated Brazilian economy. His defiance won him immense popularity within the country, but it only postponed several tough economic policy decisions, many of which were not made until the military seized control and executed a stabilization program with brutal efficiency in 1964.

In retrospect, it seems clear that the Brazilian economy grew steadily during the 1950s largely because of a policy of import substitution encouraged by high tariffs and favorable exchange rates. With the help of foreign capital and imported business practices, the production of consumer durables, machinery, and transportation equipment increased by approximately 50 percent between 1949 and 1964. By 1964, approximately one-third of Brazil's manufacturing industries were owned by foreigners. Equally important, after World War II the government increased its production of goods and services by expanding the operations of public enterprises in banking, transportation, petroleum and petrochemicals, steel, and public utilities. It was primarily the combination of foreign and government investment, supplemented by domestic private efforts in agriculture and commerce, that launched Brazil along the path of rapid economic growth. It was accomplished, however, with rapidly rising public expenditures and wages, which contributed to an annual average inflation rate of 52 percent between 1959 and 1963. Uncertainty followed, as the per capita growth rate fell to less than 0.5 percent in 1962 and 1963; soon thereafter the military stepped in, blaming the populist demagoguery and managerial incompetence of President João Goulart for the sudden decline.

When they took over in 1964, the armed forces claimed that their most immediate objective was economic, not political. Politics was primarily a means to the end of economic modernization through the use of state, foreign, and domestic private capital. They were confident that under appropriate leadership Brazil would prosper. In 1964 that meant a strong government that could get inflation under control, restore investor confidence, and extract and sell the country's abundant resources. Civilian economists were ready and waiting to tell them how to do it. Consequently, once it had terminated conventional political life, it was to the economy that the government turned most of its civilian expertise.

Their approach came closest to the conservative-modernization strategy described in Chapter 5. The only difference was the extraordinary intrusion by the state into the nation's development. Already the owner of several manufacturing enterprises and utilities, the government never considered turning them over to the private sector. With the assistance of civilian economist Roberto Campos, President Castelo Branco launched a program that combined several conventional austerity measures with a system of built-in adjustments to inflation using index linking of the exchange rate, interest rates, taxes, incomes, and prices. They wanted to make all variables move at the same speed so that production and employment would rapidly and efficiently adjust to new conditions. Nevertheless, even with indexation, real wages fell and wealth became even more concentrated in the hands of the wealthy.

Table 9.2. *Brazilian economic performance, 1950–73 (average annual real growth rates)*

	1950–60	1960–5	1965–73
Gross domestic product per capita	3.1	1.2	6.0
Agricultural product per capita	1.5	1.5	1.6
Industrial product per capita	6.0	0.8	8.1
Retail price index	–	54.0	23.3

Note: Dash indicates information not given.
Source: World Bank, *World Tables 1976*. Washington, D.C., 1976, p. 396.

To the surprise of skeptics, including some within the military, the effort gradually succeeded. The flow of foreign investment grew rapidly and, with the help of government subsidization, Brazil raised its exports of manufactured goods, bringing badly needed diversification to its trade. Not only did the government bring stability to the economy, but Brazil achieved 11 percent annual growth in its national product, the fastest in its history, causing the generals to boast of having worked a miracle by taking the country from economic chaos to unprecedented prosperity. There is some evidence to support the claim, as we can see from Table 9.2. After a few years of economic stabilization, the Brazilian economy suddenly accelerated, growing at a record pace between 1968 and 1973. At the same time, inflation, which reached nearly 100 percent in 1963, was reduced to an annual average of 23 percent after 1965. However, claims of a miracle are a bit exaggerated. The government did not so much rebuild the economy as it did consolidate and expand a process of industrial development that had already gone a long way in the 1950s before stalling in 1960.

The primary beneficiaries of the military's development program were obvious. Most of them were concentrated in the southern third of the country, where industry and modern agriculture are located. Multinational corporations from the United States, Western Europe, and Japan took full advantage of the new opportunities opened to them in Brazil, as did domestic industrialists, bankers, and retailers. Commercial farmers who shifted from traditional to new export crops (e.g., from black beans to soybeans, making Brazil the world's second-largest producer), as well as the producers of coffee, grain, and other commodities, also did well under the new regime. Even the landed elites of the northeast survived with most

of their economic resources undiminished. Urban professionals, bureaucrats, white-collar workers, and others associated with public
and private enterprises also profited from the new prosperity. Less
fortunate were the factory workers and unskilled laborers, who saw
their real wages decline until the early 1970s, when the government
began compensating them for past losses. But their condition was
still better than the estimated 50 percent of the population that survived on the fringes of the modern economy. The plight of the
peasant was as ignored by the military regime as it was by previous
Brazilian governments. And though significant strides were made in
literacy and basic education, little of the country's increased wealth
trickled down to the masses. As a result, income disparities between the middle sectors and the masses increased.

Not surprisingly, Brazil was held up as an example of what the
conservative-modernization strategy could do in Latin America. Using
authoritarian methods to impose harsh austerity and then to encourage
domestic and foreign investments in industry and commercial agriculture, the Brazilians did achieve one of the highest rates of economic
growth in the hemisphere before 1973. But Brazil has also been heavily
criticized. By worshipping at the altar of growth the Brazilians postponed efforts to solve the critical social problems that still plague the
country. While they were expanding the modern sector for one-half
the population, the other half languished at or just above the subsistence level. In 1976 the poorest 50 percent of the population still
received only 11.8 percent of the national income, whereas the wealthiest 5 percent received 39 percent.

On balance, what did it accomplish? Clearly the initial effort was
impressive. No other Latin American nation matched Brazil's economic expansion during those years. But before declaring it a success,
three things should be considered. First, what the military regime
demonstrated was not the unqualified success of the conservative-
modernization strategy, but only its ability to promote rapid industrial
growth in a country that already enjoyed an established industrial
base. Post-1964 governments did not start from scratch, but only
reinforced, albeit skillfully, a growth process well under way.

Second, Brazil's performance before 1973 was attributable not so
much to free-market capitalism as to the efforts of the Brazilian government and large multinational enterprises. By 1979 the government
owned 560 enterprises employing 1.3 million people. And 60 percent
of the investments made during the boom years 1967–1973 came from

the public sector. Add to that the fact that between 1970 and 1973 investments by multinational firms in Brazil increased sevenfold. Clearly, government bureaucrats and corporate executives had made the Brazilian economy work.

Third, Brazil's economic boom cooled off some after 1973 and the entire enterprise fell apart in 1980. Disruption began with a 120-percent increase in the cost of imports after the OPEC nations' raised oil prices in 1973. Authorities tried to finance continued expansion by borrowing from the new supply of international credit made available when the oil producers deposited their earnings in North American and European banks. By 1979, $40 billion had arrived, 85 percent of it as loans that were borrowed at low but floating interest rates. Much of it went into projects intended to generate healthy rates of return in the steel, petrochemical, and fertilizer industries, and in hydroelectric power and communications.

Unfortunately, the price of imported oil rose again dramatically in 1979, upsetting all of the government's calculations. With oil prices doubling, interest rates on borrowed money shot up and the prices paid abroad for Brazilian exports fell as other oil importers cut their consumption of everything else. Desperate, the Brazilians borrowed even more and the debt rose to nearly $100 billion in three years. Obviously, something had to change, and it was still up to the armed forces to decide what that would be.

Abertura: the transition to democracy

The decision of the Brazilian military to allow free elections after displaying so much disdain toward civilian politicians for twenty years requires some explanation, especially when we learn that they were neither forced out by civilian opponents, nor were they satisfied yet with their creation. Nevertheless, they pulled back and gradually let civilians replace them.

Disagreements between military "softliners" and "hardliners" had occasionally produced shifts in policy, but until the 1970s they were kept under control. Increasingly, however, they made it difficult for the armed forces to rule the nation comfortably, causing some among them to begin looking for another way out. They also became frustrated with increasing criticism from members of the social classes who had benefited the most from their economic recovery efforts. They had originally gained considerable support from the middle and upper classes by exploiting their fear of the political left and by capitalizing on their appreciation for the economy's revival. But their support proved transitory. By destroying the political left, the armed forces ended the public's fear of it, and after a spectacular economic boom, the economy stumbled over rising petroleum prices in the mid-1970s, leaving many to doubt if the military could sustain prosperity any longer. Gradually, industrialists and business people joined the many lawyers, students, and clergy who were protesting against repression, adding complaints about the military's direction of the economy to the expanding list of transgressions that were being hurled at it. The armed forces had relied on the enthusiasm of entrepreneurs to make their rescue of the nation's economy work, but when their efforts faltered many civilians began to question the utility of governing the nation militarily.

Recognizing all of this, President Ernesto Geisel launched a "decompression" operation beginning in 1974 that was intended to prepare the nation for a return to a form of civilian government that the military could tolerate (i.e., a conservative one). But what seemed a reasonable objective and a practical solution to Geisel and his fellow officers turned out to be an objective that was far beyond their capacity to achieve.

The process was not an easy one to manage, even for a military as powerful as the Brazilian one. There are simply too many possible combinations of decisions, conflicts, and timings involved in transitions to allow one to follow a well-prepared plan. Seldom can the armed forces control a process that usually provokes disputes among military officers and between them and civilian political parties about the plan and its utility. Transitions are usually composed of two phases: one in which some liberties are restored, allowing political parties to recruit followers and campaign for election, and the next in which a democratic government is actually created by election. During the first phase the initiative sometimes shifts from the armed forces to civilians who, with public support, demand that the government replace its own calendar with one more favorable to civilian tastes, that is, shorter, and a more direct election. Pressures to do it the way civilian politicians wish grows as the election approaches and public expectations make it increasingly difficult for the military to back out. That is why the armed forces almost never consider calling off elections just before they hold them. In short, transitions from authoritarian government to democracy involve a political process with its own dynamics, one that is conditioned as much by the way the participants bargain with one another as by the laws adopted to regulate the election itself. Exiting military officers, aspiring politicians, and the general public engage one another in a contest in which each tries to advance or defend vested interests through the design and operation of the new democratic regime.

When the Brazilians began the process in the mid-1970s two separate but closely related issues had to be addressed. One involved the restoration of fundamental rights to citizens, sometimes referred to as *liberalization*. This entails such things as freedom of speech, movement, and press, habeas corpus, etc. They must be written into a document and enforced by the judicial system regardless of who governs. The other issue is *accountability* or the mechanisms and rules that make government officials responsive to all publics in their society. This may be done using various forms of election and representation. To people currently living under a liberal democratic constitution, both of these issues are closely related, but to the Brazilian military they were very separate matters, each to be resolved in its own way.

They proceeded incrementally and experimentally, addressing parts of each issue, writing new laws, assessing their results, revising them, and then moving on to the next stage. President Geisel began the process in 1978 by lifting press censorship and announcing an *abertura cronogram,* a calendar for the transition. It was accompanied by his annulling Institutional Act No. 5, which had given the president dictatorial power, including the right to suspend civil rights, censor the press and close down Congress. When General João Figueiredo replaced Geisel he focused on the issue of accountability, starting with new electoral laws that could satisfy the armed forces in their desire to prohibit certain election results (i.e., a sweeping victory by anti-military civilian politicians) without entirely alienating the opposition. It was an impossible task, but they refused to admit it.

The military started by creating a new political party out of the old ARENA party, and staffed it with civilians. Named the Social Democratic Party, its leaders focused on mobilizing voters in regions where the military had always been strong (e.g., the northeast and other rural areas). They also decided to exclude the presidency from direct elections, filling it two years after national congressional elections using

Table 9.3. *Brazilian national elections, 1982*

	% of votes	Number of seats	
		Senate	Chamber
Brazilian Democratic Movement (MDB)	44.1	21	200
Social Democratic Party (PDS)	39.4	46	235
Democratic Labor Party (PDT)	6.7	1	24
Brazilian Labor Party (PTB)	5.5	1	14
Workers' Party (PT)	4.3	0	6

Note: Each citizen voted for one party list of candidates for local office, governorships, and the two houses of Congress.
Source: The Economist, November 27, 1982, p. 60.

representatives from the national and state legislatures in an Electoral College. Second, the government encouraged the opposition to create many parties in an attempt to divide the opposition at the polls. Third, and most important, congressional districts were drawn in such a way as to permit the Social Democratic Party to secure a majority of the seats in Congress without winning a majority of the popular vote.

The government's calculations proved quite accurate and its precautions most wise. In the November 1982 congressional elections it received only 39.4 percent of the popular vote, compared with 44.1 percent for the MDB, but it retained a majority of the Senate (one-third of whose seats were contested) and held on to a strong plurality in the Chamber of Deputies. Still, their defeat was obvious and overwhelming. The Brazilian Democratic Movement, an urban-based party that had attracted people from all social classes who were united in their determination to evict the military, was the winner (see Table 9.3). In addition to their national triumph they also won control over the governorships and legislatures in all of the powerful south-central states where 75 percent of the nation's gross national product is produced, including São Paulo, Rio de Janeiro, and Minas Gerais.

Next the military turned its attention to the presidential election in the Electoral College in 1985. For insurance against defeat in the college they made some additional changes in the rules in order to increase the number of delegates from the smaller states in the north. They simply decreed that six legislators would come to the Electoral College from each state, rather than one per million citizens. As a result, the college majority that the opposition seemed to have secured by winning in the most populous states in 1982 suddenly disappeared. Machiavelli would have been impressed.

On paper the revisions were crafty, but in practice they were a dismal failure. It started with a decision by retiring President João Figueiredo to abdicate responsibility for the selection of the PDS candidate. Exhibiting a distaste for the kind of party politics that had begun to develop once the military had given civilians in its PDS major responsibilities for the party's operation, he turned the succession issue over to the party, opening the door for hosts of back-room squabbles over candidate selection among the factions that quickly developed. Some people wanted to nominate a military officer to run while others insisted on a conservative civilian.

While the PDS quarreled over its nominee, the MDB chose civilian Tancredo Neves, a seventy-two-year-old politician who had spent his life playing by Brazilian rules, reaping the benefits of clientist politics at the state and local levels for himself and his followers under military as well as civilian governments. By selecting someone so much a member of the system, the MDB hoped to attract some Electoral College members away from the PDS, a tactic that offered them the best chance of winning. Simultaneously, the MDB also tried to change the rules, seeking congressional approval of a new law that would allow the direct election of the president in 1985 instead of leaving it to an Electoral College whose majority favored the PDS. The effort failed by only 20 votes in the House of Representatives when it came to a vote.

The message was clear to the more moderate members of the PDS who worried about the new government's losing control over a highly mobilized opposition. They needed a civilian candidate and chose Paulo Maluf of densely populated São Paulo. But Maluf, an aggressive, egotistical, and to many, offensive, upper-class businessman, was not a popular person either within his party or outside it. Knowing this, Neves seized the opportunity before the Electoral College met in January 1985 to appeal to dissidents in Maluf's PDS for support. In a very Brazilian fashion, he worked out deals with several of them, promising them places in a MDB government in return for their coming over to his side. To make his point he invited conservative José Sarney to leave the PDS and become vice-president on the Neves ticket. It worked, to the dismay of many in the military, and Neves was elected president by the Electoral College, the first civilian to occupy the office in twenty-one years.

Brazilian politics is filled with unanticipated ironies, and none was more incredible than what happened next. When Neves selected Sarney he did not know that he would become ill and die just before his inauguration, leaving the presidency to none other than José Sarney who, until a few weeks before, was a member of the government's Social Democratic Party.

This would have been disastrous in a political system where legislatures devour weak presidents who were never supposed to become president. But the Brazilian game is different. Checks and balances could not operate very well in a nation so reliant on the executive branch for its direction and maintenance. As might be expected, the new legislature was weak, its members still more accustomed to involving themselves in petty disputes and playing ombudsmen for constituents who sought favors from the national bureaucracy than with writing major pieces of legislation. Moreover, they were distracted by their taking it upon themselves to write an entirely new constitution during the next three years. It also helped Sarney that neither the PDS or the MDB were well-organized, disciplined parties. Neither offered a real program for the country, and it is doubtful that their members could have stayed together long enough to implement one if they did. So it was left to Sarney, with the armed forces at his side, to govern.

While Congress busied itself with writing a constitution, Sarney devoted most of his time to managing an economy in trouble. The gross domestic product, which had grown at an annual rate of 9.0 percent between 1965 and 1980, grew by an annual average of only 1.3 percent over the next eight years. And inflation, which had averaged "only" 31.6 percent for several years before 1980, rose to 150 percent annually in the 1980s. Moreover, the Brazilian government, which had borrowed heavily in the 1970s to fund its big investments, was now paying enormous interest on a debt of $100 billion.

In February 1986, Sarney announced his Cruzado Plan, a drastic attempt to break the inflation psychology that had seized Brazil. He froze all prices, eliminated automatic monetary indexation, and created a new currency, called the cruzado, by dropping three zeros from the old cruziero. Almost immediately inflation stopped. And for a few months Brazilians celebrated by buying everything they could find. It helped that real wages had increased by 15 percent in 1985 and were lifted another 15 percent by the government at the time of the Cruzado Plan. As demand rose and industries produced at full capacity, Brazilians consumed many of the manufactured goods that they normally had exported. Consumers expressed their appreciation by giving the MDB a massive victory in the November 1986 congressional elections and in 22 of the nation's 23 governorships. But their instant prosperity was doomed to fail.

Shortages appeared everywhere, forcing Sarney to reverse course in February 1987 by freeing nearly all prices, causing the working class to lose most of what it had gained in purchasing power the year before. But, unlike in 1964, when the armed forces stepped in to "rescue" the country, they held back this time. Their reasons were quite apparent. To start with, Sarney was not Goulart; quite the contrary, he was a conservative president who had no intention of seeking a populist political solution to his plight. Instead, he consulted daily with the military high command, asking its advice and often following it. He was comfortable living within the traditional rules of the Brazilian game, even when it was becoming harder to do so. Moreover, the armed forces had no desire to rule the nation quite yet. Times were not so bad that the middle class was eager for their return; moreover, they were as befuddled as everyone else by the nation's economic plight.

Sarney did try to gain some popularity by taking a hard stand on payment of the nation's $1 billion foreign debt. Aware of the unpopularity of his paying as much as a third of the country's export earnings to foreign banks, and eager to negotiate better terms with creditors, he suspended interest payments on most of the debt in February 1987. He made it clear that he was not defaulting, as creditors feared, but merely halting payment until the country's economy recovered. He was also convinced that because of the enormity of its debt and the dependence of major foreign banks on its payment for their own solvency, they might be willing to renegotiate it on terms more favorable to Brazil.

But Brazil's creditors did not budge, determined as they were to make no concessions that might compel them to do the same for their other debtors. It helped that they were much stronger than they had been five years before when the debt crisis struck and, therefore, less reliant on Brazilian payments than they had previously been. A year passed, and then Sarney blinked first. Refusing to confess an error of judgment, he announced that Brazil would make payments again on terms more acceptable to its creditors. He was aware that the flow of foreign capital to the country had been slowed during the holdout, and he needed much more of it. It was an unwelcome conclusion that Brazilians, accustomed to rapid economic growth through intense participation in the world economy, could not avoid reaching.

Another failure of the new government was its retreat from campaign promises to implement significant agrarian reforms in many parts of the country. In a society as conservative and elitist as Brazil's one does not expect much reform, but its necessity is nevertheless obvious. One need only examine a northeastern state like Ceara to discover that the average life span of this very rural state's 6 million inhabitants is forty-two years, illiteracy is near 50 percent, and a monthly income above $450 is earned by no more than 2 percent of the population. There never are enough jobs to go around in the best of times, and there are far fewer new ones now.

It was with this in mind that MDB candidate Tancredo Neves proposed agrarian reform during his campaign, and, after his inauguration, Sarney promised to go ahead with it, transferring government property and the land of unproductive large farmers to the landless. He proposed to expropriate nearly 107 million acres, a combined area the size of Spain, and to settle around 1.4 million families on it. Owners were to be compensated at the value they declared when they paid their property taxes (an approach that saves the government money and penalizes landowners who habitually undervalue their property for tax purposes). Some land would be taken in every state, though far more in the central and north central parts of the country, all the way up to the Amazon basin.

Carefully designed not to reduce national production, the program, though huge, threatened virtually no productive farmers. Nevertheless, the largest landowners were predictably hostile, declaring the idea a violation of the Brazilian way of life. The wealthiest went to court to halt the effort, and with relative ease slowed it down substantially. After raising hopes Sarney was afraid to cancel it, but he found it increasingly impossible to come close to delivering on his promise to complete redistribution to all 1.4 million families by 1990. Brazil's rural conservatism prevailed once more and the country's 300,000 large-scale farmers survived with their properties and power intact.

Some cheer was taken from the completion of a new constitution in 1988 that reads like the wish list of nearly every progressive interest in Brazilian society. It reduced the voting age from 18 to 16, legalized strikes for all workers, nationalized all mineral mining, abolished all censorship, prohibited making law using presidential decrees, and guaranteed women 120-day maternity leaves, among other things. Enforcing it would be a monumental task in a nation like Brazil where so little respect has been paid constitutional law in the past, but many Brazilians seem convinced that it is worth a try.

José Sarney's presidency ended in 1989 with consumer prices 22,000 percent higher than they had been at his inauguration. He was forced to impose severe austerity measures on the economy before leaving office, putting an end to the indexation of prices and wages that had protected people from the worst effects of inflation, and cutting government budgets sharply. Not surprisingly, none but his closest civilian and military friends were sad to see his unusual presidency come to an end. But that was not all. With the economy in trouble for a decade, and no new "miracle" in sight, Brazilians were becoming uncharacteristically pessimistic. It seemed that nothing came easily anymore, and despite their enormous natural resources and huge economic infrastructure, more people were poorer than a decade before and many more feared that they would join them before the century ended.

Lessons from Brazil

The Brazilian case demonstrates many things about authoritarianism, capitalism, the modernizing state, and the ways they relate to one another. Given the nation's long history of reliance on a strong national government, military authoritarianism was an almost natural progression from less sophisticated forms of authoritarianism. Brazilians were accustomed to being ruled over, and twenty years of democratic government before the military ended it in 1964 did not change that. Moreover, the upper and middle classes had been looking to military officers for rescue in times of crisis since 1930, and their doing so again when a president was inciting the masses to march behind him was not surprising. Authoritarianism is part of Brazil, not the only part, but still something with which many people, even in the working class, occasionally accommodate themselves. That, more than their weapons, is what keeps the armed forces so deeply involved in the nation's affairs.

Brazil also shows how much an already powerful state apparatus facilitates the military authoritarian operation. General Castelo Branco did not have to rebuild state institutions when he presided over the nation in 1964. The armed forces merely took over the enormous structure that had managed the nation's affairs for decades. That is quite different from what happens when the military seizes control over a far less developed state in a nation like El Salvador or Honduras where governments, though at times ruthless, are weaker institutionally. Brazilian officers operate military enterprises and retire into the civilian bureaucracy when their military careers end, all of which makes supervising the state almost instinctive with them.

In Brazil, state and private enterprises worked closely together, making the government, despite its economic enormity, heavily dependent on private investors for the success of its economic programs. Regardless of how nationalistic military officers were, they relied on multinational investors to help finance the nation's development. Together they produced one of the region's productive economies, but in doing so the Brazilians also indebted themselves as never before, making it impossible for civilian governments to replicate their economic success.

Brazil is a reminder that democracy is no more than what powerful players want it to be. As was noted in Chapter 2, culture, tradition, and economic power structures always affect how the game is played no matter what the rules say should happen. This is especially so with democracy since it gives so much leeway to players who have little or no respect for its procedures. Many Brazilians wanted to create democratic government in the 1980s, but they could not wipe the cultural and social slate clean before doing so. At best they could only impose elections and new systems of representation on a society unaccustomed to living with either. People in the middle class welcomed the civil liberties that came with democracy but those in the lower classes exhibited little confidence in the persons they elected, and the wealthiest members of society had almost no respect for them. So each continued to go about its business as if elections were peripheral to their existence.

Moreover, the huge Brazilian state, which might have given democrats tremendous power, proved nearly impossible to subdue. In theory, elected representatives in Congress and the nation's president are supposed to take control over the state apparatus, putting it to work for the people who elected them. But in Brazil government corporations and military organizations were not about to yield to the latest whim of the Brazilian people. Nor did many powerful people in Brazilian society want them to. They have always worked directly with state institutions or through a system of local political machines that served them in the most undemocratic fashion, and they did not trust political parties or national legislators to take over. President José Sarney did not change this. Without a party of his own he had to deal with a Congress that was almost totally controlled by the MDB after the 1986 elections. That left it to the armed forces to become his most ardent defender, and to him to serve as the proponent of their positions on nearly all issues. In essence, then, Brazil had created little more than a government whose president and bureaucracy supervised the nation's affairs while the Congress concentrated nearly all of its energies on writing a new constitution.

Last, but certainly not least, the most recent Brazilian experience reminds us of how a country's economic dependence circumscribes its leaders when they try to mobilize resources for the nation's economic development. The form that it takes and the amount involved has varied from one nation to another. In the 1980s, enormous financial debts were the culprit, and perhaps the most costly of all. Unlike multinational corporations that invest within a country and produce goods and wages for the nation's consumers, payments extract from its limited financial resources, reducing its pool without replenishing it. Presidents are forced to send export earnings to their creditors and demand continuous sacrifice at home. The temptation to suspend interest payments, as Sarney did in 1987, is understandable, but it provides only temporary relief. Of course, Brazil's economic development will not stop, regardless of its relations with its creditors, but as far as one can see its monumental achievements will continue to be accompanied by immense poverty.

Further reading

Military authoritarianism: general

Collier, David, ed. *The New Authoritarianism in Latin America*. Princeton, NJ: Princeton University Press, 1979.

Comblin, José. *The Church and the National Security State*. Maryknoll, NY: Orbis, 1979.
Foxley, Alejandro. *Latin American Experiments in Neoconservative Economics*. Berkeley: University of California Press, 1983.
Malloy, James, ed. *Authoritarianism and Corporatism in Latin America*. Pittsburgh: University of Pittsburgh Press, 1977.
O'Donnell, Guillermo A. *Modernization and Bureaucratic-Authoritarianism: Studies in South American Politics*. Institute of International Studies. Berkeley: University of California Press, 1973.
Ramos, Joseph. *Neoconservative Economics in the Southern Cone of Latin America, 1973–1983*. Baltimore: The Johns Hopkins University Press, 1986.
Stepan, Alfred. *Rethinking Military Politics: Brazil and the Southern Cone*. Princeton, NJ: Princeton University Press, 1988.

Brazil

Baer, Werner. *The Brazilian Economy*. 2nd ed. New York: Praeger, 1983.
Bruneau, Thomas C., and Philippe Faucher, eds. *Authoritarian Capitalism: Brazil's Contemporary Economic and Political Development*. Boulder, CO: Westview Press, 1984.
Chacel, Julian, Pamela Falk, and David Fleischer, eds. *Brazil's Economic and Political Future*. Boulder, CO: Westview Press, 1986.
Evans, Peter. *Dependent Development: The Alliance of Multinational, State, and Local Capital in Brazil*. Princeton, NJ: Princeton University Press, 1979.
Flynn, Peter. *Brazil: A Political Analysis*. Boulder, CO: Westview Press, 1978.
Gómes, Gustavo Maia. *The Roots of State Intervention in the Brazilian Economy*. New York: Praeger, 1986.
Mainwaring, Scott. *The Catholic Church and Politics in Brazil, 1916–1985*. Stanford, CA: Stanford University Press, 1985.
McDonough, Peter. *Power and Ideology in Brazil*. Princeton, NJ: Princeton University Press, 1981.
Moran, Emilio F., ed. *The Dilemmas of Amazonian Development*. Boulder, CO: Westview Press, 1983.
Moreiro Alves, Maria Helena. *State and Opposition in Military Brazil*. Austin: University of Texas Press, 1985.
Morley, Samuel. *Labor Markets and Inequitable Growth: The Case of Authoritarian Capitalism in Brazil*. New York: Cambridge University Press, 1982.
Pereira, Luiz Bresser. *Development and Crisis in Brazil, 1930–1983*. Boulder, CO: Westview Press, 1984.
Skidmore, Thomas. *The Politics of Military Rule in Brazil, 1964–1985*. New York: Oxford University Press, 1988.
Stepan, Alfred. *The Military in Politics: Changing Patterns in Brazil*. Princeton, NJ: Princeton University Press, 1971.
    Authoritarian Brazil: Origins, Policies, and Future. New Haven, CN: Yale University Press, 1973.

Worth, John, ed. *State and Society in Brazil*. Boulder, CO: Westview Press, 1986.

Transition to democracy

Baloyra, Enrique, ed. *Comparing New Democracies: Transition and Consolidation in Mediterranean Europe and the Southern Cone*. Boulder, CO: Westview Press, 1987.
Drake, Paul, and Eduardo Silva. *Elections and Democratization in Latin America, 1980–1985*. San Diego: Center for Iberian and Latin American Studies of University of California, 1986.
Malloy, James, and Mitchell A. Seligson, eds. *Authoritarians and Democrats: Regime Transition in Latin America*. Pittsburgh: University of Pittsburgh Press, 1987.
Needler, Martin C. *The Problem of Democracy in Latin America*. Lexington, MA: Lexington Books, 1987.
O'Donnell, Guillermo, Philippe C. Schmitter, and Laurence Whithead, eds. *Transitions from Authoritarian Rule: Latin America*. Baltimore: The Johns Hopkins University Press, 1986.

10. Argentina: populists, authoritarians, and democrats

Argentina differs from Brazil in several ways. Brazil was a Portuguese colony and Argentina a Spanish one. Brazil is much larger, its population four times greater, more ethnically diverse, and poorer on the average than Argentina's. Yet Argentina also tried military authoritarianism, not once but twice between 1966 and 1983, after a decade of populism that was far more profound than Brazil's and certainly more enduring thanks to the adroit leadership of General Juan Domingo Perón who ruled Argentina for ten years immediately after World War II.

In 1966, two years after the Brazilian experiment in military authoritarianism began, the Argentine armed forces did likewise. But the Argentine venture lasted only seven years before new elections were held. However, the military's retreat was brief, and after three years of Peronist government, they took control once more in 1976, this time ruthlessly unleashing an assault on the Argentine people that left over 8,000 dead, nearly all of them secretly seized and killed by military security forces in civilian dress. Yet, as before, the military government lasted just seven years, this time forced out by its own embarrassment from defeat by the British in a war over the Falkland/Malvinas Islands. Then, simultaneous with the Brazilians, the Argentines began a transition to constitutional government, spending the rest of the 1980s reeducating themselves in democratic politics.

The Argentine experience raises many questions. Why, for example, did populist Juan Perón change his nation's politics more than Vargas did his, and how did he do it? And what produced military authoritarian government in Argentina? Was it simply military hostility toward Peronism, or was it a natural consequence of the way the nation developed socially and economically? And why were the Argentine armed forces unable to sustain the kind of authoritarianism that they so admired in Brazil? Did the legacy of populism make Argentina much harder to govern, or is the Argentine military incapable of running any country? To find answers to these and other questions we

249

will begin with Juan Perón and his populist politics to determine what, if anything, he contributed to the rise of military authoritarianism.

Peronist populism

General Juan Perón was a nationalist who advocated industrialization and modest social reform. He was also a consummate opportunist, skilled at adapting Argentine rules to his needs. Much more than Vargas, he gained popularity by attacking the nation's oligarchy, deepening class antagonisms already present in Argentina, and reinforcing the popular belief that the Argentine state was a partisan instrument employed by antagonists against their rivals. Juan Perón attained far more fame outside the region than did Vargas, and he is still regarded as the consummate populist. This is not surprising, for while Vargas practiced many different kinds of politics during his career, Perón stuck to just one, relying throughout his tenure on the urban working class and nationalist economics to sustain his power.

Perón rose to the presidency by mobilizing a previously disenfranchised urban working class, assisted by his wife Evita, whose demagogic appeal and political skill made the masses believe that his government was their own. His opponents were numerous, among them the rural oligarchy and foreign business, the middle-sector and upper-class political parties that he defeated in the 1945 elections, the United States and British governments, the Roman Catholic hierarchy after he legalized divorce, and factions within the armed forces that had always resented his getting so much power so swiftly.

He was successful in part because he knew how to exploit antagonisms that had accompanied the nation's economic development during the previous half century. Until World War II Argentina had been run by an agroexporter elite of several thousand families that became wealthy when Europeans began importing vast amounts of the country's meat and grain in the 1880s. Eager to purchase the grain they needed to feed their rapidly growing urban working class and to control as much world trade as possible, the British financed the construction of railways, harbors, and other utilities in Argentina, swiftly transforming the muddy port of Buenos Aires into a replica of Paris and London and a new home for several million Spanish and Italian immigrants between 1880 and 1920, much as New York had done for other Europeans at the same time. The government was run by the upper class until the middle sectors challenged them after 1900, forcing electoral reforms that allowed the opposition Radical Party to win its first presidential election in 1916 (see Table 10.1). The Radicals immediately opened the political process to their constituents but they made no effort to alter the character of the nation's flourishing export economy or to deprive the upper class of its wealth.

The 1929 depression and fear that the Radicals could not defend the traditional economic order against rising social protests prompted intervention by the agroexporter elite and its allies in the armed forces in 1930. Two years later, a conservative regime was confirmed in fraudulent elections and harsh austerity was imposed on the depression-ravaged Argentine economy. The new authorities rescued the nation from near catastrophe using methods that antagonized nationalists who resented the country's further subordination to its British trading partners. By signing the Roca–Runciman pact, the Argentine government guaranteed a market for England's manufactured goods in exchange for the latter's purchase of beef, claiming it had no choice but to accept the British terms since no other markets were available to them. But, for a vocal and expanding community of nationalists within the opposition Radical Party and the lower ranks of the military, the treaty was a distasteful reminder of Argentina's immense vulnerability, something that Perón would later exploit to win popular support.

The oligarchs also alienated the country's growing working class. Until the 1930s, Argentina's organized laborers had been few in number but militant in spirit under the leadership of socialists and anarchists, many of them European migrants. After the 1930 coup working-class militancy was met with harsh repression by a government determined to preserve the old order, and within a few years the labor movement was left impotent by the combined pressure of unemployment and government oppression. Nevertheless, the urban working class grew as a result of migration from the countryside to the cities, which accompanied the industrialization that filled the vacuum created by a shortage of imported consumer goods during the early years of depression. Consequently, by the early 1940s Argentina had an flourishing industrial work force whose attempts to organize were continually frustrated by a hostile government. This gave Perón something to exploit once he was in a position to do so after the military coup of 1943.

Table 10.1. *Argentina: historical background*

1816	Independence from Spain declared
1835	Autocrat Juan Manuel Rosas imposes order on country torn by conflicts between city and country
1852	Rosas overthrown in revolt led by rivals in upper class, who wrote a new constitution and held elections from which masses were excluded
1916	Middle-sector Radical Party defeated upper-class parties for the first time. It won presidency again in 1922 and 1928
1929	World depression hit Argentine economy
1930	Military coup supported by upper class evicted Radical president and rigged next two elections
1943	Nationalist military coup prevented election of pro-British, conservative candidate
1946	General Juan Perón won presidency with working-class support in a free election
1951	Perón re-elected president
1952	Perón's wife, Evita, died
1955	Military coup sent Perón into exile for eighteen years
1958	Arturo Frondizi of Radical Party won presidency in election in which Peronist Party was excluded
1962	Military coup ended Frondizi government
1963	Arturo Illia of Radical Party won presidency with 25 percent of the vote in election in which Peronist Party was excluded
1966	Military coup ended Illia government and military governed for next seven years, the first five under General Juan Carlos Onganía
1973	Juan Perón returned home, was elected president, and died one year later
1976	Military coup ended Peronist government and military governed for next seven years, the first five under General Jorge Videla; an estimated 8,000–10,000 citizens were killed by armed forces
1982	Military invaded Falkland/Malvinas Islands then lost war after the British retaliated
1983	Raul Alfonsín of Radical Party defeated Peronist Italo Luder in free elections and the two parties divided control over Congress during next five years
1989	Carlos Menem of the Peronist Party elected president

Political change was expedited by the incompetence of the conservative authorities. Prior to 1916, the agroexporter elite had easily dominated Argentine politics through its control over the country's economy. That feat could not be replicated after 1930 in a nation that had changed significantly during the 1920s. The middle sectors had asserted themselves and could be excluded from the government only with physical force and electoral fraud. And constant vigilance and repression were needed to contain the aspirations of a growing working class. Nevertheless, the country's conservative rulers held fast to the traditional practices that had served them so well before 1916. But by doing so they not only discredited party politics and constitutional government in the eyes of most Argentines, they also gradually undermined the confidence of the military in their ability to create a stable and durable political order. When President Ramón Castillo tried to secure military support for the reactionary *latifundista* he had nominated as his successor in 1943, the military resisted. They were equally irritated with Castillo's reluctance to take sides in World War II, and in June they evicted him.

Colonel Juan Domingo Perón did not lead the coup, but he was an active participant in it as a member of a nationalist, pro-Axis faction of young officers. He was rewarded first with the under-secretaryship of war and a few months later with the post of secretary of labor and social welfare. In February 1944 he became secretary of war, and in July of the same year was named vice-president.

Perón used his authority as war secretary and labor minister to recruit a large and devoted following. Within the War Ministry he secured the support of young officers whom he promoted in exchange for their loyalty. As labor secretary he reorganized thousands of workers and built a loyal constituency by rewarding unions that supported him with favorable collective-bargaining settlements and social security laws while punishing those who refused to accept his leadership. For Argentine laborers the advantages of the alliance were obvious. After years of being ignored or harassed by a succession of governments and poorly served by socialist and anarchist leaders who could not secure the wages and social services demanded by the rank and file, here at last was a leader who could deliver the goods almost overnight. By the middle of 1945, Perón had converted the General Labor Confederation, the nation's largest labor organization, into one of the strongest political forces in the country.

The last obstacle to Perón's ascendancy was overcome on October 17, 1945. A military faction opposed to him, in a desperate move to block his path to the presidency, persuaded President Farrell to arrest and jail him until after the elections were held. His incarceration came to an abrupt end, however, when his working-class followers, mobilized by loyal labor leaders, marched on the presidential palace and remained there until Perón was released to address them in triumph. Four months later he was swept into the presidency by defeating a hastily contrived coalition of Radicals and Conservatives in a free election.

His alliance with organized labor not only secured his election by democratic means and sustained his rule for an entire decade, but it also prevented the radicalization of the working class, something feared at the time by the armed forces, the middle class, and the rural oligarchy. Perón boasted about having saved Argentine capitalism from revolution, its worst enemy. The fact that the rural oligarchy did not appreciate the way he did it never bothered him; nor did it matter that the danger of revolution was never as great as he contended. It was a formula that worked politically, and for a time, albeit briefly, industry prospered and the working class flourished with capitalism's preservation by a paternalistic Peronist state whose managers were at home with corporatist and populist rationales for their protection of Argentine industry and organized labor.

To this day Argentines disagree over how authoritarian Perón really was. He was elected president under democratic rules and gained control over Congress when his party secured an absolute majority in nearly every province. He was immensely popular with the Argentine masses, as was his wife, Evita. An ex-radio actress of lower-class, small-town origin, she became a skilled orator who evoked intense emotional loyalty from the poor, a bond that was reinforced by her distribution of money, food, and clothing to thousands of Argentines. Her death in 1952 deprived her husband of a major asset, but by invoking memories of her leadership he exploited her popularity until his own death two decades later.

Juan Perón changed political rules once in power, but far less than it seemed at the time. Like the oligarchs who preceded him, he was content to abuse the Argentine constitution just enough to prevail over his opponents. He merely turned the tables on them, making such abuses popular with the masses who had suffered them in the past.

Argentines understood what he was doing: It was revenge, and it was instantly popular among people who admired his way of managing the crusade.

He had reason to fear his opponents. Within his populist welfare state the upper and middle classes retained substantial power, since they were an important part of what remained essentially a capitalist economy that relied heavily on private production to finance expansion. He tried to stay a step ahead of his opponents, arresting officers suspected of plotting coups, taking over newspapers that became too strident in their criticism, and unleashing goons to break up demonstrations against him. His was not a regime controlled by a highly disciplined political party, however, but rather one run by a small group of people hastily recruited by him from the military, labor leaders, and young professionals. With their help he governed in the manner of the general who knew that his subordinates would always obey his commands.

Undeniably, Perón admired European fascists, especially Mussolini, and, like him, he was nationalistic, believed in strong leadership, and advocated corporatist methods. Yet he never went as far as they did toward constructing a real fascist state. Instead he was content to intimidate factory owners, newspaper editors, and opposition politicians whenever they refused to cooperate voluntarily. It was an authoritarianism that was supported or tolerated by a majority of the population, but it was a crude variety that was built more on Perón's whims than on coherent ideology or sophisticated organization.

Corporatism, as we learned in Chapter 2, is a mode of government that stresses central control over society by leaders who exercise their authority through interest organizations representing labor, business, agriculture, and other sectors. It assumes that central direction is better established through functional organizations than through conventional legislatures. In its most extreme form it is very hierarchical and authoritarian, with the executive making decisions alone and then ordering their implementation by the leaders of sectoral associations. More moderate forms involve interest-group leaders in decision making, allowing them some influence over the executive's resolution of disputes and design of policy.

Vargas had pretended to build a corporate state in Brazil in 1937 when he launched the Estado Novo and made interest groups even more dependent on the government for their legality and subsidization than before. But Vargas never completed his corporatist project. It was even harder for Perón, because Argentina's industrial and agricultural groups were even less disposed to cooperating with their populist president than the Brazilians had been. Argentine entrepreneurs were accustomed to getting their way in the traditional game and resented being ordered about by inexperienced Peronist officials. Perón tried to control industrialists and farmers by forcing them to join a government-subsidized national association which, along with labor, was to assist in the administration of government policy. What he gained, however, was not control over the private sector but increased hostility and a sustained effort to secure his overthrow.

Perón's economics advocated accelerated industrialization and greater national economic independence using methods that he claimed would make Argentina one of the world's major postwar economic powers. That is why he paid off the nation's foreign debts, purchased the railways (at prices favorable to the English), and bought the telephone network from the International Telephone and Telegraph Company. By 1949 his buying spree had exhausted the country's abundant gold reserves, a feat that the Peronists celebrated as the first step toward their economic liberation. He also relied heavily on high tariffs to protect Argentine manufacturers from foreign competitors and an overvalued exchange rate that encouraged the importation of capital goods. Most controversial within the country was his creation of a government monopoly over all agricultural commodity trading, a device he employed to confiscate profits from commodity sales abroad. The operation was directed by the Argentine Trade Promotion Institute (IAPI), an organization that purchased beef, mutton, and grain from farmers at low official prices, sold them abroad at high postwar prices, and retained the profit to finance the programs of a rapidly growing government. Few things Perón did were more resented by farmers, large and small, than his handling of the IAPI.

Missing from the Peronist program was any commitment to agrarian reform. Perón's goal was the redistribution of rural profits, not rural property. He encouraged the purchase of land by tenant farmers by freezing rents, but he was content to leave cattlemen and farmers alone as long as they supplied the beef, mutton, and grain that would bring high postwar prices in foreign markets and finance the government's development programs. In other words, he left the rural power structure intact because he needed its produce to pay for industrialization.

Ironically, at the same time the Peronists were trying to reduce their economy's dependence on the rural sector, they were forced to rely on it to finance their scheme.

Perón wanted to launch Argentina on a course that would quickly place it among the elite of the world's industrial nations. Its dependence on foreigners was to give way to a new sense of national autonomy as the agrarian, export economy was transformed into an industrially self-sufficient one. And workers who in the past had been exploited by an insensitive economic elite were to be given the kind of social justice they deserved. But prosperity, national autonomy, and social justice eluded the Peronists, and by 1955 Argentina, the country they had tried to launch into a new era, had become a sorry paradox, divided politically and demoralized economically. Between 1945 and 1950, the per capita gross national product had increased at an annual average rate of 2.8 percent and real income at an impressive rate of 3.7 percent. But during the next five years, the per capita product declined at an annual rate of 0.2 percent and real income by 0.5 percent. The quality of the country's economic infrastructure deteriorated, and rural and industrial entrepreneurs lost confidence in the country's public authorities. Perón had tried to build a new Argentina, but he had only created a more desperate and discouraged one.

There are many explanations for the failure of Peronist policy. Its authors blame their problems on their enemies, both domestic and foreign, whom they accuse of subversion. Their critics point to economic mismanagement, government corruption, and Perón's failure to heed the warnings of his critics in the private sector. The truth, as usual, lies somewhere in between.

Several unanticipated external conditions did hurt the nation. Perón, for example, had counted on the continuation of high commodity prices in European markets to finance investment, but with the creation of the Marshall Plan and the delivery of millions of tons of American grain to Europe, Argentine trade prospects declined. To make matters worse, two of the country's worst droughts came in 1950 and 1951, further limiting production. But the Peronists must share some of the blame. They could have used their gold supply more cautiously to protect themselves against the effects of a sudden decline in exports. They also underestimated the high cost of industrialization, especially in technology and raw materials. And they contributed to the decapitalization of the private sector with their financial policies and mismanaged public enterprises, such as the nationalized railways, which became a source of featherbedding and a cause of huge fiscal deficits.

Finally, and most important, through his combative, autocratic style and often arbitrary policy decisions, Perón demoralized his country's rural and industrial entrepreneurs at the very time that he needed their cooperation to execute his programs. Although he made a valiant effort to reverse many of his policies in 1952 and 1953 by holding labor in check and allowing higher profits for farmers, it was too little and it came too late to either placate his opponents or to ignite the Argentine economy.

Populists like Perón always followed their instincts, using simple notions of government investment and regulation to promote industrialization and social welfare. They were less interested in the historical and structural roots of underdevelopment than they were in the selection of a few policies that produced swift results. However, their short-term gains could not be sustained because of errors in their design, their vulnerability to sudden drops in government income, and elite obstruction of their implementation.

The Peronist experience offers several insights into populism. It was a phenomenon prompted by rapid industrialization and urbanization. Where industrialization occurred much later, as in Venezuela, or where other popular parties were already in place, as in Mexico, populist movements were less common. But in Argentina and Brazil thousands migrated from the countryside and small towns to Buenos Aires, São Paulo, and Rio de Janeiro looking for work in factories and commerce. The transition from rural to urban life was a shattering experience for many. Consequently, when a new kind of politician appeared with promises of economic security, they responded enthusiastically. Populist movements were also the creations of skilled politicians who used their new source of power to put domestic conservatives and foreign investors on the defensive. Yet because they were loosely organized and so dependent on a single leader, they were vulnerable to equally sudden eviction from office through the temporary decapitation of their leadership by the military. And because they were unwilling to deprive entrenched elites of their real power, populist governments were always their hostage, forced to rely on their rural as well their industrial economies to sustain their nations. Populism was not an exercise in futility, however. It challenged the elite's monopoly of government and forced reassessments of national political purpose. It also ignited a debate over industrialization, its value, and means of promotion that continues today. Most important, the populists opened politics to persons who had been disenfranchised in the past. The fact that they did so in a heavy-handed and paternalistic manner rather than an orthodox democratic one does not reduce the importance of their achievement.

Military officers were divided over the value of populism. Yet without their collaboration Perón never could have taken office in 1946 and dominated Argentine government for ten years. Initially the young and more nationalistic officers were among his most enthusiastic supporters. For some, it was a matter of personal and institutional pride to support anti-status quo movements that promised to increase the nation's economic strength; others welcomed populism because it opened new opportunities for more direct military involvement in the direction of state enterprises. The support of the military proved a mixed blessing, however. Direct military involvement in the populist game helped to protect the government from its opponents; yet, by exposing their administrations to military scrutiny, populists could not conceal their abuses of authority and the incompetence that often plagued their operations. Military officers who took pride in the economic achievements of populism were quick to assail the economic crises it provoked and the inefficiencies it bred. Moreover, the participation of the officers in the populist game also increased the military politicization, touching off factionalism and bitter rivalries between officers favored by the president and those not so favored. Eventually, Argentine and Brazilian officers concluded that their countries could no longer afford the demagoguery and waste of populism and took action to bring populist rule to an end.

One player was conspicuously missing from populism. The campesinos were neither loyal supporters nor active opponents. Although Perón received many votes from Argentina's poor farmers and rural laborers, he never brought them into his ruling coalition or tried to change their condition through agrarian reform. Vargas ignored the plight of the rural poor altogether. In fact, he actively cultivated the support of the landed elite by refraining from threatening the rural power structure. The populists looked to the urban centers for the salvation of their countries and saw little to be gained, in the short run at least, from meddling with the economic and social structure of the countryside.

Military authoritarianism I: 1966–73

The military officers who expelled Perón in 1955 were determined to rid the nation of Peronism, first by beheading its movement and then by forcing the rank and file to participate in non-Peronist political parties. They tried hard but they failed dismally. Perón deserves much of the credit for their debacle. From the moment of his eviction he acted like the leader of a government in exile, constantly sending messages home from Spain, promising to return if the working class remained loyal to him and fought for his readmission to the country. By adroitly exploiting their hopes as well as their hostility toward the military governments that repressed them, Perón made it impossible for any other government, democratic or authoritarian, to survive for very long.

In the decade that followed Perón's eviction the armed forces held two presidential elections, first in 1958 and again in 1963. The Peronist Party was banned from both of them. Naturally, the governments elected in this manner were unpopular with the working class whose leaders denounced them as illegitimate. Radical Party president Arturo Frondizi responded by allowing the Peronists to participate in the 1962 gubernatorial elections, confident that his party would defeat them. But the Peronists easily won, provoking the armed forces to evict Frondizi after his miscalculation. The Radical Party government that was elected in 1963 gave it another try, only to lose to the Peronists in the 1965 congressional elections. One year later the armed forces took over again, this time making it clear that they would not hold elections again any time soon.

The military authoritarian government created by the Argentine armed forces in 1966 was headed by General Juan Carlos Onganía. Modeled after what the Brazilians had created two years before, it was actually far more elementary in its organization. Instead of re-taining a legislature as the Brazilians had done, Onganía simply closed it. Nor did he bother with rigged elections, preferring instead a simple form of autocratic rule. To his fellow Argentines he promised political order, social discipline, and economic stability if they did as they were told. It would begin with a new effort to restore growth and stability to an economy that had been plagued by inflation and recessions since 1955, followed some years later by the restoration of a constitutional government run in a far more orderly manner than what Argentina had experienced since 1945.

From the outset Onganía delegated immense authority to his minister of economy and promised to back him until inflation was under control and business confidence restored. Simultaneously he repressed the national labor movement, jailing its leaders and using force to block its protests. Assuming a regal posture, he insulated himself from interest group leaders and ignored politicians. His approach to government was more that of the technocrat than the politician, one of command rather than bargaining and compromise, of long-term economic management rather than piecemeal problem solving. Like the Brazilians, Argentine officers believed that economic attitudes had to be changed for the nation to progress. The government had become much too large and expensive, private entrepreneurs too lethargic, and the working class too selfish and contentious. It was Perón's fault, they reasoned, and it was to dismantle the economic monster that he had created that they dedicated themselves.

The military officers and technocrats who took control of Argentina in 1966 blamed Juan Perón for the country's economic decline and castigated his Radical Party successors for perpetuating it. Adalbert Krieger Vasena, General Onganía's minister of economy in 1966, believed that Argentina's industrialization could not be completed as long as the economy was plagued by high rates of inflation and a large fiscal deficit caused by bloated public enterprises and the patronage-ridden bureaucracies that the Peronists had created. The fundamental problem, he argued, was inefficiency in both the public and private sectors caused by subsidized industry, undisciplined workers, overextended welfare programs, and politicians unwilling to tighten their belts in hard times. Only a powerful government dedicated to implementing efficiency-promoting policies could solve the problems Perón had created, and it was to that task that Onganía and Krieger Vasena dedicated themselves.

Initially they did exactly what they intended. Wages were held down, inflation was reduced to its lowest level in three decades, investment rose, and organized labor's defiance of authority ceased. But appearances were deceiving, especially in Argentina where transient docility is easily mistaken for conformity with the will of the authoritarian state.

In May 1969 riots suddenly broke out in Córdoba, an industrial center in Argentina's interior. The week-long protests, which had to be repressed by the military when local police proved inadequate, never threatened the military government directly, but they made a mockery of Onganía's claim that he had subdued the Argentine masses and transformed them into compliant citizens. In the days that followed, the military could not hide disagreements among officers about how to deal with the growing militancy of an emboldened working class. Onganía favored harsh punishment, convinced that labor had to be subdued and that only more repression could achieve it. At the other extreme were officers who believed that the Peronists were unconquerable and, therefore, had to be accommodated. Most officers, however, were in the middle, opposed to the sustained physical repression of millions of workers, yet unwilling to yield to protestors. Disturbed by Onganía's rigidity and refusal to change course after the Córdoba riots, officers from this middle group removed him in 1970 and, after a year of indecision, reluctantly decided to hold new elections.

If Argentines learned anything from Onganía's departure, it was the impossibility of replicating the Brazilian experience in their country. Far stronger than the Brazilian political parties, the Argentine ones never doubted that they would eventually force the military into retreat and restore constitutional government. Nor did the economic interest groups representing agriculture, industry, commerce, and labor believe that the armed forces could really change the way they did business. Together they confined Onganía's revolution to minor adjustments in the economy that fostered new economic growth without changing the economy's structure or the behavior of those who participated in it.

They were also forced to recognize the magnitude of Perón's political achievements. Between 1946 and 1955 a generation of working-class Argentines, many of them the children of immigrants, from small towns as well as the suburbs of Buenos Aires, had been made to feel part of the nation for the first time. For them Peronism and the Argentine nation were one and the same. To be anti-Peronist was to be disloyal to the nation as they understood it. After 1955, support for their exiled leader seemed their only way of getting their nation back, and for eighteen years they kept up the struggle. Their efforts were not in vain. In 1973 a frustrated armed forces finally allowed Perón to come home. To no one's surprise the Peronists won the 1973 election, first with a stand-in candidate in March, and then with Perón himself in September.

But the golden age of Peronism was past, and the 78-year-old Perón died after one year in office, leaving the presidency to his wife Isabel, a loyal companion but one unprepared to direct the movement or govern an unruly nation. Administrative chaos, intense infighting within the Peronist movement, economic crises, and urban terrorism brought the nation almost to a halt. To no one's surprise, the military took over in 1976. The dismal performance of the second Peronist regime delighted their opponents, most of whom hoped that Perón's death and the disaster that followed would undermine the faith of the rank and file once and for all.

Military authoritarianism II: 1976–83

In assessing what had gone wrong during their first try at military authoritarianism under Onganía, some military officers concluded that the national security state was unattainable, leaving them no alternative but to return government to civilians. Other officers, however, drew the opposite conclusion: For them it was Onganía and not military authoritarianism that had failed. A more determined and better-organized effort could succeed, they believed, and they took it upon themselves to prove that, as soon as the opportunity came.

The day arrived in 1976. The economy had deteriorated rapidly in 1975 and inflation rose to record levels. To make matters worse, segments of the extreme Right and Left turned to terrorism, causing panic among the middle and upper classes. Furious with the Peronists' inability to halt it, the military took over in April 1976. They quickly banned all political parties, took over the labor movement, and unleashed a ruthless antiterrorist campaign.

The new president, General Jorge Videla, was the kind of cool professional who seemed well prepared for the ugly job, having risen up through the army bureaucracy carefully studying and teaching the national security ideology. When Perón first appeared in 1943, Videla had been nineteen years of age and in his final year at the Colegio Militar academy. He started his career as an infantry second lieutenant in 1944, ending his first decade of service in 1954 as an instructor in the Colegio Militar. Then he went on to study in the Escuela Superior de Guerra, Argentina's War College. In 1956, not long after Perón's expulsion, he began his "international" education, serving as aide to the chief of Argentina's first delegation to the Inter-American Defense Council in Washington, D.C. He returned home in 1959 to teach military intelligence courses until 1961 when he became head of cadets at the Colegio Militar, then moved up into the Army's command in 1962 which put him in the Defense Ministry. In 1964 he went abroad again, this time to learn counterinsurgency tactics from U.S. instructors in the Panama Canal Zone, then in its heyday teaching Latin American officers how to prevent more Fidel Castros. The following year he taught military strategy in the Centro de Altos Estudios, an organization for advanced instruction of new colonels. It was no coincidence that Videla later drew much of his presidential staff from colleagues and students he had known at the Centro. But that would come later; in 1973 he was given the highest honor for the consummate "professional" when he was appointed head of the Colegio Militar. From there he went on to become the Army's commander-in-chief in 1975, and then president after the coup a year later. No officer plots a career intended to end in the presidency, but had one been designed for an officer who would lead the nation in a war against terrorism, Videla would serve as a model.

He went to work right away, unleashing the three services' intelligence and counterinsurgency units to make war on the clandestine revolutionary movements whose members had been terrorizing the country with kidnappings and bombings for over three years. He accomplished it quietly and methodically, never boasting about arrests or killings. He was a professional and not a politician, one who turned loose military and civilian security forces to pick up, interrogate, and kill anyone they pleased. To his way of thinking the terrorist was the lowest form of life, a mixture of delinquent, mentally insane, and Marxist mercenary. To reward terrorism by neglecting to combat it was tantamount to treason. He did not ask civilians whether they agreed, confident that they would one day thank him for restoring order to a nation that was falling into chaos in 1976.

As Videla had anticipated, most people pretended not to notice what he was doing, going about their lives as if it would all be over quickly. But many others, most of whom had never committed acts of terrorism, lived in fear, never knowing whether or not they, too, might be taken away from their homes in one of the government's infamous, unmarked gray Ford Falcons, never to be seen again. Suspects were taken to one of 280 clandestine prisons, most of them on military bases in or near the nation's largest cities, where they were tortured and killed without any records of their deaths being kept. That the Nazis had done such things in Germany everyone knew, but Argentina was not Germany. That is why it all seemed so unbelievable to anyone who had bothered to notice.

Most Argentines deny having known at the time how far the military was going with its "war," but its deeds were never entirely hidden from public view. Though it was not until investigations in 1984 revealed how many lives were actually taken that the severity of the repression was documented, everyone knew that some people among them were disappearing, many never to be seen again. Of course, some quietly endorsed what the military was doing, convinced that the country would benefit from the extermination of its most misguided youth. It would be nearly a decade, however, before they were forced to face up to what they had sanctioned, but even then very few admitted any moral responsibility.

The military also had economic plans for the country, but unlike General Onganía, who had been content to restore business confidence in an effort to complete the nation's industrialization with foreign help, General Jorge Videla wanted to transform the country's economy and drastically reorient Argentine society. It was to become a country where the free market rather than political chicanery, patronage, and economic subsidies prevailed. This meant that the government would sell off many of its industries, tariffs would be reduced, and Argentine firms would compete with imports or go out of business.

The military's critics would claim that it was the greed of their civilian advisors, many of whom came from wealthy families, and not serious economic philosophy that motivated so drastic a change in policy. It is not easy to separate the two, ever, and even harder when the philosophy espoused favors some members of the upper class. But to stress personal motives is to ignore the economic ideas on which the program was founded, ideas then popular in Chile and Uruguay as well as Argentina, many of them taught by monetarists in the United States to Latin American students who returned home eager to put them to work. They criticized economies where populism had produced an undisciplined work force, a bloated public sector, and heavily protected industries that could not produce products at costs low enough to sell them abroad, and they promised that their policies, though painful, would eventually make them more competitive.

Complaints about industry's inefficiencies had been made before but seldom had anyone been punished for them, and industrialists could not believe that they would be this time either. But Videla's advisors were determined to prove them wrong. Their program was composed of three parts: tariff reductions that would invite competition from imported products, forcing reductions in costs and greater efficiency and productivity; the freeing of capital markets previously controlled and subsidized by government, allowing supply and demand to determine interest rates again; and reductions in the public sector deficit, which had reached 16 percent of the gross domestic product, by cutting wages, increasing taxes, and selling hundreds of public enterprises.

In capitalist systems economists try to induce desired behavior using the incentives and regulations allowed them by law and tradition. They make assumptions about profit motives and try to design policies that take advantage of them while achieving societal objectives. So it was when Economy Minister José Martínez de Hoz went to work on Argentina's economy. He wanted desperately to force Argentine entrepreneurs to adapt their thinking to greater competition, ending their reliance on government policies to subsidize their operations. It was an audacious effort that required time to work and enough incremental success to build confidence in its permanence. But suspicious Argentines had heard it all before and were as skeptical of his ability to work miracles as they had been of his predecessors. Their perspective is short term and quite rational, one educated on generations of policy failures that teach one always to be prepared for the worst. They waited and watched in 1978 and 1979 and, sure enough, things did not turn out as promised.

At first substantial progress was made. Tariff cuts and the liberation of capital markets reduced the government's subsidization of private business substantially and freezing public employee salaries brought down the deficit. But that only scratched the surface. Almost no progress was made with the sale of public enterprises, since few wanted to buy them. Nor was the military enthusiastic about reducing the size of the government if it involved the sale of firms that they had long operated.

By 1981 it was clear that Argentina was not turning into another

Table 10.2. *Argentina: economic performance, 1976–83 (annual percentage change)*

	Total investment	GDP growth	Wholesale price index
1976	6.4	-0.5	498.7
1977	19.4	6.4	149.0
1978	-15.2	-3.4	149.4
1979	7.9	6.7	149.3
1980	7.2	0.7	75.4
1981	-23.1	-6.2	109.6
1982	-15.3	-5.1	256.2
1983	-8.4	3.1	360.9

Source: Clarín, *Suplemento Económico,* 13 January 1985, p. 11.

Taiwan, able to produce many products at low costs and sell them abroad. New investments were meager and confidence in the economy low. When General Roberto Viola succeeded General Videla as scheduled at the end of March in 1981 he was greeted with the complaints of indebted Argentine businessmen who demanded the dismissal of Martínez de Hoz and his team, and a return to old policies. He tried to placate entrepreneurs, but thanks to a world recession that struck Argentina in 1981, conditions became worse rather than better, the GDP falling by 6 percent that year (and manufacturing by 14 percent). Recognizing that the overvalued exchange rate was inflicting serious damage on the country's productive base and leading to unsustainable losses of foreign exchange, Viola announced a series of large devaluations during his first six months, suspended the tariff-reduction program, reintroduced export taxes and import licensing, and reduced public expenditures, the net result of which was to push several over-extended producers into bankruptcy. Moreover, the nation's foreign debt, which had been $8 billion in 1975, grew to $27 billion by 1980, and shot up to $45 billion by the time the military left office at the end of 1983 (Table 10.2).

Dissatisfied colleagues replaced President Viola with Army Commander Leopoldo Galtieri as 1981 ended. Then, to everyone's surprise, Galtieri launched an invasion of the Falkland Islands (Malvinas Islands on Argentine maps) on April 2, 1982. It was another mistake the armed forces came to regret.

Until then, Argentine and British diplomats had failed repeatedly to resolve the issue of sovereignty over the islands. The Argentines insisted that the British had stolen them over a century and a half ago when Argentina was a young nation, incapable of defending them. But now 1,800 persons lived there, all of them loyal to Great Britain. The Argentines had threatened invasions in the past but had never been taken seriously by successive British governments, who feared the domestic political repercussions of turning the islands back to Argentina, especially at a time when it was governed by military autocrats. So the British held firm and the Argentines became frustrated.

General Galtieri wanted to force the British into making concessions and he convinced himself that a swift invasion with little violence would provoke the United Nations to demand the issue's resolution with concessions from both sides. But he was wrong. Not only did the United Nations not lend support to his cause, but the British retaliated militarily, inflicting a swift and humiliating rout on the Argentines two months later. In the end Galtieri had nothing to show for his adventure but military defeat, economic disaster, and an Argentine population that resented its deception by military leaders who had exploited their nationalism only to lie about where it was taking them.

To save face, a deeply divided military sent Galtieri into retirement, replaced the entire junta, and announced their intention to hold free national elections within eighteen months. As in 1970, when Onganía was deposed, the moderate officers picked up the pieces and called on their military colleagues to retreat.

Repetition seems to plague Argentine behavior. Within twenty years two military authoritarian regimes had tried to launch conservative revolutions only to fail, each effort ending seven years after it had begun. The causes of their failures were not identical, but neither of them changed Argentine politics or economics in the manner intended. The Peronist and Radical Parties survived repression, as did a labor movement loyal to the Peronists. The Argentine military could not secure the kind of civilian compliance that their Brazilian colleagues had enjoyed. Brazilian parties and interest groups know how vulnerable they are to their powerful armed forces, whereas Argentine politicians, in contrast, never doubted their ability to survive military efforts to devour them. Moreover, they were certain that no military government could achieve the economic success it needed to sustain public support.

Does military authoritarian government thrive under some conditions but not others? Of course it does. The military is part of an
established political process and can do only as much as the distribution of political power and its use by others allows it to do, no
matter how great its physical force. Even though it aspires to change
national politics permanently, it seems especially ill equipped to do
so. The Brazilians managed to invent devices that helped them hold
off opponents, but they were ad hoc and transitory. The Argentines
never accomplished that much. Political creativity is not an attribute
of Argentine military officers. Consequently, they could suspend the
conventional political process but never destroy or replace it.

Political conflicts ran deeper in Argentina than in Brazil. One might
have expected the opposite given Brazil's greater poverty and disparity
of wealth, but poverty, by itself, seldom generates political conflict.
Hostility between the Argentine ruling class and the working class had
existed since the turn of the century, but not until Perón led them did
the Argentine masses secure admittance to the government. Peronism
became their vehicle to the top and the means for temporarily expelling
the country's upper class from office. Rather than looking to government as the patron that dispenses some rewards to all contending
players simultaneously, as was the case in Brazil for a time, Argentines
came to see the presidency as something to be held exclusively either
by Peronists or by their opponents. The Argentine military reinforced
this when it prohibited Peronists from running for public office in
1958 and 1973. To rule Argentina, then, the military could not pretend
that it was merely a moderator among competing players as the Brazilians tried to do; instead they faced a well-organized mass movement
whose members considered the military the instrument of their rivals.
Any attempt to reconstruct the nation's political game had to deal in
some way with this reality. Repression brought temporary peace, but
it could not guarantee the Peronists' eventual acceptance of a new
order that excluded their party from power.

Democratic rules restored

Argentines are more familiar with democratic government than are
the Brazilians, though not much more. But they are also notorious for
their repeated failures to make it work. President Arturo Frondizi
lasted four years before his removal in 1962, Arturo Illia less than

three when he was tossed out in 1966, and Isabel Perón only two after succeeding her husband upon his death in 1974. Nevertheless, democratic government was embraced more enthusiastically than ever when the military pulled out again in 1983.

The military's political demise after its humiliating defeat by the British armed forces in June 1982 touched off a very swift transition during the year that followed. Recognizing the damage that the war did to military claims of political legitimacy, political party leaders refused to negotiate the terms of transition, insisting that the armed forces call elections and leave. Reluctantly the junta did, propelled as much by discord and finger pointing among the three services as by deference to civilian demands.

When they went to the polls in October 1983, most Argentines welcomed the opportunity to put seven years of military dictatorship behind them. Almost overnight political parties, themselves among the victims of persecution, returned to life to contest with each other in free elections. Civil liberties, the bane of authoritarians, were embraced enthusiastically but with unusual restraint by an electorate that appeared to appreciate the value of civil law and political liberty more than in the past. But renewed democratic vigor, though essential, was not the primary cause for optimism in 1983. Equally encouraging was the way the election reorganized relations between the powerful Peronist movement and other political parties. Since their creation in 1945 the Peronists had been monopolistic in their politics, using mobilization of the working class to create what they came to believe was a permanent majority. The military's denying them participation in elections after Juan Perón was sent into exile in 1955 only reinforced the conviction that they could be excluded from government only by force. To regain what they thought was theirs, they worked during the 1960s to debilitate governments created by their exclusion from national elections, and it worked. As we learned, Perón returned and won easily in 1973. When elections were called again in 1983, the Peronists assumed that they would win once more, even without Juan Perón to lead them. But it was not to be; when the votes were counted this time, Radical Party candidate Raúl Alfonsín had sent the Peronists down to their first defeat ever in a free presidential election.

Alfonsín attracted many young voters to his candidacy by stressing his devotion to civil liberties and social democracy, going on television every chance he could get to attack the armed forces for their brutal treatment of civilians. Almost overnight this mild-mannered ex-senator became the slayer of much-despised dragons. But even his new popularity did not guarantee him victory against the Peronists who were believed to enjoy support from a working class that guaranteed the party's candidate at least 40 percent of the popular vote. Alfonsín's fate depended in good part on how the Peronists adapted to campaigning without Juan Perón to lead them. They had always functioned as a loosely organized mass movement whose labor leaders and white-collar politicians carried out Perón's orders, but now they had to become a modern political party able to organize their constituents at a time when many of them still remembered how disastrous the Peronist government had been a decade before. Many persons in the lower middle class wanted another Peronist government but they did not want to elect one if it resulted once again in a military coup and repressive government. It was a concern that Alfonsín did his best to exploit throughout the campaign.

He sought to mobilize an anti-Peronist majority, attacking the Peronists for their past failures while suggesting that their leaders were getting involved in conspiracies with the armed forces, promising pardons to officers who had ordered the killing of citizens. He risked alienating the Peronists and reinforcing their persecution complex, but it was a chance he had to take. On October 30, 1983, it paid off. To the surprise of an electorate that had just read polls that predicted a Peronist victory, Raúl Alfonsín had pulled in 52 percent of the vote to Peronist Italo Luder's 40 percent.

The Peronists survived thanks to the efforts of their congressional candidates who did rather well, winning a slight plurality in the Senate, 22 seats to the Radicals' 19, and a strong second place in the Chamber of Deputies with 111 seats to the Radicals' 129. It was a near perfect outcome for the Argentines' re-education in democratic politics. Constitutional democracies are composed of majorities and minorities, elected officials who govern and loyal opponents who work with and against them according to rules respected by both. Argentines have never found it easy to practice politics in that manner, but they gave themselves a chance to try in 1983. This time the Peronists assumed a role to which they were unaccustomed yet one that was vital to their learning to play by democratic rules. By taking their majority away from them in a free election, Alfonsín denied the Peronists their claim to being the nation's only legitimate majority party. Since 1955 they had nurtured themselves on attacking the legitimacy of all governments that were chosen in elections from which their party was excluded. Now they were defeated by the opposition in a free election, something that denied credibility to their labeling it illegitimate. At the same time, by retaining a strong legislative position, the Peronists remained a vital part of the political process, the leader of an opposition that was in a good position to bargain over legislation with the Radicals. It was the strongest incentive yet to their living within the confines of the constitution.

The new government also benefited from the military's preoccupation with putting itself together after suffering humiliation and recrimination from its defeat in the Malvinas war. Alfonsín lost no time in making it clear that he wanted a line of command that began in the presidential office and descended through a civilian defense minister down to the joint chiefs. He also allowed the trial of the nine generals and admirals who had served in the juntas that ruled the nation between 1976 and 1983. Five of them were convicted of various crimes, including General Jorge Videla, president from 1976 until 1981, who was sentenced to life imprisonment. No one was entirely satisfied with the result, the armed forces insisting that none among them deserved sentencing in civilian courts, and human rights activists claiming that justice would not be done until several hundred officers, down to the rank of lieutenant, were tried and convicted. During Easter in 1987 a few officers staged a minirevolt to emphasize their objection to the courts going down into the lower ranks, and, with unanimous congressional support, Alfonsín limited all future trials to officers who were at the rank of colonel and above when the crimes were committed. For politicians it was a practical way to begin solving a very formidable political problem.

Alfonsín's victory over the Peronists was impressive, but it was only temporary. The Radicals hoped for a landslide victory in the 1985 congressional elections that would consolidate their tenuous control over the government, while the Peronists, still plagued by nonstop infighting, were desperate to improve on the 43 percent they had received in the 1983 presidential election. Unfortunately, nothing was decided in 1985. The Radicals could do no better than 44 percent, hardly the landslide they sought, while the Peronists did far worse, capturing only 35 percent of the popular vote – their lowest ever – and losing seven seats in the Chamber of Deputies. Clearly Argentines were unwilling to turn everything over to the Radicals just yet; nor were they prepared to welcome the Peronists back. Their desire for constitutional politics remained strong, but their trust of civilian politicians was as tentative as ever.

All of this made the next election even more crucial. In September 1987, Argentines went to the polls to elect part of the Chamber of Deputies and new governors in all twenty-two provinces. Despite continued leadership disputes within the party, reform-minded Peronists, led by Antonio Cafiero, in alliance with provincial party chieftains, put slates together that campaigned against a government that had failed to solve the nation's economic malaise after four years of trying. It secured them 41 percent of the congressional vote to the Radicals' 37 percent, an increase of 6 percent for them and a 6 percent fall for the Radicals that cost them their majority in the Chamber of Deputies. Even more startling were Peronist victories in sixteen of the twenty-two provincial governors' races, including the populous Buenos Aires province, where Antonio Cafiero was triumphant. It was a setback from which Alfonsín's popularity would never entirely recover as attention quickly turned to the election of his successor in 1989.

Argentine democracy is always threatened by the country's frequent economic setbacks. Unfortunately for Alfonsín, he inherited an economy that was in the fourth year of a deep recession and high inflation, prices increasing by nearly 400 percent just before his inauguration. Equally troublesome was a foreign debt that had risen fourfold in five years, approaching a record $46 billion in 1984, far too much for the nation's sagging economy to service. His initial efforts to restore some order to the economy were a dismal failure, and by 1985 prices were rising at a phenomenal annual rate of 1,000 percent and interest payments on the debt absorbed 60 percent of the country's export earnings, leaving very little for financing the country's economic growth. So, on June 14, Alfonsín went on television to announce his "battle plan" to "reconstruct" Argentina. What this meant concretely was terminating the Central Bank's printing money to pay the public debt (it was paying about 25 percent of it then), and raising taxes and the prices paid for government services to make up the difference. He also decreed a new currency, called the austral, dropping three zeros from the peso and pegging it at $1.28 (U.S. dollars), and froze all prices and wages. The package, designed almost entirely by a new team of professional Argentine economists who were recruited from outside the Radical Party, was exactly what the country's creditors wanted, and within a couple of months they consented to renegotiating the nation's foreign debt, then approaching $50 billion.

Even more impressive than the austral program was the public's enthusiasm for it. When it was announced, Alfonsín immediately closed the banks and waited for the inevitable outcry. But to his surprise it never came. Instead, an uncharacteristic calm fell over the nation, followed by praise from nearly every sector for his courage and common sense. Argentines, it seemed, were relieved that something had been done to stop the economic insanity into which they had descended. In a few days' trading, the stock market picked up, the dollar stabilized, and, most impressive, prices rose only 2 percent in September (compared to 30 percent in June). And as prices came down Alfonsín's popularity ascended to levels it had not seen since his election eighteen months before.

The austral plan gave Argentines another chance to get the economy under control, but as before success proved elusive. By the middle of 1988 prices were rising by 20 percent a month again and the austral, which had originally been pegged at more than $1.00, had fallen to only $0.07 (U.S.). More than ever Argentines found it hard to make payments on their enormous foreign debt, or to grow economically with so much of their income from trade going to their creditors abroad. It was an inauspicious result for a people who wanted to bring order to their troubled economy, but as before their indebtedness and the high cost and inefficiency of the government's many enterprises made swift recovery impossible.

When the Argentines held another presidential election in May of 1989 it should have been cause for celebration since it was the first time since 1928 that one civilian was elected to replace another. But, characteristically, they held back, more uncertain than ever about where their choice was going to take them.

Since the constitution prohibited Alfonsín from succeeding himself, the presidential campaign came down to a contest between Radical Party candidate Eduardo Angeloz and Peronist Carlos Menem, both of them provincial governors. Taking full advantage of economic conditions that had deteriorated unexpectedly the year before, causing inflation to soar once again and the value of the Argentine currency to decline rapidly, Menem rallied the lower classes behind him with promises to rescue them, just as Juan Perón had done long ago. It worked, and Menem gained 47 percent of the popular vote to Angeloz's 37 percent, just enough to secure a majority in the Electoral College.

In theory at least, this was a boost for Argentine democracy since it rewarded the Peronists for living by democratic rules during the previous five years and told the incumbent Radicals that they enjoyed no monopoly over the presidency. Instead, it was now their turn to become the loyal opposition in a competitive, two-party system. On the other hand, no one was certain that President Menem and the Peronists were prepared to govern the nation effectively. Some of them were sincerely dedicated to democracy while others retained their aversion to it. The Peronist Party still lacked cohesion, and there was no guarantee that Menem could keep it in line with whatever course he chose to follow.

He also inherited one of the nation's worst economic crises in several years (prices were rising 100 percent monthly just before and after the election). Poverty within the lower class, which had been rising for two decades throughout the country, accelerated in 1989. Argentina also had $60 billion in foreign debts, but too few dollars even to pay much interest on them. Alfonsín had given up trying nearly a year before he left office and Menem confessed that he could do no better unless the Argentine citizens who had been buying and sending billions of dollars abroad for over a decade brought their wealth home and deposited it in the nation's banks or invested it in local corporations. Without that, or loans from abroad, which would remain scarce as long as Argentina did not pacify its creditors by paying at least the interest on its debts, there was no way to ignite the sorry economy.

Menem started his government by seeking help from all sectors of Argentine society, taking a remarkably nonconfrontational approach for a Peronist. His populist beliefs did not prevent his inviting people from business and from the conservative opposition to take positions in his cabinet. Such moves were dramatic, but more than drama was required to restore a people's confidence in itself and to regain the capacity to feed all of the nation's citizens adequately. Few challenges have been bigger for the players in the Argentine game.

An exception in Peru?

Before concluding our inquiry into military authoritarianism we need to examine another case that was a bit different from the rest. While the militaries of Chile and Uruguay were trying to imitate what the

the Brazilians and Argentines were doing, the Peruvian armed forces followed a different course. How different they actually were is still a matter of some dispute, but they were distinct.

The coup that ended constitutional government in Peru in 1968 at first seemed like any other. The Peruvian military had previously evicted civilian presidents to protect conservative interests on more than one occasion, and it had also sustained a strong antipathy toward APRISTA, the country's primary reform party since the 1930s, because of APRISTA's strident antimilitarism. On the surface the 1968 coup appeared to be a calculated response to a probable election victory by APRISTAs in 1969. But that was not what it really was. Only after the coup occurred would it become apparent that nationalist officers were taking over out of frustration with the concessions that civilians had made to multinational corporations, and with their failure to direct a successful war against guerrillas in the countryside.

During the first half of the twentieth century Peru's conservative leaders had successfully absorbed the country's small but growing middle sectors by giving them a role in the management of the export economy and the state bureaucracy. At the same time, the leaders ignored the plight of the peasantry and dealt harshly with the labor movement and the political parties that encouraged it. But Peruvian society continued to change, prompted by the expansion of copper mining, the growth of local industry and commerce, and accelerating urbanization in the 1950s and 1960s. The conservatives' failure to adapt their policies to these changes yielded land invasions by disgruntled peasants, student protests, illegal strikes, strident nationalism, and the formation of a small but potentially disruptive guerrilla movement in the countryside during the 1960s. The election of reformer Fernando Belaunde Terry in 1964 marked the first serious attempt to adapt public policy to these new conditions. Belaunde modeled his Popular Action Party (AP) after the democratic reform movements already active in the hemisphere and campaigned on a platform of agrarian reform and economic modernization. But his ability to fulfill his campaign promises was hindered by the opposition of APRISTAs and conservatives in Congress. As a result, instead of delivering sweeping reform, Belaunde inadvertently increased the frustrations of those who desired immediate solutions to the country's growing social problems.

The military's reaction to Belaunde's travails was hard to predict at the time. In the past it might have welcomed his failures as evidence of the strength of the old order. But the military had changed during the 1960s, and many of its younger officers, fresh from battles with guerrillas in the countryside that had awakened them to the increasing political costs of defending traditional social institutions, saw Belaunde's failures as heightening the possibility of radical upheaval. No longer, it appeared, could Peru afford the kind of reformist politics that became immobilized by interparty squabbles. The only solution, some officers concluded, was the suspension of democratic politics in order to permit a more direct assault on the country's development problems by military-led state bureaucracy.

The officers who led the Peruvian coup were more audacious than either the Brazilians or the Argentines. They intended not only to control the nation's politics, but also to build a popular foundation for a reorganized Peruvian state. Though they began like the Brazilians and Argentines with the closure of political parties and the repression of potential opponents, they were not content to rely on repression alone. Instead they hastily created new campesino and labor organizations that they hoped to use to create a corporatist-type political regime capable of both improving the condition of the poor and denying the political left a base for political action.

The new regime was organized hierarchically and by economic sector, starting with government-sponsored local economic organizations, which were joined by sectoral organizations, and finally into a national body called the National System for the Support of Social Mobilization (SINAMOS), created in June 1971. Within each economic sector, production organizations were created. Under the 1969 Agrarian Reform Law, for example, the largest private holdings were reorganized into collective enterprises known as Agrarian Production Cooperatives (CAPs), and Agrarian Societies of Social Interest (SAISs). And in 1970, firms involved in manufacturing, mining, telecommunications, and fishing were forced by a new Industrial Law to admit worker participation in their ownership and management. Such measures were intended to involve the masses in the economic decisions that affect them most directly.

SINAMOS was supposed to join all social classes within the new political system and to regulate their involvement in the making and implementation of government policy. In fact, it achieved much less, never advancing beyond a means for government control over the

Peruvian masses. Social classes were actually kept divided in order to facilitate the government's regulation of each separately.

At the top of the government hierarchy was the president – until mid-1975, General Juan Velasco Alvarado – and the Presidential Advisory Committee (COAP), an all-military body charged with designing legislation and coordinating its implementation. They were advised by a host of civilian technocrats, but they did not consult directly with leaders of peasant, labor, or other mass organizations when designing their policies, as promised. They were, however, occasionally forced to revise their programs when they met resistance from such groups.

Policy innovation, more than government organization, distinguished the Peruvian officers from their neighbors. Though they called their program revolutionary, it more resembled the progressive-modernization strategy than the revolutionary one. It began with initiatives in three areas. First came the nationalization of some foreign and domestic enterprises. The petroleum and fish-meal industries, most bank and insurance companies, the import and export trade, and most utilities were placed under state control. These measures appeared quite radical within the context of Peru, but they actually did little more than raise the level of state ownership to one commensurate with that already achieved in the more industrialized Latin American countries. Second came agrarian reform. A modest program had already been begun by President Belaunde before the military overthrew him in 1968. But in three years Belaunde had expropriated only 795 estates, covering 1.5 million hectares. In a similar amount of time President Velasco expropriated 1,939 estates covering 3.2 million hectares, including the valuable foreign-owned sugar estates along Peru's Pacific coast. Only 20,000 peasant families gained land under Belaunde compared with approximately 87,000 under Velasco. The third component of Velasco's program was industrial reform. This included a scheme for joint ownership by workers and entrepreneurs. In practice this meant the government would require the country's larger firms to implement profit- and stock-sharing plans that would gradually turn over a large share of the firm to its employees.

In the short run, the bureaucrats and military officers who worked the state agencies were the principal beneficiaries of reform and the expansion of the Peruvian state. Those peasants who were fortunate enough to receive land under the agrarian reform also profited. But a majority of the rural work force, both hired laborers and subsistence farmers, were bypassed by the reforms which were restricted primarily to the transfer of the ownership of the largest latifundios to the campesinos who worked on them. The third to gain were a minority of industrial workers who participated in the profit-sharing programs required of major industries by the government.

Velasco accomplished much, but it was far less than he had sought. Like civilian reformers he repeatedly ran into obstacles, some human and others natural, and despite his power, he could not overcome most of them. Take the rural sector, for example. It might appear that the Peruvians had solved their rural development program by redistributing land to peasants and organizing the land into various types of cooperatives. But not all peasants benefited from agrarian reform. In fact, after the completion of land redistribution, 300,000 rural families remained landless because there was not enough land to go around. Only 2 percent of Peru's total area – the lowest proportion in Latin America – is under cultivation. More land could be made available, but only at high cost because the project would require the irrigation of desert regions or the clearing of tropical lowlands.

Nor did the military government escape the kinds of externally induced balance-of-payments deficits and foreign-debt burdens that plagued previous Peruvian governments. In June 1976, it faced a crisis similar to that which it had inherited in 1968. The problem was largely one of resources. Velasco and his advisers, encouraged by foreign bankers who foresaw an oil boom for Peru in the mid-1970s, borrowed heavily abroad to finance the most ambitious development program in the country's history. In a period of four years Peru took on a host of new creditors, raising its foreign debt fivefold to $5 billion (American billions) and its annual debt servicing to 43 percent of its total export income in 1976. But little oil was discovered.

Military reformism was halted in 1975 when Velasco was deposed by more conservative officers. During the next five years they supervised the gradual restoration of constitutional government, starting with a constitutional convention in 1978 and free presidential and congressional elections in May 1980. Confident that moderates would triumph, they made no effort to rig the elections as the Brazilians would do two years later. Ironically, it was moderate Fernando Belaunde, the person overthrown by Velasco twelve years before, whom the Peruvians again elected president. As expected, Belaunde announced his intention to respect the results of Velasco's agrarian reforms while disbanding all of his mass organizations.

Whatever his shortcomings, Velasco's actions remind us that the military is not always compelled to be conservative in its policies. But it also indicates that there is no reason to believe that the armed forces can achieve lasting structural reforms any more easily than civilians can. Their actions are often swifter, but seldom more enduring. Nor is the military especially adept at securing control over society, even when attempting popular measures. The Peruvian military did achieve some autonomy from the social classes usually thought to influence military authoritarians, but its control over the government was never enough to secure its complete hegemony. On the contrary, by the time he was deposed Velasco had managed to alienate all social classes either with his policies or with forced participation in the state's organizations.

Military authoritarianism: lessons learned

The military authoritarians did not transform Brazil and Argentina in any profound way. Nor did they sustain economic progress for very long after they appeared to have restored it. In fact, nothing approaching the kind of disciplined societies posited by their national security ideologies was even approximated in either country, no matter how hard they tried to create them. Instead, when they finally departed, many of the same politicians whom they had evicted were among the first to replace them.

There are several reasons for their failures, many of them by now quite obvious. To begin with, while they were well trained for counterinsurgency, they were not intellectually or organizationally equipped for much else. Military education, even in advanced war colleges, offered little preparation for the reorganization of complex economic and social institutions and the "re-education" of civilians who were never eager to live their personal lives by the gospel of national security. The military's efforts at political reconstruction resembled children trying to fly to the moon. They knew where the moon was and understood that rockets could carry you there but they had no idea about how to build a rocket. Undaunted, they tried anyway, only to be stifled before they ever took off.

It is clear why they tried. Like civilians, they were frustrated with economic instability, distrusted civilian politicians, and feared that their "enemies," if left unchecked, might rise up and demolish them the way Castro had done to Batista's armed forces in Cuba. And if they needed any encouragement, they received it from the many civilians in the middle and upper sectors who were always eager to supply it, and from United States ambassadors who were willing to either support or tolerate them.

Initially they were able to take steps that civilian politicians had often resisted, such as cutting wages, raising prices, giving concessions to foreign investors, and the like. Nevertheless, their economic rescue operations never accomplished all that was promised. Wages were easily controlled for a time but budgets were hard to cut, due in large part to the military's vested interests, both as manager of public enterprises and as purchaser of arms. And, as we learned repeatedly, though austerity measures were occasionally compelling, they never assured recovery, especially in economies where so many other forces, many of them external, influenced economic performance. The conservative modernization strategy could ignite investment and promote higher production but it did not make a nation less dependent on the world economy for markets, technology, raw materials, and capital. Instead of strengthening their economies, the militaries in Argentina and Brazil accumulated awesome foreign debts that they were in no condition to pay. It was left to civilians who tried to live by the rules of democratic politics to cope with the crippling effects of indebtedness, a handicap that the new democracies could not easily overcome.

Military authoritarianism also suffered from the fickleness of its civilian supporters. The armed forces did not require demonstrations of popular support in order to rule, but they did rely on considerable civilian collaboration to govern effectively in societies as complex and sophisticated as those in the southern cone. Initially they were welcomed by the most affluent members of their nations, not so much because they were fond of military presidents but because they wanted authorities to restrain those below them in the social structure who were demanding a larger share of the nation's wealth and political power. Many people in the upper and middle classes were also frightened by occasional terrorism and were willing to sacrifice liberty in order to eradicate it. All of this gave the armed forces a certain legitimacy, though one that was more instrumental and immediate than ideological. As long as the armed forces did what some people wanted, they welcomed them, but once they had restored order and ignited the economy, their legitimacy declined because they were no longer needed. Soon their original civilian supporters began to demand that the armed forces return to their bases, and political party leaders called for new elections. By itself this did not force the military to depart, but eventually it caused some among them to doubt their effectiveness, giving their civilian opponents an opportunity to exploit divisions among officers.

Military authoritarianism left many people more hostile to their armed forces than ever before. Few Argentines will soon regard theirs the way they had before the military unleashed its secret war on the nation's urban population. And no Chileans will forget the way General Pinochet and his colleagues built and ran a police state for over fifteen years. Everyone knows that asking the armed forces to "restore order" will always tempt them to be more ruthless than was previously thought possible. Of course, knowing that is how it might be does not by itself prevent civilians from turning to officers, or officers on their own from taking it upon themselves to govern again.

One might hope that the region's armed forces and their civilian allies have discovered the futility of their authoritarian ways, but any such conclusion is premature. No matter how much one might wish otherwise, militaries remain active players in most national political games. Whether in office or not, they are still preoccupied with their nations' governance and economic development as well as with their own institution. Many of them still doubt the feasibility of democratic government. Moreover, one generation's failure does not necessarily convince its successors that they should not try to replicate the political efforts of their predecessors no matter how little they accomplished. Civilian politicians know this and will be among the last to disregard the military as a player in the national game.

Further reading

Argentina

Corradi, Juan E. *The Fitful Republic: Economy, Society, and Politics in Argentina.* Boulder, CO: Westview Press, 1984.
Fraser, Nicholas, and Marysa Navarro. *Eva Perón.* New York: Norton, 1981.
Gillespie, Richard. *Soldiers of Perón.* New York: Oxford University Press, 1983.
Hastings, Max, and Simon Jenkins. *The Battle for the Falklands.* New York: Norton, 1983.
Mallon, R.D., and J.V. Sourrouille. *Economic Policy Making in a Conflict*

Society: The Argentine Case. Cambridge, MA: Harvard University Press, 1975.

O'Donnell, Guillermo. *The Bureaucratic Authoritarian State: 1966–1973.* Berkeley: University of California Press, 1988.

Page, Joseph. *Perón: A Biography.* New York: Random House, 1983.

Peralta-Ramos, Monica, and Carlos H. Waisman, eds. *From Military Rule to Liberal Democracy in Argentina.* Boulder, CO: Westview Press, 1987.

Potash, Robert. *The Army and Politics in Argentina, 1945–1962: Perón to Frondizi.* Stanford, CA: Stanford University Press, 1979.

Rock, David. *Argentina 1516–1982.* Berkeley: University of California Press, 1985.

Scobie, James R. *Argentina: A City and a Nation.* 2nd Edition. New York: Oxford University Press, 1971.

Turner, Frederick, and José Enrique Miguens, eds. *Juan Perón and the Re-shaping of Argentina.* Pittsburgh, PA: Pittsburgh University Press, 1983.

Waisman, Carlos H. *Reversal of Development in Argentina: Postwar Counterrevolutionary Policies and Their Structural Consequences.* Princeton, NJ: Princeton University Press, 1987.

Wynia, Gary W. *Argentina: Illusions and Realities.* New York: Holmes & Meier, 1986.

Argentina in the Postwar Era: Politics and Economic Policy in a Divided Society. Albuquerque: University of New Mexico Press, 1978.

Peru

Becker, David G. *The New Bourgeoisie and the Limits of Dependency: Mining, Class, and Power in "Revolutionary" Peru.* Princeton, NJ: Princeton University Press, 1983.

Booth, David, and Bernado Sorj, eds. *Military Reformism and Social Classes: The Peruvian Experience.* New York: St. Martin's, 1983.

Cleaves, Peter S., and Martin Scurrah. *Agriculture, Bureaucracy, and Military Government in Peru.* Ithaca, NY: Cornell University Press, 1980.

Fitzgerald, E.V.K. *The State and Economic Development: Peru since 1968.* Cambridge University Press, 1976.

Long, Norman, and Bryn Roberts. *Mines, Peasants, and Entrepreneurs: Regional Development in the Central Highlands of Peru.* New York: New York: Cambridge University Press, 1984.

Lowenthal, Abraham, ed. *The Peruvian Experiment.* Princeton, NJ: Princeton University Press, 1976.

McClintock, Cynthia, and Abraham Lowenthal, eds. *The Peruvian Experiment Reconsidered.* Princeton, NJ: Princeton University Press, 1983.

Stepan, Alfred. *The State and Society: Peru in Comparative Perspective.* Princeton, NJ: Princeton University Press, 1978.

11. Cuba: a communist revolution

Revolutions are quite rare in Latin America. This may seem surprising given the magnitude of economic and political torment throughout a region where social structures are often rigid and repressive, the exploitation of the many by the few quite common, and the frequent subordination of national to foreign economic interests a fact of life. Whether one's theory holds that revolution is caused by imperialism, class conflict, "relative deprivation," or merely the escalation of political conflict, Latin America has always seemed ripe for it. Nevertheless, real revolutions are infrequent, though not for a lack of trying. In the past half century insurgents have succeeded only in Cuba and Nicaragua.

Why so few? To begin with, conditions for revolution are seldom as optimal as they appear to the outside observer. The poor do not revolt just because they are poor; quite the contrary: Resignation to their fate and fear of persecution often prevent their recruitment to revolutionary causes. Equally obstructive is the ability of ruling elites to defend themselves against rebels. They may dispute issues with one another and with the middle class, but such discord seldom prevents their banding together to protect one another. Furthermore, the armed forces have learned how to fight against insurgents. Since Fidel Castro's triumph in Cuba over three decades ago, thousands of Latin American soldiers have been taught counterinsurgency warfare by experts from the United States, France, Israel, and elsewhere. Although their training never guarantees battlefield triumph as Anastasio Somoza's National Guard discovered in Nicaragua in 1979, it does make waging revolutionary wars more formidable and costly in human lives than ever before, as is currently evident in El Salvador where rebels have been fighting without victory for over ten years.

Revolutions are also rare because they involve much more than the defeat and expulsion of ruling elites. Many who have claimed revolution as their goal have actually achieved little more than marginal modifications in their societies. A real revolution requires the transformation of a nation's politics, social structures, and economic institutions, a monumental task not easily achieved anywhere.

To succeed, revolutionaries must defeat the ruling elite and their defenders, create a new government and enforce new rules, and radically reconstruct social and economic institutions. Evicting incumbents may involve anything from a brief insurrection to a protracted and costly guerrilla war. The path taken is dictated by the relative political and military strengths of both rebels and the incumbents as well as their tenacity. Mass insurrections, small-unit or *foco* guerrilla warfare, and terrorism directed at selected targets have all been tried, though none has proven foolproof. We now know that what matters most is not the government's military strength, but the degree to which the urban and rural publics actively oppose it and the price authorities are willing to pay to defend themselves. Nothing illustrates this better than the Nicaraguan experience where, after a decade of failing, the Sandinistas finally triumphed because they were joined by almost the entire population in their war against Somoza, swiftly isolating his National Guard and making it impossible for them to win.

Triumph on the battlefield is necessary but hardly sufficient for achieving revolutionary reconstruction. Celebrations by the victorious warriors must be followed by the creation of a new government that can secure control over the nation in the face of inevitable opposition to its radical agenda from within the country and from neighbors who fear the example that it might set. In nearly every revolution during this century the evicted elites have launched "counterrevolutions" against the new regime, some of them being quite brief as was the invasion of Cuba at the Bay of Pigs by exiles in 1961, two years after the guerrillas triumphed, and others lasting several years, as did the U.S.-financed Contra war against Nicaragua's Sandinista government. That is one reason, though certainly not the only one, why revolutionary authorities seize tight control over the nation's police and military forces as quickly as they can and strip their most prominent opponents of power. What seems cruel and autocratic to the opposition is regarded as mere necessity by revolutionaries who want to reconstruct their societies. Power and its use for radical ends, not personal freedom, is their primary objective. If that means riding hard over members of the old society who are not comfortable in the new one, so be it.

Equally important to creating a new society is the government's winning and retaining the support of the masses whom they claim to serve. Ideological "reeducation" is supposed to achieve this end, but it must be accompanied by the social services promised the poor and the redistribution of property in a manner that convinces them that the revolution's objectives are their own. Political democracy is less the goal of socialist revolution than mass participation in the implementation of a plan designed by the revolution's leadership. Accomplishing all of this is never as easy as it might seem since the ways that revolutionary authorities go about building the new society are frequently offensive to rural and urban masses who resent supervision by political authorities who often become intolerant of any opposition to their plans.

Finally, turning the revolutionary vision of the new society into reality is a never-ending project. No Marxist–Leninist, for example, has achieved true communism, though each believes that he or she will one day. Their vision may be utopian, or, at worst, a convenient device for rationalizing whatever authorities choose to do, but its achievement requires continuous effort long into the future. Revolutionary authorities can either hold firm to a plan conceived and implemented early in their nation's transformation or revise their plans periodically, as many revolutionary socialist governments began doing in the 1980s with their loosening of central control over their economies. But no matter how routine and entrenched their revolutions become, they will always argue that their society's transformation is still in progress.

The revolutionary state brings with it many problems that are inherent in its creation, none more apparent than its own kind of conservatism after taking control. Historical experience demonstrates that revolutionary elites, once secure, do not welcome attempts to distribute political power more widely. The revolution creates a state bureaucratic structure that tends to resist reform from within or without. Yet, change is often needed to complete society's transformation, whether it be to achieve real communism or improve mass participation. Nevertheless, rather than moving swiftly toward the creation of citizen-controlled communal political institutions, most modern revolutionary regimes are still governed by a vanguard that speaks for the proletariat. The consequences of such practices merit close scrutiny in our examination of the Latin American experience.

Cuba and Nicaragua exemplify variations in contemporary revolutionary politics. Each tells us something about the possibilities for a radical rewriting of the rules and the price that is paid to achieve it. Moreover, by comparing the two cases we can also learn about the options available to revolutionaries, the choices they make, and how much they achieve.

The 26th of July Movement

Explanations of why rebels triumphed in Cuba differ substantially, as does the granting of praise and blame for what came afterwards. The history of the period is rewritten frequently to bolster the causes of victors and vanquished alike. While some credit insurgents in the nation's largest cities for Fulgencio Batista's defeat, others claim that the war was won by a guerrilla army in the Sierra Maestra Mountains known as the 26th of July Movement. Led by Fidel Castro, the 26th of July Movement made its way down from the mountains at the east end of the island in 1958 to fight its way to Havana, only to see Batista flee long before they arrived. The dispute would be of interest only to historians were it not for the fact that so many Latin American revolutionaries have studied the Cuban experience diligently to determine how they can replicate it in their own countries (see Table 11.1).

In many ways Cuba was not the prime candidate for revolution in the late 1950s. It was neither the poorest Latin American nation nor the most industrialized. Its per capita income placed it third in Latin America, just behind Argentina and Venezuela, and far more Cubans lived in towns and cities than in the countryside. Yet they were an insecure people. Their fate was tied to sugar and, as in any monoculture economy, economic growth fluctuated with the performance of the primary export crop. The Cuban class structure was also conditioned by the sugar economy, being most noted for its rural proletariat of seasonal laborers who divided their time between six months in the sugar harvest and six months of unemployment. Ever since Cuba's "liberation" from Spain by its northern neighbor during the Spanish American War in 1898, sugar had tied the Cuban economy and polity to the United States. Alongside wealthy Cubans, American business reigned supreme over the island economy, American tourists played in its capital and on its beaches, and the American underworld ran the country's flourishing gambling and prostitution industries. That an intense nationalism would result from such outside domination is

Table 11.1. *Cuba: historical background*

1898	Cuba achieves independence from Spain during Spanish American War Cuba occupied by U.S. troops until 1902
1901	Platt Amendment to new Cuban constitution gives the United States the right to intervene in Cuba to "maintain government adequate for the protection of life, property, and individual liberty"
1906	American governor appointed to replace Cuban president
1909	José Miguel Gómez elected president
1913	Mario García Menocal elected president; United States continues to intervene frequently with troops and advisers
1921	Alfredo Zayas elected president and advised by American General Enoch Crowder
1925	Gerardo Machado becomes president and rules in dictatorial manner
1933	Machado overthrown by popular revolt
1934	U.S. President Franklin Roosevelt abrogates Platt Amendment Provisional government overthrown by "sergeants' revolt" led by Fulgencio Batista
1940	Batista elected president under new constitution
1944	Opposition candidate, Grau San Martín, elected president
1948	Carlos Prio Socarras elected president
1952	Fulgencio Batista takes over government in a coup
1953	Young rebels, led by Fidel Castro, attack Moncada military barracks in Santiago and are captured and jailed
1955	Batista declares amnesty and Castro flees to Mexico
1956	In July, rebels led by Castro travel by boat to east end of Cuba but only a dozen escape battles with armed forces and take refuge in Sierra Maestra Mountains
1958	Guerrilla war starting in mountains spreads and defeats Batista's force at end of year
1959	Castro creates coalition government with party politicians in January In June moderates in cabinet resign, leaving effective control to Castro and 26th of July guerrillas
1961	In January, United States breaks relations with Cuba and imposes trade embargo Invasion at Bay of Pigs by CIA supported by Cuban exiles is defeated by Cuban Army
1962	United States confronts Soviet Union over its placement of missiles in Cuba; "Missile Crisis" ends with Soviets pulling missiles out in exchange for U.S. promise never to invade Cuba
1965	Cuban Communist Party formed
1975	First Communist Party Congress called
1976	New system of local, provincial, and national assemblies created (Poder Popular)
1989	Cubans celebrate the revolution's thirtieth anniversary

hardly surprising; that it would lead to a successful revolution *was,* however, especially to the North Americans who watched in disbelief as it happened.

If there was a catalyst in the Cuban revolution, it was the increasingly brutal dictatorship of Fulgencio Batista. He was an old hand at Cuban politics, ascending from his leadership of the "sergeants' revolt" in 1934 to victory in a fair presidential election in 1940 under a democratic constitution that he helped compose. More populist and opportunistic than genuinely democratic, Batista endeavored to please the North Americans on whom his nation had come to rely economically while placating his nationalist critics by securing the abrogation of the Platt Amendment, which since 1901 had permitted North American intervention into Cuba's governance. He also promoted the nation's economic growth through the Sugar Act and Reciprocal Trade Agreement of 1934, which guaranteed Cuban access to the United States market. He even stepped down on schedule when a successor from the opposition was elected president in 1944. But that was the extent of his democracy. After two well-meaning (but corrupt and patronage-ridden) reformist administrations proved themselves incapable of providing Cuba with a progressive, well-managed government, an autocratic Batista took over in 1952. Backed by foreign investors, the United States government, and the sugar industry, he rejected political democracy, preferring this time to give orders and punish anyone who disobeyed them. That left democrats in Cuba only one real choice: Either submit to Batista or fight him.

The war against Batista was waged on several fronts after 1952, the two most prominent being the urban resistance in major cities and the guerrilla campaign of the 26th of July Movement in the Sierra Maestra Mountains at the east end of the island. Both were led by the idealistic generation of 1953 who, as university students and young professionals, had opposed Batista's return to power and his perpetuation of a corrupt, elite-dominated regime subservient to the Americans. Because it was more diffuse and produced no leaders to match the charisma of Fidel Castro, the urban resistance has received less credit than it deserves for the war against Batista. While Castro was trying to consolidate his position in the Sierra Maestra in 1957 in preparation for his assaults on the Cuban army, many Cubans were already bombing government installations, assassinating police, and undermining public confidence in the Batista regime. Several thousand of them were killed and many jailed and tortured by police forces between 1953 and 1959.

The other front belonged to Fidel Castro and his guerrilla army. His campaign to rule over Cuba began with an ill-fated attack on the Moncada military barracks in Oriente province on July 26, 1953, a disaster that resulted in his capture and imprisonment. Before his conviction, however, he delivered his famous "History Will Absolve Me" speech announcing his commitment to the overthrow of Batista and the creation of a nationalistic, reform-oriented social democracy to replace his dictatorship. A general amnesty in mid-1955 allowed Castro to flee to exile in Mexico, where he met Argentine Marxist Ernesto ("Ché") Guevara and prepared for his return to Cuba and the guerrilla struggle that followed. After a near-disastrous battle when they landed on the Cuban shore in the now-famous Granma boat on December 2, 1956, from which only twelve of Castro's eighty-two-man force escaped to flee into the Sierra Maestra Mountains, the guerrilla struggle was launched.

Most remarkable about the 26th of July Movement was its military success after so meager a start. It did not begin its attacks on government outposts in earnest until early 1958, yet, less than a year later, Batista had fled the country and Castro was welcomed as a national hero in Havana. Several factors accounted for his unexpectedly brief campaign, including an American embargo on arms sales to Batista, a decision that hurt the government's morale more than its military strength; the persistent agitation of the urban resistance; middle-sector disaffection with and opposition to the repressive Batista regime; and, most important, the incompetence and corruption of Batista's army and the ability of the 26th of July Movement to exploit this weakness through the use of guerrilla tactics that harassed and demoralized government troops.

The government's demise began in May 1958, when it overextended itself in an all-out offense against the guerrillas in the Sierra Maestra. The turning point was a ten-day battle in Jigue when the rebels surrounded a government battalion camped at a river fork and, despite aerial bombardments and army reinforcement, defeated the government's expeditionary forces. It broke the Army's spirit, and soldiers fled from the Sierra Maestra. Seizing the opportunity, Castro sent his troops on the attack, two columns moving westward toward Havana while he descended on Santiago where he had failed to liberate the Moncada barracks five years before. Led by Ché Guevara and Camilio Cienfuegos, the forces that went west defeated army defenses in late November and again in late December, the last battle just outside the city of Santa Clara. The Army collapsed, leaving Batista with no reliable defenses around Havana. Dictators need armies, and, without one to defend him, Batista fled on December 31, much sooner than Castro had anticipated. The final victory came so swiftly, in fact, that several days were required for Fidel Castro to organize his triumphal ride across the island from Santiago to Havana to join Guevara and his victorious colleagues on January 8, 1959.

To a large degree the insurrection was uniquely Cuban. It was not the kind of mass-based revolutionary war that occurred in China a decade before when Mao Tse Tung led millions to victory over Chiang Kai-shek and his Nationalists. Although several thousand people had fought against Batista in the cities, and many joined the 26th of July Movement as it approached Havana, it had only 800 fighters as late as August 1958, when the final campaign began. Nor was it a peasant uprising like those led by Zapata in Mexico or Ho Chi Minh in Vietnam. To be sure, Castro could count several peasants among his guerrilla army, and some peasant farmers did assist guerrillas with food and communications. However, it was not campesinos or the rural proletariat that Castro led; his was a guerrilla force of students, professionals, and workers, drawn primarily from the middle sectors. Had the struggle lasted longer, a peasant army might have become necessary, but victory came swiftly, making it irrelevant. And finally, the Cuban insurrection was not an urban proletarian revolution. Organized labor, which was largely controlled by the Communist Party (PSP), opposed the guerrilla struggle until near its conclusion, when labor leaders belatedly lent their support to Castro. Consequently, when we strip away the rhetoric and revolutionary mythology, we are left with a focused, armed insurrection by a small band of dedicated revolutionaries who were supported by elements of the urban middle sectors and rural poor who sought to expel a corrupt tyrant. That the effort would become something far more ambitious than many who witnessed the revolt had expected would not be evident until Castro and his colleagues were firmly in control, a year later. Meanwhile, the Cubans celebrated while Castro plotted a very ambitious transformation of Cuban society.

The new political order

In Cuba the consolidation of power came more rapidly than most observers anticipated, but it was never as automatic as it appears in retrospect. The almost complete domination over Cuba by Fidel Castro and his cohorts since the early 1960s should not obscure the challenge that Castro faced when he entered Havana in January 1959. The swiftness of his victory and the involvement of so few Cubans in it had left much of the old political power structure intact. Only Batista and a few thousand army officers, police, and bureaucrats fled the island. Most of the landowning elite, foreign and domestic entrepreneurs, professionals, clergy, and other powerful groups remained behind, hopeful that they could thrive under the new regime by influencing the course that it followed. Castro had to contend with the expectations and power of such players, while at the same time fulfilling his pledge to supporters to create a more just political order and a more equitable economic system.

After the celebration had ended, Cuba's revolutionary leaders turned their attention to the consolidation of their control over the Cuban state and the initiation of a program of radical social and economic reform. Neither could be accomplished without a confrontation with the many players who were opposed to real revolutionary change. To deal with them Castro needed a political strategy for winning inevitable confrontations as consistently as possible. His approach emerged gradually through a process of trial and error during the first half of 1959, and involved the isolation of his potential opponents one by one, followed by their forced withdrawal from the new regime. At first glance, Castro's strategy appears to have been inspired by political genius, but in retrospect it is obvious that good fortune and the ineptness of his opponents had as much to do with his success as did the brilliance and ruthlessness of his tactics.

Castro's political choices essentially came down to three options: First, he could use his triumph over Batista to propel himself to the head of a broad coalition of anti-Batista groups, and then begin the slow process of creating a new democratic regime that he would likely head as a president; second, he could ignore all other players and create a government drawn entirely from the 26th of July loyalists; third, he could take a position somewhere between these two extremes, creating a smaller coalition of those groups who shared his vision of radical reform and using them to consolidate enough control to isolate and defeat his opponents.

He began with the first option, adopted some reform policies, and then, after his enemies had identified themselves through their outspoken opposition to such measures, moved to the third strategy, dropping other players one by one from his coalition until only the 26th of July loyalists and the remnants of the Communist Party (PSP) were left in the government. By then, however, he had consolidated his support among the rural and urban masses through a host of popular reform measures and had organized a revolutionary army large enough to defend him from most enemies, both domestic and foreign. What made the strategy so successful was Castro's ability to avoid a confrontation with all opponents at the same time. By dealing with each separately, he prevented their organization into a united opposition that might have stopped the march of his small band toward the execution of a Marxist revolution.

He relied on four fundamental policy decisions to flush out his opponents. First came the use of revolutionary tribunals in early 1959 to judge and then execute approximately 500 members of Batista's police and security agencies. The tribunals not only fulfilled a need for revenge, but also forced many of those who had been associated with the dictatorial regime to seek refuge abroad. At the same time, they prompted moderates who were opposed to the crude process of revolutionary justice to disassociate themselves from the regime. Second came the long-awaited announcement of an agrarian reform program in June 1959. Moderates in the cabinet, such as acting president Miguel Urrutia, resigned in protest, taking much of the leadership of the old democratic parties and landed elite into exile with them. And as the moderates began leaving the cabinet their places were taken by 26th of July loyalists, giving Castro increasing control over the bureaucracy. Third was the alliance he formed with the PSP in late 1959. Castro did not completely trust the PSP and refused to be dominated by it, but he recognized it as a source of political operators who could staff his talent-starved agencies. He also knew that his collaboration with the old Communists would drive the remaining democrats from his regime.

Finally, Castro decided to seek Russian allies, a decision that helped drive the United States from the island. From mid-1959 until the United States broke relations with Cuba in January 1961, Castro skillfully baited the U.S. government and then used its often clumsy reprisals to justify even more drastic anti-American measures. After cutting U.S. relations with Cuba, the United States made one last try to evict him, with the ill-conceived Bay of Pigs invasion in May 1961. But Castro's defeat of the invaders only increased his standing among Cuban nationalists and rid the country of its most feared opponent.

The swift consolidation of power was also aided by the small size and relative homogeneity of Cuba. It is one thing to establish political control over a nation as large as Mexico or Brazil and quite another to do the same on a small island nation like Cuba. It has always been a relatively homogeneous nation, traditionally controlled from Havana. For Castro political consolidation was not a matter of uniting a heterogeneous society but one of defeating potential opponents in the Cuban elite and middle sectors, a difficult task, but something that required a less mammoth effort than what was undertaken in Mexico in 1917.

By a process of elimination Castro drove his rivals from the government and quickly consolidated his personal control over Cuba: First Batista and his army left, then North American business and the U.S. government, Cuban plantation owners, and moderates in his government. Finally in control, Castro proceeded to build a new regime with the help of allies in the 26th of July Movement, the leadership of the PSP, the new revolutionary army, and the laboring masses whose support he had cultivated with his charismatic appeal, strident nationalism, and economic reforms.

Communist rules

Revolutionaries rely heavily on three things when they govern: an ideology, a mass-based political organization, and strong and loyal civil and military bureaucracies. Ideology is used to unite the government and to convert the masses to new political beliefs. It instructs citizens on the new rules of the game, motivates them to work for common ends, and gives them a new political ethic for determining right and wrong. Adhesion to the normative values of the ideology, rather than physical force or personal charisma, are supposed to become the primary source of the government's authority. A mass-based political organization spreads the ideology, mobilizes supporters, and isolates opponents of the regime. The political party is the preferred form of organization, but, unlike political parties in liberal democracies, the revolutionary party does not limit itself to campaigns, elections, and legislative politics. None of these activities is as important as the mobilization of mass support for the regime. Finally, revolutionaries must have a strong and loyal bureaucracy to implement government policy and supervise public conduct. Working closely with the official party, government agencies carry the burden of reorganizing social and economic institutions and coordinating diverse efforts to achieve revolutionary goals. Because the revolutionary state controls much, if not all, of the economy, state agencies find themselves with enormous power and incredible responsibilities. How effectively they use these often determines the fate of the revolution.

Many Cubans are convinced that they have discovered a superior way of doing politics. Without denying their many errors along the way, they are certain that Marxist socialism has more to offer a society than does capitalism, Christianity, Islam, or any other belief system about good and evil, progress and development. Many of them are quite sincere; that is why it would be a mistake to regard their professions of socialism as just a facade that is intended to disguise a personal political tyranny. But they do insist on total conformity with official interpretations of the Marxist gospel. Claiming that Marxism–Leninism derives its wisdom from the scientific study of human life, they insist on the absolute truth of its conclusions. There is no "halfway" in a Cuban society that is more tightly disciplined by its leadership and its ideology than almost any other nation in the communist world.

Castro is not only determined to eliminate the vices of capitalist society but he also wants to eradicate many features of his nation's Hispanic culture, like machismo, political disobedience, and the habit of equating success with luxury. He claims to be creating the "New Man," a person who places community above self, work above pleasure, and socialism above individualism. That is why he continues to criticize his people for reverting to their old, selfish, individualistic habits, victims of their own indiscipline and unwillingness to sacrifice for their nation's future.

Any failure to recognize the truth of Marxist–Leninist ideology is due, Castro insists, to a person's bourgeois origins, inadequate education, and intellectual decadence, rather than to deficiencies in the ideology. To make certain that everyone understands this, the revolutionary government has built an elaborate apparatus dedicated to educating society in its new secular religion and overseeing its application to virtually everything in life. It is a dramatic change from past Cuban practice by any account, and asks more of the nation than anything previously done in Latin America. Even Roman Catholicism at the peak of its power never made such demands for conformity on its members.

Yet, as mighty as it is, ideology has never been enough to sustain revolutionary government in Cuba. From its creation, the government has also relied on Fidel Castro and his popularity among the masses to remain in power. In few Latin American countries has a leader enjoyed as much trust among the lower classes as has Castro. Since the beginning he has been their benefactor, conveying the impression that he is more dedicated to serving them than himself. Unlike the pompous, aloof leaders of prerevolutionary Cuba, Castro always speaks in simple language to huge crowds in plazas, and for hours on television and radio, reminding everyone that he was one of them. To persons exhausted by terror and violence, bitter about government corruption, and ashamed of their domination by the American underworld, Castro was refreshing in 1959. Even without knowing where he would lead them, many Cubans found it easy to believe that his direction would be a vast improvement over Batista's.

Castro's personality contrasted sharply with that of Ché Guevara, the revolution's inspirational leader and principal ideologue. Guevara, the Argentine expatriate who had fought with Castro in the Sierra Maestra, was a disastrous administrator, never at home running government agencies after the revolution. A very private and ascetic individual, Ché was once described as a person who combined the idealism of Mahatma Gandhi with the aggression and zeal of Leon Trotsky. His cause was liberation, not governance, and it was in fighting for it that he was killed by North American-trained counterinsurgency forces in Bolivia in 1967. All revolutions have a Ché Guevara and a Fidel Castro, leaders with contrasting personalities whose individual strengths initially complement each other. But it is the Castros, the ambitious politicos, who always prevail in the end over the more idealistic Guevaras. It is they who know how to use their political skill and popularity to outfox some opponents and deal ruthlessly with others.

The nation's armed forces, built from the 26th of July Movement, were also pivotal to the revolution's implementation. Today a very

professional organization of 250,000 combatants and 190,000 re-
servists, its officers have often staffed government agencies and played
a direct role in mobilizing the Cuban work force for special production
efforts. No organization has been more loyal to Castro or more useful
in his establishment of effective command over Cuban society whenever resistance from within or without occurred. More recently it has
also become an instrument of Cuban foreign policy. Long eager to
assist less affluent Marxist regimes, the Cubans aided Ethiopia in 1978
in its battles with the Somalians, and they have kept 25,000 troops
in Angola throughout the 1980s to defend its revolutionary government against the UNITA rebels who were backed by the South Africans. Castro takes great pride in Cuba's sharing its military, medical,
and technical expertise with nations that have undertaken revolutions
similar to his own.

To penetrate Cuban society with the revolution's ideology and mobilize the population to live by it, civilian organizations were also
necessary. Most prominent at the beginning were the Committees for
the Defense of the Revolution (CDRs). Originally designed in 1960
for security purposes, the CDRs acted as the eyes and ears of revolutionary leaders in each neighborhood, reporting on the activities of
counterrevolutionaries and enforcing government policy. At their peak
they numbered 3 million members, but, as the counterrevolutionary
threat declined in the mid-1960s, the CDRs were gradually transformed into smaller organizations responsible for neighborhood
ideological education and social organization, communicating government decisions to the masses, and quelling serious dissent.

Neither the military nor the CDRs were enough to institutionalize
revolutionary supervision of the country, however. That task was given
to the Cuban Communist Party (PCC), created in 1965. The party's
origins can be traced to July 1961, when Castro formalized his alliance
with the existing, prerevolution Communist Party (PSP) through the
creation of the Integrated Revolutionary Organization (ORI). The ORI
was transitional, temporarily assisting in the implementation of the
initial socialist phase of the revolution. With 16,000 members, in
February of 1963 it was reorganized as the United Party of the Socialist
Revolution (PURS), which the Soviet Union, Cuba's principal foreign
ally and financier, recognized as a legitimate Communist Party. The
final stage of party development began in October 1965 with the
launching of the Cuban Communist Party, an organization modeled

after the Soviet one, with a small Politburo at the top composed primarily of 26th of July veterans and a few from the prerevolutionary Communist Party, a Central Committee of a few hundred members, and a national party congress that was to meet every five years to ratify official policy.

Actually little really changed at first. Castro did not call the first party congress until 1975, governing until then just as he had before, using well-tested chains of command. But after 1975 the party's responsibilities grew and by 1980 party members occupied nearly all of the important positions within the ministries, the armed forces, and the education system. It was, however, like other communist parties, an elite organization whose membership included no more than 5 percent of the population initially.

Lenin would recognize the way Cubans are governed today, and most Cubans would be honored that he did. What appears to be a dictatorship to one accustomed to constitutional democracy and capitalist economics is a dictatorship with a declared purpose. Creating an egalitarian society is the end that justifies the means employed by the Communist Party and the government that it supervises. But as in the Soviet Union, political power is wielded by professionals, not the rank and file. The people who lead the party are the educated offspring of workers, professionals, and military officers. Of those serving on the Communist Party Central Committee in 1986, 78 percent had received a university education; half of them were either government bureaucrats or full-time party officials; and 30 percent were military officers. (Only 20 percent of the committee members were women, a figure some consider low given the regime's dedication to sexual equality.)

Party members are selected carefully in order to be certain that they will dedicate themselves to doing whatever the revolution's leaders ask of them. They are expected to be rather puritanical in their personal lives, and industrious in everything they do. Most of them start early, beginning as Young Pioneers when teenagers, then becoming Young Communists when they enter adulthood, and finally party members a few years later. Their material rewards are said to be meager, yet everyone knows that they are favored by easier access to housing and consumer goods, and are allowed more travel abroad. They form an elite in what is supposed to be an egalitarian society, and have no problem justifying their greater power and privilege to anyone who dares question it, claiming that they are the vanguard that society needs to lead its march toward communism.

The Cuban government has never functioned as smoothly nor as efficiently as its creators intended, however. During the early years costly planning and administrative mistakes were made, some owing to the zeal of the country's new leaders, others to Castro's capricious meddling with policy, and still more to the difficulty of organizing a centrally controlled economy. In one attempt to improve performance in 1975 Castro proposed more popular participation in policy implementation, calling the new system Poder Popular. Still in operation today, it is composed of municipal, provincial, and national assemblies that are assigned the task of supervising government agencies within their jurisdictions. The first elections were held in late 1976. Photographs and information about each candidate were posted publicly and secret ballots cast to elect 10,743 delegates to 169 municipal assemblies. They, in turn, chose from among their members delegates to 14 provincial assemblies (1 for every 10,000 citizens), whose members in turn chose delegates to a national one. Each assembly then selected an executive committee to supervise the day-to-day implementation of government policy, the entire assembly meeting for only a few days each year to review the committee's performance. Responsibilities are divided among the levels of government, with municipal assemblies focusing on local schools, hospitals, retail stores, hotels, public utilities, and sports programs, whereas at the provincial level transportation and trade receive the most attention.

The system does not negate the influence of the Communist Party. Over half of those who were originally elected at the municipal level were party members, and of the 481 delegates first elected to the National Assembly, 441 were party members. Moreover, the Council of State, which serves as the executive arm of the National Assembly, is chaired by Fidel Castro, who is assisted by his brother Raúl, head of the armed forces, as first vice-president, and five other vice-presidents, three of whom are veterans of the 26th of July Movement. Voters may prefer party members for a variety of reasons, the most obvious being their greater clout within the bureaucracy. Or they may simply resign themselves to the party's monopoly over most things in the nation's socialized economy. But whatever their reasons, Cubans testify to the system's utility: It does not make much policy, but its members do keep an eye on those who implement it, often demanding and securing minor revisions in the way they deliver services.

Socialist economics

Cubans take socialism seriously. Everything but a small portion of the nation's farms is owned and run by the government: all manufacturing, retail sales, and human services. It is an enormous undertaking and Cubans admit to still being deeply involved in the learning process.

Some of their achievements are obvious. Anyone who reaches Cuba from Mexico, Central America, or one of the Andean countries is impressed by the absence of abject poverty. Nearly all Cuban children go to school and can advance to universities if qualified, free of charge. And minimal medical services are provided for everyone, as is enough retirement income to guarantee a comfortable if humble way of life. By Latin American standards it is a very impressive achievement for an entire nation. On the other hand, Cubans are not affluent. The supply of manufactured goods (e.g., stoves, washing machines, automobiles, and the like) is far below demand. And housing is still insufficient. While there is usually enough rice, milk, and root vegetables to go around, meats and citrus fruits are frequently in short supply, or are deliberately priced too high for average citizens to buy so that the government can export them. As a result, though they are economically secure, most Cubans are no better off materially than labor union members in Mexico. Repeatedly Castro has tried to convince them that dedication to the common good is far more rewarding than monetary wages, but most people continue to want material as well as political rewards.

What the Cubans have done must be viewed within the context of their desire to end United States domination over the Cuban economy regardless of how much it would cost them. Americans owned substantial property and industry in Cuba and controlled much of its foreign trade, making the Cuban economy more dependent on decisions made in New York and Miami than almost any other country in Latin America. If economic reform was to succeed, Castro believed, the Americans would have to leave, which they did soon after disagreements arose over the Cubans importing crude petroleum from the Soviet Union late in 1959, and the refusal of American and British oil companies to refine it. Castro retaliated by expropriating the refineries, after which President Eisenhower cut the volume of sugar imported from Cuba. Finally, in one sweeping move the Cubans expropriated nearly all U.S. assets in the country, causing the United States government to break relations and impose an embargo on trade with Cuba. It hurt Cuba economically, but the embargo did give Castro an excuse for the country's slow development that he continues to exploit thirty years later.

The Cubans have tried to compensate for their losses by accepting the aid and trade that was offered them by the Soviet Union, then eager to find some friends in the Western Hemisphere. Castro insisted that Cuba's reliance on the Soviet Union was far less onerous than dependence on the United States had been. The Russians have pumped from $3 billion to $4 billion into the Cuban economy annually ($11 million a day during the 1980s, which is equal to more than $1 per head daily for Cuba's 9.8 million people), an amount that is nearly one-fourth of the Cuban gross domestic product. It takes many forms: soft loans, cheap oil supplies, and generous prices for one-half of Cuban sugar exports. More recently Cuba has begun increasing its trade with the West, raising it to 23 percent of its total in 1982, in order to earn the hard currency it needs to purchase many modern technologies. It has also borrowed from banks and governments in Europe and Japan, accumulating a debt of $3.3 billion by 1988. Due to the fall of world prices for sugar, nickel, and tobacco, Cuba, like nonsocialist Venezuela and Mexico, was forced to reschedule its debts repeatedly in the 1980s.

The socialization of the Cuban economy was not hard to accomplish; once the government's authority was established, the expropriation of property came rapidly. Managing the economy was far more difficult, involving choices with enormous impact (e.g., dividing resources between agriculture and industry, capital investment and consumption, and defense and nondefense activities). The Cubans never found a perfect formula to guide them; instead, they have experimented with many different mixes, occasionally shifting course in order to deal with obstacles imposed by nature, foreigners, and their own mistakes.

Distributive objectives were stressed in an effort to gain mass support during the first phase of the revolution (1959–1960). Driven more by revolutionary ardor than a clear plan of attack, Fidel Castro and his colleagues from the 26th of July Movement concentrated their energies on agrarian reform, health care, education, and public housing. As a result of their zeal and inexperience, technical errors, bureaucratic waste, and disorganization accompanied the implementation of most policies. The second phase (1961–1962) began with an increase in central control through the emulation of the Soviet model of economic development with its emphasis on economic planning, bureaucratic regulation, capital accumulation, and industrialization. A third phase (1963–1967) resulted from a reassessment of the high costs of industrialization and a decision to return to an emphasis on agricultural rather than industrial growth. Again, Soviet planning methods were applied, but now their goals were agricultural production and diversification. The fourth phase (1968–1970) saw a shift to more radical methods, such as the use of revolutionary ideology and moral incentives, to inspire the Cuban masses to greater effort in the implementation of the government's economic and social programs. This "revolutionary offensive" culminated in an unsuccessful attempt to produce a record 10-million-ton sugar crop in 1970 and a reassessment of the development effort. Since then greater emphasis has been placed on material incentives, more realistic objectives, and the improvement of economic administration using Poder Popular.

After three decades of socialist development, agriculture remains the driving force in the Cuban economy. The original agrarian reform of 1959, which authorized the expropriation of all properties over 995 acres, created a dual system of tenure composed of private farms owned by ex-tenant farmers who had been given their land by the state, and a cooperative sector composed of expropriated sugar plantations and cattle ranches. In 1963 the second agrarian reform converted most cooperatives into state farms and authorized the expropriation of the remaining large private farms. It left an estimated 200,000 farms of less than 168 acres each – or 30 percent of the country's arable land – in private hands. These private owners, for whom prices and marketing regulations are set by the government, have been encouraged to enter the socialized sector, and slowly they are doing so, often joining cooperatives. Still, the anomaly of nearly 100,000 private farms in 1980 still operating in an otherwise socialized economy will likely continue for a decade or two longer.

Nothing illustrates the problems faced by planners and administrators better than the ill-fated campaign to produce a 10-million-ton sugar crop in 1970. Cuba had averaged 5 to 6 million tons of sugar in its annual harvest prior to the revolution. After a decline to only 3.8 million at the end of the intense industrialization campaign in 1963, production rose again to 6.2 million in 1967. To raise it above that level required the reallocation of resources from other activities, a risky endeavor that threatened the production of other goods and offered no guarantee of a 10-million-ton harvest. Nevertheless, Cuban leaders decided to take the risk and, beginning in 1965, they implemented an investment plan designed to modernize the sugar industry in preparation for the 1970 harvest. In addition, they initiated a "revolutionary offensive" to mobilize the Cuban people to an all-out assault on the sugar-production problem. Yet, despite unprecedented human effort, the heavy involvement of the Army in the production process, and the expenditure of record amounts of public funds, they could only produce 8.5 million tons. Administrative problems, technical difficulties, and inflated expectations all contributed to the disappointing results. The experience was a sobering one. Reassessments of the campaign led to the abandonment of several other grandiose plans and the initiation of a more balanced and pragmatic approach to agricultural development.

During the 1970s Cuba's economic fortunes rose and fell with the international price of sugar, much as they had before the revolution. Two-thirds of the crop was committed through trade agreements to the Soviet Union and Eastern Europe at a price of 32 cents a pound, with the remainder being sold on the open market. The sudden rise of the world price to 65 cents a pound in November 1974 gave the Cuban economy its biggest boost since the revolution began. Immediately, the Cubans increased the share placed on the world market to 50 percent of their crop and soon thereafter revised public investment plans upward with the expectation that the added income would accelerate the pace of the country's development. But, alas, prices fell in 1976, descending to only 8 cents a pound, making Cuba once again the victim of its reliance on sugar. As a result, the goals of the ambitious 1976–1980 development plan were revised, and proposals for immediately improving the general standard of living were set aside.

Cuban leaders did not have to be reminded by collapsing prices of their excessive dependence on sugar exports. Although they have been forced by short-term financial exigencies to return to sugar repeatedly since 1959, they have not given up their campaign for agricultural diversification and self-sufficiency in food production. Since 1970 they have been trying to lay the foundation for a major breakthrough in agricultural production. Thousands of technicians and managers have been trained at home and abroad, experiments in plant and animal genetics have reached advanced stages, and new production processes have been tested successfully. New feeds created from domestically produced molasses and fish meal have been developed to reduce dependence on imported grains, and new breeds of livestock more compatible with the tropics were created. The long-term objective of the program was the doubling of livestock, dairy, and poultry production by 1980, an ambitious objective that they did not achieve. Instead, the rationing of many basic foods has continued.

To make matters worse, Cuba, like so many of the region's nations, was hard pressed internationally during the late 1980s. With sugar prices down, even Soviet and East European subsidies and loans were not enough; nor did it help that oil prices fell in 1986 just as the Cubans were beginning to earn hard currencies by re-exporting Soviet oil at prices higher than they had paid for it. They had no choice but to reduce their hard-currency imports by half the following year, from $1.2 billion (U.S. dollars) to $600 million, diminishing supplies of imported foods and manufactured products that were already scarce. Then, at the end of 1987, Castro announced an even tougher austerity program to compensate for a 50-percent decline in foreign exchange earnings and for cuts in Soviet subsidies. It was not all that different from what debt-ridden capitalist nations like Mexico, Brazil, and Argentina suffered, though on a smaller scale, but that did not make it any more welcome.

Castro responded by increasing central control over the troubled economy, giving more power to national planners and less to provincial officials. The prices of electricity and transportation were raised; the supply of milk, beef, and kerosene to consumers was cut; and potatoes were substituted for rice in some provinces. He even reverted to "moral incentives" to incite people to work harder since he could not pay them more for additional effort. It was like watching a newsreel from twenty years ago when Ché Guevara and Fidel had stressed "will" over material rewards, urging all Cubans to display their communist spirit by working harder even if it earned them less income. If there is one thing that Fidel and many of his closest colleagues cling to, it is their belief that politics more than economics is what makes a socialist society work, especially on an island that is forced by its climate to rely so much on sugar.

Its policy reversals made Cuba something of an anachronism within the communist world, a nation that saw fit to retreat into tight central management at a time when the Soviet Union, China, and other socialist nations were experimenting with economic diversity and decentralization. In 1988 Castro made a point of telling the Cuban people that what the Chinese and the Russians were doing to open their economies and permit more competition to promote growth was totally inappropriate for Cuba. As revolutionaries in those countries had done (e.g., Stalin and Mao Tse Tung), Castro refused to change the system that he and his 26th of July colleagues had designed over two decades before. If there is a Gorbachev in the Cuban bureaucracy waiting for a chance to reform the nation's economic system, the opportunity will not come until after the first generation has passed on. With Fidel reaching 64 years of age in 1990, and his brother Raúl near the same, the second generation will probably have to linger in their offices for another decade or so before replacing them and charting a new course.

Cuba's future

The accomplishments of Cuban socialism are no longer in doubt, but neither are its deficiencies. It has not generated affluence, but it did eradicate poverty, provide minimal economic security, and restore some dignity to lower-class Cubans. At the same time, the gains of the Cuban masses have come at the expense of those who owned and managed the economy before 1959. Individual diversity and private competition for economic gain have been replaced by political orthodoxy and conformity to the dictates of a bureaucratic elite. Moreover, Cuba has not overcome the economic predicament caused by its reliance on sugar. As a result, it must depend on the Soviet Union to sustain it financially and must limit its own consumption far more than its people want. The Cuban experience does not offer other Latin Americans the solution for all of their development problems; at best it suggests a different way for redistributing the burdens of coping with underdevelopment, poverty, and economic dependence.

The revolution has changed Cuban life, though not as much as its founders had hoped. The Roman Catholic religion, never as strong in Cuba as in other Latin American countries, has withered but not disappeared: About 5 percent of the population continues to attend church and their numbers are slowly growing again. Prostitution, gambling, and organized crime have been drastically reduced if not totally eliminated. Monogamy is stressed in sexual relations, and homosexuality and lesbianism condemned by authorities as unnatural. The family is regarded as the basic cell of society, yet birth control is encouraged, abortion permitted, and divorce legal. Today an estimated 40 percent of all marriages end in divorce, initiated almost as often by women as by men.

Women have gained substantially from the revolution but they still do not share real political power with men. Cuban law instructs men to divide home care and child rearing with their spouses and encourages women to seek employment. It is in the work force that women have made the greatest progress to date, though most continue to find employment in the lower-paid service sector, the most outstanding exception being the medical profession, where women may soon become the majority. Two things are obvious, however: Few women are rising to the top of the Communist Party, and most Cuban men resist assuming more domestic responsibilities. Because machismo does survive in Cuba, neither of these shortcomings is surprising; yet Cuban women, though proud of their achievements, especially when they are compared to the plight of women in the rest of the hemisphere, remain dissatisfied.

The development of the Cuban economy will continue to be plagued by difficulties, among them the nation's limited resources. Many of those who suffered the most under the old economic system now enjoy an improved living standard, even under socialist austerity. Nevertheless, because a relatively small proportion of the national income is allowed for current consumption, citizens will continue to do without a wide range of goods. Labor is often employed inefficiently, as is common in a socialism that achieves full employment by command. Waste and temporary labor shortages in critical economic sectors are also common. And third, materials are still allocated in uneconomical ways that impair production. Without market prices that accurately reflect shortages or real demand for materials, planners labor under far too little constraint, as even Castro has often confessed. But none of these problems seriously threatens the basic nature of the Cuban revolution. It is a socialist country that is run by a disciplined political organization whose leaders are still convinced that they are setting a example for other Third World nations.

The Cuban "game" is unlike any other that we have examined. Its rules were imported and adapted to the needs of revolutionaries in this insular society, and they were enforced with a thoroughness unprecedented in the region. Many remnants of the older culture survive, but their manifestations are more tightly regulated than in any other Hispanic society. A people once known for their defiance of authority have become incredibly compliant with it, some because they believe in it and others because they fear punishment for nonconformity. It is because of the latter that we cannot be certain just how well entrenched socialist politics have become. Nevertheless, as in China and the Soviet Union, no one expects that an eventual liberalization of the nation's economy, should it ever come, will sweep away the Communist Party and end its monopoly over the nation's politics.

Further reading

Azieri, Max. *Cuba,* New York: Printer Publishers, 1988.

Bonachea, Ramón L., and Marta San Martín. *The Cuban Insurrection 1952–1959.* New Brunswick, NJ: Transaction Books, 1974.

Brundenius, Claes. *Revolutionary Cuba: The Challenge of Economic Growth with Equity.* Boulder, CO: Westview Press, 1983.

Dumont, René. *Cuba: Socialism and Development.* New York: Grove Press, 1970.

Is Cuba Socialist? New York: Viking Press, 1974.

Debray, Regis. *Revolution in the Revolution.* New York: Grove Press, 1967.

del Aguila, Juan. *Cuba: Dilemmas of a Revolution.* Boulder, CO: Westview Press, 1984.

Dominguez, Jorge I. *Cuba: Order and Revolution.* Cambridge, MA: Harvard University Press, 1978.

Guevara, Ernesto "Ché." *Reminiscences of the Cuban Revolutionary War.* New York: Grove Press, 1968.

Liss, Sheldon. *Roots of Revolution: Radical Thought in Cuba.* Lincoln: University of Nebraska Press, 1987.

MacEwan, Arthur. *Revolution and Economic Development in Cuba.* New York: St. Martin's, Press, 1981.

Marshall, Peter. *Cuba Libre: Breaking the Chains.* Boston: Faber and Faber, 1987.

Mesa Lago, Carmelo. *Cuba in the 1970s: Pragmatism and Institutionalization.* Revised edition. Albuquerque: University of New Mexico Press, 1978.

Revolutionary Change in Cuba. Pittsburgh: Pittsburgh University Press, 1974.

The Economy of Socialist Cuba. Albuquerque: University of New Mexico Press, 1981.

Pérez, Louis A. *Cuba: Between Reform and Revolution*. New York: Oxford University Press, 1988.

Roca, Sergio G. *Socialist Cuba: Past Interpretations and Future Challenges*. Boulder, CO: Westview Press, 1988.

Szulc, Tad. *Fidel: A Critical Portrait*. New York: Morrow, 1986.

Thomas, Hugh. *Cuba*. New York: Harper & Row, 1971.

Zimbalist, Andrew, ed. *Cuban Political Economy: Controversies in Cubanology*. Boulder, CO: Westview Press, 1988.

12. Nicaragua: revolution the Sandinista way

When access to authorities is callously denied a people, as it was in Nicaragua by the Somoza family and its National Guard, they can either acquiesce to dictatorial rule, resist it nonviolently, or take up arms against it. Acquiescence was a way of life in Nicaragua until 1978, when people turned to strikes and boycotts to protest their abuse by authorities. Then, under the leadership of well-armed guerrillas, they went to war against the Somoza tyranny and won at the cost of 50,000 lives. Twenty years after Fidel Castro and the Cuban guerrillas had won their war with Batista, the Nicaraguan people evicted dictator Anastasio Somoza Debayle, the youngest of the three Somozas who had ruled over Nicaragua for four decades. In July 1979, one of the hemisphere's poorest and most repressed peoples celebrated an unprecedented opportunity to rebuild their nation.

The rebellion

The Somoza dynasty was launched in 1938, when Anastasio Somoza García, head of the Nicaraguan National Guard, became president. He ruled the nation without interruption until he was assassinated in 1956. His eldest son, Luis, succeeded him only to die of a heart attack a decade later, leaving the reins of government to his younger brother, Anastasio Somoza Debayle, who, some years before, had assumed the leadership of the National Guard after completing his education at West Point in the United States. He ruled until the revolution in 1979.

From the beginning the Somozas were supported by the United States government. The United States considered building a canal across the country at the turn of the century, and though they never did, interest in Nicaragua never ended. U.S. banks lent money to the Nicaraguan government before World War I and frequently called upon officials in Washington to help them collect what was owed them when the bickering Nicaraguans were slow in meeting their obligations. The U.S. president sent the Marines to pacify the country in

Table 12.1. *Nicaragua: historical background*

1838	Gained independence from the Central American Confederation
1856	North American William Walker took over the country and governed it for a few months
1909	U.S. naval forces intervened when two U.S. citizens were executed
1912	U.S. Marines occupied Nicaragua until 1933 except for brief absence in 1925
1916	The Bryan–Chamorro treaty gave the United States rights to build a canal through Nicaragua
1927	César Augusto Sandino led uprising against U.S. Marines that continued until they left five years later
1934	General Anastasio Somoza García, made head of Nicaraguan National Guard by departing U.S. forces, killed Sandino and overthrew President Juan Batista Sacassa
1956	President Somoza is assassinated and is succeeded by his oldest son, Luis
1963	President Luis Somoza dies of heart attack and is succeeded by puppet president René Schick
1967	Youngest son, General Anastasio Somoza Debayle, became president
1972	Earthquake destroyed most of Managua, the nation's capital
1978	Pedro Joaquín Chamorro, editor of opposition *La Prensa* newspaper, is assassinated; public blames Somoza and protests with strikes and boycotts for several days
1979	Rebels, led by Sandinista FSLN, triumph and Somoza flees on July 17
1981	In January United States halts aid to Nicaragua
	Attacks from outside Nicaragua by CIA-sponsored Contra army begin before year ends
1984	Presidential election for a six-year term won by Sandinista Daniel Ortega; Sandinista FSLN also wins majority in Congress
1987	Agreement among Central American nations to negotiate an end to civil wars in region is signed by Nicaraguans in Guatemala in August; truce declared between Contras and Nicaraguan government and negotiations are begun

1909, and they stayed for most of the next quarter century until President Franklin Roosevelt finally withdrew them in 1933. But before it was decided that the Marines should leave, an American-trained National Guard was created to replace them, and Anastasio Somoza Garcia made its commander (see Table 12.1).

Starting 1927 the National Guard worked with the Marines in their effort to subdue guerrilla forces that were led by anti-American populist August César Sandino. When President Roosevelt pulled the Marines out in 1933 Sandino signed a truce with the government, only to be murdered by General Somoza. It would be another forty years before rebels using the symbolism of Sandino rose up and defeated what was left of the ruling Somoza dynasty.

The first Somoza was ambitious and enterprising, employing his political power to erect a personal economic empire that gave his family control over nearly one-third of the nation's economy. It was built not just on plunder but also on some modernization of the economy, first by increasing the land devoted to cotton and sugar production, and later through the construction of cotton gins, sugar refineries, banks, insurance companies, a steel mill, a national airline, and many complementary enterprises, most of them owned by the Somozas. It was this veneer of national development that made it easy for many Nicaraguans and foreigners to rationalize the Somozas' rule as necessary for the nation's modernization. But as their enterprises multiplied, so did the family's control over the country, and eventually most Nicaraguans found themselves more dependent on decisions made either by the government or by Somoza enterprises than they could tolerate.

If the Somoza regime was so strong, then how was it defeated in 1979? The political ineptitude displayed by the youngest Somoza son after he succeeded his brother Luis in 1967 was one reason. Anastasio Somoza Debayle proved to be even greedier than his father and brother, and much less willing to share the spoils of economic development with other members of the elite or with the growing middle sectors. Nothing evidenced this greed more than the way he handled relief efforts after an earthquake destroyed much of Managua, the nation's capital, in 1972. Rather than distributing reconstruction projects among the nation's entrepreneurs, he kept nearly all of them for himself and pilfered most of the emergency aid sent from abroad before it reached those in need. When the public protested, Somoza's National Guard smashed them. As repression increased, moderate Nicaraguans, originally unsympathetic with the tactics of anti-Somoza guerrillas, moved closer to them, gradually giving up any hope of nonviolent solutions to the Somoza problem. Like Porfirio Díaz in Mexico over half a century before and Fulgencio Batista in Cuba, Somoza became increasingly isolated from his own society, and in the end could rely on only the National Guard to protect him against the entire nation.

Another cause of the Somozas' demise was the way the rebels took advantage of the opportunities he gave them in 1978 and 1979. The guerrilla opposition was led by the Sandinista National Liberation Front (FSLN), an organization created in 1961 by university students and Nicaraguan socialists, who took their inspiration from Castro's triumph in Cuba two years before. Frequently defeated in skirmishes with the National Guard, they initially were forced to retreat into the countryside from where they quietly built support networks in the capital and in some remote areas. Only 1,000 in number, they limited their efforts to bank robberies, kidnappings, and encouraging student and union protests against the government until the late 1970s, when the opportunity for bolder initiative finally arose.

Revolutionaries do not always take up arms, dash to the hills, and fight wars, Fidel Castro notwithstanding. They had fought various little wars in Nicaragua for almost two decades with no success, becoming institutionalized as more of an annoyance than a threat to the Somoza regime. Part of the Sandinistas' difficulties derived from fundamental disagreements among themselves over tactics. The FSLN, which was launched in 1961 by Carlos Fonseca Amador, Tomás Borge, and Silvio Mayorga, split into factions in 1975, each differing from the others more on strategy and tactics than over a desire to achieve revolutionary change in Nicaragua. During the next two years the three groups operated virtually independently of one another. One of them, called the Prolonged People's War (GPP) and led by Tomás Borge, Henry Ruiz, and Bayardo Arce, stressed a slow accumulation of revolutionary forces among the rural proletariat, along the lines of Vietnam. Another, the Proletarian Tendency (TP), piloted by Jaime Wheelock and Carlos Nuñez, wanted to create an orthodox Marxist–Leninist party and from it mobilize the urban poor for guerrilla warfare in the largest towns and cities. In contrast, the Third Force of Daniel and Humberto Ortega was less patient, and favored multiclass alliances devoted more to evicting Somoza than to ideological purity.

In addition to hating Somoza, the three factions shared an intense nationalism that sought to end the nation's subservience to the United States. A lingering resentment of the nation's occupation by U.S. Marines for two decades after the turn of this century, foreign support for the Somozas regardless of how ruthless they became, and decades of pandering to the United States generated a bitter resentment among them and a desire to step out of the North American network. Nationalism was never simply a facade employed to disguise a Marxist revolution; it was one of several important motives for revolution. If there was one thing that the Marxists and non-Marxists, Christians and atheists who made up the FSLN shared, it was their desire to stand up to the North Americans who had for so long taken their subservience for granted.

The FSLN benefited from changes in Nicaraguan society that bred discontent among the masses during the 1970s. It was not a country of foreign-run sugar or banana plantations, nor of large, antiquated haciendas, but one with farms of all sizes and a relatively small landless rural proletariat that annually harvested crops like coffee and cotton. After World War II, cotton became a major export crop, being grown on commercial farms that were managed in modern ways. Still one of Central America's poorest countries, Nicaragua's economic development accelerated when it joined with its neighbors to form the Central American Common Market in 1958. Manufacturing, which accounted for only 16 percent of the nation's gross domestic product at the time, grew to 24 percent by 1979. Greater urbanization followed, some people coming to Managua looking for jobs, others because cotton producers had forced them off their land, and by 1979 over half of all Nicaraguans lived in towns and cities (in contrast to less than a third in Honduras and El Salvador). But what such movement created were not cities that provided full employment, but places where a rapidly growing class of urban poor were forced to work on the edges of the modern economy. It was among the children of these people and those of petty traders, as well as among the lower middle class, that the Sandinistas recruited the little army that they would need to lead less well-armed members of society through the final phase of their insurrection.

Most remarkable about Somoza's defeat was how fast it occurred. Before 1977 the masses were passive, attempting few strikes or other forms of protest. Except for a few labor unions, they had almost no organizations to express their discontent, and, though admired by some of them for its bold attacks on the government, the FSLN had not yet mobilized many people. But during the next two years all that changed; first tentatively, then aggressively, the Nicaraguan middle and lower classes began to protest, provoking the kind of retaliation from Somoza that incited a real rebellion, much of it occurring without any instruction from the FSLN.

In January 1978, popular opposition newspaper editor Pedro Joaquín Chamorro was assassinated and everyone blamed the intemperate Somoza for it, though no proof was ever found. Instantly Nicaraguans took to the streets in protest, starting with 30,000 persons who attended Chamorro's funeral and a "civil stoppage" by the business community that halted 80 percent of the nation's commerce for two weeks. In May, opposition political parties, professionals, and business people created the Broad Opposition Front (FAO) in the hope of securing Somoza's departure and replacing him with moderates from their ranks. While they busied themselves with matters of strategy, the FSLN struck again in August, sending twenty-five disguised guerrillas into the National Palace where they held the nation's legislature and most of Somoza's cabinet hostage until they were paid a $500,000 ransom, imprisoned guerrillas were freed, and the culprits were allowed to drive away triumphantly amid the cheers of thousands who saw them off at the national airport.

The FSLN was still not in control as 1979 began. In fact, it was not until March that its three factions formally reunited and agreed to take a single position in their negotiations with the less radical FAO. Together the two organizations formed a broadly based National Patriotic Front that incorporated nearly everyone in the country, but the National Guard, against Somoza. Their final offensive came in June; it was intense and bloody, as guerrillas, students, and anyone else who wanted to join with them seized the city of Leon; the National Guard shelled them with artillery and bombed them from the air, killing thousands of innocent civilians, then retreated to Managua. An estimated 15,000 people died during the last six weeks of combat, but the FSLN overcame the guard's superiority in numbers, mobility, and air power, encircled them in Managua, and defeated them. On July 17, Somoza fled to Miami and three days later the FSLN's ragged columns marched into the rubble of Managua that Somoza had left behind. Eventually he settled in Asunción, Paraguay, where he was assassinated by persons who were never caught.

Sandinista political reconstruction

Assessing the Sandinista regime is not easy. Part of the problem stems from the very partisan political debate that has raged in the United States since the regime's creation. The ways people appraise events in Nicaragua too often stem less from close observation than from a compulsion to defend or assail the Sandinistas by labeling them either freedom-seeking social democrats or Leninist totalitarians. But nothing is quite so simple, even in this little nation of 3 million persons.

The Sandinistas have also contributed to the confusion, supplying their enemies and defenders with enough material to confirm almost anything they want to believe. They are revolutionaries who want to change Nicaragua drastically, and, as such, they are stubborn defenders of their right to supervise the nation's transformation. To justify revolutionary change they draw on V. I. Lenin, Ché Guevara, and the New Testament, among other sources, claiming that their revolution was also uniquely Nicaraguan and not a thoughtless copy of any other. Unlike the Cubans who liquidated nearly all private enterprise quite swiftly, the Sandinistas preferred to regulate and torment their bourgeoisie, taking bits and pieces of its property without entirely destroying it. For some this was evidence of a novel "pragmatism" that is part of a truly unique kind of revolution, while to others it merely illustrates how a revolutionary vanguard can take a few steps backward now and then during its long march toward socialism. Whichever it is, there is no doubt that from the moment they marched into Managua the Sandinistas were determined to make Nicaragua a place that the Somozas' friends would no longer recognize.

Victorious rebels cannot afford to spend much time in celebration, knowing as they do that a dictatorship's destruction creates a political vacuum that must be filled quickly. The unity built on the battlefield is always short-lived, causing problems from the outset for the victors who instantly need to create a new political chain of command, fill bureaucratic posts, and assure that the people's immediate economic needs are met. So it was in Nicaragua in July 1979.

Initial decisions are made even more important by the fact that once the new rules are set, they are not easily reversed. Vested interests quickly develop around them and those who challenge the new rules are often excluded from the new political system by those dedicated to defending their new political acquisitions. This is why the people who seize the initiative and define the rules usually govern for a long time. In Cuba, Castro used his personal popularity and his small, disciplined army to secure control over the nation, one by one evicting all of his rivals outside and inside his movement. In Mexico it took much longer, nearly a decade, but revolutionary generals like Calles and Cárdenas built a new power structure that has ruled Mexico ever since. Nicaragua falls somewhere in between Cuba and Mexico in this regard, for there was no charismatic leader like Castro to capitalize on his personal popularity, but there was the FSLN, a stronger and more disciplined organization than anything the Mexicans had when they began.

The FSLN's gaining control over the new government was not automatic. Nearly the entire society had joined in the war against Somoza and each group had its own vision of how the country would be governed in the post-Somoza era. Traditional political parties wanted elections, business wanted a moderate government that would allow them larger shares of the market than Somoza had permitted, organized labor wanted immediate economic benefits and political influence, and campesinos wanted land or better wages. But the leaders of the FSLN had plans of their own. They were determined to establish a strong government, one able to implement vital economic reforms swiftly and to defend the nation against counterrevolutionaries from within the country and from outside it. The FSLN alone, they were convinced, had to lead such an effort if it were to avoid interruptions by its less revolutionary rivals.

Like most revolutionaries, FSLN leaders were reluctant to define clearly the new government's organization until they knew how their competitors might respond to their agenda for the nation's reconstruction. Though they claimed to believe in democratic government, they refused to hold free elections at first, fearing that political parties that were less devoted to social reform than they were might upset their program before it had a chance to prove itself. Naturally the parties cried foul, claiming that the FSLN was denying them the rights they had fought for, but the FSLN held firm.

Gradually a new government was created, composed of the Governing Junta of National Reconstruction, the Cabinet, and the Council of State. Initially the junta was broadly representative, one member coming from the FSLN and the other four from business, opposition parties, and other sectors. The Cabinet was composed of technocrats and Sandinistas who were placed in charge of government ministries, including a couple of sympathetic Catholic priests. It was their job to implement the junta's policies. The Council of State, which was created in May 1980, was given a kind of legislative role, though a very weak one. Its forty-seven members were to be consulted by the junta regarding its legislation, though the council's approval was not always required. Representation was corporatist in nature, with delegates coming from the FSLN, other parties, labor, peasants, and the private sector.

What made the government work, however, was the FSLN. Most initiatives did not originate in the junta but in the FSLN Joint National Directorate, the movement's collegiate leadership which designed nearly all policies, controlled the armed forces, the police, and the judicial system. Their control was far from complete, however. Most business people and private landowners, conservative clergy, opposition parties – conservative, liberal and communist – and some dissident unions were highly critical of FSLN methods and its refusal to hold elections. They were a minority since the FSLN continued to enjoy considerable popularity among the masses, but they were initially outspoken and eager to see the government fail. But as long as the FSLN was able to meet the basic needs of the poor and exploit their fear of Somocistas's return from exile, their grass roots support remained intact.

The government was reorganized in 1984. The Council of State was abolished, a president elected, and a national legislature created, with its members elected from geographical districts rather than economic and social sectors as was the case with the Council of State. The change seemed to please none of the Sandinista critics, however. The Reagan administration claimed that the elections were unfair despite the fact that foreign observers found the counting of ballots straightforward and honest. Some alleged that it was impossible to defeat an incumbent party that controlled the media and the police as much as the Sandinistas did. But regardless, Daniel Ortega, the victor with 67 percent of the popular vote, was inaugurated president, and the FSLN majority in the new legislature, along with legislators from minority parties, was sworn in. Nevertheless, the same government that many had accused of being undemocratic because of its governing through a weak Council of State whose members were not selected in general elections, was now condemned for the way it had used conventional election procedures to win a national contest.

But the victory was not entirely due to the efforts of the FSLN. The opposition also helped by being so disorganized. Six parties ran against the Sandinistas in the 1984 elections, among them the old conservative and liberal parties, communist and Christian democratic ones, and a few new parties, none of which received more than 15 percent of the vote. Another hastily created party, the Coordinadora, refused to participate in the elections altogether. Equally active in the opposition is the national organization of business people, called COSEP, which does not hide its desire to force the Sandinistas to abandon their journey toward socialism, no matter how slowly they are going. Opposing the government in the Sandinista state is no easy task, however, since authorities exercise so much control over the media and police, and declare so much of what their opponents do to be off limits. While from time to time they have allowed others to criticize them on the radio and in newspapers, they remain reluctant to permit organized protests, claiming that they are less intended to force changes in policy than to promote rebellion against the revolution. And to some degree they are correct, but even if the opposition could not overthrow the government, the government would remain reluctant to allow its obstruction of the reforms that the Sandinistas are determined to accomplish.

The FSLN is a relatively small organization with an estimated 25,000 members, or about 1 percent of the Nicaraguan population, but direct representation was not the Sandinistas' primary concern when they began. They considered themselves unique, "the only party with a truly national program," as they frequently said. They had led a revolt, set new objectives for the nation, and trained young people to implement them. As Defense Minister Humberto Ortega put it, "Our elections will seek to perfect revolutionary power, not hold a raffle among those who seek to hold power." The Sandinistas insisted that the creation of a more egalitarian society required that they retain enough power to assure that "oligarchs and traitors, conservatives and liberals" did not ever again rule over the nation in pursuit of their own narrow interests. In short, they declared that their economic and social ends justified their political means. Objections by their opponents fell on deaf ears; only if they recognized the right of the FSLN to supervise the revolution and its programs and to retain control over the police and armed forces could they be considered part of the same revolution.

Political friends and enemies

Nicaragua is too poor and its economy too badly damaged by the United States embargo, its war with the counterrevolutionary Contras, and the government's occasional mistakes to achieve much on its own. But the Sandinistas knew that it would be difficult when they began and did not hesitate to look everywhere for assistance. Most, but certainly not all, of it came initially from Cuba and its Russian and East European allies. The Cubans were eager to assist with the country's charting a new course that included social revolution and nationalism among its goals, providing economic planners, military advisors, and intelligence services, as well as teachers and doctors. By the mid-1980s an estimated 3,000 Cuban civilians and 1,000 military personnel were still working in Nicaragua, along with several thousand individuals from nations all over the world, including many from the United States whom the Nicaraguans refer to as *internationales* to distinguish them from the U.S. government.

The Soviet Union and several East European countries have supplied oil and machinery, along with helicopters and tanks to bolster the nation's defenses. They also provide several thousand scholarships to Nicaraguans for technical and professional training, primarily in the USSR and its neighboring countries. But from the outset they made it clear that Nicaragua would not be given the amount of assistance that goes to Cuba. It is simply not worth it to the Russians strategically. Under Gorbachev the Soviets are even less enthusiastic about making Nicaragua their ward since they now prefer to keep more of their resources at home. The Sandinistas are left with little choice but to diversify their trade and to seek more help from social democrats in Western Europe. But regardless of from where it comes, everyone knows that it will not be enough to improve economic conditions in the country any time soon.

Cubans working in Nicaragua complain of indiscipline among Sandinistas, whom they find more idealistic and romantic in their revolution than the Cubans were in theirs. It seems that part of the Sandinista mind wants perpetual liberation of the spirit and continued celebration, while the other part knows that it can no longer afford such pleasures. This is not unique to Nicaragua, of course; most revolutionaries begin quite idealistic only to become far more realistic as their problems increase. What makes Nicaragua different is how reluctant many Sandinistas are to resolve it in the manner of the far more disciplined and regimented Cubans. They act like they believe that revolution should involve constant celebration rather than the endless toil that is required to improve the condition of the nation.

Relations between church and state also distinguish Nicaragua from Cuba. The Roman Catholic Church, which today counts no more than 10 percent of the Cuban population among its members, remains a strong, though divided, institution in Nicaragua. Like many clergy in Latin America, there were some in Nicaragua who embraced liberation theology and exhibited new dedication to social justice as defined by Church officials at the Medellín meetings in 1968. A few of them became the FSLN's most ardent supporters, convinced that revolution was necessary to liberate the Roman Catholic masses from economic and political tyranny. From the outset they never doubted that they could find a place alongside Marxists within Sandinismo. Believing that they could make contributions to a revolutionary society without sacrificing their faith, they seldom questioned the wisdom of their alliance. Ten years later some clergy still worked for the Sandinista government and assisted with its programs all over the country.

Not all clergy agreed with the founders of this revolutionary *Popular Church,* however, least of all the Nicaraguan bishops. Though they too had championed Somoza's removal, they feared Sandinismo and its ability to draw the masses out from under the traditional church organization using Marxist ideology and new theologies. As a result, the Roman Catholic Church in Nicaragua became deeply divided with many clergy ending up on both sides. Disagreements over theology, religious practice, and the legitimacy of the Sandinista government are intense today and their resolution is not imminent.

Pope John Paul II espouses justice for the poor, but he has refused to relinquish Vatican authority to the clergy who administer to them. He may appear to preach "liberation" but he is always quick to reprimand theologians who disagree with his interpretation of it. It has been an intense dispute within the Church but one over which the Vatican ruled supreme until Nicaragua. Now dissidents within the clergy not only have a concrete cause to champion, but they also have a political regime that supports their efforts to do it. The Pope demands a separation of church and state, including a prohibition against the clergy taking jobs in governments, but in Nicaragua some clergy have defied him, laying down a challenge to his authority. He responded by elevating Nicaraguan Archbishop Obando y Bravo to the position of Cardinal in 1985 and authorizing him and other anti-Sandinista clergy to denounce defiant members of the Popular Church and to support the political opponents of Sandinismo, including the Contras.

It is a conflict that no one is winning. Many Nicaraguans, from the lower classes as well as the bourgeoisie, remain loyal to the traditional Church and its Pope, and look upon the Popular Church with fear and disdain. Others, nearly all of whom are from the rural and urban poor and the clergy, have found a new home in the Popular Church, taking great pride in their building this dynamic new religious community. Claims of membership vary immensely, though it is certain that neither side can count more than 60 percent of the population among its most devoted members. But regardless, Catholicism still thrives in Nicaragua. Even if they wished to imitate Fidel Castro's dismantling of the Church, the Sandinistas could not accomplish it. Accommodation is the only solution to their religious conflicts, and as the revolution approached its tenth anniversary there were signs that some persons on both sides were realizing it.

The Sandinistas also had a counterrevolutionary war to contend with after 1981. It should be recalled that the Central Intelligence Agency organized and financed the effort, and was determined to keep it going as long as necessary to prevent the Sandinistas from achieving anything resembling peace and order within the country. The Contras, as the counterrevolutionaries were called, were recruited from veterans of Somoza's National Guard, middle-class opponents of Sandinismo, and campesinos who were unhappy with the way the government pushed them around when it tried to reconstruct the rural economy. Once organized and funded by the United States government, as many as 10,000 of them operated out of neighboring Honduras, crossing into Nicaragua in small guerrilla units to attack local Sandinista officials, school teachers, and anyone else who defended the government, and then retreat back across the border. They frightened the Nicaraguans whom they did not kill, and forced the government to devote enormous resources to keeping its army chasing them. Especially unpopular was the military draft that the Sandinistas used to increase the size of their armed forces.

Frustration with the war eventually led President Daniel Ortega to join with the other four Central American presidents in signing an unprecedented accord that was designed to create a process for negotiating settlements among governments and rebels. The agreement signed in Guatemala City in August 1987 was unusual in its insistence that governments within the region increase their democratization in order to accommodate all opponents in their midst, and that all of them (and hopefully the United States, which was not invited to the meeting) cease giving aid to insurgents in neighboring countries. An amazing chain of events followed. The Sandinistas, who said they would never negotiate with the Contras, agreed to meet with them, first outside the country and then in Managua itself. To communicate their intentions, they also allowed the opposition La Prensa newspaper and the Catholic radio station to operate once more, promising more liberty for the regime's peaceful opponents as long as they did not take the revolution away from the FSLN.

With the fighting halted and the troops of both sides still in the field, they tried to reach an agreement during the year that followed, but it proved elusive. The Contras wanted several things done before their troops, numbering around 8,000, handed in their weapons. They demanded that the Sandinista government release all of its political prisoners, dismantle its control over the courts, separate the Sandinista Party from the state (e.g., give up control over the police and Army), allow the opening of independent television stations with their own news programs, permit strikes by labor unions, and guarantee private property rights. They promised that all arms would be handed in after all of this was *implemented*. For their part, the Nicaraguan government promised to negotiate an agreement that might include some of these items, but would agree to it only if the Contras gave up their weapons when the agreement was *signed*. This difference was a fundamental one. The Contras feared that the Sandinistas would not comply once military pressure was withdrawn, while the Sandinistas were convinced that the Contras would keep their weapons and demand even more concessions after the agreement was implemented.

The Sandinistas were plagued by a real dilemma. They did not want to yield control over their revolution to persons less dedicated to its achievement than they were, but they were tired of spending half of their budget to defend themselves. Their economy was in serious trouble in 1988, causing discontent among people in all social classes, and more war would only sustain a decline in popularity, especially with opponents eagerly exploiting their predicament. Yet if they gave the opposition the latitude that the Contras demanded, they invited their mobilizing the masses against the government. Concessions were risky in the short run, no matter how they were assessed. However, in the long term the Sandinistas stood to gain from economic recovery, something they might achieve more rapidly if war was ended. The decision was crucial, but, surprisingly, it was the Nicaraguan electorate and not the FSLN who actually made it.

Daniel Ortega and the FSLN were defeated in the February 1990 elections by Violeta Chamorro and the newly formed National Opposition Union (UNO), a coalition of fourteen parties ranging from communists to conservatives, that received 55 percent of the vote. When she agreed to disband the Contras, the FSLN accepted her as president, hoping that this would relieve the weary Nicaraguans of war and economic blockades. Nevertheless, no one was certain what would follow this sudden change.

An economic struggle

From the beginning the Sandinistas took a more cautious approach to economic revolution than the Cubans had. Where the latter turned immediately to socialism and state planning, the Nicaraguans chose to mix capitalist economics with the socialization of certain parts of the economy much as the Mexicans had done under Cardenas in the 1930s. Their decisions were dictated as much by economic necessity as by philosophy. Sandinistas wanted a more equitable economic system for Nicaragua; some among them preferred Marxist economics while others were less dogmatic about the form socialism should take, recognizing that need, not utopian visions, must guide policy.

Whatever their economic faith, the Sandinistas' job was not an enviable one. Nicaragua is one of Latin America's poorest nations ($660 per capita income in 1979), one that was badly damaged by an earthquake in 1972 and the war in 1979. To make matters worse, when Somoza fled, he took most of the Nicaraguan treasury with him, leaving his successors nothing but huge foreign debts. Moreover, unlike the Cubans who marched into cities virtually untouched by combat, the Sandinistas inherited thousands of homeless, unemployed persons to care for.

In poor countries socialists always face a cruel choice between either quickly redistributing the nation's property and wealth to those most in need or promoting capital development, something that may require their asking the masses to sacrifice in order to improve conditions for future generations. In the euphoria of victory one is always tempted to divide the spoils instantly, but experience elsewhere has taught just how disastrous that can be. The FSLN designed its own mix of welfare and capital development, making substantial effort to improve public health, sanitation, and basic education, relying primarily on the labor of volunteers from Nicaragua and abroad, while at the same time devoting some resources to restoring the nation's production.

What made the Nicaraguan effort unique was the new government's inheriting 25 percent of the economy that was previously owned by the Somozas, which altogether made it the nation's largest entrepreneur overnight. Moreover, to assure its control over the nation's development the government also nationalized all enterprises involved in mining, lumber, and fishing, and services like banking and insurance. The private sector was allowed to retain ownership of two-thirds of the nation's internal commerce, over half its agriculture, and three-fourths of industry. Thus, about 60 percent of the national product remained in private hands. As a result, thereafter the state and private entrepreneurs were locked into a relationship that both disliked but neither was in a position to change: The government could not manage the entire economy on its own and the private sector could not reduce the will or the power of the government to direct the nation's development according to its own plan. Not surprisingly, business repeatedly accused the government of sabotaging its enterprises with regulations and controls, and officials charged entrepreneurs with trying to use their economic power to undermine the reform effort.

The government did not waste any time in addressing the issue of agrarian reform, but it could not have done otherwise because it inherited all of the Somozas' properties, some 1,500 estates that made up 20 percent of the country's arable land. They decided to turn most of them into state farms rather than divide them among campesinos, convinced that government-run enterprises were necessary to increase production immediately. In what would become one of their most controversial ploys, they tried to keep the rural labor force free enough to harvest crops annually rather than turn them into farmers tied to their own plots. Predictably, many campesinos protested, using the Sandinista Rural Workers' Union to demonstrate against the government's failure to distribute more property. Authorities finally responded in 1981 by announcing a second agrarian reform law that promised to redistribute some of the properties under government control. But instead of expropriating the farms that held the other 80 percent of the nation's arable land as Castro had done in Cuba, they took a more cautious approach, seizing only properties that had been abandoned by owners who lived in exile and large plots from farms that were not being put into productive use. Several hundred thousand acres were given to campesinos and rural workers who agreed to form cooperatives, and to the families of persons who had been killed during the insurrection. Nevertheless, dissatisfaction continued among the landless and in 1985 a third phase was begun. This time government began giving individual titles to farmers without insisting that they join cooperatives. One reason for their letting up on the individual ownership issue was the ability of the Contras to recruit soldiers from among the rural poor in the north who were unhappy with the government's failure to give them land. Collective farming and cooperatives were foreign to the rural Nicaraguan, and the government's promises of social justice and higher production did not make them any more popular in the countryside. Some compromise was necessary between the government's desire to assure production of exportable commodities and the campesinos' desire for more autonomy. The result is a very intricate mixture, a rural sector composed of state farms, large and medium private farms, small ones within cooperatives, and small, individually owned ones. As long as the war with the Contras continued there was no hope of restoring production to the levels achieved before the revolution, but even if the war had been ended, it would have been some time before this reorganized rural economy became more productive than it had been before 1979.

The Sandinistas also contended with an uncooperative international economy. Rather than defaulting on their debts and cutting themselves off from the capitalist nations, they renegotiated or paid them. Agricultural production declined sharply during the insurrection, but when it rose again a couple years later, world prices for coffee, cotton, and sugar had dropped precipitously, forcing the Nicaraguans to borrow even more heavily abroad, just as their neighbors had done. And when the Reagan administration cut off foreign assistance, ostensibly to punish them for encouraging revolutions in neighboring countries, the Nicaraguans borrowed wherever they could, both in Western and Eastern Europe and from the Soviet Union.

The economy, badly damaged by civil war, grew some in 1981 and again in 1983, only to stagnate after that (Table 12.2). It was plagued by a severe shortage of foreign exchange, a large government budget deficit, an inflation rate that reached 220 percent in 1985, and a continuous decline of about 12 percent annually in real wages. Agriculture was hurt as much by the Contra war as it was by agrarian

Table 12.2. *The Nicaraguan economy, 1982–7*

	1982	1983	1984	1985	1986	1987
GDP growth (%)	−0.8	4.6	−1.6	−4.1	−0.4	1.7
Real wages (%)	−12.7	−12.7	−5.1	−14.3	n.a.	n.a.
Exports (millions, US$)	382.5	428.3	385.7	301.5	239.2	299.0
Imports (millions, US$)	681.6	779.1	799.6	878.2	714.4	837.9
Terms of trade	79.2	83.0	105.0	97.0	109.0	86.0
(Index: 1980 = 100)						

Source: Inter-American Development Bank, *Economic and Social Progress in Latin America, 1986 and 1987.*

reform, and manufacturing slowed because it could not get the foreign exchange it needed to purchase the raw materials that went into its products. Shortages in basic consumer goods grew, creating a huge black market in which most Nicaraguans traded for food and home supplies despite repeated government efforts to shut it down. This might have been more bearable were it not for the fact that 60 percent of the population was urban not rural, placing enormous burdens on the government to generate housing and basic supplies that urban dwellers could not produce for themselves. As before, most persons found ways to get by, but frustrations grew.

The Nicaraguan economy went into an even faster tailspin in 1988 when inflation rose to an annual rate of over 1,000 percent. The government had no choice but to attack inflation using rather conventional measures (e.g., knocking 3 zeros off its currency, the cordoba; reducing the budget deficit by cutting expenditures more than 10 percent; eliminating subsidies for many products; and declaring a war on speculation and black marketeering). President Daniel Ortega explained his choice of such unsocialistic emergency measures this way: "We are obliged to be creative and take economic steps necessary for survival in these difficult moments when the fundamental task is the defense of revolutionary power. For geopolitical reasons, we have not taken profound steps like those taken in Cuba, where private property has been abolished." In short, the Sandinistas could not afford to take over their economy as long as they did not have the financing that was needed to operate it.

The Sandinista economy suffered from the nation's poverty, the government's inexpert policies, war, the U.S. embargo, and insufficient help from abroad. Like so many before them, the new authorities discovered that they could not just sit down and reconstruct an economy in any way they wished, no matter how noble their intentions. They yearned to serve the masses in their struggle against the bourgeoisie, but they could not operate the economy without relying far more than they wished on the nation's private sector to produce goods that the government and the population consume. The arrangement satisfies no one. The FSLN cannot force private business to conform to its rules, and entrepreneurs, who want as much freedom as their peers enjoy in the other Central American countries, cannot get the government to abdicate.

There is no easy way out for the Nicaraguans, even if the counter-revolutionaries give up their fight. The nation is blessed by a low population/land ratio, rich soils, good metal mining potential, and some decent roads, but it has no petroleum, and the commodities that it exports are, like those of its neighbors, subject to wide price fluctuations. With few new investments being made by any institution but the government the nation does not have any more capacity to produce now than it did a decade ago. That is why authorities swallowed hard and announced in 1988 that they would soon open beach resorts on the Pacific coast and advertise for tourists all over the world.

Nicaragua's prospects

The Sandinistas wanted Nicaraguans to operate by rules that they had written and intended to enforce over the objections of any opposition. They espoused dedication to achieving national independence and social justice, and they have raised the literacy rate from 54 percent to 74 percent in less than a decade, improved basic health services, built many schools, redistributed some farmland, and unleashed feelings of national pride seldom expressed before. But Nicaraguans are a very poor people: The per capita national product that had reached $979 (U.S.) in 1960 was only $879 in 1987. The poorest may not suffer as much as they did before the revolution, but they remain weak and dependent, and increasingly, with essential goods unavailable, they are becoming an unhappy people. Even their Cuban guests feel sorry for them and see no swift escape from their economic predicament.

Unpleasant economic realities have forced the FSLN to tolerate many more capitalists than they would prefer, something that has put them on the defensive politically from the outset, since they are convinced that as long as their opponents have any power, they will use it to prevent the revolution's completion. As a result, Sandinistas behave like a small elite that is willing to debate how it implements its revolution but not its right to exercise control over it. Though they are very self-conscious about how easy it is to abuse authority, that does not prevent their doing so from time to time in order to preserve their control. But opposition does exist and not all of it comes from abroad. How large it is and how unhappy it is with the Sandinista regime is not easy to determine amid the confusion caused by the variety of opponents that exist within and outside the nation.

No one could hide the fact that 1988, the revolution's tenth year, was its worst. Prices rose over 20,000 percent that year and the gross domestic product continued to shrink. The Nicaraguan economy simply was not working and no one, neither the Cubans, the Russians, nor the Europeans, was willing to pay many of its bills or supply most of its goods. Even the people who still praised the Sandinistas for launching the revolution expressed disappointment in the way of life they had created. In desperation President Ortega announced an unprecedented cutback in public expenditures in 1989 that included his firing 15 percent of the government's employees at a time when unemployment was already over 30 percent. He also promised new national elections for 1990, allowing the opposition an opportunity to compete with the Sandinistas. Nevertheless, few expected that any party but the FSLN would be governing the nation thereafter.

Obviously many persons in all social classes are disappointed with the way the economy is being managed and want more freedom to do as they wish. Yet, as much as Nicaraguans complain of adverse conditions, they are hard pressed to indicate who else could govern the nation today. There are no obvious candidates in the nation's other political parties or among its citizens who live in exile. Nicaraguans were not raised on heavy doses of democracy but on dictatorship, and many fear that were the Sandinistas to go, dictators from the Somoza school would likely replace them. No speeches about democracy's virtues given in Washington, D.C., or elsewhere are enough to assure them that they can create real democratic government in Nicaragua. Distrust has always run high in the country, and it will not be easy to replace it peacefully with greater trust and cooperation. They also know that if the Sandinistas were forced to flee Managua tomorrow, civil war would likely follow for a long time. Moreover, few Nicaraguans believe that any foreign nation, least of all the United States, would guarantee them the economic and political security that they want. In short, whatever their faults, and they are abundant, many Nicaraguans fear that the Sandinistas' successors, should they ever come, might only be worse.

The revolutionary game: lessons learned

Revolutions have many causes and take several forms, making any single theory inadequate to explain them. Each one requires separate study if it is to be understood. Yet, though their differences were many, the Cubans and the Nicaraguans did share a few things when their revolutions began. One was the general discontent with the maldistribution of wealth and the cruelty of the ruling classes who nearly monopolized it. Another was the elite's smug denial of political participation to potential rivals who refused to accept complete subordination to those in power. In each case armed rebellion became an effective means for gaining admission to the game, not just for peasants and workers but also for the middle-sector intellectuals, students, and politicians who led them.

What makes armed revolt against dictatorships so likely is the apparent impossibility of accommodation between the dictator and his opponents. The autocrat always fears that compromise will lead to his own demise rather than to his opponents' subservience. Since the dictator has nothing to rely on for his ultimate authority except the power of intimidation, he believes that concessions will be taken as evidence of weakness, provoking only more challenges to his rule. So the dictator holds his ground, but in doing so only forces his opponents to launch an all-or-nothing violent struggle. Dictatorial government can survive for many years this way, but eventually the autocrat, be he a Díaz, Batista, or Somoza, will meet a violent end.

Today few of the old dictators remain. Does this mean that the era of armed rebellion is over? Not at all. Many revolutionary movements, like the Tupamaros in Uruguay in the early 1970s and the Montoneros in Argentina a few years later, have been crushed, but the revolutionary's cause is far from hopeless. The risks are greater and the probability of success anywhere but in Central America is lower than before, but there is nothing to prevent revolutionaries from adapting their tactics to changing conditions, thereby improving their chances of victory, just as they did in the past. But whether movements like the Sendero Luminoso in Peru can actually do that remains to be proven.

The performance of revolutionary governments is another matter. Nothing as controversial as a revolutionary regime is ever praised by everyone. Personal beliefs shape our assessments of revolutions even more than they do other kinds of politics because of the intensity of feelings about both the means and the ends of radical change. Nevertheless, judge them we must, just as we do the other types of government in Latin America.

Revolutionaries are not the only ones who demand substantial political conformity, but they expect much more of their people than do the leaders of nonrevolutionary regimes. They demand that people change their ways, often substantially, in order to become part of a society held together by a new, community-based ethic. And, because their vision of the new order is quite precise, they expect conformity in the details of social life. Moreover, like those they deposed, they face antagonists eager to expel them from power. Revolutions always create enemies, both foreign and national, who resent being deprived of their property and privileges. Unlike constitutional democrats who take their chances with the rules of competitive politics, revolutionaries want to control their own fate totally, if possible. Consequently, internal and external security absorbs much of their attention and, when threatened, they often turn their society into a fortress dedicated to the revolution's defense.

Each revolutionary regime develops its own ways of achieving conformity with its values. Once the Cubans had chosen the Marxist–Leninist model to guide their construction of the Cuban state, very specific rules were written and enforced in economic as well as political affairs. Strict conformity became common because doctrine and discipline were taken seriously. In Nicaragua the Sandinistas have not been as rigid as the Cubans, and that is why describing their regime remains an inexact science. So far they have been content to allow a mixed, but highly regulated, economy while devoting much effort to defending their regime against counterrevolutionaries. But they still toy with elections and other means of public participation under their own supervision, so it remains to be determined just how much control the Sandinistas will exercise over their society.

The other distinguishing feature of revolutionary government is the way it provides social services and promotes economic development. Leaders quickly learn that the redistribution of wealth, no matter how equitably it is done, will not by itself meet the needs of their people. Like everyone else, revolutionaries must also increase their nation's product in order to provide adequately for all. How to do that without abandoning the revolution's social welfare objectives poses one of the toughest problems faced by revolutionary governments throughout the Third World. And few of them have dealt with it in the same way.

The Cubans concentrated on improving working-class welfare; as a result, in no Latin American country are education, medical care, and sanitation available to a larger proportion of the nation's citizens than in Cuba. It is such achievements that the Cubans point to when defending themselves against critics from the more capitalistic Latin American countries whose economies have grown much faster than Cuba's. Revolutionary economics, as the Cubans readily admit, has not brought affluence to their society, but it has mobilized the nation's resources for national development and rationed goods that are still in short supply. Cuba remains a modest, tropical island heavily dependent on the export of sugar, a few minerals, and other agricultural crops for its economic survival, and it must rely on its Soviet allies for capital and technology. But the old oligarchs are gone, the United States government and the multinational firms enter the country only on the terms dictated by the Cubans, and the Cuban leadership feels free to send its troops anywhere in the world where ideology and geopolitics suggest a need for them. Middle-class Mexicans would not enjoy life in Cuba, but one wonders how uncomfortable Mexican slum dwellers would find it.

The plight of Nicaragua is grimmer than that of Cuba. There is nothing that the Sandinistas can do to increase the country's wealth significantly in the short run. They have raised literacy and have given some relief to a people whose economic productivity remains low. But to expect them to achieve even as much as the Cubans did is to ignore how little they have to work with. The principal task facing them after a decade is the same as it was when they began, namely, producing enough to employ and feed all Nicaraguans, using private, state, and borrowed capital.

What are we to conclude about the revolutionary game? Clearly its appeal is strong to anyone who resents how conservative modernization increases foreign penetration of an economy without improving the condition of the poor significantly, or who is displeased with the way reformers make concessions to the defenders of the old order while failing to deliver on their promises of a better life for the masses. And it will always be an enticing option for young persons who want to rule their countries but believe they must change the rules in order to do so. But, as the Cubans and Nicaraguans have discovered, revolutionary politics are neither cheap nor easy. Costly mistakes are often made, disappointments are common, and substantial personal freedom may be sacrificed. To dismiss the latter as an expendable bourgeois luxury only ignores the fact that most people, regardless of their social class, covet the opportunity to do some things as they wish. Of course, they also want liberation from oppression, and as long as they do, revolutionary politics of the socialist variety will retain its appeal.

Looking ahead

It is tempting to think that we really know where Latin Americans are going in the future, if only because we have grown so accustomed to labeling them democrats or authoritarians, good governments or bad ones. Such distinctions and judgments are not irrelevant, to be sure. The Argentine government did kill more than 8,000 of its citizens, a war has lasted for more than a decade in El Salvador, and democrats contend with authoritarians nearly everywhere. All of this matters. But we must be careful with our labels, for they make it far too easy to pretend that we know even more about Latin Americans than they know about themselves. Politics in Brazil will always be very different from what it is in Portugal or India even when they claim the same definition for their forms of government. And a democratic Costa Rica will never resemble a democratic Greece, nor will a socialist Nicaragua become just an Hispanic Yugoslavia. We may think ourselves wise because we know something about politics in this perplexing and ever-changing part of the world, but we still know very little.

Actually, our theories about political change in the region have never lasted very long. One need only recall that during the 1960s it was popular to believe that the region was abandoning old-fashioned dictatorships for modern democracy, clumsily and sporadically, to be sure, but indubitably. Democracy, it was thought, accompanied economic and social modernization. But it did not turn out that way. Instead, modern militaries took over and authoritarianism became the new way of life. Thereafter, it came to be preferred to insist that authoritarianism, not democracy, was the natural product of modernization in such deeply dependent societies. But it was not long before revulsion for autocratic government brought freer governments back to life, calling into question notions about authoritarianism's inevitability.

Theories of any kind are scarce today. Instead, it is the region's variety and complexity that seem to command everyone's attention. But even without satisfactory explanations of politics in Latin America, we must continue our search for them, if only to understand better how the games are played by the people most affected by them. If we have learned anything during the past half century, it is the necessity of searching for those explanations within the region itself, among the people who live and work there and know it best. I hope you have found this volume a useful first step in preparing for just such an assignment.

Further reading

Belli, Humberto. *Breaking Faith: The Sandinista Revolution and Its Impact on Freedom and Christian Faith in Nicaragua.* Westchester, IL: Crossway Books, 1985.

Booth, John. *The End of the Beginning: The Nicaraguan Revolution,* 2nd ed. Boulder, CO: Westview Press, 1986.

Burns, E. Bradford. *At War in Nicaragua: The Reagan Doctrine and the Politics of Nostalgia.* New York: Harper & Row, 1987.

Cabezas, Omar. *Fire from the Mountain: The Making of a Sandinista.* New York: Crown, 1985.

Close, David. *Nicaragua: Politics, Economics, and Society.* New York: Pinter Publishers, 1988.

Colburn, Forest D. *Postrevolutionary Nicaragua: State, Class and the Dilemma of Agrarian Policy.* Berkeley: University of California Press, 1986.

Dunkerley, James. *Power in the Isthmus: A Political History of Modern Central America.* New York: Verso, 1988.

Pastor, Robert A. *Condemned to Repetition: The United States and Nicaragua.* Princeton, NJ: Princeton University Press, 1987.

Spalding, Rose, ed. *The Political Economy of Revolutionary Nicaragua.* Winchester, MA: Allen & Unwin, 1986.

Vanderplaan, Mary B. *Revolution and Foreign Policy in Nicaragua.* Boulder, CO: Westview, 1986.

Vilas, Carlos M. *The Sandinista Revolution.* New York: Monthly Review Press, 1986.

Walker, Thomas W. *Nicaragua: The First Five Years.* New York: Praeger, 1985.
  ed. *Nicaragua: The Land of Sandino,* 2nd edition. Boulder, CO: Westview Press, 1985.
  ed. *Reagan versus the Sandinistas: The Undeclared War on Nicaragua.* Boulder, CO: Westview Press, 1987.

Appendix: Tables

Table A.1. *Latin American demographics*

	Area (sq. miles)	Population, 1987 (millions)	Average annual population growth, 1981–7 (%)
Argentina	1,072,000	31.1	1.4
Bolivia	424,000	6.7	2.7
Brazil	3,286,000	141.4	2.2
Chile	292,000	12.5	1.7
Colombia	440,000	30.0	2.2
Costa Rica	20,000	2.3	2.9
Cuba	44,000	11.0	1.8
Dominican Republic	19,000	6.7	2.4
Ecuador	109,000	9.9	2.9
El Salvador	8,000	4.9	1.2
Guatemala	42,000	8.4	2.9
Haiti	11,000	6.1	1.8
Honduras	43,000	4.7	3.6
Mexico	762,000	83.0	2.4
Nicaragua	50,000	3.5	3.4
Panama	29,000	2.3	2.2
Paraguay	157,000	3.9	3.2
Peru	496,000	20.7	2.6
Uruguay	72,000	3.0	0.7
Venezuela	352,000	18.2	2.8

Source: Inter-American Development Bank, *Economic and Social Progress in Latin America 1988 Report*. Washington, D.C., 1988, p. 534.

Table A.2. *Latin American economic and social conditions*

	Per capita gross domestic product, 1987 (1986 dollars)	% Population with safe water, 1979	% Literacy rate	% Population urban 1987
Argentina	2,745	57	94	86.3
Bolivia	721	38	63	49.6
Brazil	2,428	47	69	72.2
Chile	2,213	87	92	83.0
Colombia	1,581	62	82	70.8
Costa Rica	2,011	80	90	49.6
Cuba	–	98	95	–
Dominican Republic	1,401	61	70	59.6
Ecuador	1,326	46	85	53.2
El Salvador	900	44	70	47.7
Guatemala	1,376	42	57	39.2
Haiti	300	10	37	25.9
Honduras	782	59	60	41.4
Mexico	2,423	55	88	69.6
Nicaragua	879	41	74	58.7
Panama	2,549	82	86	50.5
Paraguay	1,402	17	92	40.6
Peru	1,517	53	86	68.3
Uruguay	2,733	83	96	85.0
Venezuela	4,107	91	90	78.5

Note: Dashes indicate figures not available.
Sources: Ruth Leger Sivard, *World Military and Social Expenditures, 1982.* Leesburgh, Va.: World Priorities, 1982; Inter-American Development Bank, *Economic and Social Progress in Latin America 1988 Report.*

Table A.3. *Latin America and the Caribbean: selected economic indicators*

	Average 1970–1979	1981	1982	1983	1984	1985	1986	1987
Per capita real GDP[a]	3.1	−1.9	−3.4	−4.7	1.1	1.3	1.6	0.2
Terms of trade[a]	3.8	−4.6	−4.7	−3.0	3.8	−2.7	−14.3	−0.9
Debt service ratio[b]	–	41.8	51.6	40.8	40.9	40.3	45.0	35.5

[a]Annual changes in percent.
[b]In percent of exports of goods and services.
Source: International Monetary Fund, *World Economic Outlook*, October 1988.

Index

Acción Democrática (AD) party (Venezuela), 77, 169; economic policies of, 196, 199, 200–3, 204–5, 208; political strategy of, 68, 164, 193–6, 197, 198, 205, 207, 209

Agrarian Production Cooperatives (CAPs) (Peru), 277

Agrarian Societies of Social Interest (SAISs) (Peru), 277

Alessandri, Jorge, 177, 179, 180

Alfonsín, Raúl, 270–1, 272, 273, 274, 275

Alianza Popular Revolucionaria Americana (APRISTA) party (Peru), 77, 276

Allende, Salvador, 175, 211; economic program of, 178, 182–5, 186, 188; as socialist leader, 79, 173, 174, 176, 180, 181–2, 186, 187, 189–90

Anaconda corporation, 178, 183

Angeloz, Eduardo, 274, 275

Angola, 81, 297

Anti-Reelectionist party (Mexico), 140

Arce, Bayardo, 312

Argentina, 74, 75, 80, 217; agrarian reform in, 256–7, 259; agroexporter elite of, 250, 251, 253, 254; austral program, 273–4; Córdoba riots, 262; and democratic government, 132, 212, 249, 254, 260, 269–75; economy of, 132, 135, 251, 256–8, 263, 266–7, 273–4, 275; elections in, 250, 251, 254, 260, 262–3, 270–1, 272–3, 274–5; entrepreneurs in, 53, 256, 257, 258, 267; foreign debt of, 132, 256, 267, 273, 274, 275, 281; foreign investment in, 250, 256, 275; foreign trade, 86, 95, 133, 204, 251, 256, 257; guerrilla movement in, 33, 79, 329; industrialization in, 251, 256–8,

265; inflation in, 263, 273, 274, 275; middle sectors, 57, 58, 76, 251, 253, 255, 263, 271, 281; military, 73, 81, 83, 86, 259, 262, 270, 272, 280, 282; and military authoritarian government, 41, 214, 218, 249, 260–9, 280–2; military coups in, 36, 213, 251, 253, 260, 262, 263, 267, 272; multinational firms in, 256; nationalism in, 250, 251, 257; and Peronist populism, 249, 250–60; presidency of, 36–7, 73, 269; repression in, 28, 41, 79, 249, 251, 255, 263, 264–5, 277, 282; and the Roman Catholic Church, 250; technocrats, 261; upper class, 263, 269, 281; working class, 250, 251, 253, 254, 260, 262, 269, 274

Argentine Trade Promotion Institute (IAPI), 256

authoritarian government, 14, 38, 43–4, 69, 329; monarchies as, 7–8, 27, 218, 222

Aztecs, 7

Azuela, Mariano, 142

Barrios, Gonzalo, 197

Batista, Fulgencio, 287, 289, 290, 291, 293, 311

Bay of Pigs invasion, 285, 294

Belaúnde Terry, Fernando, 276–7, 278, 279

Betancourt, Rómulo, 195–6, 197, 199, 200, 202, 208–9, 210

Bolivia, 31, 67, 135, 212, 296

Borge, Tomás, 312

Braden Company, 178, 183

Brasília, Brazil, 224

Brazil, 53, 73, 80; agrarian reform in, 50, 226, 228, 243; campesinos, 228, 232, 235, 259; Cruzado Plan, 241–2; democratic transitions, 218–20, 229, 236–44, 245; economy of, 56, 106–7,